BEYOND ROSWELL

The Alien Autopsy Film, Area 51, & the U.S. Government Coverup of UFOs

Michael Hesemann
Philip Mantle

BEYOND ROSWELL

The Alien Autopsy Film, Area 51,
& the U.S. Government Coverup of UFOs

Marlowe & Company
New York

Published by Marlowe & Company
632 Broadway, Seventh Floor
New York, NY 10012

Library of Congress Cataloging in Publication Data

Hesemann, Michael.
    Beyond Roswell: the alien autopsy film, area 51, and the U>S. government coverup of UFO's / Michael
Hesemann and Philip Mantle.
        p. cm/
    Includes bibliographical references and index.
    ISBN 1-56924-781-1
    ISBN 1-56924-709-9 (paper)
    1. Human-alien encounters. 2. Unidentified flying objects-Sightings and encounters—New Mexico—
Roswell. 3. Unidentified Flying objects—Sightings and encounters. I. Mantle, Philip. II. Title.
BF2050.H47 1997
001.942—DC21   96-28934
                                                                                              CIP

Manufactured in the United States of America

Acknowledgments

The authors would like to thank everyone who helped make this book a reality. This includes eye-witnesses, UFO investigators, UFO researchers, and others too numerous to mention. Nearly all of them have been interviewed in person for this book (if not otherwise mentioned, by Michael Hesemann), and we owe them special thanks for adding their testimony to an already growing amount of documentation.

Listed below are those individuals that we would like to thank for helping in a variety of ways with *Beyond Roswell*.

Master Sgt. Bob Allen, Colin Andrews, Maurizio Baiata, Prof. Pierluigi Baima Bollone, Johannes von Buttlar, Ole Jonny Braenne, Cristoforo Barbato, Chris Cary, Prof. Hoang-Yung Chiang, Col. Gordon Cooper, Hub Corn, Theresa Carlson, Dr. Sergey Chernouss, Charles D., CMSgt. Robert Dean, Glenn Dennis, MSgt. Richard Doty, Don & Vicki Ecker, Robert Eveleth, Nucl.-Phys. Stanton Friedman, Adriano Forgione, Timothy Good, Jim Goodall, Bill Hamilton, Jr., Lt. Walter Haut, Noryo Hayakawa, Sappho Henderson, Derek Henessey, William Holden, Linda Moulton Howe, Antonio Huneeus, Rick Jones, Frank Joyce, Frank Kaufmann, Tom King, George Knapp, Steve Kaeser, Helga Kuppers-Morrow, Robert Lazar, John Lear, Dr. Roger K. Leir, Max Littell, Ted Loman, Dr. Bruce Maccabee, Prof. Corrado Malanga, Susan Mantle, Dr. Jesse Marcel, Jr., Howard Marston, Bill McDonald, William L. Moore, Robert Morning Sky, Sean David Morton, Dennis Murphy, Captain James McAndrews, Carl Nagaitis, Bob Oechsler, Ron Pandolfi, Dr. Roberto Pinotti, Col. Dr. Yurii Platov, Dr. Marina Popovich, Major Virgil Postleweith, Reg Presley, Loretta Proctor, Kevin Randle, Frankie Rowe, Odd-Gunnar Roed, Nick Redfern, Ray Santilli, Don Schmitt, Gary Schultz, Jaime Shandera, Bob Shell, Lt. Robert Shirkey, Gary Shoefield, Jack S., the autopsy cameraman, Derrel & Doris Sims, Dan Smith, Lt. Col. Wendelle Stevens, Leonard Stringfield, Sgt. Clifford Stone, John Spencer, Mark Spain, Johsen Takano, Theresa and three other Laguna Indians, Bill Uhouse, Col. Colman VonKeviczky, Dr. Jacques Vallee, Hanspeter Wachter, George Wingfield, Llewellyn Wykel, and Natalia Zahradnikova.

Our special thanks to Certified Engineer L. Subramanyan, Gelsenkirchen, for his excellent transla-tion of Hesemann's (original German) manuscript and to our friend and literary agent, John White.

Michael Hesemann & Philip Mantle

Contents

BEYOND ROSWELL

The Alien Autopsy Film, Area 51,
& the U.S. Government Coverup of UFOs

FOREWORD

By Jesse A. Marcel, M.D.

A new day dawned for me in the middle of the night that first week of July 1947, when I was eleven. I was a witness to an event which, when fully acknowledged by the powers that be, will be a turning point for all humanity.

I could not believe what I was seeing on the kitchen floor that night. The fogginess of being awakened from a sound sleep at 2:00 A.M. rapidly faded as I examined the strange debris which my dad, a major in the intelligence operations at Roswell Army Air Field in Roswell, New Mexico, had brought in from a crash site on a nearby ranch . The big question was: the crash of what? This was certainly not from a known aircraft, and certainly not the debris from a balloon with its radar target. This debris had properties which I had never seen before or since. My dad was very excited and wanted my mother and me to have a close look at what I am sure he called parts of a "flying saucer."

Initially he wanted us to look for any electronic components such as vacuum tubes, resistors, condensers or wires. At least in the portion of the debris which I saw, there was nothing of that description. What I saw was a bewildering collection of metal-like foil, bakelite or plastic shards and beams. To complete the picture of weirdness, there were even symbols of strange geometric forms and designs of a metallic violaceous hue printed along the length of the I-shaped beams.

What this has meant for me is the realization that we are not alone in our galaxy and that there are advanced civilizations using principles of which we have no concept. Certainly there is a broad spectrum of civilizations "out there," ranging from those just entering their stone age to those who are capable of transporting themselves intergalactic distances perhaps in the wink of an eye, using unimaginable knowledge. I surmise that we are somewhere between the extremes on the scale of knowledge and scientific development of sentient beings in the universe. It may very well be that our "cousins" who visit us from time to time are not at the zenith of scientific development, and that there are others far more advanced who would appear godlike to us if we could even recognize them as a form of intelligence. They would be so far advanced that they no longer need a physical body and in reality are states of pure radiant energy devoted entirely to intelligence. This may sound like poppycock, but who is to say that there isn't some element of truth to this far-fetched idea?

What is certain is that there are a few individuals in the "need to know" loop of the major world powers who have the knowledge that our planet is being studied by extraterrestrial civilizations. Perhaps the reason to keep this a supreme secret hidden from the common people is the realization that we are really not in control of our skies and by extension, our very destiny. The thought of this would be very unsettling and could disrupt the very fabric of our civilization. That would be reason enough for people in the "need to know" loop to take extreme measures to keep this fact buried so that "ordinary" people would be insulated from the knowledge that "we are not alone" and that in fact we are an object of study by one or more advanced nonhuman societies.

This fact does not disturb me and I feel it would not be that disruptive for my bothers and sisters on this planet to have this same knowledge. That, of course, contradicts the theme of some very popular science fiction movies based on a "space invader" concept which depicts us in a life-and-death struggle with extraterrestrials.

I do believe that government conformation of this knowledge would broaden human horizons profoundly and enlarge our concept of our place in the universe. Last of all, it would place God in a higher plane because we would no longer limit Him creating just us in His image, whatever that image happens to be.

I am delighted to offer this, my first written public statement, in support of Michael Hesemann and Philip Mantle's book. Their research and that of others is gratifying to me because personal conviction is not the same as public demonstration. Although I am personally convinced of ET visitations, with *Beyond Roswell* we now have possible public demonstration of the long-rumored notion that alien life forms have come here. Let's call upon Government to end the cover-up now and tell us the truth. We have the right to know. My father thought as much for mom and me that night in 1947; even more so it is the case for all us citizens of planet Earth half a century later.

Jesse A. Marcel, M.D.
August 1, 1996.

Introduction

*Time's glory is
to calm contending kings,
to unmask falsehood
and bring truth to light.*
-William Shakespeare

Belfast, Ireland, 1 December 1995. For the first time a president of the United States of America commented on Roswell. And what he said was as trivial and unsatisfying as everything else that the government of the U.S.A. had till then revealed about the greatest mystery of the twentieth century. President Clinton's official visit to Ireland was a gesture of goodwill and American appreciation of the emerging accord in the conflict in Northern Ireland. The reference to Roswell was perhaps meant only to lend a popular note to his speech in connection with the illumination of a Christmas tree. He had recently received a letter from a thirteen-year-old Belfast boy, Clinton said, before addressing himself directly to the boy, *"Ryan, in case you are out there, here is your answer: No! As far as I know, no extra-terrestrial spaceship crashed at Roswell, New Mexico, in 1947."* The crowd laughed. *"If the Air Force really recovered any extra-terrestrial bodies, they did not tell me,"* added the president with a broad grin, *"and I want to know!"*[1]

Apparently the Air Force could tell him nothing more about Roswell, because "someone" had removed and destroyed all reports connected with the incident in the files of 1947, without any orders or official notes in any files to justify the action. At least, that was the outcome of an official inquiry into the Roswell case, conducted during 1994/1995 by the General Accounting Office, the investigating arm of the U.S. Congress, at the instigation of a congressman from New Mexico. Could this have been an attempt to hush something up.[2]

Derision and suppression of facts have played a big role in the story of Roswell right from the beginning. On the very next day after the press officer of the Roswell Army Air Fields announced the salvaging of a "flying saucer" by the 509th Bomb Group, General Roger Ramey, Commanding Officer of the U.S. 8th Air Force, declared that the object retrieved was only a weather balloon.[3]

At the time the American public swallowed this explanation, but the mightiest man of the other superpower, namely the Russian dictator Joseph Stalin, did not. He was informed about the incident by the KGB, the Soviet Secret Service, and the KGB was convinced that the "weather balloon" declaration was a political feint. The Bomb Group 509 was considered the best-trained unit of the U.S. Air Force and had repeatedly been employed in secret missions. Members of this unit had discharged the atom bombs on Hiroshima and Nagasaki, flew the most recent aircraft and certainly would have been capable of distinguishing a weather balloon from a "flying saucer." In order to clarify the situation, Stalin ordered three of his best scientists to investigate if the object in question could be a threat to the security of the Soviet Union.

The three specialists were the prominent mathematician Mstislav Keldysh, the chemist Alexander Topchiev and the physicist Sergei Korlyov, who, as a Soviet counterpart of Wernher von Braun, was to construct the rocket in which the first Sputnik and finally Yuri Gagarin were transported into space. All three men were top scientists of the U.S.S.R., and, during the following years, each one of them occupied the office of president or vice president of the Academy of Sciences. When Stalin received them personally a few days later, they all had come to the conclusion that the "flying saucers" were not foreign secret weapons and did not represent a serious threat to the Soviet Union, but were, nevertheless, real phenomena. They therefore recommended that Stalin initiate a scientific study in order to gather more information about them.[4]

This resulted in a whole series of official UFO studies by the Soviets, of which the West has learned only recently, after the collapse of the Soviet Union. The last of these studies was not only intended to discover the origin and intentions of the mysterious interlopers, but also had an ulterior motive. The Russians suspected—not without reason—that most of the "stealth technology" of the "invisible" bombers of the USA had been developed from research on crashed UFOs. They now hoped to locate a crashed UFO, so as to analyze it and catch up with the Americans' advanced technology. *"If we discover the secrets of the UFOs we shall be in a position to win the race against the potential enemy, using the extra-terrestrial know-how regarding speed, materials and camouflage"*, said Colonel Boris Sokolov to the American journalist George Knapp. And Sokolov must have known what he was talking about: he was head of

the UFO Office of the Defense Department in Moscow.[5]

President Clinton too may soon learn the truth about the Roswell incident. No lesser person than Laurance Rockefeller, multimillionaire and philanthropist, is determined to do everything possible to make the public aware, during his lifetime, of what the government has long known about UFOs. At his behest leading UFO investigators compiled a 150-page study. A thousand copies were made with the intention of sending a copy to every congressman, senator, and scientific adviser in the U.S.

In this "Rockefeller Report," which also deals with testimonies from ex-officers and astronauts *"who contradict the statement of the Air Force denying the landing of extraterrestrials,"* the Roswell incident marks the central theme. Leading Roswell investigators Stanton Friedman, William Moore, Kevin Randle, and Don Schmitt so far have interviewed over three hundred eyewitnesses.[6]

Or perhaps we shall learn the truth through another channel. In the summer of 1995 the British film producer Ray Santilli created a worldwide sensation with his statement that he had acquired film material from a former photographer of the U.S. Army Air Force, showing the salvaging of the Roswell wreck and the autopsy performed on two extraterrestrials. The discussion about the authenticity of these films is still going on, but meanwhile preparations have begun to mark the fiftieth anniversary of the Roswell occurrence on July 4, 1997. According to inside rumors Steven Spielberg is making a big movie for that date, which would also include original material.

"Spielberg to Expose UFO cover-ups," said the headlines above the first announcement regarding this project in the British newspaper *Daily Mirror*, which goes on to report that the world-famous director and producer of *E.T.* and *Close Encounters of the Third Kind* is working on an eighty-million-dollar movie dealing with *"the UFO crash and the political intrigue that followed."* Known to insiders only as Project "X," the film will apparently include *"previously unseen film footage of the flying saucer crash scene taken by a military officer,"* which have been passed on to Spielberg.[7]

When six weeks later another newspaper, the *Daily Star*, repeated this announcement in its movie section[8], British UFO researcher Philip Mantle asked the paper's acting editor in chief, Michael Hellicar, where he had got this information. The answer was:

> *"Our story about Steven Spielberg acquiring footage of the UFO crash in Roswell is one hundred per cent accurate. It comes from a source who is involved in the projected movie about the crash. The working title, the meaning of which will be known to you, is Majestic-12. I know little more than that, except that Spielberg's production company, Amblin, is trying to keep the movie secret, because they fear another studio will beat them to it. However, a rival version will be lacking in one sensational detail: the official crash pictures.*
>
> *One aspect of the story which I tried to check, but couldn't confirm, is that the U.S. government may have deliberately leaked the film to Spielberg.*
>
> *The theory is that by letting him include it in a glossy Hollywood movie, the awesome truth—that We Are Not Alone—will be watered down. . . .*
>
> *Thus, you can either believe a Spielberg movie as fact, or treat it as a bit of Hollywood hype which makes you think, like* Close Encounters. [9]

We can only wait and see what comes out of all these rumors about impending revelations. Perhaps the powers that be, which were behind the hushing up of the Roswell occurrence, will prevent the truth from ever getting out. But it is also possible that "someone" is permitting the truth to leak out piece by piece. Santilli's film, *The Roswell Autopsy*, genuine or otherwise, could be the first step in this direction, and the Spielberg film, if it is not prematurely blocked by restrictions, could be the next. But no matter when the truth about the happenings at Roswell comes to light, it will bring about a change in all of us.

Michael Hesemann and Philip Mantle.

[1] AP announcement of 1 December 1995.

[2] United States General Accounting Office, "Results of a Search for Records Concerning the 1947 Crash near Roswell, New Mexico" (GAO/NSIAD-95-187), Washington, D.C., 1995.

[3] *Roswell Daily Record*, Roswell, NM, 8 and 9 July 1947.

[4] *Rabotshaya Tribuna*, Moscow, 13 August 1991.

[5] Gresh, Bryan, "Soviet UFO Secrets," in: *MUFON UFO Journal*, Seguin, TX, October 1993.

[6] *New York Daily News*, New York, 18 December 1995.

[7] *Daily Mirror*, London, 22 December 1993.

[8] *Daily Star*, London, 1 February 1994.

[9] Letter by Michael Hellicar, Assistant Editor, *Daily Star*, to Philip Mantle, 3 February 1994.

1.

The Birth of the Flying Saucers

Tuesday, June 24, 1947. Time: 2:57 P.M. Place: the area around Mount Rainier in the state of Washington, USA. Slowly, buzzing loudly and monotonously, the twin-engined propeller aeroplane was flying in the clear steel-blue sky, circling around the snow-capped peak of the mighty volcano. The pilot, thirty-two-year-old businessman Kenneth Arnold, was carefully searching the slopes for a missing C-46 transport plane belonging to the U.S. Army Air Force. At Chehalis Airport, Washington, he had come to know that the AAF was offering a reward of $5,000 for finding this machine. The reward was a tempting incentive to Arnold, who, as a member of the Idaho Search and Rescue Flyers, had often won rewards for locating lost aircraft. And since he would in any case pass by the Mount Rainier massif on his return flight to Yakima, Washington, he decided to spend an hour searching for the C-46 transporter.

There were no clouds at all in the sky. Ideal flying weather. As Arnold was scanning the terrain in search of the crashed aircraft, he suddenly noticed a flash of light reflected by the side of his own plane. For a moment he was frightened: this could mean that he was on a collision course with another aircraft, which he had not been aware of. But there was no other plane in

Kenneth Arnold

his vicinity. Only far away near the horizon could he see a lonely DC-4 flying on the air route from San Francisco to Seattle. Somewhat irritated, he was trying to think of a possible source for the flash of light, when he saw a second flash. He looked at once in the direction that the light came from, and what he saw there took his breath away.

From the North, in the direction of Mount Baker, a formation of bright objects was approaching him at an unbelievable speed. Some of them shot out of the line, flashed in the sunlight, and returned to their positions. They still were about 100 miles away, too far to make out details. But they were flying towards Mount Rainier. Soon he was able to count them—there were nine of them, flying in a straight line one behind the other, the largest in the middle. They were too fast, even for jet-propelled craft. Was he watching a test flight of the latest secret weapon of the United States? Or a Russian attack? Arnold looked at his watch. It was 2:59 P.M., and the chain of objects was now at a distance of about fifty miles from him.

Soon he could make out details. With amazement he noted that the flying objects did not seem to have any protrusions—whether bulges, wings, or tails. They looked far more like flat discs, rounded in the front and a bit truncated and slightly curved at the stern. And they radiated a bright bluish white light.

A new type of aircraft? To see them better, the pilot pushed up his window and looked out. He could easily make out their shapes against the snow—covered slopes. He had never seen aircraft with such capabilities-aircraft that could shoot past the peak at so close a range. They then flew along the ridge between Mount Rainier and Mount Adams. Arnold noticed that the first object was just at the southern end of the ridge as the last reached the northern end. This meant that the chain must have stretched over a distance of at least five miles. Arnold looked at his watch again as the objects were about six miles away from him. The chain must have flown over a distance of fifty miles within one minute and forty-two seconds. He later calculated from this a speed of over 1700 miles per hour. It was incredible!

Arnold sighted the mysterious squadron once more, after it had already passed Mount Adams. Soon after that it disappeared completely in the horizon. According to his watch it was 3:02 P.M. The show was over. The entire spectacle had lasted just about five minutes. Arnold was no longer in the mood to continue the search for the C-46 and he could not care less about the $5,000 reward. He just wanted to go to Yakima and tell everybody what he had seen. And just in case the Russians had been responsible, he felt it was his patriotic duty to inform the authorities as well.

Arnold's drawing of the observed objects

The first reporters learned about his experience on the very same day. No matter what the objects were, their journalist's intuition told them that the story was worth a headline. The witness seemed honest. *"They were flat as a plate and so smooth that they reflected the sun like a mirror,"* said Arnold, describing the discs. *"You can call me Einstein or Flash Gordon or just a crazy nut. But I know what I saw. The things flew like saucers when you make them skip on a lake."* That gave the press its cue, and the catchy name "flying saucers" came to life.[1]

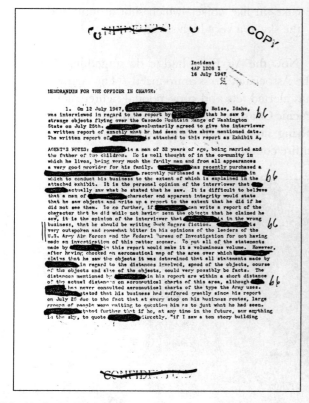

U.S. Air Force Memorandum on Kenneth Arnold: "It is difficult to believe that a man of (Arnold's) character and apparent integrity would state that he saw objects and write up a report to the extent that he did if he did not see them."

Shortly afterwards the Air Force also began to take interest in the occurrence. In a confidential report dated July 16, 1947 the investigating officer made this concluding remark: *"It is difficult to believe that a man of (Arnold's) character and apparent integrity would state that he saw objects and write up a report to the extent that he did if he did not see them."*[2]

There proved to be a second witness to the strange phenomenon. An elderly gold digger from Oregon had read about the sighting in the newspapers and declared that he too had seen the "saucers" a few minutes after Arnold, circling above the Cascade Mountains. *"While the discs were flying around above me my compass needle went wild,"* he said to the journalists.[3]

But it did not stop there. During the following weeks the USA was plagued by a downright epidemic of "flying saucer hysteria." Suddenly they were everywhere, reports of sightings came in from all over the country. UFO researcher Ted Bloecher was able to collect over 850 announcements from the national press[4], there could have been over 2,000 in the local papers. Among the witnesses were:

- A married couple in Redding, California, who saw a big, shining triangular flying object gliding silently north.
- An employee of the Marine Airfield at Santa Rosa, California, who saw an object "like a gigantic pocket watch, without any protrusions, as if made of a silvery metal similar to aircraft aluminum,"[5] between five and seven meters in diameter, crossing the northern end of the runway, at a height of about a thousand feet.
- A dentist, Dr. R. W. Nelson, who had also seen the "shining silvery" object.[6]

On July 3, 1947, the U.S. Air Force for the first time made an open statement regarding these sightings. An

AAF spokesman declared, *"If a foreign power is sending flying discs over the U.S.A., it is our duty and responsibility to be aware of this and to take appropriate steps."*[7]

The Air Technical Intelligence Center (ATIC) at Wright Field near Dayton, Ohio, announced, *"German scientists, many of them experts from research laboratories, whose existence had been kept secret with the greatest care by the Nazis . . . are shaking their heads in wonder over the reports about the 'flying saucers' that are flitting through the skies in over a dozen states."*[8] The writer of a letter to the *Los Angeles Examiner* accused the Soviets, saying the discs were *"newly invented Russian atom powered planes, aircraft, that left deadly radioactive clouds in their wake."*[9]

On the other hand the Russian vice-consul at Los Angeles, Eugene Tunantzev, declared: "Russia respects the sovereignty of all nations and by no stretch of the imagination would it use another country for a proving ground . . . Russia has plenty of territory of its own for any scientific experimentation."[10] According to United Press, high-ranking U.S. Army officers agreed with him: until then the "flying saucers" had not even once been detected by radar.[11]

The number of sightings reached a peak on—of all days—July 4, 1947, with a number of interesting reports from reliable witnesses:

- "Five discs are tearing past above us, weaving up and down," reported patrolling policeman K. McDowell from Portland, Oregon, on the radio. Minutes later two other patrol cars confirmed his observation, and they were soon joined by the harbor police and dozens of civilians. They all saw how twenty metallic discs, sparkling in the sunlight, soared, dived, circled, shot off, and then returned, fell into formation, and broke off again. The show lasted for a minute and a half and was also seen from the Portland office of the news agency INS.[12]
- In Hauser Lake, Idaho, some 200 people at a football game saw a disc carrying out maneuvers above the city for about thirty minutes.[13]
- More than sixty people taking part in a picnic to celebrate Independence Day observed three groups of "shining discs," each in V-formation, while separate "saucers" circled around them.[14]
- In Bakersfield, California, witnesses saw a "shining, cake-tin like object, which shot around and crossed the sky at a very high speed."[15]

Now the Air Force had to do something. On July 6 the Associated Press announced, "The Army Air Force has alerted jets and conventional fighter planes on the Pacific Coast . . . in the hope of solving the riddle of the 'flying saucers,' which in 12 days has challenged the entire country."[16]

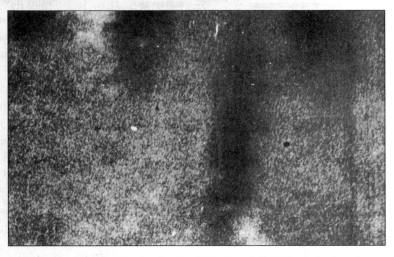

UFO photo 4 July 1947, taken by Frank Ryman of the U.S. Coast Guard near Seattle, Washington.

While some of the interceptor planes were equipped with cameras, others were provided with ammunition. As the *Chicago Daily News* reported, "Capt. Tom Brown of the Air Force Public Relations staff in Washington confirmed that the Air Force has decided there was something to the saucer reports and has been actively investigating the mystery for ten days without much result."[17]

Army Air Force Commander General Carl Spaatz flew suddenly and unscheduled to Seattle and Tacoma, Washington, officially to make a speech, to inspect an airfield, and to go fishing. A Pentagon spokesman emphatically denied that the trip had another purpose, saying, *"He is not going there to investigate flying saucers...."*[18]

Soon a pattern could be seen in the activities of the unknown intruders. Their main target was New Mexico, the state which at that time was the center of the world's military armament technology. It was here that, two years before, the first atom bombs had been tested. Los Alamos was here, the secret laboratory in the highlands of New Mexico, known to insiders as "the Mountain," that reminded one of a monastery, difficult to reach and secluded from the world. And here lived a steadily growing community of top level scientists, who, between 1943 and 1945, developed the atom bomb under what went down in history as the Manhattan Project. In 1947 Los Alamos was a "secret city," a cordoned-off area which only those people could enter who had the proper clearance and permit pertaining to top secret projects.[19]

The same applied to White Sands Proving Grounds, the vast chalky desert, which borders in the north on the black lava basin where once the Mescalero-Apaches hid their treasures and which they had named "Jornada del Muerto," "Journey of Death." The ancient Path of Death crossed another very old road, "El Camino de Diablo," "The Devil's Road," in this alchemic landscape. Yes, New Mexico is indeed "the land of enchantment," the land of magic. Not far from this mystical road-crossing is a spot which like no other is connected with the Devil, death and alchemy. Marked today by an obelisk out of volcanic rock, it is Ground Zero, the heart of the "Trinity Site," at which in a flash of light, on July 16, 1945, at 5:49:45 A.M., the atomic age was born.

It was the day on which for the inhabitants of Carrizozo, thirty miles eastward, the sun rose in the west and shortly after disappeared below the horizon, followed by a mighty gale, which was reminiscent "of

"The great shatterer of the worlds". Photograph of the first atomic explosion on the Trinity Site on the White Sands Proving Grounds on July 16th, 1947. Was it a coincident that New Mexico became the favorite target of unknown flying objects?

the appearances of God in he Old Testament," as Bill Laurence of the *New York Times* wrote.[20] Robert Oppenheimer, the great physicist known as the Father of the bomb, who was also a Sanskrit scholar, quoted the *Bhagavad Gita*, the holy book of the Hindus:

"divi surya sahasrasya bhaved yugapad utthita"

yadi bhah sadrsi sa syad bhasas tasya mahatmanah

. . . lelihyasr grasamanah samantal lokan samagran vadanair jvaladbhih

tejobhir apurya jagat samagram bhasas tavograh pratapanti visno

. . . sri bhagavan uvacu:

kalo smi loka-ksaya-krt pravrddho lokan samahartum iha pravrtthah."

"Brighter than a thousand Suns radiated the glory of the deity supreme in His universal form

. . . oh deity, I see how you devour all mankind from all directions with your flaming mouths

With your shining glory you penetrate the whole universe. You are radiating frightful, parching heat . . . .

The supreme deity spoke:

Time am I, the great shatterer of worlds, and I come to exterminate all mankind."[21]

On that very day, on which the sun rose twice, the USA had won for the first time the military race for the most sophisticated technology, and one month later Hiroshima and Nagasaki ended the Second World War. Within four years the Soviet Union broke the U.S. atomic monopoly, and a forty-year race of fear began. A further development began in those days at the White Sands Missile Range, north of the Alamogordo Air Base (Army Air Field in those days.) The captured German V-2 rockets were brought here, examined, and tested. The knowledge gained thereby led not only to the evolution of remote-controlled missiles, but also of rockets that put the first satellites into orbit and finally took man to the moon.

If extraterrestrials did visit the earth in 1947, New Mexico would have been their first choice of area to investigate. There, and nowhere else, were the fundamental bases established for the technological, political and military developments for the next forty years.

And indeed, since June 25, 1947, UFOs had been seen in New Mexico almost every day:

JUNE 25: The dentist Dr. R. F. Sensenbaugher sees a saucer-shaped object, one and a half times as big as the full moon, south of Silver City, New Mexico.

JUNE 27: At about 9:50 A.M., W. C. Dobbs sees a "white disc, glowing like a bulb" over Pope, New Mexico. Minutes later, the same object is reported by Capt. E. B. Detchmendy, above the White Sands Testing Area. Lt. Col. Harold R. Turner received this report. As one Mrs. Appelzoller saw the same body over San Miguel and informed White Sands about it, Turner took action. He informed the press that the object was a "daylight meteorite."

JUNE 28: A pilot, Capt. F. Dwyn, sees, near Alamogordo, New Mexico, "a ball of fire with a blue, flaming tail" shooting off from under his plane.

JUNE 29: Pilots of the Army Air Force investigate a rumor according to which an object had crashed in the neighborhood of Cliff, New Mexico, around noon. They find nothing, but register a strange smell.

JUNE 30: The railwayman Price observes thirteen silvery discs in a row, flying over Albuquerque, New Mexico, changing their direction of flight more than once. Price informed his neighbors, who could confirm the strange maneuvers.

On the same day at about 11 P.M. a disc flies at a very high velocity over the house of Helen Hardin in

Tucumcari, New Mexico.

JULY 1: Max Hood, Chairman of the Albuquerque Chamber of Commerce, reports seeing a blue disc flitting in a zigzag course across the sky.[22]

At 11:30 P.M. the commander of the military police of the Army Air Fields at Roswell, Major Edwin Easley, called to the chief of the Intelligence Department, Major Jesse Marcel, "Come here, quick!" But on the way to the base the Major already observed a perfect V-formation of lights flying across the city in a southerly direction. "Our planes are not that fast," was his first thought. As he learned later, no U.S. planes had been in the air that night. Some GIs and MPs also saw the spectacle.[23]

In spite of all efforts made by the Air Force to track down the "flying saucers" and to photograph them, it was given to a civilian, on July 7, 1947, to take the first picture of the mysterious aircraft. William A. Rhodes of Phoenix, Arizona, was just on his way to his workshop behind his house, when he heard a noise which sounded as if it came from a jet-fighter flying very low. The enthusiastic hobby photographer had long waited for this opportunity. He ran quickly into the house to bring his new camera and photograph the jet. But when he came out of the house, there was no plane in the sky. Instead, he saw a strange flying object, which was almost circular, without wings or projections, flat and with a light in the middle of its back. It must be one of those "flying saucers" about which he had read in the papers, thought Rhodes and pointed his camera at the approaching object. When it was about 2,000 feet away he took the first picture of it. Instead of coming nearer, the object now veered off and started moving away from him. Rhodes took a second picture, before it accelerated and silently flew off westwards, disappearing behind a blanket of thick clouds.

Rhodes developed the film the same day in his own laboratory and offered the successful shots to the local newspaper, *The Arizona Republic*.[24] Two days later they

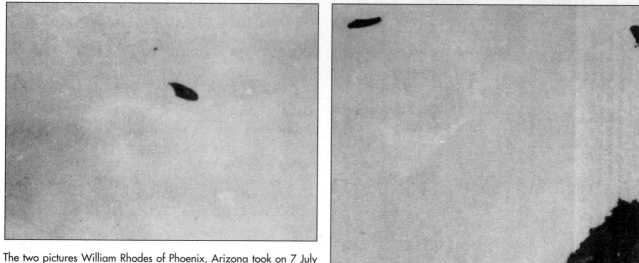

The two pictures William Rhodes of Phoenix, Arizona took on 7 July 1947

were published under the headline "Saucer Flits in the Sky at Unbelievable Speed." As Kenneth Arnold saw the photos, he expressed his conviction that they must be genuine. It was exactly the same type of "saucer" that he had seen, although he had never described them so minutely to the press.[25]

This caught the attention of the Air Force and of the FBI as well. *"The FBI appeared within 48 hours after I published the news item,"* said William Rhodes later, *"a civilian official called Mr. Ledding and Lt. Col. Beam from the Air Force were the interrogators. They confiscated the negative and said I would get it back soon. But that never happened. Years later when I called the FBI, they denied all knowledge of the incident."*[26]

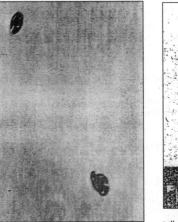

Two discs over Pontiac, Michigan, photographed by Albert Weaver

Bill Turrentine's photo of a flying disc "bigger than an Automobile" over Norfolk, Virginia, 8/7/47.

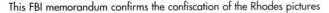

This FBI memorandum confirms the confiscation of the Rhodes pictures

We know today that this was clearly a lie. The FBIs extensive UFO files, which were released during the presidency of Jimmy Carter, confirm the confiscation of the negatives on July 11, 1947 and their being sent to the Intelligence Department of the Army Air Force.[27]

Rhodes's photographs were not the only shots of a "flying saucer." On the same day Albert Weaver photographed two discs above Pontiac, Michigan[28], and a day later the thirteen- year-old boy Bill Turrentine got a picture of a "gigantic metallic football, followed by two smaller bodies," over Norfolk, Virginia.[29] But what really should have been a sensation, namely three photos of decent quality, from three different states, went unnoticed by the media, owing to another set of headlines. For on July 8, 1947 a spokesman of the Roswell Army Air Field announced that the riddle of the mysterious interlopers had been solved by a sensational find:

"The many rumors regarding the flying discs became a reality

yesterday when the intelligence office of the 509th Bomb Group of the eighth Air Force, RAAF, was fortunate enough to gain possession of a disc through the cooperation of one of the local ranchers and the sheriff's office of Chaves County.

The flying object landed on a ranch near Roswell sometime last week. Not having phone facilities, the rancher stored the disc until such time as he was able to contact the sheriff's office, who in turn notified Major Jesse A. Marcel of the 509th Bomb Group Intelligence office.

Action was immediately taken and the disc was picked up at the rancher's home. It was inspected at the RAAF and subsequently loaned by Major Marcel to higher headquarters."[30]

This announcement, published by Associated Press (AP), did not go unnoticed. The 509th Bomb Group was the AAFs elite unit, the only unit in the world with atomic weapons, the unit that had dropped the atom bombs on Hiroshima and Nagasaki. Every one of its pilots had spent thousands of hours in a bomber. Each one of them was a veteran, many had been in Europe during World War II and later in the Far East. Everyone in the unit had been checked for security. Its Intelligence Department was first rate and had the best counterintelligence officers of the Army Air Force. This applied especially to Major Marcel. In 1943 he had graduated from the Air Intelligence School in Harrisburg, Pennsylvania, then flew heavy bombers in New Guinea, before being trained in the latest radar technology at Langley Field, Virginia. After he had been made familiar with "more or less everything that flies, whether ours or theirs," he was promoted to the rank of major and attached to the 509th Bomb Group. He took part in the first atom-

Roswell Army Air Field—Home of 509th Bomb Group, 1st Air Transport Unit. Sign at the base gate

ic tests in the Bikini Atoll, before being transferred to Roswell. No wonder his statement made a big stir. What came from the 509th Bomb Group had nearly as much impact as something from the Pentagon.

But hardly had the news made headlines in the country's evening papers, than it was followed by a correction on the teleprinters:

DISC SOLUTION COLLAPSES. "Flying Saucer" Find Turns Out to Be a Weather Balloon. Ramey Broadcast.

There was immediately much telephoning from the Pentagon in Washington, and then Brigadier General Roger M. Ramey, commanding the Eighth Air Force at Fort Worth, said the object had been identified as the wreckage of a high-altitude weather observation device.

General Ramey later made a radio broadcast further to deflate the excitement caused by the first announcement.

Originally he said, it consisted of a box-kite and a balloon. "The wreckage is in my office right now and as far as I can see there is nothing to get excited about," he said.

The device, a star-shaped tinfoil target designed to reflect radar, is incapable of speeds higher than the wind.

The mysterious flying discs which have been "seen" all over the Nation (except Kansas which is dry) have been described as traveling at speeds up to 1,200 miles an hour.[31]

For the media and the public the matter was settled for the time being. Nobody, really no one, asked himself how the chief of the Intelligence Department of the best bomber unit of the U.S. could have mistaken a simple weather balloon for a mysterious "flying

The Atomic Blast, the base newspaper of the 509th Bomb Group

saucer." At best, one held the press announcement as the peak of hysteria or the overreaction of a profile-seeking officer, trying to make a career. Thirty years were to go by till the truth about the Roswell incident came out into the open and General Ramey's disinformation was shown to be the beginning of one of the most elaborately organized cover-ups of the twentieth century.

Perhaps this young nation, the USA, which had

"RAAF CAPTURES FLYING SAUCER ON RANCH IN ROSWELL REGION ": With this headline of the *Roswell Daily Record* of 8 July 1947 the Roswell story began.

"GEN. RAMEY EMPTIES ROSWELL SAUCER"—the cover-up began just one day later, on 9 July 1947

General Roger Ramey, Commander of the 8th Air Force

tic radio play about the landing of Martians in New Jersey and set off mass panic.

It was decided that such a situation should never arise again. No matter what happened, the citizens of the USA must feel secure under the protection of their government, army and intelligence. That the U.S. could deal with any situation—and easily at that—had been proved by the victories over Germany and Japan. But the price that was paid for this apparent security was high—it was the abandonment of democratic virtues. People had to be intimidated and forced into silence. So perhaps that 8th day of July, 1947, will be remembered as the beginning of the darkest chapter in the history of the United States, the day on which this young nation lost her innocence.

become the world's leading power after its glorious victories in the Second World War, was unable to face the situation. Or perhaps the decision was made out of the need to attain national stability after the years of depression and war and a justifiable fear that panic would break out and governmental authority would be lost if the truth were revealed. Memories of the Halloween night of 1938 were still vivid, when the young director Orson Welles broadcast his very realis-

[1] Arnold, Kenneth and Ray Palmer, *The Coming of the Saucers*, Amherst, 1952.

[2] Army Air Force Telex of 16 July 1947.

[3] Arnold/Palmer, 1952.

[4] Bloecher, Ted, *The Report on the UFO Wave of 1947*, Washington, D.C., 1967.

[5] *Chico Record*, 7 July 1947.

[6] *Press Democrat*, Santa Rosa, CA, 8 July 1947.

[8] *Santa Maria Times*, 3 July 1947.

[9] *Los Angeles Examiner*, 5 July 1947.

[10] *The Memphis Press-Scimitar*, 5 July 1947.

[11] *Tacoma Times*, 8 July 1947

[12] *The Denver Post*, 6 July 1947.

[13] *Mercury Herald*, San Jose, CA, 5 July 1947 / *Examiner*, San Francisco, 5 July 1947.

[14] *The Clearwater Sun*, 6 July 1947.

[15] *Mercury News*, San Jose, CA, 6 July 1947.

[16] *The Bakersfield Californian*, 5 July 1947.

[17] Associated Press, 6 July 1947.

[18] *Chicago Daily News*, Chicago, 7 July 1947.

[19] Los Alamos Historical Society, "Los Alamos—Beginning of

[20] an Era," Los Alamos, 1986.

[20] Borwolf, Adalbert, *Die Geheimfabrik,* Munich, 1994 .

[21] *Bhagavad Gita,* 11.12.

[22] Berlitz, Charles and William Moore, *The Roswell Incident,* New York, 1980.

[23] Pratt, Bob, Interview with Col. Jesse Marcel, 8 December 1979.

[24] *The Arizona Republic,* 9 July 1947.

[25] Arnold/Palmer, 1952.

[26] Ibid.

[27] FBI-Telex of 11 July 1947.

[28] Arnold/Palmer, 1952.

[29] Ibid.

[30] *San Francisco Chronicle,* 9 July 1947.

[31] Ibid.

2.

The Debris Field

Wednesday, 2 July 1947, Roswell, New Mexico, around 9:50 P.M. Dan Wilmot and his wife were sitting on the porch of their white-painted wooden house and were looking at the sky, deep in thought. Suddenly Dan noticed a big glowing object coming from a south-easterly direction at a very high speed. He called the attention of his wife to it, saying, "Look, darling, what is that?" They went down the porch steps into the front garden, from where they could see it better. "It was oval and looked like two saucers put together," Wilmot said later, as he was being interviewed by a reporter for the *Roswell Daily Record,* the local paper, "or like two of the old-fashioned washbasins," added his wife. "The whole thing seemed to glow," Dan went on, "not as if it was being lit up from below, no, it glowed from within." It flew very low, only 1,500 feet high, at a speed of about 400 to 500 miles per hour, in his estimate, and its size must have been between fifteen and twenty feet in diameter. "It was absolutely silent," he maintained, but his wife contradicted, saying, "For a short time I heard a kind of hissing." Dan, finishing his description, said, "It disappeared after that in the direction of the Six-Mile Hills." "We discussed about it the whole weekend, whether it was one of those 'flying saucers,' about

which one now reads everywhere," continued his wife, "and we asked ourselves whether other people had seen it too. So my husband decided to call you." The call took place only a few minutes before the official announcement of the salvaging of a "flying disc" made by the public relations officer of the 509th Bomb Group, as the *Roswell Daily Record*—an evening paper—of July 8 emphatically stated.[1] It seemed as if there was a connection between the two incidents, although there was nothing to prove it. But there were other mysterious sightings around Roswell during the early days of July 1947.

William M. Woody, son of a farmer and at that time fourteen years old, declared later in an affidavit:

One hot night during the summer of 1947, probably in early July, my father and I were outside on the farm. It was well after sundown and quite dark. Suddenly, the sky lit up. When we looked up to see where the light was coming from, we saw a large, very bright object in the south-western sky, moving rapidly northward.

The object had the bright white intensity of a blow torch and had a long flame-like tail with colors like a blow-torch flame fading down into a pale red. Most of the tail was this pale red color. The tail was very long, equal to about 10 diameters of a full moon.

We watched the object travel all the way across the sky until it disappeared below the northern horizon. It was moving fast but not as fast as a meteor, and we had it in view for what seemed like 20 to 30 seconds. Its brightness and colors did not change during the whole time, and it definitely went out of sight below the horizon, rather than winking out like a meteor does. My father thought it was a big meteorite and was convinced it had fallen to earth about 40 miles north of Roswell.[2]

Rancher W. Mac Brazel in July 1947, when he found the debris

The Franciscan nuns who served as nurses at St. Mary's Hospital noted in the night of July 4 between 11:15 P.M. and 1:30 A.M. the appearance of *"a flaming object that came down in a curve, north of Roswell."*[3]

On this night a heavy storm was raging in the vicinity of Corona, New Mexico, seventy-five miles northwest of Roswell. Rancher William W. "Mac" Brazel, leaseholder of the Foster Ranch in Lincoln country, his family, and his neighbors heard a loud explosion. Jim Ragsdale and his girlfriend Trudy were camping somewhere in the desert some forty-five miles northwest of Roswell. They had been attracted by the loneliness and peace the place offered, far away from civilization. Yet that night was anything but peaceful. Lightning flashed and thunder rolled, a gale was blowing, dust and rain battered on the tent, in which they lay huddled against each other in their sleeping bags, watching the spectacle of nature. Suddenly *"we*

observed a bright flash and what appeared to be a bright light source moving towards southeast," Ragsdale said later, describing their sighting. It happened at about 11:30 P.M.[4]

Early next morning rancher Brazel, accompanied by William "Dee" Proctor, the seven-year-old son of a neighbor, rode out to see what damage the storm had done. Often enough a heavy rain had let loose whole avalanches of mud, which had torn down his fences, or the wind had damaged his windmills, or lightning had struck a sheep or two. Time and again it had happened that the animals thronged against the fence, frightened by the thunder and trying to find shelter from the rain. One found them lying knotted together in heaps, one over the other, the ones at the bottom crushed to death by the weight of the ones on the top. "Sheep are always stupid," Brazel used to say. The ride took them over his grazing land, which was covered by rocks, thickets, and wild buffalo grass, to a terrain some five miles south of the ranch house, where one of his herds had been grazing.

The sight that met the eyes of Mac Brazel and Dee was awful, even from a distance. Beginning directly behind a dried-out riverbed and spreading over a hill was "a field of debris." Fragments of metallic parts lay there, covering a strip of land three quarters of a mile long and 200 yards wide. Something must have crashed there. A plane? It must have exploded. A weather balloon? Impossible. Brazel had already found over a dozen weather and test balloons on his land and as a rule informed the meteorological office or the University of New Mexico. This much was clear to him: it was something very different.

Together with Dee he rode over to the wreckage, dismounted, and looked at the pieces one by one. Some of them had a silvery shine, but most of them were a dull metallic. There were very large and also many tiny parts. Some were so light that they fluttered in the wind. There were rods, covered with hieroglyphs, as light as balsa wood. But as he tried to cut them with his pocket knife, he could not even make a scratch on them. He lit a match and tried to burn them, but they would not burn.

The bleating of his sheep brought him back to pressing realities. They were on one side of the field of destruction, but their watering place was on the other side. Obviously they were afraid to cross the debris. "I shall have to get them over with the truck this afternoon," Brazel said rather disgustedly to Dee, "or they'll go and die of thirst!" He then picked up a few of the fragments and stuffed them into his saddle bags. "I'll show them to your parents," he said, "and see what they say about it." They then rode back to the ranch house.

At lunchtime Brazel brought Dee home to his parents, Floyd and Loretta Proctor, and showed them what he had found. On May 5, 1991 Loretta Proctor declared in an affidavit, *"In July 1947, my neighbor William 'Mac' Brazel came to my ranch and showed my husband and me a piece of material he said came from a large pile of debris on the property he managed. The piece he brought was brown in color, similar to plastic. He and my husband tried to cut and burn the object, but they weren't successful. It was extremely light in weight. I had never seen anything like it before. 'Mac' said the other material on the property looked like aluminum foil. It was very flexible and wouldn't crush or burn. There was also something he described as tape which had printing on it. The color of the printing was kind of purple. He said it wasn't Japanese writing; from the way he described it, it sounded like it resembled hieroglyphs."*[5] She confirmed this account when we interviewed her personally in July 1995 . She still lives in the same little white ranch house north of the Foster Ranch in which she and her family lived in 1947. When we wanted to interview her son, who is now fifty-five years old, she dissuaded us from doing so. "Dee says he can't remember anything now. He was too young then," she said, "only once, as we rode through the Foster land, he showed me a strip above a dried-up riverbed and said it was there that he and Mac had found the wreck of the 'saucer.'"[6]

The Proctors had too many pressing chores on their ranch to accept Mac's offer to show them the wreck. They advised him, however, to report it to the authorities. "Maybe it is again one of these military tests and they are looking for it. There is usually a reward for this sort of thing." When the rancher finally came home for lunch, he showed his family the things he had found. On the same afternoon he went with his fourteen-year-old daughter Bessie and twelve-year-old son Vernon to "clear up the place," as he called it. They rode over to the field of wreckage, at least to gather the fluttering pieces, that were frightening the sheep.

Bessie Schreiber (Brazel's daughter, now married) said in an affidavit dated 22 September 1993:

> *Most of it was a kind of double-sided material, foil-like on one side and rubber-like on the other. Both sides were grayish silver in color, the foil more silvery than the rubber. Sticks, like kite sticks, were attached to some of the pieces with a whitish tape. The tape was about two or three inches wide and had flower-like designs on it. The "flowers" were faint, a variety of pastel colors, and reminded me of Japanese paintings in which the flowers are not all connected. I do not recall any other types of material or markings, nor do I remember seeing gouges in the ground or any other signs that anything may have hit the ground hard. The foil-rubber material could not be torn like ordinary aluminum foil can be torn. I do not recall anything else about the strength or other properties of what we picked up.*
>
> *We spent several hours collecting the debris and putting it in sacks. I believe we filled about three sacks and we took them back to the ranch house.*[7]

But the three sacks represented only a very tiny percentage of the debris that still lay around. There was no sense in trying to collect them. The sheep were thirsty.

He drove back to the spot in his truck to transport the sheep in small groups to the watering place. In the evening he drove to Corona to do some shopping. He talked about his find to friends there and heard for the first time about the "flying saucers" that had been making news recently. "Who knows, maybe one of those things has come down on your land. There is a reward of $5,000 for anyone who helps to solve the riddle of the saucers. You say there is writing on the things. Perhaps it's something from the Russians or the Japanese. Go to Roswell tomorrow and inform the sheriff."

On Sunday, 6 July 1947, Mac Brazel got up early as usual. After a good breakfast he set off in his truck at about 7:30 A.M., intending to drive to Roswell. In those days, owing to bad roads, it was a three-and-a-half-hour journey through the bare and rocky desert of New Mexico. He arrived at the office of the Sheriff, George Wilcox, at about 11 A.M. The sheriff was not particularly impressed as Brazel, a typical cowboy in dirty trousers, leather boots, and wearing a stained leather hat, entered his office. "Sheriff, I believe a flying saucer has crashed on my ranch." "Really?" "I have brought a few pieces of it with me: they are in my truck outside. At home I have a whole field—bigger than a football field—covered with the stuff. It looks as though the grass got burnt as it came down."

Wilcox went out with Brazel, had a look at a piece about thirty-five inches wide, took a few small pieces with him inside, and ordered a couple of deputies to "drive out there and have a look." To Brazel he said, "I think we should inform 509th Bomb Group." At that moment the telephone rang. At the other end was Frank Joyce, radio correspondent of the KGFL station, who had just started his usual forenoon calls to snap the latest for the twelve-o'clock news. "Hi, Sheriff! Who was drunk last night?" he asked jocularly. Instead of that, Wilcox told him about the rancher who was in his office at the

Sheriff Wilcox

moment. Joyce talked to Brazel.

"He spoke of things that made me skeptical," Joyce told me when I interviewed him in December 1993 at Albuquerque, New Mexico, *"as a radio correspondent one is confronted by all sorts of strange stories. So I recommended him to tell the Army at Roswell Army Airfield, since they were the experts on everything that flies."*[8] So Sheriff Wilcox called the base and was immediately connected with the office of the Intelligence Corps Officer, Major Jesse A. Marcel. "What is the matter, Sheriff?" he asked. "I have here a man who is telling me something very strange." "I am all ears!" answered the major and was put on to Brazel. *"He said that he had found something on his ranch that had crashed down either on the previous day or the day before that, and that he did not know what it was,"*[9] Marcel declared later. He promised to go over to the sheriff's office immediately after lunch—it was twelve noon then. Meanwhile Wilcox showed the pieces from the wreck to his wife and children.

Major Marcel turned up at about 12:50 P.M. He looked carefully at the pieces, loaded the largest one into the trunk of his car and drove back to the base. But before leaving he requested Brazel to stay at the sheriff's office: he would soon be back. At the base Marcel took the fragment directly to the commanding officer, Colonel William Blanchard. "What would you advise me to do?" asked the major. The olonel looked at the piece carefully and said, "My advice is that you drive out to the site. How much of this stuff is there?" "According to what the guy says, there's plenty." "Now, you have three counterintelligence agents at your disposal. Take one of them with you for support." Marcel called up Captain Cavitt, the highest-ranking man in the counterespionage corps of the base. They decided to meet at the sheriff's office. Marcel took his 42-model Buick, Cavitt drove a Jeep from the base. At 5 P.M. they left for the site, followed by Brazel.

Meanwhile, Blanchard had informed Brigadier General Roger Ramey, commander of the 8th Air Force, to which the 509th Bomb Group belonged, at the Fort Worth Field in Texas. He, in turn, forwarded the news to the Pentagon in Washington. At 3:00 P.M. local time (CT), when it was 2:00 P.M. (MT) at Roswell, Ramey's chief of staff, Colonel Thomas Jefferson DuBose, received a call from the Pentagon from General Clements McMullen, Vice-Commander of the Strategic Air Command, with orders to send the fragment brought by Brazel in a sealed container via Fort Worth to Andrews Air Field near Washington, where General McMullen would receive it personally. Colonel DuBose at once contacted Colonel Blanchard, who immediately prepared an aircraft for takeoff. The plane left for Fort Worth at 3:00 P.M. with the fragment on board. It was received there at about 6 P.M. (CT) by the commander of the base, Colonel Al Clark, personally and carried by him to a B-26 aircraft which was waiting to take it to Washington, D.C. Soon after it started, Colonel DuBose called General McMullen to announce the arrival of the plane. "Thanks, Colonel," answered the general, "I shall send it with a personal courier to General Chidlaw at Wright Field. And please remember: the entire operation falls under the highest level of secrecy."[10] General Benjamin Chidlaw was commanding general of the Air Materiel Command.

At about the same time the sheriff's deputies who had gone to inspect the crash site came back. They had not found the area where the wreckage lay, but had discovered a "large, circular black spot" in which "the sand had melted into glass and turned black."[11]

It was already getting dark as Brazel, Marcel, and Cavitt reached the Foster ranch. Brazel showed the officers the other pieces of the wreck, which he had taken to the ranch with him and stored in a shed outside. The biggest was about ten feet in diameter. "One doesn't know if the stuff is radioactive," he remarked. "That we'll find out right now," replied Marcel, went to his car and brought a Geiger counter with him. When he held the sensor near the pieces, there was no indication of radiation. "Negative," said Marcel, "the things are not dangerous . . . whatever they are." Brazel promised, "We'll ride over to the place early in the morning." They dined on canned beans and crackers and went to sleep.[12]

At seven o'clock, right after breakfast, Brazel saddled the horses. While Cavitt, called "Cav" by his friends, came from Texas and had learned riding at his parents' ranch, Marcel had never sat on a horse before and felt queasy about it. "I'd rather drive in the jeep behind you," he said, interrupting Brazel as he was about to saddle the third horse, "we can load a bit right away and save time."

They could see the field of wreckage from quite a distance. *"The debris was spread over a wide area,"* Marcel said, meanwhile promoted to the rank of colonel, in an interview on 8 December 1979, three years before his death,

maybe three-quarters of a mile long and a few hundred feet wide . . . it was all evenly spread out, as if something had exploded in the air and fallen down on the ground. What impressed me was that one could clearly see which direction it came from and where it was going. It flew from northeast to southwest. One could see where it began, and also where it ended. Although we didn't go over the whole area, I could see that it was broader where we started and became narrower towards the southeast end.... We found some very small metallic pieces, but most of what lay around was very difficult to describe. I had never seen anything like that before, and even today, I don't know what it was. We picked them up one by one.... I wanted to see if the material would burn, and me being a heavy smoker, I had a cigarette lighter with me. So I held the lighter flame under some of the pieces, but they didn't burn.... Some of them had signs on them, which I just call hieroglyphics. I couldn't read them and don't know whether they have been deciphered or not.... There were some rods as well, which we couldn't bend or break. They didn't feel like metal, looked more like wood. There were differ-

ent sizes of them. If I remember right, they were about three inches by two-and-a-half inches in girth and in various lengths. None of them was very long, the biggest was about a yard long ... and almost weightless. One could hardly feel that one had anything in his hand—like with balsa wood—and along the length they had marks on them, in two different colors, that looked to me like Chinese writing....

I was familiar with every kind of gadget that we used in the army for meteorological observations, but I couldn't identify any of the stuff as being part of any such thing.... I was in fact fairly familiar with almost everything that went into the air in those days, not only our own military aircraft, but also those belonging to other countries. I still believe that it was not a terrestrial object. It came to the earth, but not from the earth...."[13]

In a television interview in 1979 he gave more details about the pieces that formed the major portion of the debris: "Then there was a kind of parchment, brown and very tough, as well as many bits of metallic foil, that looked like, but was not, aluminum, for no matter how often one crumpled it, it regained its original shape again. Besides that, they were indestructible, even with a sledgehammer."[14]

The three men spent the whole day loading Cavitt's Jeep and the trunk of Marcel's car with the wreckage. They gave

Drawing of one of the "I-Beams" and reconstruction of the "hieroglyphs" by Dr. Jesse Marcel Jr.

Airways Authority. In an affidavit dated 6 March 1991 he described what he had seen on the kitchen floor: *"There were three categories of debris: a thick foil of metallic gray material; a rough plastic-like, brown-black in color . . . and pieces of I-sectioned rods. On the inner surface of these I-members was a kind of lettering. The writing was in purple and seemed to be in relief. The letters were curved, geometric figures that had no resemblance to Russian, Japanese, or any other foreign language. They looked like hieroglyphs, but had no pictures of animals."*[16]

Dr. Jesse Marcel Jr. with author Michael Hesemann

up when it was getting dark, and at about nine P.M. they left for Roswell. Marcel had to confess, *"We have collected only a tiny fraction of the lot."*[15]

But before Marcel went to the base he stopped at his house, to show his wife and eleven-year-old son Jesse Jr. what he had found. He took a few bits with him inside, and spread them on the kitchen floor for them to see. "That is something very special," he said to his son, "it doesn't come from this world. I want you to remember this all your life!"

Today Jesse A. Marcel, Junior is senior consultant in an ear, nose and throat clinic. He served as helicopter pilot in the Vietnam War and has been a member of the National Guard since 1978 as a Flying Doctor. He is also a certified crash investigator of the Federal

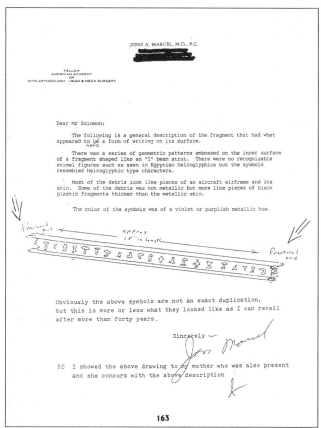

Jesse Marcel's drawing of debris fragment.

[1] *Roswell Daily Record*, 8 July 1947.

[2] Affidavit of William M. Woody, 28 September 1993.

[3] Randle, Kevin D. and Donald R. Schmitt, *The Truth about the UFO Crash at Roswell*, New York, 1994.

[4] Affidavit of James Ragsdale, 27 January 1993.

[5] Affidavit of Loretta Proctor, 5 May 1991.

[6] Personal Interview with Loretta Proctor, 3 July 1995.

[7] Affidavit of Bessie Schreiber née Brazel, 22 September 1993.

[8] Personal Interview with Frank Joyce, 8 December 1993.

[9] Pratt, Bob: "Interview with Col. Jesse Marcel, 8 December 1979," in Karl Pflock, *Roswell in Perspective*, Mount Rainier, MD, 1994.

[10] Affidavit of General Thomas Jefferson DuBose, 16 September 1991.

[11] Fund for UFO Research (FUFOR): "Interview with Elisabeth Tulk," in *Recollections of Roswell*. (Video) Mount Rainier, MD, 1993.

[12] FUROR: "Interview with Phyllis Mcguire" in *Recollections of Roswell*.

[13] Pratt, Bob: "Interview with Col. Jesse Marcel."

[14] FUROR: "Interview with Col. Jesse Marcel."

[15] Pratt, Bob: "Interview with Col. Jesse Marcel."

[16] Affidavit of M.D. Jesse A. Marcel, Jr., 6 March 1991.

3.

The Cover-Up

Tuesday, 8 July 1947. Early in the morning at six o'clock Major Marcel and Captain Cavitt reported to Colonel Blanchard at his house, which was on the base. They told him what they had seen and showed him the bits of wreckage that they had brought. He looked at them fascinated. He then ordered Cavitt to go back to the Foster Ranch at once, cordon off the field of debris and arrange for the salvaging of the whole wreckage. He was also to bring Brazel back with him to Roswell. Marcel was to stay at the base.

Cavitt returned to the crash site, accompanied by CIC-Agent Master Sergeant Lewis S. Rickett and four MPs in another vehicle. They had hardly left Roswell behind them, when they were stopped by a road blockade put up by the Military Police. The vehicle with the MPs was waved through, but the two CIC plainclothesmen had to identify themselves. "Sorry, Captain, but something has landed there," said one of the MPs, apologizing, as he looked through their papers. At the exit for Corona there was a second blockade.

At the farm there were about thirty men who had already collected most of the debris under the personal supervision of Major Edwin S. Easley. Rickett saw a piece of metal still lying on the floor. *"It was a slightly curved piece of metal, very light. It was about six inches wide and* *a foot long. I leaned down and tried to bend it,"* Rickett remembered during an interview with the Roswell researcher Mark Rodeghier. *"My boss laughed out loud and said, 'Clever boy! He's now trying to do what we have been trying in vain all this time!' What is the thing made of? I asked myself. It didn't feel like plastic, and I had never seen a piece of metal that thin that I couldn't bend. As we went around, my boss said to me, 'You and I were never here. You and I saw nothing. You saw no soldiers here, you understand?' And I answered, 'Yes, you are right. We never left the office.'"*[1]

Col. William H. Blanchard, commander of the 509th Bomb Group and the Roswell Army Air Fields 1947. He ordered his PIO, Lt. Haut, to inform the press about the recovery of the "saucer." Shortly after, he was promoted to general and became deputy chief of staff of the USAF until his death in 1966.

Lt. Walter Haut, the Public Information Officer (PIO) of the Roswell Army Air Field.

They then found Brazel and took him to Roswell. And there, meanwhile, all hell was loose. At nine o'clock in the morning Colonel Blanchard had requested the Press Officer of the base, Lieutenant Walter Haut, to come to his office. There Blanchard dictated an announcement and instructed Haut to take it to the two local newspapers and radio stations personally.[2] When interviewed in June 1993 (by one of the authors), he remembered, *"I got back to my office and typed up the press statement. It had more or less exactly the same phraseology as Blanchard had used. He was very particular that everything should be given out exactly as he had dictated."*[3]

At about eleven A.M. Lieutenant Haut first drove to the radio stations KGFL and KSWS, then to the local papers *Roswell Daily Record* and *Roswell Morning Dispatch*. The *Daily Record,* an evening paper, published the text on the same day under the headline "RAAF Captures Flying Saucer on Ranch in Roswell."[4] KSWS cabled the news to Associated Press, KGFL passed it on through Western Union to United Press. Then the news went around the world. During the following hours the broadcasting stations, Sheriff Wilcox's office, and Roswell AAF were bombarded with calls from all over the world, among others from Rome, London, Paris, Hamburg, Hong Kong, and Tokyo.[5]

The spokesman at KGFL who received the statement was Frank Joyce, whom I personally interviewed in December 1993. He said,

I looked at it very cursorily and didn't attach much importance to it, perhaps because I was busy with something else at that time. About a half an hour later I looked at it more carefully. It said that the U.S. Army Air Force had actually salvaged a flying saucer. . . I went at once to the telephone and called the Press Officer (Haut) and said, Listen, I know how things go in the Army, and I tell you, you can't write something like this. The Army won't allow you for it is a factual statement, "The U.S. Army declares it has," do you understand? If I were you, I wouldn't do it. But he only answered, "That's OK. The base commander has allowed it. You can send it ."

```
DXR 54
      MORE FLYING DISC (DXR 53)
                    -o-
     THE INTELLIGENCE OFFICE REPORTS THAT IT GAINED POSSESSION OF THE
"DIS:" THROUGH THE COOPERATION OF A ROSWELL RANCHER AND SHERIFF
GEORGE WILSON OF ROSWELL.
     THE DISC LANDED ON A RANCH NEAR ROSWELL SOMETIME LAST WEEK.  NOT
HAVING PHONE FACILITIES, THE RANCHER, WHOSE NAME HAS NOT YET BEEN
OBTAINED, STORED THE DISC UNTIL SUCH TIME AS HE WAS ABLE TO
CONTACT THE ROSWELL SHERIFF'S OFFICE.
     THE SHERIFF'S OFFICE IN TURN NOTIFIED A MAJOR OF THE 509TH
INTELLIGENCE OFFICE.
     ACTION WAS TAKEN IMMEDIATELY AND THE DISC WAS PICKED UP AT THE
RANCHER'S HOME AND TAKEN TO THE ROSWELL AIR BASE.  FOLLOWING
EXAMINATION, THE DISC WAS FLOWN BY INTELLIGENCE OFFICERS IN A SUPER-
FORTRESS TO AN UNDISCLOSED "HIGHER HEADQUARTERS."
     THE AIR BASE HAS REFUSED TO GIVE DETAILS OF CONSTRUCTION OF THE DISC
OR OF ITS APPEARANCE.
     RESIDENTS NEAR THE RANCH ON WHICH THE DISC WAS FOUND REPORTED
SEEING A STRANGE BLUE LIGHT SEVERAL DAYS AGO ABOUT THREE O'CLOCK IN
THE MORNING.
      J241P 7/8
```

Telex of 8 July 1947 regarding the Roswell incident

Now, in those days . . . I grew up in very poor circumstances, during the Great Depression, so I always thought of the costs. Today one would have cameras and all sorts of things at once there. But I thought a while before I said to myself, Now that looks like a big story. Do I send it out at once or tonight? At night it was cheaper to use the telex. But I decided to send it out at once. One gets such a story only once in a lifetime. So I sent it out at once, at the higher costs . . . I took the press announcement over to the Western Union office and sent it word for word on the ticker to United Press . . . Then I folded it, took it to the station and put it into the drawer of my writing table.

Then I had a call from Washington. A person who identified himself as Colonel Johnson was very angry, and I was the object of his anger. Whether I had sent out the press announcement? I naturally answered, "Yes." "Did you say yes?" "Yes." I don't know what he said after that, but I knew that I was in trouble. I said I was a civilian, but he yelled out that it made no difference. I didn't want to put my friend the press officer in trouble, but finally I had to say where I got the story from. "Listen, I sent the story out but I got it from an official source." He began to boil. "From where?" I told him and he banged the receiver down. The next call I had was from the press officer: "Frank, you were right, I shouldn't have given the story out." Later they came into my office and took away the announcement.[6]

Lt. Walter Haut today.

the radio station KSWS, drove towards the Foster Ranch to get an idea of the situation and do a bit of first-hand investigation. But he got only as far as the blockade north of Roswell. From the next telephone booth he called up Lydia Sleppy, the telex secretary of the sister broadcasting station KOAT, Albuquerque. Since KSWS did not have its own telex machine, he asked Lydia to send his report to ABC News in Hollywood. "One of these flying saucers crashed here, north of Roswell," began his report. "Witnesses related that they looked like big dented washbasins."

On 14 September 1993, Lydia A. Sleppy declared in an affidavit:

As I typed McBoyle's story, a bell rang on the teletype indicating an interruption. The machine then printed a message something to this effect: 'THIS IS THE FBI. YOU WILL IMMEDIATELY CEASE ALL COMMUNICATION.' Whatever the precise words were, I definitely remember the message was from the FBI and that it directed me to stop transmitting. I told McBoyle the teletype had been cut off and took the rest of his story in shorthand, but we never put it on the wire because we had been scooped by the papers.

I never again discussed the matter with McBoyle, but the next day he told Mr. Lambertz the military had isolated the area where the saucer was found and was keeping the press out.

He confessed to the Program manager of KSWS, "I received a call from the Defense Department and they told me, 'Shut up!' 'That is unusual,' said Walsh, 'had they corrected the report or is someone else responsible for the press?' I don't know that, my orders are, I quote, 'Shut up!' end of quote. . . ."[7]

An official called up the *Roswell Morning Dispatch* as well and declared that the press announcement was an error and that the salvaged object was a weather balloon.

Immediately after Lieutenant Haut gave him the statement, Johnny McBoyle, reporter and part-owner of

He told Lambertz he saw planes come in from Wright Field, Ohio, to take the thing away. . . .[8]

Other people also came across the road blockade. William Woody and his father decided to look for the "meteorite," which they had seen "falling some fifty miles north of Roswell three nights ago." Woody stated, in an affidavit on 28 September 1993,

He took me with him in our old flatbed truck. We headed north through Roswell on U.S. 285. About nineteen miles north of town, where the highway crosses the Macho Draw, we saw at least one uniformed soldier stationed beside the road. As we drove along we saw more sentries and Army vehicles. They were stationed at all places-ranch roads, crossroads etc.—where there was access to leave the highway and drive east or west, and they were armed, some with rifles, others with sidearms. I do not remember seeing any military activity on the ranchland beyond the highway right of way.

We stopped at one sentry post and my father asked a soldier

U.S. 285 north of Roswell.

what was going on. The soldier, whose attitude was very nice, just said his orders were not to let anyone leave 285 and go into the countryside.

As we drove north we saw that the Corona road (State 247), which runs west from highway 285, was blocked by soldiers. We went on as far as Ramon, about nine miles north of the 247 intersection. There were sentries there, too. At Ramon we turned around and headed south and home.

I remember my father saying he thought the Army was looking for something it had tracked on its way down. He may have gotten this from the soldier he spoke with during our drive up 285, but I am not sure.[9]

Brazel's neighbor, the rancher J. O. Bud Payne, was also stopped by the police. In an affidavit made on 14 September 1993 he declared:

When I heard about the flying saucer coming down on the Foster ranch a few days after it happened in early July 1947, I decided to see if I could get a piece of the thing. The site where the saucer came down was about two or two and a half miles east of the east boundary of our pasture. I drove over there in a pickup truck. Before I reached the site I was stopped by two soldiers in an army truck parked beside the ranch road I was on. They were in field uniforms and they may have been armed, wearing pistols. There were more vehicles and soldiers on higher ground beyond where I had been stopped.

I told the two soldiers who stopped me I was going to where the flying saucer came down. They said, "We know where you're going but you can't go in there." I said, "Well, all I want is a little piece of that material." They said, "We know what you want but there's the road you came up. You go back down that road." They were nice, jolly old boys. They did not threaten me but they had their instructions to turn everybody back.[10]

Even two deputies of Sheriff Wilcox, sent by the sheriff to have another look at the ranch, were stopped at the blockade and sent back.[11] The barriers were there at least till the afternoon of July 9, as reported by George "Jud" Roberts, manager of KGFL, Roswell: *"In an attempt to drive to the crash site and see it with our own eyes, we were stopped by the army and compelled to turn back, since we, as they said, were on forbidden area."*[12]

But two journalists had more luck, since they came from the north through Corona, and the access to the Foster Ranch had not been closed. Jason Kellahin was at that time working as a reporter for AP in Albuquerque. As soon as the news of the crash came there, he was sent out with the photographer Robin D. Adair to visit the Foster Ranch. On 20 September 1993 he affirmed in an affidavit,

At the ranch house, we found William "Mac" Brazel, his wife, and his small son. It was Brazel who made the find in a pasture some distance from the house. He was not happy about the attention he was getting and the people traipsing around he place. He said if he ever found anything again he would not tell anyone unless it was a bomb.

Brazel took Adair and me to the pasture where he made his discovery. When we arrived, there were three or four uniformed army officers searching some higher ground about a quarter to a half a mile away. Apparently, they had been there for some time.

There was quite a lot of debris, the site pieces of silver-colored fabric, perhaps aluminized cloth. Some of the pieces had sticks attached to them. I thought they might be the remains of a high altitude balloon package, but I did not see anything, pieces of rubber or the like, that looked like it could have been part of the balloon itself. The way the material was distributed it looked as though whatever it was from came apart as it moved along through the air.

After looking at the material, I walked over to the military men. They said they were from RAAF and were just looking around to see what they could find. They said they were going back to Roswell and would talk with me further there. They had a very casual attitude and did not seem at all disturbed that the press was there. They made no attempt to run us off.

Adair and I, Brazel, and the Army men then drove down to Roswell, traveling separately. Late that afternoon or early evening we met at the offices of the Roswell Daily Record, *the city's afternoon newspaper. The military men waited on the sidewalk out front while I and a* Record *reporter named Skeritt interviewed Brazel and Adair took his picture. (Adair also took photos of Brazel and the debris at the ranch, but these were never used.) Walter E. Whitmore, owner of KGFL, one of Roswell's two radio stations, was also present during the interview. Whitmore did his best to maneuver Brazel away from the rest of the press.*

After interviewing Brazel, I spoke with the military people outside and then went over to see Sheriff George Wilcox, whom

Roswell main street in 1947

I knew well. Wilcox said the military indicated to him it would be best if he did not say anything. I then phoned in my story to the AP office in Albuquerque. The next morning Adair transmitted his photos on the portable wirephoto equipment.[13]

The next thing was that Whitmore took Brazel to the radio station, accompanied by two soldiers, to be interviewed by Frank Joyce, who in December 1993 told us:

He came to the station and I sat there in my ugly announcer's cabin—wholly self-made—and he told me a story entirely different from what he had told me two days ago on the phone (from the sheriff's office). After the interview, just as he was about to leave, I said, "One moment, you know with whom you have spoken, don't you?" He replied, "Yes." "And you know that this story you have told me today has nothing to do with what you related on the telephone." He looked at me for a few moments—you know, the guy was one of those old Wild West, dirt-in-the-pores types whom one meets on the ranches—and said, "Look, Son. Keep it to yourself. They told me to come here and tell you this story, or I would get into serious trouble." "And what about the little green men?" I asked. "Only that they weren't green," he said, opened the door and went out, where the two soldiers were waiting for him.[14]

But Walt Whitmore was not satisfied with that: he had the feeling that the army was trying to cover up something. Since the GIs had only received orders to take Brazel to Roswell to make his statements, they did not object to Brazel's spending the night at Whitmore's home in Roswell. There Whitmore recorded another interview with Brazel. Early next morning two MPs came to Whitmore's house and took Brazel with them. He had to stay in Roswell till July 15, at the guest house of the RAAF, "in the custody" of the Army. Once his neighbor Floyd Proctor, who, according to a statement made by his wife Loretta Proctor on 5 May 1991, had

Walter E. Whitmore, owner of the Radio station KFGL

gone to Roswell with his brother and a friend, caught a glimpse of Brazel. Mac *"was surrounded by soldiers. He walked right by them, without speaking a word . . . when he got back, he said that the Army had told him the object he found was a weather balloon. "If I see another one, I won't report it," he said. He was upset about them keeping him from home that long. He wouldn't talk about it after he got back."*[15]

His neighbor Marian Strickland remembered how he had once spoken about the bad treatment he had received at Roswell. *"He made it clear that he was not permitted to talk to anyone about it. He was a man of integrity. He felt definitely hurt, misused and disrespectfully treated. He was more than angry. He was under great stress and felt he was being pushed around. They had threatened him that if he opened his mouth he would be sent to the most remote prison.*[16]

To others he only hinted at being kept as if in prison and that he had been asked the same questions again and again. But what made some of his neighbors wonder was why he now suddenly seemed to have come into money. Whereas before he had been *"so poor that he couldn't rub two nickels together,"* he now returned from Roswell driving a new truck and had enough money to buy a new house for his family at Tularosa and a coldstore at Las Cruces. *"A few months later he had enough money to invest in big meat deals,"* recalled Alma Hobbs, daughter of the Proctors. And Brazel's sister, Lorrene Fergusson, wondered about it too: *"Where did he get the money from?"*[17]

Otherwise he kept quiet. Tommy Tyree, a ranch worker whom Brazel hired after the incident, remembered how he saw a piece of wreckage swimming on a pool, while out riding with Mac Brazel. *"That is a piece of what came down then,"* said Mac and shortly and quickly changed the subject.[18] *"My Dad found this thing and he told me a little bit about it . . . not much,"* said Mac's older son Bill, who lived in Albuquerque in those days, *"because the Air Force asked him to take an oath that he wouldn't tell anybody in detail about it. He went to his grave and he never told anybody. He was an old-time Western cowboy and they didn't do a lot of talking. My brother and I had just gone through World War II (him in the Army and me in the Navy) and needless to say, my dad was proud. Like he told me, 'When you guys went in the service, you took an oath, and I took an oath not to tell.' The only thing he said was, 'Well, there's a big bunch of stuff, there's some tinfoil, some wood, and on some of that wood there was Japanese or Chinese figures.'"*[19]

That someone wanted to prevent Brazel from broadcasting his story uncensored became clear soon after the MPs had taken him away from Whitmore's house. The telephone rang at the KGFL radio station and George "Jud" Roberts, the manager, picked up the call. He declared on 30 December 1991 in an affidavit, *"The next morning, I got a call from someone in Washington, D.C. It may have been someone in the office of Clinton Anderson or Dennis Chavez. This person said, 'We understand that you have some information, and we want to assure you that if you release it, it's very possible that your station's license will be in jeopardy, so we suggest that you not do it.' The person indicated that we might lose our license in as quickly as three days. I made the decision not to release the story."*[20]

Two further calls from Washington, from Senator Chavez and the Secretary of Telecommunications, T. J. Slowie, personally, to Whitmore gave him the same message: he would lose his license if he broadcast the interview with Brazel.

The official version of the interview was published in the *Roswell Daily Record* on July 10 and read:

Brazel stated that on June 14 he and an 8-year-old son, Vernon (sic), were about 7 or 8 miles from the ranch house of the J. B. Foster ranch, which he operates, when they came upon a large area of bright wreckage made up of rubber strips, tinfoil, a rather tough paper and sticks.

At the time Brazel was in a hurry to get his round made and he did not pay much attention to it. But he did remark about what he had seen and on July 4 he, his wife, Vernon and a daughter, Betty, age 14, went back to the spot and gathered up quite a bit of the debris (sic). The next day he

Radio station KGFL in Roswell

Harassed Rancher who Located 'Saucer' Sorry He Told About It

W. W. Brazel, 48, Lincoln county rancher living 30 miles south east of Corona, today told his story of finding what the army at first described as a flying disk, but the publicity which attended his find caused him to add that if he ever found anything else short of a bomb he sure wasn't going to say anything about it.

Brazel was brought here late yesterday by W. E. Whitmore, of radio station KGFL, had his picture taken and gave an interview to the Record and Jason Kellahin, sent here from the Albuquerque bureau of the Associated Press to cover the story. The picture he posed for was sent out over AP telephoto wire sending machine specially set up in the Record office by R. D. Adair, AP wire chief sent here from Albuquerque for the sole purpose of getting out his picture and that of sheriff George Wilcox, to whom Brazel originally gave the information of his find.

Brazel related that on June 14 he and an 8-year old son, Vernon were about 7 or 8 miles from the ranch house of the J. B. Foster ranch, which he operates, when they came upon a large area of bright wreckage made up on rubber strips, tinfoil, a rather tough paper and sticks.

At the time Brazel was in a hurry to get his round made and he did not pay much attention to it. But he did remark about what he had seen and on July 4 he, his wife, Vernon and a daughter Betty, age 14, went back to the spot and gathered up quite a bit of the debris.

The next day he first heard about the flying disks, and he wondered if what he had found might be the remnants of one of these.

Monday he came to town to sell some wool and while here he went to see sheriff George Wilcox and "whispered kinda confidential like" that he might have found a flying disk.

Wilcox got in touch with the Roswell Army Air Field and Maj. Jesse A. Marcel and a man in plain clothes accompanied him home, where they picked up the rest of the pieces of the "disk" and went to his home to try to reconstruct it.

According to Brazel they simply could not reconstruct it at all, but could not do that and could not find any way to put it back together so that it would fit.

Then Major Marcel brought it to Roswell and that was the last he heard of it until the story broke that he had found a flying disk.

Brazel said that he did not see it fall from the sky and did not see it before it was torn up, so he did not know the size or shape it might have been, but he thought it might have been as large as a table top. The balloon which held it up, if that was how it worked, must have been about 12 feet long, he felt, measuring the distance by the size of the room in which he sat. The rubber was smoky gray in color and scattered over an area about 200 yards in diameter.

When the debris was gathered up the tinfoil, paper, tape, and sticks made a bundle about three feet long and 7 or 8 inches thick, while the rubber made a bundle about 18 or 20 inches long and about 8 inches thick. In all, he estimated, the entire lot would have weighed maybe five pounds.

There was no sign of any metal in the area which might have been used for an engine and no sign of any propellers of any kind, although at least one paper fin had been glued onto some of the tinfoil.

There were no words to be found anywhere on the instrument, although there were letters on some of the parts. Considerable scotch tape and some tape with flowers printed upon it had been used in the construction.

No strings or wire were to be found but there were some eyelets in the paper to indicate that some sort of attachment may have been used.

Brazel said that he had previously found two weather observation balloons on the ranch, but that what he found this time did not in any way resemble either of these.

"I am sure what I found was not any weather observation balloon," he said. "But if I find anything else, besides a bomb they are going to have a hard time getting me to say anything about it."

"HARASSED RANCHER WHO LOCATED 'SAUCER' SORRY HE TOLD ABOUT IT," the *Roswell Daily Record* reported on 10 July 1947. In the presence of the military Brazel told a completely different story—and claimed he already found the wreckage on June 14.

first heard about the flying disks, and he wondered if what he had found might be the remnants of one of these.

Monday (sic) he came to town to sell some wool (sic) and while here he went to see Sheriff George Wilcox and "whispered kinda confidential like" that he might have found a flying disc.

Wilcox got in touch with the Roswell Army Air Field and Maj. Jesse A. Marcel and a man in plain clothes accompanied him home, where they picked up the rest (sic) of the pieces of the "disc" and went to his home to try to reconstruct it.

According to Brazel they simply could not reconstruct it at all. They tried to make a kite (sic) out of it, but could not do

that and could not find any way to put it back together so that it would fit.

Then Major Marcel brought it to Roswell and that was the last he heard of it until the story broke that he had found a flying disk (sic).

Brazel said that he did not see it fall from the sky and did not see it before it was torn up, so he did not know the size or shape it might have been, but he thought it might have been about as large as a table top (sic). The balloon which held it up, if that was how it worked (sic), must have been about 12 feet long, he felt, measuring the distance by the size of the room in which he sat. The rubber was smoky gray in color and scattered over an area about 200 yards (sic) in diameter.

When the debris was gathered up the tinfoil, paper, tape, and sticks made a bundle about three feet long and 7 or 8 inches thick, while the rubber made a bundle about 18 or 20 inches long and about 8 inches thick. In all, he estimated, the entire lot would have weighed maybe five pounds.

There was no sign of any metal in the area which might have been used for an engine and no sign of any propellers of any kind, although at least one paper fin had been glued onto some of the tinfoil.

There were no words to be found anywhere on the instrument, although there were letters on some of the parts, considerable Scotch tape and some tape with flowers printed upon it had been used in the construction. No strings or wires were to be found but there were some eyelets in the paper to indicate that some sort of attachment may have been used.

Brazel said that he had previously found two weather observation balloons on the ranch, but that what he found this time did not in any way resemble any of these. "I am sure what I found was not any weather observation balloon," he said. "But if I find anything else beside a bomb they are going to have a hard time getting me to say anything about it."[21]

Brazel's son Bill, who, as mentioned before, lived in Albuquerque with his wife, learned about his father's predicament for the first time from the papers. "I got up one morning. . . got the paper and looked at it and here's my dad's picture. I said to Shirley, What the hell did he do now? So I proceeded to the ranch. I think it was two or three days before Dad showed up." Bill had meanwhile helped his mother with the chores on the ranch and now decided to stay on for a few weeks.[22]

Fascinated by the story, about which his father wouldn't say a word, he went again and again to the crash site. "I rode out there (the field where the debris was found) on the average of once a week, and I was riding through that area, I was

lookin'. That's why I found those little pieces," he recalled in a talk with Roswell researcher and nuclear physicist Stanton Friedman.

Not over a dozen pieces—I'd say maybe eight different pieces—but there was only three (different) items involved: somethin' on the order of balsa wood, something on the order of heavy-gauge monofilament fishing line, and a little piece of—it wasn't tinfoil, it wasn't lead foil—a piece about the size of my finger. Some of it was like balsa wood: real light and kind of neutral color, more of a tan. To the best of my memory there wasn't any grain in it. Couldn't break it—it'd flex a little. I couldn't whittle it with my pocket knife.

The "string," I couldn't break it. The only reason I noticed the tin foil (I'm gonna call it tin foil) I picked this stuff up and put it in my chaps pocket. Might be two or three days or a week before I took it out and put it in a cigar box. I happened to notice when I put that piece of foil in that box, and the damn thing just started unfolding and just flattened out! Then I got to playin' with it. I'd fold it, crease it, lay it down and it'd unfold. It's kinda weird. I couldn't tear it. The color was in between tin foil and lead foil, about the [thickness] of lead foil . . . .[23]

He showed it to his neighbors and friends, including the Stricklands, who lived in a neighboring ranch. Sally Strickland-Tadolini, nine years old at that time, recollected this in her affidavit on 27 September 1993:

What Bill showed us was a piece of what I still think of as fabric. It was something like aluminum foil, something like satin, something like well tanned leather in its toughness, yet it was not precisely like any of one of those materials. While I do not recall this with certainty, I think the fabric measured about four by eight or ten inches. Its edges, which were smooth, were not exactly parallel, and its shape was roughly trapezoidal. It was about the thickness of very fine kidskin glove leather and a dull metallic grayish silver, one side slightly darker than the other. I do not remember it having any design or embossing on it.

Bill passed it around and we all felt of it. I did a lot of sewing, so the feel made a great impression on me. It felt like no fabric I have touched before or since. It was very silky or satiny, with the same texture on both sides. Yet when I crumpled it in my hands the feel was like that you notice when you crumple a leather glove in your hand. When it was released it sprang back into its original shape, quickly flattening out with no wrinkles. I did this several times, as did the others. I remember some of the others stretching it between their hands and "popping" it but I do not think anyone tried to cut or tear it.[24]

Bill showed the strange material around in the billiards room of the Bar at Corona. That was about a month after the crash. Bill:

I was in Corona, in the bar, the pool hall—sort of the meeting place-domino parlor . . . . That's where everybody got together. Everybody was askin' . . . they'd seen the papers (this was about a month after the crash) and I said, "Oh, I picked up a few little bits and pieces and fragments." So, what are they? "I dunno."

Then, lo and behold, here comes the military (out to the ranch, a day or two later). I'm almost positive that the officer in charge, his name was Armstrong, a real nice guy. He had a [black] sergeant with him that was real nice. I think there was two other ensigns. They said, "We understand your father found this weather balloon." I said, "Well, yeah!" "And we understand you found some bits and pieces." I said, "Yeah, I've got a cigar box that's got a few of 'em in there, down at the saddle shed."

And this (I think he was a captain), and he said, "Well, we would like to take it with us." I said, "Well . . . " And he smiled and he said, "Your father turned the rest of it over to us, and you know he's under an oath not to tell. Well," he said, "we came after those bits and pieces." And I kind of

smiled and said, "OK, you can have the stuff, I have no use for it at all."

He said, "Well, have you examined it?" And I said, "Well, enough to know that I don't know what the hell it is!" And he said, "We would rather you didn't talk very much about it."[25]

The Air Force had become aware of the astonishing properties of the fragments, right after Major Marcel had brought in the first few pieces on July 8. He told Stanton Friedman,

But something that is more astounding is that the piece of metal that we brought back was so thin, just like the tinfoil in a pack of cigarette paper. I didn't pay too much attention to that at first, until one of the GIs came to me and said, "You know the metal that was in there? I tried to bend that stuff and it won't bend. I even tried it with a sledgehammer. You can't make a dent on it." He said, "It's definite that it cannot be bent and it's so light that it doesn't weigh anything." And that was true of all the material that was brought up. It was so light that it weighed practically nothing.

This particular piece of metal was, I would say, about two feet long and perhaps a foot wide. See, that stuff weighs nothing, it's so thin, it isn't any thicker than the tinfoil in a pack of cigarettes. So, I tried to bend the stuff [but] it wouldn't bend. We even tried making a dent in it with a sixteen-pound sledgehammer and there was still no dent in it."[26]

On the same day, 8 July 1947, Marcel received orders from Colonel Blanchard, in the presence of Lieutenant Colonel Payne Jennings, to fly to Fort Worth and report the matter to General Ramey. The recollections of flight security officer First Lieutenant Robert Shirkey about his observations as the plane was loaded, as recorded in an affidavit recorded on 30 April 1991, were as follows

I was in the Operations Office when Colonel Blanchard arrived. He asked if the aircraft was ready. When he was told

From the 1947 RAAF Base Yearbook: Lt. Robert Shirkey, after parachuting with his cocker spaniel.

it was, Blanchard waved to somebody, and approximately five people came in the front door, down the hallway and on to the ramp to climb into the airplane, carrying parts of what I heard was the crashed flying saucer.

At this time, I asked Colonel Blanchard to turn sideways so I could see what was going on. I saw them carrying what appeared to be pieces of metal; there was one piece that was 18 x 24 inches, brushed stainless steel in color. I also saw what was described by another witness as an I-beam and markings."[27]

When interviewed in July 1993 (by Hesemann) he said, *"I could see the hieroglyphs clearly, the signs were in relief and stood out."*[28]

One of the five men who carried the fragments to the aircraft was Flight Engineer Master Sergeant Robert P. Porter. He stated in an affidavit on 7 June 1991:

On this occasion, I was a member of the crew which flew parts of what we were told was a flying saucer to Fort Worth. The people on board included: Lt. Col. Payne Jennings, the Deputy Commander of the base; Lt. Col. Robert I. Barrowclough; Maj. Herb Wunderlich; and Maj. Jesse Marcel. Capt. William E. Anderson said it was from a flying saucer. After we arrived, the material was transferred to a B-25. I was told they were going to Wright Field in Dayton, Ohio.

I was involved in loading the B-29 with the material, which

was wrapped in packages with wrapping paper. One of the pieces was triangle shaped, about 2 ½ feet across the bottom. The rest were in small packages, about the size of a shoe box. The brown paper was held with tape.

The material was extremely light-weight. When I picked it up, it was just like picking up an empty package. We loaded the triangle shaped package and

Lt. Robert Shirkey today.

three shoe-box-sized packages into the plane. All of the packages could have fit into the trunk of a car.[29]

The B-29 took off at three P.M. and at the same time a plane from Washington arrived at the RAAF, which was loaded with more pieces of the wreck before it too left Roswell.

At about five P.M. the B-29 landed at Fort Worth. *"After we landed at Fort Worth, Colonel Jennings told us to take care of maintenance of the plane and that after a guard was posted, we could eat lunch. When we came back from lunch, they said they had transferred the material to a B-25,"* Porter said in his statement.[30]

Major Marcel was taken to General Ramey. He made his report and showed the general a few of the pieces. Ramey wanted Marcel to show him the place where they were found on a map, and so they went to the map room. When they returned, the base photographer made two pictures, and after that Marcel was sent to the officers' mess for dinner.

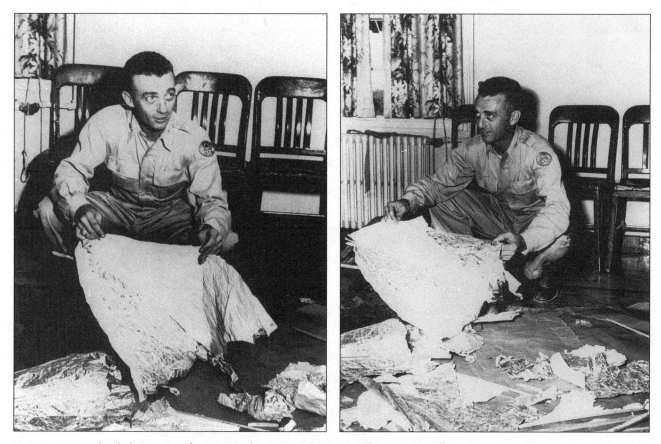

Major Jesse Marcel with the remains of a Rawin radar target at the press conference in the office of General Roger Ramey on 8 July 1947. (Photos. James B. Johnson)

General Ramey had called a press conference at six P.M., which Marcel was to attend, whereas his companions were sent back to Roswell at once.

Around 5:45 P.M., J. Bond Johnson, reporter of the *Fort Worth Star Telegram* came to the general's office. He had been given the job of making pictures of the "crashed saucer" for Associated Press. On the floor of the office lay "a heap of junk," as Johnson later described the remains of burnt rubber, aluminum foil, and balsa wood. The pieces from the wreck had disap-

peared from the office and in their stead there were now the remnants of a weather balloon. He took four pictures: one of Ramey, one of Ramey with his chief of staff, Lieutenant Colonel Thomas Jefferson DuBose, and two of Marcel. "We have found out that it was a weather balloon," declared Ramey. Ten minutes later Johnson was on his way to his office. On arrival he cabled the photos round the world. Later he regretted having taken only four shots. *"The papers were crazy after them. Everyone wanted an exclusive and I'd taken only two pieces*

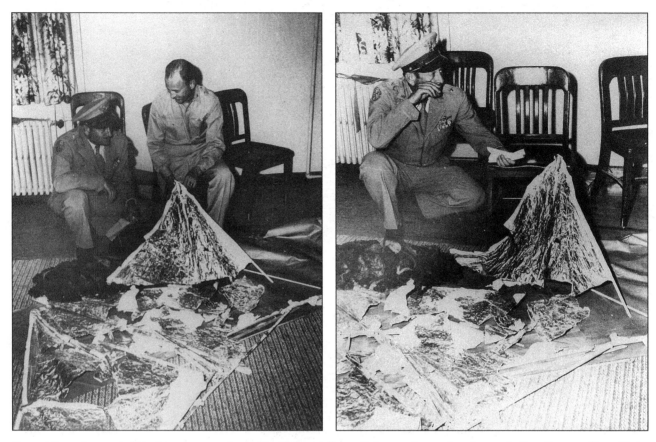

General Roger Ramey and his deputy commander, Lt. Col. Thomas Jefferson DuBose at the press conference in Gen. Rameys office with the remains of the Rawin target of a weather balloon. Reporters were told this was the Roswell wreckage. Later, after promoted to general, DuBose said in an affidavit, "The weather balloon explanation for the material was a cover story to divert the attention of the press."

of film (two holders with two shots each, MH). *I could have retired very early* (but) *I only I had those* (four) *pictures so I had nothing to sell.*"[31]

For the press conference, General Ramey had thought up a special effect: on-the-spot-identification of the "wreckage." He had left instructions for Irving Newton, the meteorological officer, to come over. Newton tried to excuse himself, saying that he could not leave the weather station unattended. But Ramey called

him up personally and said, "Get your ass over here. If you don't have a car, take the first one with a key!"

The reporters came in after that. They were not allowed into the office, but had to crowd up at the door. At first Marcel related honestly about how Brazel came to the sheriff's office, how he went with him to the ranch and salvaged the wreckage. Newton came in just then, pushed himself past the six reporters, and was shortly introduced to them. "Irving Newton, our meteorological officer. Now, Newton, can you tell us what you see here?" There was no doubt about that. "A Rawin target balloon," answered Newton. "Thanks, Newton, thank you, gentlemen. You see that all the excitement is for nothing. Colonel DuBose, cancel the flight to Wright Field."[32]

Marcel kept silent. Orders were orders. Even if he now stood there like an idiot who had mistaken a simple weather balloon for a flying saucer! As early as December 1947 he was promoted to the rank of lieutenant colonel and transferred to Washington, D.C. There he was attached to the Special Weapons Program, which tested air samples from all over the world for radioactivity, to tell whether or not Russians had the atom bomb. And when this finally happened, it was he who wrote the official announcement of the discovery for the White House.

Thirty-three years later, for the first time ever, at a veterans' party of Bomb Group 509, he revealed to Walter Haut that *"the stuff exhibited at General Ramey's office was not what he had salvaged,"* as Haut affirmed in his statement.[33]

This was confirmed in an affidavit by General Ramey's chief of staff, Lieutenant Colonel (later General) Thomas Jefferson DuBose: *"The material shown in the photographs taken in General Ramey's office was a weather balloon. The weather balloon explanation for the material was a cover story to divert the attention of the press."*[34]

With success. "Ramey Empties Roswell-Saucer," said the headlines in the *Roswell Daily Records* the next evening.[35]

"We all knew that the declaration of the HQ of the 8th Air Force was false . . . ," said First Lieutenant Robert Shirkey, when interviewed by one of the authors in Roswell in June 1993, *"for what we saw had nothing to do with any of the weather balloons we had. The I-beams had signs on them like hieroglyphs. We saw all the material and nothing was a part of a*

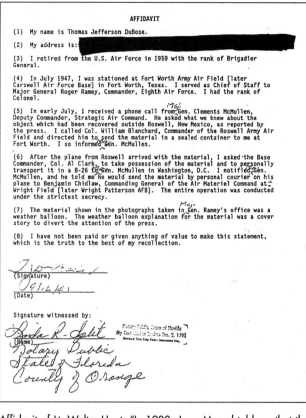

AFFIDAVIT

(1) My name is Thomas Jefferson DuBose.

(2) My address is: ████████████

(3) I retired from the U.S. Air Force in 1959 with the rank of Brigadier General.

(4) In July 1947, I was stationed at Fort Worth Army Air Field [later Carswell Air Force Base] in Fort Worth, Texas. I served as Chief of Staff to Major General Roger Ramey, Commander, Eighth Air Force. I had the rank of Colonel.

(5) In early July, I received a phone call from Maj. Gen. Clements McMullen, Deputy Commander, Strategic Air Command. He asked what we knew about the object which had been recovered outside Roswell, New Mexico, as reported by the press. I called Col. William Blanchard, Commander of the Roswell Army Air Field and directed him to send the material in a sealed container to me at Fort Worth. I so informed Gen. McMullen.

(6) After the plane from Roswell arrived with the material, I asked the Base Commander, Col. Al Clark, to take possession of the material and to personally transport it in a B-26 to Gen. McMullen in Washington, D.C. I notified Gen. McMullen, and he told me he would send the material by personal courier on his plane to Benjamin Chidlaw, Commanding General of the Air Materiel Command at Wright Field [later Wright Patterson AFB]. The entire operation was conducted under the strictest secrecy.

(7) The material shown in the photographs taken in Maj. Gen. Ramey's office was a weather balloon. The weather balloon explanation for the material was a cover story to divert the attention of the press.

(8) I have not been paid or given anything of value to make this statement, which is the truth to the best of my recollection.

_____
(Signature)

9/16/91
(Date)

Signature witnessed by:

Linda R. Splitt
(Name)
Notary Public
State of Florida
County of Orange

Notary Public, State of Florida
My Commission Expires Dec. 2, 1991
Bonded Thru Troy Fain - Insurance Inc.

Affidavit of Lt. Walter Haut: "In 1980, Jesse Marcel told me that the material photographed in Gen. Rameys office was not the material he had recovered."

balloon. We knew that something very important had happened and that was covered up. . . . "[36]

"General Ramey had given me orders under no circumstances to talk to the reporters," Colonel Jesse Marcel had revealed in 1978 to Roswell investigator Bill Moore. *"At first I had orders to take everything to Ft. Worth. I was taken off the flight by Ramey . . . and somebody else took the stuff to Wright Field."*[37]

Actually, there is an official document that shows that the press conference in General Ramey's office was only a farce and that the flight to Wright Field had not been canceled at all. For, simultaneously, at 6:17 P.M. a telex message was sent from the Dallas office of the Federal Bureau of Investigation to its director J. Edgar Hoover and a special agent in Cincinnati, Ohio. It says: [Note: %%%%%% indicates areas blacked out by marker in the record. Spelling as in the original.]

TELETYPE
FBI DALLAS   7-8-47 6-17 PM %%%%%
DIRECTOR AND SAC, CINCINNATI URGENT %%%% FLYING DISC INFORMATION CONCERNING %%%%% HEADQUARTERS EIGHTH AIR FORCE, TELEPHONICALLY ADVISED THIS OFFICE THAT AN OBJECT PURPORTING TO BE A FLYING DISC WAS RECOVERED NEAR ROSWELL, NEW MEXICO, THIS DATE. THE DISC IS HEXAGONAL IN SHAPE AND WAS SUSPENDED FROM A BALLOON BY CABLE, WHICH BALLOON WAS APPROXIMATELY TWENTY FEET IN DIAMETER. %%%%%% FURTHER ADVISED THAT THE OBJECT FOUND RESEMBLES A HIGH ALTITUDE WEATHER BALLOON WITH A RADAR REFLECTOR, BUT THAT TELEPHONIC CONVERSATION BETWEEN THEIR OFFICE AND WRIGHT FIELD HAD NOT %%%%%%%%% BORNE OUT THIS BELIEF. DISC AND BALLOON BEING TRANSPORTED TO WRIGHT FIELD BY SPECIAL PLANE FOR EXAMINATION INFORMATION PROVIDED THIS OFFICE BECAUSE OF NATIONAL INTEREST IN CASE. AND FACT THAT NATIONAL BROADCASTING COMPANY, ASSOCIATED PRESS, AND OTHERS ATTEMPTING TO BREAK STORY OF LOCATION OF DISC TODAY. %%%%%%% ADVISED WOULD REQUEST WRIGHT FIELD TO ADVISE CINCINNATI OFFICE RESULTS OF EXAMINATION, NO FURTHER INVESTIGATION BEING CONDUCTED.
WYLY
RECORDED
end"[38]

Sometime in October 1947, Arthur R. Mcquiddy, a personal friend of Blanchard, asked him about the affair. *"I'll tell you this and nothing more,"* he replied. *"The stuff I saw, I've never seen anyplace else in my life."*[39] And his wife confirmed, long after his death, *"He knew it was not a weather balloon. At first he thought it was something from the Russians, but then it became clear to him that it was something quite different."*[40] The Roswell occurrence did not damage his career. On the contrary—he was made a Four Star General when he was only forty-eight years old, sent to the Pentagon, and finally appointed vice chief of staff of the Air Force. He might have even become chief of staff——the highest military post—if he had not died of heart failure in his Pentagon office.

[1]Randle, Kevin and Donald Schmitt, *UFO Crash at Roswell*, New York, 1991.

[2]Affidavit of Walter Haut, 14 May 1993.

[3]Personal Interview with Walter Haut, 25 June 1993.

[4]*Roswell Daily Record*, 8 July 1947.

[5]FUROR-Interviews with Phyllis McGuire and Elisabeth Tulk, in *Recollections of Roswell* (Video), Mount Rainier, MD, 1993.

[6]Personal Interview with Frank Joyce, 10 December 1993.

[7]Affidavit of George Walsh, 13 September 1993.

[8]Affidavit of Lydia A. Sleppy, 14 September 1993.

[9]Affidavit of William Woody, 28 September 1993.

[10]Affidavit of J. O. Bud Payne, 14 September 1993.

[11] Randle, Kevin and Donald Schmitt, *The Truth About the UFO Crash at Roswell*, New York, 1994.

[12]Affidavit of George "Jud" Roberts, 30 December 1991.

[13]Affidavit of Jason Kellahon, 20 September 1993.

[14]Personal Interview with Frank Joyce, 10 December 1993.

[15]Affidavit of Loretta Proctor, 5 May 1991.

[16]Friedman, Stanton T. and Don Berliner, *Crash at Corona*, New York, 1992.

[17] Randle/Schmitt, 1994.

[18]Ibid.

[19]Friedman/Berliner, 1992.

[20]Affidavit of George "Jud" Roberts, 30 December 1991.

[21]*Roswell Daily Record*, 10 July 4197.

[22]Randle/Schmitt, 1991.

[23]Friedman/Berliner, 1992.

[24]Affidavit of Sally Strickland-Tadolini of 27 September 1993.

[25]Friedman/Berliner, 1992.

[26]Ibid.

[27]Affidavit of Robert Shirkey, 30 April 1991.

[28]Personal Interview with Robert Shirkey on 25 June 1993 and 3 July 1995.

[29]Affidavit of Robert P. Porter, 7 June 1991.

[30]Ibid.

[31]Schmitt, Don and Kevin Randle, "The Fort Worth Press Conference," in Eberhart, George M. (ed.): *The Roswell Report*, Chicago, 1991.

[32]Affidavit of Irving Newton, 21 July 1994.

[33]Affidavit of Walter Haut, 14 May 1993.

[34]Affidavit of General Thomas Jefferson DuBose, 16 September 1991.

[35]*Roswell Daily Record*, 9 July 1947.

[36]Personal Interview with Robert Shirkey on 25 June 1993.

[37]Berlitz, Charles and Bill Moore, *The Roswell Incident*, New York, 1980.

[38]FBI-Telex of 8 July 1947.

[39]Affidavit of Arthur R. McQuiddy, 19 September 1993.

[40]Moore, William L., "Crashed Saucers: Evidence in Search of Proof," presented at 1985 MUFON Symposium, St. Louis, MO, June 1985.

4.

Not from This Earth

Monday, 7 July 1947, Roswell, New Mexico, time: 1:15 P.M. While Major Marcel and Captain Cavitt were gathering the debris at the crash site, some eighty miles away to the southeast, Glenn Dennis was sitting in his office at the Ballard's Funeral Home in Roswell. It was the biggest firm of undertakers in the city and had a contract with the Roswell Army Air Force, to deal with cases of death on the base. Dennis was also responsible for the emergency service of the town and drove its only ambulance vehicle. He was on emergency duty that afternoon, when a mortuary officer from the base called him on the telephone and asked, "Glenn, how small are the smallest caskets you can furnish, that can be hermetically sealed?" "Four feet," answered Dennis. "How many do you have in stock?" "I always have one child's casket here, but can get more by morning. Has there been an accident?" asked Dennis. "No, no. We are having a meeting here and discussing provisions for future eventualities. I'll call you when I need a coffin," said the officer and terminated the conversation.

Three-quarters of an hour later came the second call: "Glenn, how would you prepare a body that has been lying out in the desert?" the mortuary officer asked this time. But before Dennis could answer, the

officer went on, "What would you do if you don't want to change any of the chemical contents, destroy any blood, destroy anything that might be very important down the road? What would you do not to change the chemical contents? Would they change the chemical contents . . . ?" "The chemical we use most is a strong solution of formaldehyde in water, and that will be sure to change the composition of the body. In a case like that I would lay the body in dry ice and freeze it for transport and storage," replied Dennis, adding, "I can come out and help you." But the officer turned down the offer, saying, "Thanks, Dennis, there's no need for that. This is only for future reference." An hour later came the third call, also from the base. An accident: a GI had been injured on the head and probably had a broken nose. "Please come at once!"

Dennis drove over, rendered first aid and transported the soldier to the base hospital. He got there at about five P.M. Although Dennis was a civilian, he had free access to all areas of the base, for he was well known there.

"I wanted to park the car in front of the infirmary, as usual, but there were three field ambulances there, so I parked a bit further," he told us in December 1993. *"When I walked to the infirmary I passed an ambulance, the door of which was open. I*

could see that they had loaded aluminumlike material, that looked like stainless steel, that was not damaged or dented. It had a bluish tinge. Another piece was formed like the bottom of a canoe, about three feet long, and had four-inch-high characters that reminded me of Egyptian hieroglyphs. There was the same kind of stuff in the other two ambulances as well. Two MPs stood there. I then went in and did the paperwork for the soldier who was to be brought in."[1] What happened after that he described in an affidavit dated 7 August 1991:

> I checked the airman in and went to the staff lounge to have a Coke. I intended to look for a nurse, a second Lieutenant, who had been commissioned about three months earlier right out of college. She was twenty-three years of age at the time (I was twenty-two). I saw her coming out of one of the examining rooms with a cloth over her mouth. She said, "My gosh, get out of here or you're going to be in a lot of trouble." She went into another door where a captain stood. He asked me who I was and what I was doing here. I told him, and he instructed me to stay there. I said, "It looks like you've got a crash; would you like me to get ready?" He told me to stay right there. Then two MPs came up and began to escort me out of the infirmary. They said they had orders to follow me out to the funeral home.
>
> We got about ten or fifteen feet when I heard a voice say, "We're not through with that SOB. Bring him back!" There was another captain, a redhead with the meanest-looking eyes I had ever seen, who said, "You did not see anything, there was NO crash here, and if you try anything you could get into a lot of trouble." I said, "Hey, look, mister, I'm civilian and you can't do a damn thing to me." He said, "Yes, we can; somebody will be picking your bones out of the sand." There was a black sergeant with a pad in his hand who said, "He would make good dog food for our dogs." The captain said, "Get the SOB out." The MPs followed me back to the funeral home.[2]
>
> The next day, I tried to call the nurse to see what was going on. About eleven A.M., she called the funeral home and said, "I need to talk to you." We agreed to meet at the officers, club. She

was very upset. She said, "Before I talk to you, you have to give me a sacred oath that you will never mention my name, because I could get into a lot of trouble." I agreed.

She said she had gone to get supplies in a room where two doctors were performing a preliminary autopsy. The doctors said they needed her to take notes during the procedure. She said she had never smelled anything so horrible in her life, and the sight was the most gruesome she had ever seen. She said, "This was something no one has ever seen." As she spoke, I was concerned that she might go into shock.

She drew me a sketch of the bodies, including an arm with a hand that had only four fingers; the doctors noted that on the end of the fingers were little pads resembling suction cups. She

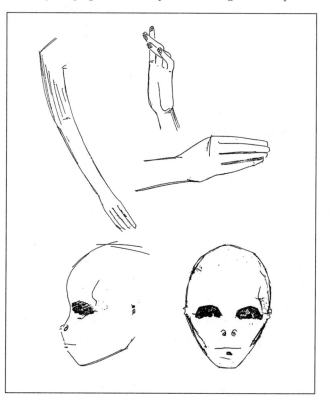

Glenn Dennis' sketch of the entities, how the nurse drew them

said the head was disproportionately large for the body; the eyes were deeply set; the skulls were flexible; the nose was concave with only two orifices; the mouth was a fine slit, and the doctors said there was heavy cartilage instead of teeth. The ears were only small orifices with flaps. They had no hair, and the skin was black—perhaps due to exposure in the sun. She gave me the drawings.[3]

There were three bodies; two were very mangled and dismembered, as if destroyed by predators; one was fairly intact. They were three-and-a-half to four feet tall. She told me the doctors said: "This isn't anything we've ever seen before; there's nothing in the medical textbooks like this." She said she and the doctors became ill. They had to turn off the air conditioning and were afraid the smell would go through the hospital. They had to move the operation to an airplane hangar.

I drove her back to the officers' barracks. The next day I called the hospital to see how she was, and they said she wasn't available. I tried to get her for several days, and finally got one of the nurses who said the Lieutenant had been transferred out with some other personnel. About ten days to two weeks later, I got a letter from her with an APO number. She indicated we could discuss the incident by letter in the future. I wrote back to her and about two weeks later the letter came back marked "Return To Sender—DECEASED." Later, one of the nurses at the base said the rumor was that she and five other nurses had been on a training mission and had been killed in a plane crash.

Sheriff George Wilcox and my father were very close friends. The sheriff went to my folks' house the morning after the events at the base and said to my father, "I don't know what kind of trouble Glenn's in, but you tell your son that he doesn't know anything and hasn't seen anything at the base." He added, "They want you and your wife's name and they want you and your children's addresses."[4]

But it was only when he got back to his office that Dennis realized completely what had occurred. He

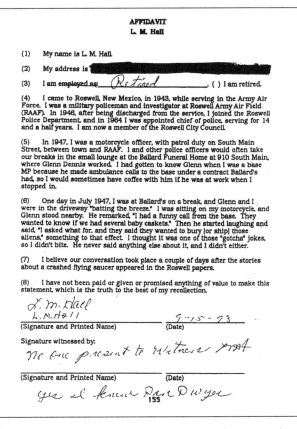

Affidavit of L. M. Hall, former Roswell Police chief. He remembered how Dennis told him in 1947 about the calls from the base.

found the *Roswell Daily Record* in his mailbox, with the headlines "RAAF Captures Flying Saucer on Ranch in Roswell Region."[5]

Glenn Dennis's revelation made the Roswell story appear in a new light. Corpses of beings, possibly of nonterrestrial origin, already picked up while Marcel and Cavitt were still salvaging pieces of debris at the ranch. There are no reasons for doubting the integrity of Dennis.

A few days after the incident he made some remarks

to a friend about the coffins and the extraterrestrials. This friend, L. M. Hall, was then a young patrolman who later became chief of police at Roswell. On 15 September 1993 he stated in an affidavit:

One day in July 1947, I was at Ballard's on a break and Glenn and I were in the driveway "battin the breeze." I was sitting on my motorcycle, and Glenn stood nearby. He remarked, "I had a funny call from the base. They wanted to know if we had several baby caskets." Then he started laughing and said, "I asked what for, and they said they wanted to bury (or ship) those aliens," something to that effect. I thought it was one of those "gotcha" jokes, so I didn't bite. He never said anything else about it, and I didn't either.

I believe our conversation took place a couple of days after the stories about a crashed flying saucer appeared in the Roswell papers.[6]

The existence of the young nurse at that period is also indisputable. The toxicologist David N. Wagnon, who was working as a laboratory technician at the base hospital in 1947, remembers her. In an affidavit dated 15 November 1993 he described her as *"small, attractive, in her twenties, and, I believe, a brunette. I seem to recall that she was transferred from the RAAF while I was still stationed there."*[7]

Dennis was not the first person who attested that on July 7, 1947 corpses of extraterrestrial beings had been recovered. On 24 October 1978 the nuclear physicist and UFO investigator Stanton Friedman gave a lecture at the University of Bemidji in Minnesota. After he had finished speaking and answered questions, the audience left the room one by one, some lingering to ask one more personal question. An elderly couple waited till everyone else was gone and Friedman started packing his things. "Mr. Friedman," began the man hesitatingly, "have you ever heard of a flying saucer that they say crashed in New Mexico . . . with alien bodies?" "I have heard rumors about that," countered Friedman, "tell me what you know about it." The couple introduced themselves as Vern and Jean Maltais. A friend of theirs, meanwhile deceased, "a very upright man, you know," had told them a very strange story. One day—they just could not remember the year, but it was during the end of the '40s—this man, "Barney"—Barnett was his name, he was an engineer who worked for the government—had seen a crashed flying saucer and dead aliens. Then came the Army and blocked everything off.

The story fascinated Friedman. The couple seemed so conservative that he could rule out that they were leading him up the garden path. Barnett was a field engineer in the Soil Conservation Service. While out on duty he came upon a "large metallic object," sticking halfway in the ground, which had just then been discovered by a group of four or five archaeologists. According to Vern Maltais, Barnett *"noticed they were standing around looking at some dead bodies that had fallen to the ground, I think there were others in the machine, which was a kind of metallic instrument of some sort—a kind of disc. It seemed to be made of stainless steel. The machine had been split open by explosion or impact.*

"The beings were like humans, but they were not humans. The heads were round, the eyes were small (sic), and they had no hair. The eyes were oddly spaced. They were quite small by our standards and their heads were larger in proportion to their bodies than ours. Their clothing seemed to be one piece, and gray in color. You couldn't see any zippers, belts, or buttons. They seemed to be all males and there were a number of them."[8]

Maltais added to this in an affidavit dated 23 April 1991 that Barnett had said, *"While we were looking at the bodies, a military officer drove up in a truck with a driver and took control. He told everybody that the Army was taking over and to get out of the way. Other military personnel came up and cordoned* off the area. We were told to leave the area and not to talk to anyone else about what we had seen . . . that it was our patriotic duty to remain silent." Maltais added, "Mr. Barnett was a man of great personal integrity and would never tell a false story."[9]

Barnett had died in 1969 and his wife in 1976. But Friedman was able to locate Barnett's niece, Alice Knight. She affirmed formally that she too had been told by Barnett about the crashed disc. Since Barnett himself could not be interviewed, one does not know where the disc had crashed. The Roswell researchers Kevin Randle and Donald Schmitt believe that it was near Roswell, but Stanton Friedman and Bill Moore refer to Alice Knight, who believes that it was near Datil, in the western part of New Mexico. That would mean that a second saucer crashed on the plateau of San Augustin, west of Magdalena, at about the same time as the first, and was salvaged by the Army. Since Barnett had often been to that area in the course of his work, this possibility cannot be ruled out. On the other hand, it has not been possible to trace any archaeological team that had worked in that area during the period in question, whereas there were archaeologists who attested to having found a crashed saucer north of Roswell.

The first tip came from a nurse in September 1989. She had seen a part of a TV series, *Unsolved Mysteries,* in which Barnett's story was told and reenacted. She called NBC at once and related what she had heard about the incident, from a woman archaeologist who was lying on her deathbed. Nurse Mary Ann Gardner of the Community Hospital in St. Petersburg, Florida, later said in a filmed interview:

I had a cancer patient once. She had terrible pains and was often kept on pain-killing drugs. But sometimes she felt better and was fully conscious. One day she seemed very suspicious
and wanted to know if we were alone in the room. She said there was something she wanted to tell somebody, a secret she had kept for years. Many years before, she had gone "stone-hunting" with friends. She wished she had never gone. In the desert there was a big shining object. They went to take a closer look at it. It was partly stuck in the ground and around it were tarpaulins. They wanted to see what was under them, and when they lifted them they saw small beings lying there. She couldn't believe it. Things like small people, with big heads, very large eyes, wearing a kind of shining material. She thought the clothing was bluish. But then she got excited and said, "Don't tell anyone about it, for they can find you everywhere." I asked who could find me, and she replied, "The Government!"[10]

This was, according to Gardner, in 1976 or 1977.

A second tip also came in as a result of the TV show. A certain Iris Foster, who had once owned a café near Tacos in New Mexico, rang up the station. She remembered the words of an old amateur archaeologist, whom she had known only as "Cactus Jack." He had told her that when he was a young student he had found an object, *"round and not very big."* Near that lay four little creatures. Their blood was *"like tar, thick and black,"* and was sticking on their silver-colored uniforms. Foster's sister Peggy could actually remember Cactus Jack's real name, Larry Campbell. This too remained a nonverifiable track.[11]

On 15 February 1990 Kevin Randle received a call from a man who claimed to have been one of the archaeologists concerned. He requested that his name be kept confidential. *"Yes, we were looking for signs of occupation that predated the arrival of the white man."* They had just reached the top of a hill when they saw, about three-quarters of a mile further down, *"something that looked like a crashed airplane without wings."* There was a man already there, who was inspecting the wreck. He could see that *"it wasn't a plane, it was more rounded,"* but it was so damaged that he could not make out what it was. He also saw three bodies. They were small, with large heads and big eyes. They lay on their bellies, so that it was difficult to see their faces. They wore silver-colored *"flight suits."* Shortly after that, according to him, the army appeared on the scene. Some had pistols, some had rifles also. The archaeologists were ordered to get away from the wreck and turn their backs to it. The commanding officer explained to them that in the interests of national security they should forget what they had seen. He then wrote down their names and those of the universities they worked for, and threatened that the government grants for their institutions would be stopped if they spoke about the affair. They were then taken off the site under armed escort. On a nearby road there was a blockade and soldiers ordered all approaching traffic to turn back.[12]

This report too could not be verified, but soon after this came the breakthrough, when the anthropologist and Roswell investigator Tom Carey took up the "search for the lost archaeologists." More by accident he found out that the father of an acquaintance, C. Bertrand Schultz, had over the years repeatedly told

Prof. C. Bertrand Schultz

the same tale of a crashed "saucer." Schultz is Professor Emeritus of Geology and Paleontology at the University of Nebraska, now eighty-six years old. In the faculty he is considered an authority, the leading paleontologist of the New World. Some time before July 10, 1947 he came to Roswell. As he was

driving towards the Town on Highway 285 he saw a lot of military activity and noted that all exits had been blocked and were guarded by armed sentries. He did not think much of this, having other things on his mind, until he got to Roswell and met his friend, a fellow archaeologist, Professor W. Curry Holden,

Prof. W. Curry Holden

a much respected expert on the pre-Columbian cultures in the southwestern part of the U.S. Holden explained to Schultz the reason for the barriers and told him how he and his team had come upon a crashed flying disc, which they at first thought was a Russian secret weapon, until they saw the strange little bodies. Soon after that the military had come and driven them off from the spot. Schultz remembered that the incident was reported in the papers and over the radio shortly thereafter.

Professor Holden was still alive when Carey spoke to Schultz. Thus this was the first track that did not turn out to be a blind alley. Dr. W. Curry Holden was Professor Emeritus of History at Texas Technical University. During the twenties and thirties he built up the Department of History and Anthropology—the most renowned one in the States—at the university. After the war he began with the excavation of an archaeological site in Hondo Valley, west of Roswell. In 1950 he actually transferred the headquarters of his Field Research Institute to Roswell. It is therefore quite likely that he searched for signs of pre-Columbian settlements in the other arroyos around Roswell, including the Cienega Arroyo, northwest of Roswell, near which the wrecked saucer was found.

Texas Tech archaeological team in the 1930s. W. Curry Holden is on the left.

Holden's colleague William Pearce became uncommunicative as soon as Carey mentioned the name "Roswell," but he was able to verify that Holden had been in Roswell between July 3 and 9, 1947. So Carey forwarded this information to Kevin Randle, who in November 1992 went to Lubbock, Texas, to have a talk with Holden. Although over ninety-six years old, and physically weak, Holden was mentally fully alert. And indeed he said to Randle affirmatively, *"Yes, I was there and saw everything."* Was he there personally, when the discovery was made? *"Yes, I saw everything."* More than that he could not or would not say. He died five months later.[13]

The fact is that when Holden's wife permitted Randle to look through Holden's bank statements for the year 1947—to see if he had made any payment by check at Roswell during the period in question, which would confirm his presence there—he discovered that a check for $4,834 (a small fortune in those days!) had been *deposited* into his account on 15 July 1947. Had "somebody" bought his long-lasting silence? The origin of the check could not be traced. His private archives

showed all his yearly income-tax returns from the thirties to the seventies with one exception: the one for the year 1947.[14]

Carey then interviewed another colleague of Professor Holden, Dr. George Agogino. After much humming and hawing Agogino finally admitted having heard the story from Holden. As Carey read to him the report of the anonymous archaeologist (see above), Agogino affirmed, *"That's what he told me too."* But he was not ready to name the other archaeologists, because he *"did not want to get them into trouble."*[15]

But who was the person whom the anonymous archaeologist had mentioned, who at first was at the crash site? Was it Barnett? Perhaps. Or was it Jim Ragsdale, who, together with his girlfriend, had seen an object come down during the stormy night and on Monday morning, on his way back to Roswell, discovered the wreck, as stated by him on 27 January 1993, in a notarized affidavit? *"I and my companion came upon a ravine near a bluff that was covered with pieces of unusual wreckage, remains of a damaged craft and a number of smaller-bodied beings outside tile craft. While observing the scene, we watched as a military convoy arrived and secured the scene. As a result of the convoy's appearance we quickly fled the area."*[16]

Ragsdale's statement gives us at least a hint about the time of the discovery. It must have happened on Monday, July 7. The presence of the archaeological team fits in with this: the scientists and the students would most probably have been away during the "long weekend" from July 4 to 6. Barnett was away on an assignment. Professor Schultz drove to Roswell to do shopping. He saw the roadblocks that had been witnessed since Monday. He said that he heard the radio news about the crash, which came after Lieutenant Haut made his announcement in the afternoon of July 8. According to Glenn Dennis, the inquiries from the RAAF about the burial caskets and conserving of bodies were made on the afternoon of July 7. Therefore the bodies were already in the base by then and the first autopsy was being conducted. This means that the corpses had been recovered long before Major Marcel returned from the Foster Ranch, at about 2:00 a.m. on July 8th.

But how had the Army located the wreck? Frankie Rowe, the then twelve-year-old daughter of a fireman of the Roswell Fire Department, related that one night her father had gone out to put out a fire some thirty miles north of Roswell. He returned in the early hours of the morning and at breakfast had told her about his strange mission. *"He said that something had crashed that was not from this earth. Owing to the crash a large number of pieces of a strange metal were lying around, besides that he saw two little corpses and one person running around . He said they were from another planet . . . didn't look like us . . . were like ten-year-old kids, very small ears, rather big black eyes, without any hair at all. They wore single piece suits. The two dead ones were put into bodybags. The other one looked so lost and frightened that he felt sorry for it."*[17]

Her father also told her later that a friend of his,

Herbert Ellis, who worked as a painter at the base, had seen how *"the surviving creature was taken on its own into the hospital."* It had *"looked like a child, rather lean."* As a matter of fact, a number of such rumors went around Roswell during those days. One of them said that the army had recovered Martians and one of them had been alive. He had shrieked the whole night like an animal. According to another, one of the "green men" had escaped and run through the city all night, until the Air Force captured him again.

There are no witnesses for either of these stories. Three or four days later, when Frankie Rowe visited her father at the fire station, a policeman came in and said he wanted to show the firemen something. He took out a piece of metal from his pocket, which, he said, he had picked up at the crash site. It looked like mercury, as it was lying on the table. *"It was a bit bigger than the hand of the trooper. It had jagged edges and was silver-gray. I took it in my hand. One could hardly feel it. It was so thin, like hair. The firemen tried to cut it or tear it, but they couldn't.*[18] In her affidavit she added, *"It was dull gray and like aluminum, when wadded into a ball, it would unfold itself.*[19]

The Roswell Fire Department.

A few days after that, when her father was at the station, there stood three MPs and an officer at the door of their house:

A few days later, several military personnel visited the house, telling my younger brothers and sisters to wait outside. My mother and I were told to sit at the dining room table where I was questioned about the piece of metal I had seen. I was told that if I ever talked about it, I could be taken out into the desert never to return, or that my mother and father would be taken to "Orchard Park," a former POW camp, or to the concentration camp for the Japanese at Artesia, and we could also be sent to other camps or sent out east for adoption. But if they found out that we had said anything, we would just be taken into the desert and shot, where nobody would ever find us again.[20]

Frankie's sister Helen Cahill affirmed Frankie's story in a second affidavit.[21]

The reference to the policeman suggests that the sheriff's office was also concerned. Was Sheriff Wilcox, in the night after Mac Brazel's visit, once more involved in a UFO crash? His daughters remember only the presence of the Army men at the sheriff's office and their father's injunction never to speak to him about the incident. After his death his widow Inez Wilcox—known in the family as "Big Mom"—lived with their granddaughter, Barbara Dugger. Shortly after the publication of the book *The Roswell Incident* by Charles Berlitz and Bill Moore, Inez Wilcox wrote an article about the incident, which she sent to *Reader's Digest* and the Roswell Historical Society. It ended with the words: *"Till today we do not know whether it was really a flying saucer, since they had forbidden my husband to speak about it."*

One day Inez and Barbara together watched a TV program about UFOs. "Barbara, tell me, do you believe that there is life out there in space?" asked Inez. "Big Mom, you know I do," replied Barbara. "I must tell you something. But you must promise me that you will never talk to anyone else about it." She then said that her husband, Sheriff Wilcox, knew a great deal more than what Mac Brazel had told him in his office. She continued reluctantly, "Please keep this to yourself. For when all that happened, the Military Police came to us in the sheriff's office and declared that if we, George and I, ever said a single word about the affair to anyone at all, they would kill not only us but also the whole family." "Did you hear that yourself, Big Mom?" "Yes, I was there, and that is exactly what they told us."

In Barbara's words:

She said someone had come to Roswell and told him about this incident. My grandfather went out there to the site; it was in the evening. There was a big burned area, and he saw debris. He also saw four "space beings." One of the little men was alive. Their heads were large. They wore suits like silk.

After he returned to his office, my grandfather got phone calls from all over the world—including England. M.P.s came to the jail. A lot of people came in and out of the jail at the time.

. . . . However, if she said it happened, it happened."

The various telephone calls came in to the sheriff's office after Walter Haut had handed over his statement on July 8. The MPs must, therefore, have come between Brazel's visit in the morning of July 6 and noon of July 8, most probably during the night between July 6 and 7. Perhaps it was Wilcox who first notified the fire department and told them to bring sacks to transport the bodies.

The intimidation by the Army turned Wilcox into a broken man. He was disillusioned and lost his faith in his job and his duties, and he did not run for reelection as sheriff. Inez was a candidate, but the times were not ripe for a woman sheriff in Chavez county. One of Wilcox's deputies, Tommy Thompson, confirmed that after all these events Wilcox had been "finished." *"My grandmother was a very loyal citizen of the United States, and she thought it was in the best interest of the country not to talk about the event. . . . she said nothing,"* explained Barbara Dugger. Shortly after she had entrusted her secret to her granddaughter, Inez Wilcox died at the age of ninety-three.[22]

Whether the army had been informed about the crashed disc or discovered it independently, we do not know. The statement given by Frank Kaufmann supports the latter probability. According to his own testimony, Kaufmann was a member of a highly qualified team of experts, which detected the falling disc on radar and searched for it in the appropriate area. Kaufmann told us, when we interviewed him in July 1995, that from 1941 to 1945, as a member of the Western Flying Training Command with headquarters at Santa Ana, California, he was in active military service under Brigadier General Martin F. Scanlon. After the war Scanlon was attached to the Strategic Air Command (SAC) and Kaufmann was transferred to Roswell as a paramilitary member of a special team for secret service and counterespionage work. From 1945 to 1948 he was, among other things, responsible for the control and security of the Norden-bomb-aiming device—at that time one of the most vulnerable and highly classified items of American military technology—which had been installed in the bombers of the SAC at Roswell. After his discharge from active duty, he stayed on at Roswell, where, from 1948 till 1972, he was a vice-president of the Chamber of Commerce. For two years after that he was a consultant for development initiatives for the Chamber, before taking up the post of industrial and economic consultant to a company in Texas.

On June 20, 1947, according to Kaufmann, he, being a member of the SAC special team, was informed that the radar at White Sands base had picked up strange echoes, which literally jumped across the screen. The radar at Roswell had also received the "blips," but only when they were above the Capitan Mountains, which lay between Roswell and White Sands and acted as a natural barrier for radar reception. Acting on orders from General Scanlon, he went to White Sands, where he and two others watched the radar

Brigadier Gereral Scanlon

screen in rotating shifts. During one night, when a violent storm was raging, one of the signals on the screen remained stationary, and apparently struck by lightning, flickered up as if it had exploded, before diving down. A triangulation with the bearings taken by the radar sta-

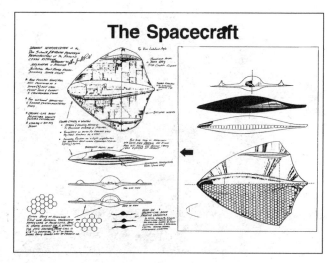

The wreckage, drawn by Bill McDonald based on Frank Kaufmann's description.

tions at Roswell and Kirtland AAF showed that it must have come down somewhere northwest of Roswell.

During the long weekend the base was undermanned, and one did not want to arouse too much attention. The CIC Warrant Officer Robert Thomas was flown in from Washington, D.C. to lead the action. Thus the search began only on Monday, 7 July 1947, soon after sunrise. Planes were probably sent out first, but at any rate a military convoy set off on Highway 285 driving north. After about thirty-five miles they turned west, on to an "old ranch road." They were very perturbed, as Kaufmann learnt, "on seeing that civilians were on the site of the crash." Soon they found the object, "in an arroyo." The sight that met the eyes of the soldiers was overwhelming: the crashed spacecraft was stuck in the desert sand at the foot of a cliff, a creature like a small human being cowered on a rock. A corpse lay on the ground near the wreck, another was hanging out of the wrecked ship, the legs sticking out of

The wreckage, drawn by Bill McDonald based on Frank Kaufmann's description.

a hole in the side. Kaufmann could see into the ship through this hole. A dead being was still sitting on a seat, but fallen to one side. The corpses, four altogether—a fourth was found inside the vessel—and the living being wore "very close-fitting single-piece silvery uniforms" and a sort of belt. They looked like human beings, with other proportions, bigger heads and eyes, smaller noses, mouths and ears, hairless. The bodies were slim, about five feet tall, the skin pale.

The salvage team put the area at once under security, swore the civilians in to secrecy. A photographer and a cameraman who had been flown over with Thomas—according to Kaufmann a "technical sergeant and a master sergeant . . . real professionals who knew their business"—made pictures of the scene before the retrieval operation started. Ambulance men, MPs, equipment and more crew were requested over the wireless, instructions were given for planes to fly over the area, make aerial photographs, and search for more wreckage and bodies. The bodies were put into bodybags and brought to Hangar 84. The hangar was cleared "in thirty minutes," the corpses brought in and placed where "a bright floodlight from above shone directly upon them," and were then left heavily guarded. Later some 100 MPs from Kirtland AAF turned up. They watched over the recovery operation in shifts of twenty men each, and were transferred to another base immediately after that, before they knew too much. At the Roswell Base a preliminary examination of the cadavers was performed by two pathologists at the base hospital. Major Sanford from the Beaumont General Hospital in Fort Bliss and Major Sullivan from Chicago. After that two bodies were flown to Fort Worth and from there to Andrews AAF near Washington, D.C., before finally being taken to Wright Field.

The long stopover in Washington served to give topranking army personnel the opportunity to see the bod-

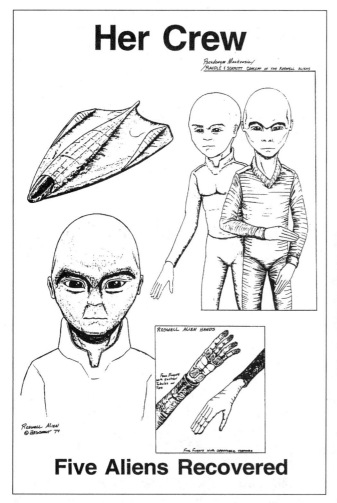

Her Crew

Breakdown Mackenzie/
RANDLE & SCHMITT Concept of the Roswell Aliens

ROSWELL ALIEN HANDS

Four Fingers
with gristle
Tubules on
Tips

Roswell Alien
© Bergamini '74

Five Fingers with opposable thumbs

Five Aliens Recovered

The alien crew drawn by William McDonald based on description by Frank Kaufmann.

ies. Amongst the visitors were President Truman, Defense Secretary Forrestal and the Army's chief of staff, later President Dwight D. Eisenhower. A second plane took the remaining bodies to Fort Worth and from there at once to Wright Field. The wreck, about twenty-four feet long, fifteen feet wide, and with no

more than about six feet, was taken on the back of a transporter truck to the base. It did not have any recognizable source of energy on board, except a set of "cells" like a beehive, in the belly.[23]

The arrival of the experts and MPs from Washington has been confirmed by various witnesses. "Everything changed as soon as the people from Washington came," said Joe Briley, later chief of operations at the RAAF. "Before that one heard stories and rumors. After they came, everything was covered up."[24] Robert E. Smith of the first Air Transport Unit, who was stationed at the

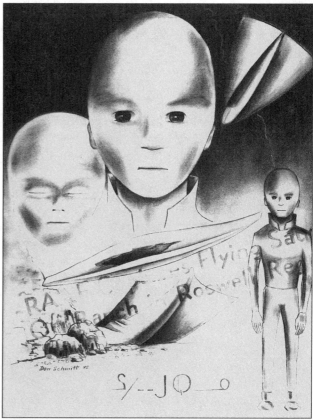

The wreck and its inhabitants as illustrated by Donald Schmitt.

RAAF at that time, said in an affidavit that a number of people in civilian clothes appeared on the base. *"There were a lot of people in plain clothes all over the place. They were 'inspectors,' but they were strangers on the base. When challenged, they replied they were here on Project So-and-So, and flashed a card, which was different from a military ID card."*[25]

One of the photographers who came from Washington meanwhile could be identified. In November 1990 Roswell researcher Stanton Friedman was able to interview him. F. B. (he wished to remain anonymous) was stationed at the Anacostia Marine Airport near Washington, D.C. as photographer for the AAF. One morning he and his colleague A. K. received the order, "Pack your things. We have the cameras for you." On board a B-29 bomber, which had been waiting for them, they were given press cameras. They were not told where they were flying, but after several hours they landed at Roswell AAF. Staff cars were waiting for them, with trucks behind them, on to which the cargo of the B-29 was loaded. They then proceeded towards the north and arrived at their destination after a journey of one and a half hours.

We got out there, and there was a helluva lot of people out there, in a closed tent. You couldn't hardly see anything inside the tent. They said, "Set your camera up to take a picture fifteen feet away." A. K. got in a truck and headed out to where they was pickin' up pieces. All kinds of brass runnin' around. And they was tellin' us what to do: Shoot this, shoot that! There was an officer in charge. He met us out there and he'd go into the tent and he'd come back and tell us, "OK." He'd stand there right besides us and say, "OK, take this picture!"

There was four bodies I could see when the flash went off, but you was almost blind because it was a beautiful day . . . sunny. You'd go in this tent, which was awful dark. That's all I was takin': bodies. These bodies was under a canvas, and they'd open it up and you'd take a picture, flip out your flash-bulb, put another one in [take another picture] and give him the film holder (each holder held two sheets of four-by-five-inch cut film) and then you went to the next spot.

I guess there was ten to twelve officers, and when I got ready to go in, they'd all come out. The tent was about twenty by thirty foot. The bodies looked like they was lyin' on a tarp. One guy did all the instructions. He'd take a flashlight and he'd come down in there: "See this flashlight." Yes, sir! "You're in focus with it." Yes, sir! "Take a picture of this." He'd take the flashlight away. We just moved around in a circle, takin' pictures. Seemed to me [the bodies] were all just about identical. Dark—complicated. I remember them as thin, and it looked like they had too big of a head. I took thirty shots. . . . I think I had about fifteen [film] holders. It smelled funny in there.[26]

In the meanwhile A. K. had photographed the wrecked pieces. He was then brought back in a pickup truck full of debris, and they were taken back to Roswell. At four in the morning they were woken up, given breakfast at the officers' mess and taken to their B-25, which flew them back to Anacostia. There they were taken to the commanding officer, who swore them in to absolute silence on the subject. "Whatever you think you saw in New Mexico—you have not seen it. It just never happened. You did not leave Anacostia at all!"

For the salvaging there are witnesses too. The first one who spoke out was Sergeant Melvin E. Brown, called "Brownie" by his friends. During the course of his service in the U.S. Army he had married an Englishwoman, and after his discharge from the Army he migrated to the United Kingdom. In 1979 he confided for the first time to his family what he had seen at Roswell in those days. The worldwide best-seller *The Roswell Incident* by Charles Berlitz and Bill Moore had just appeared in bookstores and the *Daily Mirror* published a lengthy review. Brownie read this and showed it to his family, saying, "I was there. Everything in the article is true," according to his daughter Beverly Bean, who was interviewed in August 1995 by one of the authors.

All available men had been drummed up on that day, Brownie had said, to protect the crash site. They had formed a ring around the wreck while it was being loaded on to a transporter. Trucks came, loaded with dry ice, which Brownie did not quite understand. "They want to keep something cool," he thought to himself, but did not know what it was. Together with a companion, he was then ordered to sit in the back of a truck and watch some stuff which was to be taken to one of the hangars on the base. Whatever the freight was, it was packed in the dry ice and covered with a sheet. "Don't ever look under the sheet," had been their orders, "or you'll get into serious trouble." But curiosity won: during the journey Brownie and his companion had a quick peep under the sheet. What they saw gave them a shock: there were three bodies under the plane. . . .

"He said they didn't look frightening," said his daughter Beverly to the British researcher Timothy Good, *"they looked friendly, they had pretty faces, Asiatic-looking, with big heads and no hair. They had slanted eyes."*[27] Later, in an interview with Friedman, she added, *"They were smaller than normal people, only four feet tall. . . . once I asked him if he hadn't been frightened by them, but he said, "Certainly not, they looked nice and friendly."*[28]

Luckily Sergeant Brown's family had kept all his papers intact after his death in 1986, so that Timothy Good was able to verify that Brown had really been at the RAAF during the summer of 1947 and had held the rank of sergeant, with technical qualifications. He had been decorated many times during the Second World War, and owing to his capabilities in May 1948 was promoted to the rank of staff sergeant. He was later entrusted with intelligence work.

A further witness to the transport, Sergeant Thomas Gonzales, met Don Ecker, chief editor of the American *UFO Magazine,* rather by chance, during a visit to the UFO Museum at Roswell. Gonzales had heard of the museum through television and wanted to visit once more the place where he had had perhaps the most moving experience in his life. After he had found his picture in the base's 1947 yearbook, he told his story:

Gonzales said he was one of the men sent out to protect the crash site while the wreck was being salvaged. The craft had appeared to him more like a wing than a conventional disc. Then he had seen what he called

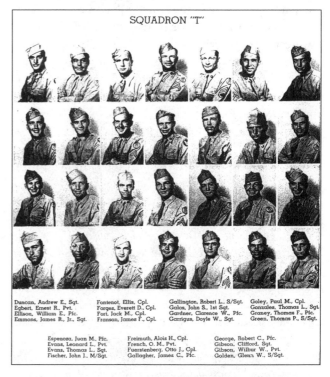

SQUADRON "T"

Duncan, Andrew E., Sgt.
Egbert, Ernest R., Pvt.
Ellison, William E., Pfc.
Emmons, James R., Jr., Sgt.

Fontenot, Ellis, Cpl.
Forges, Everett D., Cpl.
Fort, Jack M., Cpl.
Franson, James F., Cpl.

Gallington, Robert L., S/Sgt.
Galos, John S., 1st Sgt.
Gardner, Clarence W., Pfc.
Garrigus, Doyle W., Sgt.

Goley, Paul M., Cpl.
Gonzales, Thomas L., Sgt.
Graney, Thomas F., Pfc.
Green, Thomas P., S/Sgt.

Espenoza, Juan M., Pfc.
Evans, Leonard L., Pvt.
Evans, Thomas L., Sgt.
Fischer, John J., M/Sgt.

Freimuth, Alois H., Cpl.
French, O. M., Pvt.
Fuerstenberg, Otto J., Cpl.
Gallagher, James C., Pfc.

George, Robert C., Pfc.
Gibson, Clifford, Sgt.
Gibson, Wilbur W., Pvt.
Golden, Glenn W., S/Sgt.

From the 1947 RAAF base yearbook: the T-Squadron, which participated in the retrieval operation. The fourth in the second row is Sgt. Thomas Gonzales, who later described four extraterrestrials.

"the little men from Mars." They were basically like human beings, he emphasized, only their heads and eyes had been much bigger. What makes Gonzales's evidence even more interesting is his statement that he was still in possession of a piece of the "crashed spaceship." As long as he lived in his own house—after the death of his wife he went to live with his son—it was on top of the TV and must now be in one of the boxes, he thought. He did, in fact, show Ecker a few family photos, where the TV can be seen, with some metallic object lying on it. Gonzales's children also confirmed that their father had said the "stone," as they called the piece, came from a crashed spaceship. One could not make a dent on it with the heaviest hammer or scratch it with the best knife. Shortly after the incident he was transferred overseas and that was the start of hard times for him and his family. The stress of having to live with a secret became too much for him, but he got over it after a period. . . . But till today, the metal piece he had could never be found again.[29]

Kaufmann's statement that the bodies had been kept in a hangar—Hangar 84—was confirmed by Sergeant Brown, who was ordered to guard the entrance to the hangar. *"He told us . . . his commanding officer came up and said, '. . . Let's both have a look at it' . . . but they didn't see anything, as everything was packed away to be flown out next day,"* recalled his daughter Beverly. *"He'd shut up if we questioned him about it. . . . He wanted to tell people about it, but if you started asking questions, he was completely off it. . . . Even when he was asleep he was mumbling about it. . . . Dad was absolutely no liar. He was a smashing bloke and loved his country."* She asks herself even today whether his silence was perhaps bought. *"Shortly before his death he told my two brothers-in-law that he had a trustee account at a place called Roswell, New Mexico, and that there was a lot of money in it, for he had done something very secret for Uncle Sam. They joked, asking, 'Come, Brownie, what did you do? Robbed a bank?' He*

became quite angry at that and replied, 'I have never done anything bad for my country. But I want you to find the money and give it to your mother.'"[30] The money could never be located. Instead, after his death his family received a service medal and a letter of condolence from President Reagan, which Beverly showed to Timothy Good: *"That makes me wild. Was that their thanks for his being afraid to talk about it till his death? They should have apologized for what they did to him. . . . I think he deserved something more than this hypocritical letter."*[31]

"Brownie" is not the only witness for the transport and the storing of the bodies in the hangar. Robert E. Smith of the first Air Transport Unit said in his affidavit dated 10 October 1991: *"There was another indication that something serious was going on: several nights before this, when we were coming back to Roswell, a convoy of trucks covered with canvas passed us. The truck convoy had red lights and sirens. When they got to the gate, they headed over to this hangar on the east end, which was rather unusual."*[32] First Lieutenant Robert Shirkey too, in his affidavit dated 30 April 1991, stated: *"I learned later that a sergeant and some airmen went to the crash site and swept up everything, including bodies. The bodies were laid out in Hangar 84. Henderson's flight contained all that material. All of those involved, the sergeant of the guards, all of the crewmen, and myself, were shipped out to different bases within two weeks."*[33]

Ruben Anaya was at that time a cook at the Officers' Club of the RAAF. Like many Hispanic citizens of New Mexico, he supported New Mexico's lieutenant governor Joseph Montoya, who, himself a Hispanic, fought for the needs of the Spanish-speaking minority in the State. Anaya was one of Montoya's most active campaign helpers and was proud of also being one of his close friends. Anaya told the researcher Stanton Friedman the following story:

One evening, Anaya and his brother Pete were sitting with two guests, Moses Burrola and Ralph Chaes, when

Affidavit of Lt. Robert Shirkey: "I learned later that a sergeant and some airmen went to the crash site and swept up everything, including bodies. The bodies were laid out in Hangar 84. Henderson's flight contained all that material."

the telephone rang. At the other end was Montoya, "with a panic-stricken voice." "Ruben," he said, "I am at the Base. I must get out of here! Get your car and pick me up here." Anaya asked him where exactly he was. "I am near the big hangar. We'll meet there. Hurry up!" At once all four sprang up, got into Ruben's car and drove to the Base. Ruben had been discharged from the Army recently, but since he still worked at the Officers' Club he had a pass for his car and was simply waved through at the entrance to the RAAF.

They stopped at Hangar 84 and wanted to go in to meet Montoya. But they were not allowed to enter. *"They had MPs . . . and city police there. Then he [Montoya] came out. That man was as white as a sheet, really shook up. He said, 'Come on, let's get out of here.' I asked him if he wanted us to take him to his hotel but he said, 'No. Just take me to your house. I need a drink bad.'"*

After they arrived at the Anaya home, Montoya *"sat on the couch and drank down a quart bottle of Jim Beam three-quarters full. We said, 'Take it easy.' He said, 'No. I've got to calm myself down.' The four men demanded to know what had happened. Anaya told me Montoya replied, 'You're not going to believe it. There was a flying saucer*—un plato muy grande con una machina en la media *[a big saucer with a machine in the middle]—that came down by Corona. There were four little men not from this world. One was alive.'*

"He said they were little, came up only to his chest—and Montoya was a little guy [he was known as Little Joe]. . . . He described them wearing silvery suits, with big eyes and a very little mouth. . . . We thought, This guy, he's out of whack. . . . Then he called his wife and talked with her about it and then called the Nixon Hotel (where he was staying) and got a friend and his brother, Tom Montoya . . . to come and get him. . . . About ten-thirty the next morning we went to the hotel and talked to him. He told us, 'Confidentially, they shipped everything to Texas, and those guys are in the hospital. Look, if any of you guys say I talked about this, I'm going to say you're a bunch of liars.'"[34]

Pete Anaya too remembered this incident. During the drive to the town Montoya had sat motionless in his seat and stared into the distance. Later, he had described the object as "a plane without wings," which "moved like a dish." He also remembers the description given by Montoya of the four creatures. They were small, with disproportionately big heads. They had lain on a table in the middle of the hangar. One of them had still been alive, had sighed and moved its hand slowly. Its legs were bent. Since doctors were standing around the table, Montoya could not get closer. But he could clearly see that the beings had no hair on their heads, that their skin was white and that they wore one-piece suits which resembled those worn by divers. As far as he could make out, they had four long fingers on each hand and big eyes. Shortly after that the beings were taken to the base hospital.

Meanwhile pieces from the wreck were brought in. They were only metallic fragments, none of which had looked like a big craft. Montoya requested the Anaya brothers to pick him up at his hotel the next morning and drive him to the base, from where a flight to the Kirtland Air Base near Albuquerque had been scheduled. Pete's wife Mary confirmed this story, as did the widow of Moses Burrola when she was interviewed by Kevin Randle.[35]

Later, according to Ruben Anaya, all four of them—he, Pete, Burrola and Chaes—were called personally to the telephone by Senator Chavez—who had also called Frank Whitmore of the radio station KGFL—and told, *"Joe Montoya was a damn liar. He didn't see anything. . . . It was a very, very secret project, it could hurt us with Russia and Germany [if it came out]."*[36]

On July 8, 1947, the day after the recovery, all hell was let loose at the base, remembers Kaufmann. At 7:30 A.M. there was a staff meeting at the office of Lieutenant Colonel Blanchard, "where decisions were made." General Scanlon had flown over especially to attend the meeting, General Ramey came from Fort Worth, and even Charles Lindbergh was there, a total of fifteen officers, to discuss further action. According to Kaufmann they decided in favor of a truly Macchiavellian maneuver to deviate attention from the incident. It was too late to deny that anything unusual had happened in the Roswell region: the road blockades were facts that no one could overlook, Brazel's story had spread. It was decided to concede openly that "a flying saucer" had been found, but to transfer the site of the crash to the Foster Ranch, which was actually only a secondary site, a field full of minor debris, with neither saucers nor bodies. One could gather the debris quickly, so that, should the press appear, everything would already be over. And so that the announcement could be completely deflated, General Ramey would later on the same day issue a statement to say that there had been a big misunderstanding: the alleged flying saucer was only a crashed weather balloon.

In August 1995 the army historian Joe Stefula succeeded in finding a witness for the clearing up operation. Captain Chester Barton was in military service from 1929 till 1954, and during the war was stationed at Fort Worth and Roswell. There he served in a security squadron. He received orders from Major Easley, whose office was directly at the main entrance to the Base, to go to the crash site and report how far the clearing up had progressed. Together with Captain Beverly Teripp, chief of the Military Police and a driver, he drove north in a jeep. Chester: *"It took about forty-five minutes, then we were there. It was out in the middle of the wilderness. It looked like there had been a fire there, but somehow different. The landscape was flat. Some 100 yards before the spot we were stopped by the guard . . . . We looked around. We saw unmarked wreckage, which looked as if it had come from a burnt-out plane. As I tried to pick up a piece to have a closer look, I was not allowed to do so. We had no radiationproof suits on. The MPs had Geiger counters and had detected radiation. . . . We stayed an hour or so there, then we were taken back to Easley's office. He told us to come back at 8:30 A.M. next morning. But then everybody came back from the site and reported that everything had been finished. We were sworn to silence."*

Asked whether he knew what had crashed, Chester replied, *"There were rumors at that time that it was a flying saucer. There were only a few pieces lying there. The whole site was as big as a football field. At first I thought that a B-29 had crashed but I could see no pieces to show that. I heard very little about the bodies. They were taken to the base hospital. . . . It was all so quick. . . . I never heard anything about it after that, not even a crypto-message."* Although Chester still believes that it was a crashed plane, a particular part of his description suggests that he was actually a witness of the Roswell incident. *"I heard at that time that some archaeologists were at the site . . . ,"* he told Stefula.[37]

On the evening of July 10 the recovery operation was completed, all signs of the crash erased. One day later, on July 11, all the soldiers who had taken part in the operation were briefed. They were taken to a room in small groups, in which an officer told them: "That was a matter of national security and stands under absolute secrecy. Speak to nobody about it. Forget everything that happened and all that you saw. Nobody will believe you, anyhow. Officially the whole affair never happened." Within a month all the MPs and the majority of those who were involved in the salvaging were transferred to other bases: a measure taken to prevent them from talking about and discussing the event, perhaps telling their families about it and citing colleagues as witnesses. A soldier new to a base would be isolated and without supporting witnesses for tales he could tell. Thus any breach of secrecy could be most effectively prevented, or detected and dealt with.[38]

Meanwhile the Roswell AFB was visited with surprising frequency by top-ranking scientists, generals and aviation experts, who apparently made studies on the spot. This tallies with Kaufmann's statement about his having met General Ramey and Charles Lindbergh on July 8 at Colonel Blanchard's office.

However fantastic Kaufmann's story may sound, even this element could be verified. General Ramey

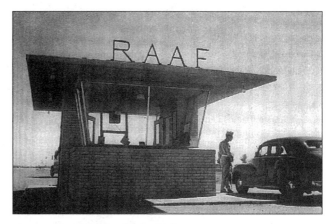

The gate at Roswell Army Air Field, 1947.

and Charles Lindbergh were, in fact, visiting the Base during this period. The bartender at the Officers' Club, Earl Zimmerman stated in an affidavit on 3 November 1993: *"I heard many rumors about flying saucers in the club and around the base, including something about investigating the discovery of one under the guise of a plane crash investigation. At about this time I saw Eighth Air Force commander General Roger Ramey in the Officers' Club more than once. On a couple of these occasions, he had Charles Lindbergh with him and I heard they were on the base because of the flying saucer business. There was no publicity about Lindbergh's visits, and I was very surprised to see him in the club."*[39]

The memory of the alien corpses haunted Kaufmann for the rest of his life. That was perhaps the reason why he remained at Roswell for so long. Occasionally he went back to the crash site. *"Once, about 25 years ago, I had a funny kind of feeling, a terrible feeling, and I had to get away. I couldn't stay there any longer."* After a pause he said to me, *"You see, I can't forget the expression on the faces of the beings. It was so peaceful and quiet. It seemed to me as if they could do nobody any harm. It was clear to anyone who saw them, that they could never be a danger or threat to us. They looked as if they had found a deep peace in themselves."*[40]

[1] Personal Interview with Glenn Dennis on 8 December 1993.

[2] Affidavit of Glenn Dennis, 7 August 1991.

[3] Personal Interview with Glenn Dennis on 8 December 1993.

[4] Affidavit of Glenn Dennis, 7 August 1991.

[5] *Roswell Daily Record*, 8 July 1947.

[6] Affidavit of L. M. Hall, 15 September 1993.

[7] Affidavit of David N. Wagnon, 15 November 1993.

[8] Friedman, Stanton and Don Berliner, *Crash at Corona*, New York, 1992.

[9] Affidavit of Vern Maltais, 23 April 1991.

[10] FUROR, *Recollections of Roswell* (Video), Mt. Rainier, MD, 1993.

[11] Randle, Kevin and Don Schmitt, *The Truth about the UFO Crash at Roswell*, New York, 1994.

[12] Ibid.

[13] Carey, Thomas, "The Continuing Search for the Roswell Archaeologists," in *International UFO Reporter*, Vol. 19, No.1, Chicago, 1994.

[14] Randle/Schmitt, 1994.

[15] Carey, Thomas, 1994.

[16] Affidavit of Jim Ragsdale, 27 January 1993.

[17] Pflock, Karl T., *Roswell in Perspective*, Mt. Rainier, MD, 1994.

[18] Affidavit of Frankie Rowe, 22 November 1993.

[19] Ibid.

[20] Affidavit of Helen Cahill, 22 November 1993.

[21] FUROR, 1993.

[22] Randle/Schmitt, 1994.

[23] Personal Interview with Frank Kaufmann, 12 July 1995 and Pflock, Karl, 1994.

[24] Randle/Schmitt, 1994.

[25] Affidavit of Robert E. Smith, 10 October 1991.

[26] Friedman, Stanton and Don Berliner, *Crash at Corona*, New York, 1992.

[27] Good, Timothy, *Alien Liaison*, London, 1991.

[28] Friedman/Berliner, 1992.

[29] Ecker, Don, in *UFO Magazine*.

[30] Interview with Beverly Brown in Video *UFO Secret: The Roswell Crash*, New Century Productions, 1993.

[31] Ibid.

[32] Affidavit of Robert E. Smith, 10 October 1991.

[33] Affidavit of Robert Shirkey, 30 April 1991.

[34] Pflock, Karl, 1994.

[35] Ibid.

[36] Ibid.

[37] Filer, George and Joe Stefula, *Roswell-Witness*, Report of 11 September 1995.

[38] Randle/Schmitt, 1994.

[39] Affidavit of Earl L. Zimmermann, 3 November 1993.

[40] Personal Interview with Frank Kaufmann, 12 July 1995.

5.

Under Strict Secrecy

Hardly had the news of the recovery of the spacecraft reached Washington, action was started at the highest level. On July 7, 1947 at 1:55 P.M. EST (11:55 A.M. at Roswell), according to official records, there was a meeting at the Pentagon between General Curtis LeMay, the vice-chief of staff of the Air Force for Research and Development, and General Hoyt Vandenberg, chief of staff and vice-commander of the Air Force. The subject of the meeting was "Flying saucers."[1]

At the same time General Nathan Twining, Commanding General of the Air Technical Intelligence Corps (ATIC) at Wright Field, canceled his scheduled departure to the West Coast on July 10 and flew totally unannounced to the Kirtland Air Base at Albuquerque, New Mexico. At his office, reporters of the *Oregonian* and the *Houston Chronicle* were told that he "had perhaps been ordered to go to Washington, D.C.,"[2] which we know today to be a blatant lie. Actually he flew from Kirtland to the Alamogordo Field and back to Kirtland. On July 10 he left New Mexico, to report at Washington, D.C. On July 16 he paid Roswell AAF a surprise visit, before returning that same evening to Wright

![Major General Curtis LeMay with Brigade General Roger M. Ramey during WWII in India.]

Major General Curtis LeMay with Brigade General Roger M. Ramey during WWII in India.

Lt. Gen. Hoyt S. Vandenberg, Deputy Commander of the U.S. Army Air Forces 1947

General Nathan F. Twining, commanding general of the Air Materiel Command in 1947. He suddenly changed his travel plans to supervise the retrieval operation in New Mexico.

Field. On that very day he wrote a letter of apology for having canceled a scheduled visit to the Boeing factory in Wichita, Kansas on July 10—he was supposed to view the XL-15 project—to the Boeing vice-president J. E. Schaefer. "Due to important and sudden matters that developed here," he had been compelled to change his travelling plans. It was only now that he could write, for "he had been travelling quite a bit during the last two weeks."[3]

In fact he even referred to the UFO theme during this period. The *Albuquerque Journal* of July 9 quotes his words: "*. . . the flying saucers are definitely not the result of experiments made by the armed services. . . . neither the AAF nor any other component of the armed forces has any aircraft, or guided missile or other aerial device under development that could be mistaken for a saucer or formation of flying discs. . . . some of these witnesses evidently saw something. . . . we don't know what we are investigating.*"[4]

Late in the evening of July 8 Colonel Blanchard left the RAAF. Officially he had gone on leave for a few days. But there are witnesses to prove that he had actually gone to the crash site to supervise completion of the recovery and clearing operation.[5]

At Roswell, meanwhile, the recovered wreckage was packed for further transport, and doctors conducted preliminary autopsies on the bodies, perhaps also attempted to keep alive the alien who had survived the crash. Altogether nine planes left the RAAF loaded with the wreckage between July 6 and 9, bound for different destinations:

1. Sunday, July 6, 3:00 P.M.: The material brought by Brazel was flown to Fort Worth in a B-29. There Colonel Alan D. Clark received the material personally and took it with him in a B-26 to Andrews Army

BOEING AIRPLANE COMPANY

WICHITA DIVISION

WICHITA 1, KANSAS

July 17, 1947   17 July 1947

JCS:cm

Dear Earl:

I have received your letter in which you asked us to drop by at Wichita for a brief visit. With deepest regrets we had to cancel our trip to the Boeing factory due to a very important and sudden matter that developed here. All of us were considerably disappointed as Mr. Allen had planned a very fine trip for us; however, we hope to go out at a later time. Will remember your invitation and get out to see you just as soon as we can, as I am very anxious to see the XL-15.

I have been away quite a bit the last couple of weeks so have not had a chance to submit any information to you that you asked for in your round robin letter. I will get on this very shortly.

Best regards,

N. F. TWINING
Lieutenant General, U.S.A.

P.S. Unification looks like a sure thing now.

Mr. J. E. Schaefer
Boeing Airplane Co,
Wichita, Kansas

Twining's letter to Earl Schaefer of Boeing Airplane Co.: "With deepest regrets we had to cancel our trip to the Boeing factory due to a very important and sudden matter that developed here." Instead, Gen. Twining flew to New Mexico on July 7, 1947—officially for a "routine inspection."

Airfield near Washington, where it was picked up by a courier from the SAC Commanding General, Clements McMullen.[6]

2. Tuesday, July 8, 4:00 P.M.: A B-29 left for Fort Worth, fully packed with wreckage. On board, amongst others, the vice-commander of the RAAF, Lieutenant Colonel Payne Jennings, and Major Jesse Marcel. At Fort Worth the cargo was transferred to a B-25 and flown to Wright Field near Dayton, Ohio, the head-quarters of the Air Materiel Command.[7]

3. Tuesday, July 8, 4:00 P.M.: Simultaneously a plane from Washington landed at the RAAF, which brought personnel for supervising the recovery, amongst them the intelligence officer Raymond deVinney, who "more or less as a representative of President Truman" (R.E. Smith) supervised the operations. The plane returned, loaded with wreckage.[8]

4.–7. Wednesday, July 9, 8:00 A.M.: Four C-54 trans-porters were loaded with wreckage. Armed MPs and "inspectors" from Washington watched the proceed-ings. Robert E. Smith of the first Air Transport Unit, who was stationed at Roswell and took part in the load-ing, declared in an affidavit dated 10 October 1991:

The Roswell Army Air Field, as it was in 1947.

My involvement in the Roswell incident was to help load crates of debris on to the aircraft. We all became aware of the event when we went to the hangar on the east side of the ramp. Our people had to remeasure the aircraft on the inside to accommo-date the crates they were making for this material. All I saw was a little piece of material. The piece of debris I saw was two to three inches square. It was jagged. When you crumpled it up, it then laid back out; and when it did, it kind of crack-led, making a sound like cellophane, and it crackled when it was let out. There were no creases. One of our people put it in his pocket.

The largest piece was roughly twenty feet long; four to five feet high, four to five feet wide. The rest were two to three feet

long, two feet square or smaller. The sergeant who had the piece of material said that was the material in the crates. There were words stenciled on the crates, but I don't remember what they were; however, the word "section" appeared on most of the crates. The entire loading took at least six, perhaps eight hours. Lunch was brought to us, which was unusual. The crates were brought to us on flatbed dollies, which also was unusual.

A lot of people began coming in all of a sudden because of the official investigation. Somebody said it was a plane crash; but we heard from a man in Roswell that it was not a plane crash but it was something else, a strange object. Officially, we were told it was a crashed plane, but crashed planes usually were taken to the salvage yard, not flown out. I don't think it was an experimental plane, because not too many people in that area were experimenting with planes—they didn't have the money to.

We were taken to the hangar to load crates. There was a lot of farm dirt on the hangar floor. We loaded it on flatbeds and dollies; each crate had to be checked as to width and height: We had to know which crates went on to which plane. We loaded crates on to three or four C-54s. It took the better part of the day to load the planes. One crate took up the entire plane; it wasn't that heavy, but it was a large volume.

This would have involved [Oliver W.] "Pappy" Henderson's crew. I remember seeing Technical Sergeant Harbell Ellzey and Technical Sergeant Edward Bretherton and S. Sergeant William Fortner; Elszey was on "Pappy's" crew.

We weren't supposed to know the destination, but we were told they were headed north. Wright Field at that time was closed down for modernization; therefore, I would deduce that the next safest place was Los Alamos, the most secret base available and still under the Manhattan Project. There were armed guards present during the loading of the planes, which was unusual. There was no way to get to the ramp except through armed guards. There were MPs around it, and our personnel were between them and the planes.

There were a lot of people in plain clothes all over the place; they were "inspectors," but they were strangers on the base. When challenged, they replied that they were here on project so-and-so and flashed a card, which was different than a military ID card.

A lot of the people involved in the event believe that they should go to their deathbeds without telling anything about it. We were told: "This is a hot shipment; keep quiet about it."

I'm convinced that what we loaded was a UFO that got into mechanical problems. Even with the most intelligent people, things go wrong.[9]

L to R: Capt. Sales, AC; Capt. Toler, CP; Capt. Bockman, Nav.; T/Sgt. Seymour, RO; T/Sgt. Miller, Eng.

R to L: Lt. Frazier, AC; Lt. Winningham, CP; Lt. Curley, Nav.; S/Sgt. Murphy, Eng.; M/Sgt. Watkins, RO.

L to R: Lt. Brunson, AC; Lt. Henninger, CP; T/Sgt. Nickell, Eng.; T/Sgt. Newhouse, RO.

L to R: Capt. Henderson, AC; Lt. Fields, CP; T/Sgt. Bretherton, Eng.; T/Sgt. Ellzey, RO.

L to R: Lt. Eddington, AC; Lt. Ricks, CP; T/Sgt. Place, Eng.; 1st/Sgt. Nielen, RO.

AIR CREWS

From the 1947 RAAF base yearbook: In the middle Capt. Henderson's crew which transported the wreckage to Wright Field.

While R. E. Smith assumed that the cargo was to be delivered to Los Alamos or the Kirtland Base—where General Twining was just then present—one of the pilots has stated that the destination at least of his plane was Wright Field. The pilot was Captain Oliver W. Henderson, known to his comrades as "Pappy," because he was older and his hair had gone gray prematurely. Pappy was a war hero. During the Second World War he had flown for the 446 Bomber Squadron thirty B-24

AFFIDAVIT

(1) My name is Sappho Henderson.

(2) My address is: ████████████████████

(3) I am retired.

(4) My husband was Oliver Wendell Henderson, who was called "Pappy," because he was older than the other ~~enlisted men~~ PILOTS in his squadron during World War II and had prematurely gray hair. We met during World War II, when he flew with the 446th Bomb Squadron; he flew B-24s and had 30 missions over Germany, for which he received two Distinguished Flying Crosses and the Air Medal with Four Oak Leaf Clusters.

(5) After the war, he returned home and was sent to Galveston Air Force Base, then transferred to Pueblo AFB, and then sent to Roswell (later Walker AFB), where we stayed for 13 years.

(6) While he was stationed at Roswell, he ran the "Green Hornet Airline," which involved flying C-54s and C-47s, carrying VIPs, scientists and materials from Roswell to the Pacific during the atom bomb tests. He had to have a Top Secret clearance for this responsibility. After separating from the service, he operated a construction business in Roswell. He died on March 25, 1986.

(7) In 1980 or 1981, he picked up a newspaper at a grocery store where we were living in San Diego. One article described the crash of a UFO outside Roswell, with the bodies of aliens discovered beside the craft. He pointed out the article to me and said, "I want you to read this article, because it's a true story. I'm the pilot who flew the wreckage of the UFO to Dayton, Ohio. I guess now that they're putting it in the paper, I can tell you about this. I wanted to tell you for years." Pappy never discussed his work because of his security clearance.

(8) He described the beings as small with large heads for their size. He said the material that their suits were made of was different than anything he had ever seen. He said they looked strange. I believe he mentioned that the bodies had been packed in dry ice to preserve them. He was not aware of the book [The Roswell Incident] that had been published about this event at the time he told me this.

(9) I have not been paid or given anything of value to make this statement, which is the truth to the best of my recollection.

Sappho Henderson
(Signature)

July 9, 1991
(Date)

Signature witnessed by:
Steve Gcode
(Name)

PERSONA APPEARED MRS. SAPPHO HENDERSON

Subscribed and sworn to before me this 9th day of July, 19 91.

Notary Public in and for the County of Los Angeles State of California

OFFICIAL SEAL
GUADALUPE DIAZ
Notary Public - California
Principal Office in
LOS ANGELES COUNTY
My Commission Expires 157

Affidavit of Sappho Henderson, the widow of Capt. Oliver "Pappy" Henderson: "He described the beings as small with large heads for their size."

flights over Germany, for which he received two of the highest military decorations. After the war he was first transferred to Galveston, then to Pueblo and finally to Roswell, where he stayed for thirteen years. At Roswell he was in charge of the "Green Hornets Airline," the secret transport unit of the first atom-bomb unit of the world. He and his pilots took top military officers, politicians, scientists and journalists to the atom tests in the Pacific in their C-54 and C-47 transporters. His access level was "Top Secret," which meant that he himself could be sent on missions requiring highest secrecy. One trusted Pappy, who "had flown practically everything that has wings."

Captain Henderson kept his silence till 1981. He was then living in San Diego with his wife Sappho. Once while going shopping, "Pappy" saw a newspaper which reported about the Roswell incident—the book by Berlitz and Moore had just appeared. . . . The paper was the *Globe* of 17 February 1981. He studied the article carefully and showed it to his wife: "I want you to read this article, for it is a true story. I am the pilot who flew the wreckage to Dayton, Ohio. Now that they have brought it out in the papers, I think I can tell you about it. I've been wanting to tell you for years. . . ."

He knew about the crash of the disc north of Roswell and also that "small creatures" had been found, which he—perhaps while they were lying in the hangar—had seen with his own eyes. *"He described the beings as small with large heads for their size. He said the material that their suits were made of was different than anything he had ever seen. He said they looked strange. I believe he mentioned that the bodies had been packed in dry ice to preserve them,"* recalled Sappho in an affidavit dated 9 July 1991.[10]

He had, however, already told the story to the dentist Dr. John Kromschroeder, with whom he had built up a business, although under oath of silence. He trusted Kromschroeder, who was himself a retired army officer. He not only spoke to the dentist about "spaceship fragments" and the "little men," but also showed him a piece of metal, which he said was a part of the debris. *"I had a good look at it and came to the conclusion that it was an alloy, which we don't have here,"* Kromschroeder, who knows metallurgy, said during an interview. *"It was a gray, shining metal that looked like aluminum, but lighter and harder. Its edges were sharp and serrated."*[11] The metal piece could lie somewhere in

"Pappy's" possessions, but to date, his widow Sappho has not been able to find it.

Stanton Friedman found out that Henderson had talked about his mission to a number of old flight companions at a veterans' meeting at Nashville in 1982. *"It was in a hotel room that he told us the story of the UFO and his role in it ,"* cited an anonymous witness to Friedman. *"Pappy told us that he flew the plane to Wright Field. He mentioned the bodies. . . . they were small and different from us."*[12]

When Mary Kathryn Goode, Henderson's daughter, visited her parents in 1981, her father showed her the article: *"He told me that he saw the crashed craft and the alien bodies described in the article, and that he had flown the wreckage to Ohio. He described the alien beings as small and pale, with slanted eyes and large heads. He said they were humanoid looking, but different from us. I think he said there were three bodies. He said the matter had been top secret and that he was not supposed to discuss it with anyone, but that he felt it was all right to tell me because it was in the newspaper,"*[13] she said in an affidavit. Then she recalled that her father had always made certain hints. *"When I was growing up, he and I would often spend evenings looking at the stars. On one occasion, I asked him what he was looking for. He said, 'I'm looking for flying saucers. They're real, you know.'"*[14]

As a matter of fact, Henderson's statement that the wreckage went to Wright Field is confirmed by no less a personage as the later vice-commander of the base, Brigadier General Arthur E. Exon. Lieutenant Colonel Exon—which he was at the time—had been transferred to the RAAF shortly before the incident occurred. *"We heard the material was coming to Wright Field,"* he said to Kevin Randle on 19 July 1990. *"The testing was done in various laboratories. . . everything from chemical analysis, stress tests, flexing. . . the boys who tested it said it was very unusual. . . some of it could be easily ripped or damaged. . . others very thin but awfully strong and couldn't be dented with heavy hammers. . . . it was flexible to a degree. . . . Some of it was flimsy but* *tougher than hell and other almost like foil but strong. It had them pretty puzzled. . . . They knew they had something new in their hands. The metal and material was unknown to anyone I talked to. Whatever they found, I never heard the results. A couple of guys thought it might be Russian but the overall consensus was that the pieces were from space.*[15]

8. Wednesday, July 9, 4:00 P.M.: Two of the ET-bodies were flown to Fort Worth, accompanied by Major Edgar Skelley, a crew of eight members, and four MPs. There they picked up Major Jesse Marcel, who had spent the night there. One of the crew members, Robert A. Slusher, described this flight in an affidavit dated 23 May 1993 as follows:

I was stationed at the Roswell Army Air Field from 1946–1952.

On July 9, 1947, I boarded a B-29 which taxied to the bomb area on the base to get a crate, which we loaded into the forward bomb bay. Four armed MPs guarded the crate, which was approximately four feet high, five feet wide, and twelve feet long. We departed Roswell at approximately 4 P.M. for Fort

Wright Field in the late 1940's.

Worth [later Carswell AFB]. Major Edgar Skelley was the flight operations officer.

The flight to Ft. Worth was at a low level, about four to five thousand feet. Usually we flew at 25,000 feet, and the cabin is pressurized. We had to fly at a low level because of the MPs in the bomb bay.

On arrival at Fort Worth, we were met by six people, including three MPs. They took possession of the crate. The crate was loaded onto a flatbed weapons carrier and hauled off.

Their MPs accompanied the crate. One officer present was a major, the other a first lieutenant. The sixth person was an undertaker who had been a classmate of a crewman on our flight, Lieutenant Felix Martucci. Major Marcel came up to our plane in a jeep and got on board. We were at Ft. Worth about thirty minutes before returning to Roswell.

The return flight was above 20,000 feet, and the cabin was pressurized. After returning to Roswell, we realized that what was in the crate was classified. There were rumors that they had carried debris from a crash. Whether there were any bodies, I don't know. The crate had been specially made; it had no markings. . . .

The flight was unusual in that we flew cargo and returned immediately. It was a hurried flight; normally we knew the day before there would be a flight. The round trip took approximately three hours, fifteen minutes: it was still light when we returned to Roswell. Lieutenant Martucci said, "We made history."[16]

In an interview with Kevin Randle in 1990, John G. Tiffany said that his father had been a part of the crew of the flight that had started from Wright Field to pick up the material at Fort Worth. Investigation showed that Tiffany's father had in fact been stationed at Wright Field at that time. After landing at Fort Worth they had loaded the wreckage and amongst these a big container that looked like a giant thermos bottle. The material had been very light, but very tough, with a glassy surface. During the whole flight the crew had tried to bend, break or scratch it, but in vain. When the "weather balloon" declaration appeared in the papers, they could only laugh out loud. Later on, his father had also heard about three bodies, two mutilated, one intact. They had had gentle features and a soft skin and worn a kind of flying suit. One of them, he had heard, had been part of his load.

That filled the crew with misgivings. After the flight they had all felt *"that they would never be clean again."* On landing, everything was loaded onto trucks. After that a high-ranking officer had instructed them never to speak to anybody about the incident. *"It never happened!"*[17]

General Exon affirmed that he had heard about this transport to Wright Field. But he emphasized that the debris came from a site—Foster Ranch—other than that where the bodies had been found. *"(It was) probably part of the same accident, but there were two distinct sites. One, . . . as I remember flying over the area later, that the damage to the vehicle seemed to be coming from the southeast to the northwest, but it could have been going in the opposite direction, but it doesn't seem likely. So the farthest pieces found on the ranch, those were mostly metal. . . . There was another location where . . . apparently the main body of the spacecraft was . . . where they did say there were bodies. . . . they were all found in fairly good condition. . . . they weren't broken up a lot."*[18]

9. Wednesday, July 9, 4:00 P.M.: More or less at the same time a second plane started with other bodies and Frank Kaufmann on board with destination Andrews Air Field near Washington, D.C.[19]

Bustling activity at the highest level followed. On the morning of July 9 General Leslie Groves, commander of the Weapons Development Project at Los Alamos together with General Robert Montague, commander of the Remote-Controlled Rockets School of the U.S. Army at Fort Bliss, Texas, flew unannounced to Washington. Apparently their specialist's opinion was required. On the same day, between 10:30 and 11:00

President Harry S. Truman

A.M., President Truman received a visit from Senator Carl Hatch of New Mexico. At the same time Lieutenant General James Doolittle and the vice-commander of the Army Air Force, General Hoyt S. Vandenberg, conferred with the Air Force secretary Stuart Symington at the Pentagon. At 10:48 A.M., while Hatch was still at the White House, Vandenberg called the president. A few minutes later they went together into the office of the chief of staff of the Army, General Dwight D. Eisenhower. The meeting, obviously to discuss a crisis, lasted till 12:12 P.M. At 12:50 P.M. General Vandenberg and Secretary Symington met to attend a meeting of the joint chiefs of staff of the Forces, which lasted till 2:15 P.M. A quarter of an hour later Vandenberg and Symington conferred again with each other till 3:10 P.M. Whereas all these meetings are carefully registered and documented in the U.S. National Archives, oddly enough, in all these cases the purpose and agenda of the meetings is missing. Apparently one discussion of a crisis followed the other, without any record being kept as to what it was all about![20]

This continued during the following days. On July 10 the newly arrived Generals Groves and Montague met Generals Vandenberg and LeMay at 10:30 A.M. at the Pentagon. At 12:15 P.M. Generals Vandenberg and Doolittle met the president, officially to sign an Air Force declaration. Defense Secretary Robert P. Patterson and Generals Groves and Montague met at the Pentagon at 2:40 P.M. Montague was placed in command of the Sandia Base, a super-secret research center southeast of Albuquerque. On the same day the scientific adviser of the president, Dr. Vannevar Bush, left Washington for an unknown destination. His secretary said, in a letter written to General Spaatz on July 17, that "he was not expected to be back till the beginning of September."[21] He was back in Washington on September 16. On the 24th he met the president, together with the new Defense Secretary James Forrestal . . .

Also on July 10, an internal memorandum was sent to FBI Director J. Edgar Hoover. Subject: "flying saucers." Brigadier General George F. Shulgen, chief of

Award-winning security poster of the Defense Intelligence Agency (DIA) from 1984.

Memorandum of 10 July 1947 to FBI Director J. Edgar Hoover regarding the request of Brigadier General Schulgen of the Army Air Corps Intelligence, to cooperate with the FBI in the investigation of the "flying discs." "I would do it," Hoover replied, "but before agreeing to it we must insist upon full access to discs recovered."

the Army Air Corps Intelligence, had requested the FBI for assistance on 9 July 1947. *"General Schulgen indicated that the Air Corps has taken the attitude that every effort must be undertaken in order to run down and ascertain whether or not the flying discs are a fact and, if so, to learn all about them. According to General Schulgen, the Air Corps Intelligence are utilizing all of their scientists in order to ascertain whether or not such a phenomenon could in fact occur. . . . all Air Corps installations have been alerted to run out each reported sighting to obtain all possible data to assist in this research project. . . . (he) indicated that it . . . has been established that the flying discs are not the result of any Army or Navy experiments, the matter is of interest to the FBI."*[22]

"I would do it," replied Hoover in handwriting, referring to the offer of cooperation with the AAF, *"but before agreeing to it, we must insist upon full access to discs recovered."*[23]

The cooperation was agreed upon, the Air Force promised Hoover that in the future his people could deal with "discs found on the ground." How seriously this offer was meant can be seen from an instruction sent out by the headquarters of the Air Defense Command to the commanding generals of the first, second, fourth, tenth, eleventh and fourteenth Air Forces (interestingly enough, NOT to General Ramey of the eighth) on 3 September 1947, meant to define which cases were to be handed over to the FBI: *"The Federal Bureau of Investigation has agreed to assist Air Force Intelligence personnel in the investigation of 'flying disc' incidents in order to quickly and effectively rule out what are pranks and to concentrate on what appears to be a genuine incident. . . . the FBI would investigate incidents of so called 'discs' being found on the ground . . . in order to relieve the numbered Air Forces of the task of tracking down all the many instances which turned out to be can covers, toilet seats and whatnot."*[24]

On September 19, 1947 a lieutenant colonel who was responsible for the contact with the FBI handed over a copy of these instructions to the deputy director of the FBI, D. M. Ladd, who immediately sent a report to Director Hoover. *"In the first place, the instructions issued by the Army Air Forces in this letter appear to limit the type of investigations which the Bureau will be asked to handle and secondly it appears to me the wording of the last sentence in the second paragraph mentioned above is cloaked in entirely uncalled for language tending to indicate the Bureau will be asked to conduct investigations only in those cases which are not important and which are almost, in fact, ridiculous.*

"The thought has occurred to me the Bureau might desire to discuss this matter further with the Army Air Forces both as to the types of investigations which we will conduct and also object to the scurrilous wordage which, to say the least, is insulting to the Bureau in the last sentence of paragraph two."[25]

Internal Memorandum of the AAF of 3 September 1947 regarding the cooperation with the FBI in the investigation of "flying discs": The services of the FBI were enlisted "in order to relieve the numbered Air Forces of the task of tracking down all the many instances which turned out to be ash can covers, toilet seats and whatnot."

Hoover was furious when he got this report. On September 27 he wrote to the Air Force deputy chief of staff Major General George C. McDonald: *"I cannot permit the personnel and time of this organization to be dissipated in this manner.*

"I am advising the Field Divisions of the Federal Bureau of Investigation to discontinue all investigative activity regarding the reported sightings of flying discs, and am instructing them to refer all complaints received to the appropriate Air Force representative in their area.[26]

Only three years later did Hoover learn how far he had been misled, after an "investigator for the Air Force" reported to Guy Hottel, chief of the FBI office in Washington, *"that three so-called flying saucers had been recovered in New Mexico. There were described as being circular in shape with raised centers, approximately 50 feet in diameter. Each one was occupied by three bodies of human shape but only 3 feet tall, dressed in metallic cloth of a very fine texture. Each body was bandaged in a manner similar to the blackout suits used by speed flyers and test pilots.*

"According to Mr. XXX informant, the saucers were found in New Mexico due to the fact that the Government has a very high-powered radar set-up in that area and it is believed the radar interferes with the controlling mechanism of the saucers."[27]

However generalized this statement is, there is enough to suggest that some weeks before the Roswell occurrence another crashed UFO already had been found by the Air Force. This explains the panic in the army circles. What had originally looked like a lone expedition to the earth from outer space, now looked like an invasion.

In the autumn of 1990 the Californian UFO researcher Timothy Cooper came in contact with a former army colleague of his father, who had once been stationed at the Hollomon Base near Alamogordo in New Mexico. During the summer of 1947 he had been technical sergeant at Hollomon and had occasion to see pictures and documents concerning a UFO crash in 1947. Bob—that was his first name—was in charge of the printing press at the base. One day in July 1947 the base commander Colonel Paul F. Helmlek, accompanied by a cohort of MPs, came to the press and ordered all those present there to go home, except Bob. He then gave Bob a document and said, "Print it!" The sergeant looked at the papers. There were about fifty pages, illustrated with a number of black-and-white photographs. "That is not so easy," said Bob, "it will take a few days." "Impossible!" shouted the colonel. "You'll do it now, straight-away! And avoid taking note of the contents or photos. It is all top secret!"

Bob started on the work immediately, but naturally could not avoid registering the fascinating contents of the document. It dealt with the crash of a "flying disc" near the White Sands Proving Grounds. And while focusing the repro camera, he could only too clearly see the saucer-shaped metallic object that had dashed against a cliff. The object reflected the sunlight and showed no markings on it or signs of an external propulsion system. Bob finished the job on the same day. He was instructed to deposit the papers in the safe, from where security officers would pick them up.

"What exactly did you see on the photos?" asked Cooper.

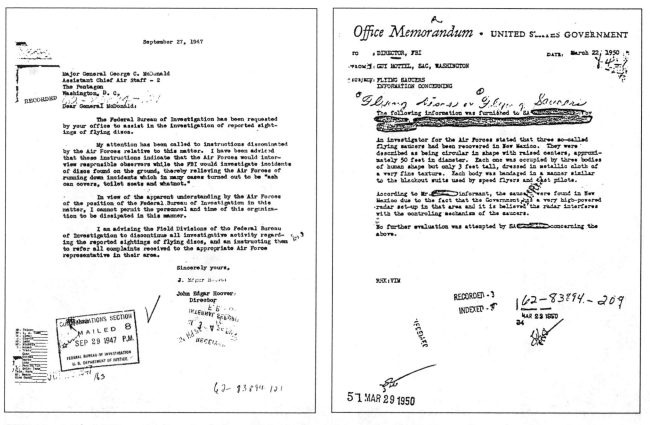

FBI Director J. Edgar Hoover sent this angry letter on 27 September 1947 to General Major George C. McDonald in the Pentagon: Hoover couldn't "permit the personnel and time of this organization to be dissipated in this manner" but wanted access to the real discs.

Memorandum to FBI Director Hoover from 22 March 1950: "Three so-called flying saucers had been recovered in New Mexico."

"I remember a dozen or more 8 X 10 B&W glossies of the craft resting near a hillside. It appeared slightly tilted. The craft appeared to be a large, round dome-shaped, almost egg-shaped disc with a flat bottom. It looked bigger than a B-29 in size. The personnel in the foreground gave a sense of scale to it. I guess it'd be approximately 100 ft. in diameter and about 15 to 20 ft. high at the center. I saw a rim or a dihedral edge near the bottom of the craft in one photo. I saw no landing gear, exhaust ports or windows. I did see one access opening or door-like opening that seemed to open outward. Some stills are of the base technical personnel surrounding the craft. Some were wearing suits. They were climbing on top. There were some close-ups of the craft's structure but I can't recall what it looked like."

"What do you remember of the technical report itself?"

"It was a technical description of the craft. It was prepared for the AMC and the ATIC. It did not analyze but record dimensional, structural, and material specifications. The report also contained radar data. There was a section that included the possible flight path, guidance and navigation systems, propulsion theory, and flight controls. Part of the report was done by a German scientific team headed by Ernst Steinhoff and Wernher von Braun. There were a few aeronautical engineers flown into Holloman (Alamogordo Field) from ATIC. I did not read the report itself, but recall some topics it covered. It was approximately 50 pages with a lot of photographs. I did not process any motion picture film at that time." Bob remembered a comrade, a pilot, First Sergeant Robert G. Baines, who had flown in some very important Air Force generals, amongst them Twining, Canon, LeMay, Vandenberg, Doolittle and Wainwright. Another general, Groves, was flown in with the sci-

White Sands Proving Grounds, New Mexico.

Twinings Air Accident report on Flying disk crack near White Sands proving grounds, New Mexico 16 July 1947.

entists Robert Oppenheimer, Vannevar Bush, John von Neuman and Theodor von Karman. Timothy asked him whether all this to-do was in connection with the Roswell affair. Bob denied this, saying, "Roswell is only one of a number of UFO crashes in New Mexico."[28]

Bob's story is confirmed by a document sent to UFO researcher Leonard Stringfield in 1993 by a Secret Service insider. In this technical report AMC commander General Nathan F. Twining summarizes the results of the first examinations carried out at Wright Field. Since this report bears clearly the heading "Air Accident Report on Flying Disc Aircraft That Crashed Near White Sands Proving Ground, New Mexico," it has nothing to do with the Roswell incident, but refers to another crash, which must have occurred at some time before this report, with the code name D 333.5 ID, was written. It originates from "Headquarters Air Materiel Command, Wright Field, 16 July 1947" and is addressed to the "Commanding General of the Army Air Force, Washington 25 (Pentagon) D.C.—Air Defense Command; ATTN: Ac/15-2."

Since it has not been officially released, we naturally do not know whether it is genuine or forged. At least the dates would seem to be acceptable. General Twining was back at Wright Field on the evening of July 16. A "directive from the president, dated 9 July 1947" is possible. The document also specifically mentions Fort Bliss, whose commander General Montague was specially ordered to go to Washington on July 9, which suggests that his equipage was involved in the investigations. We also find in the document the names of those German "Paperclip" scientists—top Nazi experts from the V-2 program, including Wernher von Braun, who from then on worked for the U.S. rocket projects. The paper says:

WSPG UFO INCIDENTS OF 1947: A PRELIMINARY REPORT

1. As ordered by Presidential Directive, dated 9 July 1947, a preliminary investigation of a recovered "Flying Disc" and remains of a possible second disc, was conducted by the senior staff of this command. The data furnished in this report was provided by the engineer staff personnel of T-2 and Aircraft Laboratory, Engineering Division T-3. Additional data furnished by the scientific personnel of the Jet Propulsion Laboratory, CIT, and the Army Air Forces Scientific Advisory Group, headed by Dr. Theodore von Karman. Further analysis was conducted by personnel from Research and Development.

2. It is the collective view of this investigative body, that the aircraft recovered by the army and air force units . . . are not of U.S. manufacture for the following reasons:

a. The circular, disc-shaped "platform" design does not resemble any design currently under development by this command nor of any Navy project.

b. The lack of any external propulsion system, power plant, intake, exhaust either for propeller or Jet propulsion, warrants this view.

c. The inability of the German scientists from Fort Bliss and White Sands Proving Ground to make a positive identification of a secret German V weapon of these discs. Though the possibility that the Russians have managed to develop such a craft, remains. The lack of any markings, ID numbers or instructions in Cyrillic, has placed serious doubt in the minds of many, that the objects recovered are not of Russian manufacture either.

d. Upon examination of the interior of the craft, a compartment exhibiting a possible atomic engine was discovered. At least this is the opinion of Dr. Oppenheimer and Dr. von Karman. A possibility exists that part of the craft itself comprises the propulsion system, thus allowing the reactor to function as a heat exchanger and permitting the storage of energy, unlike the release of energy of our atomic bombs. The description of the power room is as follows:

1) A doughnut shaped tube approximately thirty-five feet in diameter, made of what appears to be plastic material, surrounding a central core (see sketch in Tab. 1). This tube appeared to be filled with a clear substance, possibly a heavy water. A large rod centered inside the tube, was wrapped in a coil of what appears to be of copper material, ran through the circumference of the tube. This may be the reactor control mechanism or a storage battery. There were no moving parts of the spaces examined.

2) This activation of an electrical potential is believed to be the primary power to the reactor, though it is only a theory at present. Just how a heavy water reactor functions in this environment is unknown.

3) Underneath the power plant, was discovered a ball-turret, approximately ten feet in diameter. This turret was encompassed by a series of gears that has an unusual ratio not known by any of our engineers. On the underside of the turret were four circular cavities, coated with some smooth material not identified. These cavities are symmetrical but seem to be movable. Just how is not known. The movement of the turret coincides with the dome-shaped copula compartment above the power room. It is believed that the main propulsion system is a bladeless turbine, similar to current development now underway at AMC and the Mogul Project. A possible theory was devised by Dr. August Steinhoff (a Paperclip scientist), and Dr. Wernher von Braun and Dr. Theodor von Karman: as the craft moves through the atmosphere, it somehow draws the hydrogen from the atmosphere and by an induction process, generates an atomic fusion reaction (see Tab. 2). The air outside the craft would be ionized, thus, propelling the craft forward. Coupled with the circular air foil for lift, the craft would presumably have an unlimited range and air speed. This may account for the reported absence of any noise.

e. There is a flight deck located inside the copula section. It is round and domed at the top. The absence of canopy, observation windows / blisters, or any optical projection, lends support to the opinion that this craft is either guided by remote viewing or is remotely controlled.

1) A semi-circular photo-tube array (possibly television).

2) Crew compartments were hermetically sealed via a solidification process.

3) No weld marks, rivets or soldered joints.

4) Craft components appear to be molded and pressed into a perfect fit. [29]

In December 1995 Michael Hesemann was able to interview the daughter of a German scientist who had lived in America. She confirmed that her father too had been ordered to investigate the Roswell UFO. Helga Kueppers-Morrow is the daughter of Friederich August Kueppers, a physicist who worked for the aircraft builders Martin Co. (later Martin Marietta), then for the government military projects. He knew Wernher von Braun, John von Neumann, and others. Helga grew up in a milieu of scientists of German origin in Baltimore, so exclusive that as a child she thought everyone had the title of "doctor." "I can remember the day in summer 1947, I was twelve years old at that time," she said, *"my mother and I were in the kitchen. Daddy called, as usual from a place he was not allowed to divulge. He was enthusiastic, said, 'At last we can prove that extraterrestrials exist.' I jumped for joy. Mother could foresee what effect that would have on our church and faith. On the next day daddy called again. That was the day the army took back the story (8 July 1947). 'Liars, damned liars,' he said angrily, 'we know better. Don't believe them. They do exist!' Daddy was away long, but called*

Albert Einstein

regularly. When he came for Christmas he held my hands, then grabbed my shoulders. He said, 'Everything you have learned is false, only lies.' 'Where were you, Daddy?' I wanted to know. He said he was not permitted to say, only when he was dying. We knew that he was in New Mexico, for the lady on the telephone exchange said so automatically every time he called. That Christmas I did ask him one question: 'If these people from another world exist, does God exist? and who is He?' He answered:, 'Yes, but he is most probably naked and not an old man.'"[30]

If we trust the words of a professor of chemistry from Florida—whom Len Stringfield gave the pseudonym Edith Simpson—another scientist was also flown over, a man whom we can unhesitatingly designate as the greatest scientist of this century, Albert Einstein. In 1947 Edith Simpson was a highly gifted student of natural sciences and had been chosen from a large number of candidates to work as assistant to Einstein during the summer, between semesters. She described Einstein as *"warmhearted, sympathetic and friendly to all his students,"* and apparently he had developed a fondness for the very promising and highly intelligent young lady. In order to work for Einstein she had to go through an intensive security check, for her job automatically put her in a very sensitive position. She had access to all his research projects, he took her with him everywhere, and so she accompanied him when he was invited by the U.S. government to attend a crisis conference of top scientists and army officials, which was to take place at an Air Force Base in a southwestern State.

They flew from Princeton to Chicago on a regular flight, where they took another flight and landed at a small civilian airport. Edith remembers that it was raining when they landed and a colonel in a trenchcoat picked them up. They then drove in a military vehicle some fifty to seventy-five miles through the desert to the base. There they were taken to a strongly guarded old hangar, where they saw the extraterrestrials for the first time. *"Some of the specialists were allowed closer looks, including my boss. To me they all looked alike, all five of them. They were about five feet tall, without hair, with big heads and enormous dark eyes, and, yes, their skin was gray with a slight greenish tinge, but for the most part, their bodies were not exposed, being dressed in tight-fitting suits. But I heard they had no navels or genitalia. One of the aliens stood out above the rest. It had a bilious green fluid oozing from its nostrils. But it was strange: after exposure to the air, the ooze gradually became bluish, suggesting maybe a copper or cobalt base. I'm guessing, but it might have seeped from a gallbladderlike organ. In fact, I wondered if it was still alive, but I wasn't close enough to see any body movement or hear any comments from the medics."* Simpson told the local UFO researcher Sheila Franklin, who first came into contact with her and later interviewed her on Stringfield's behalf.

The wrecked spacecraft had been stowed in the same hangar, at the other end. *"It was disc-shaped, sort of concave,"* said Simpson, *". . . its size took up about one fourth of the hangar floor."* To her disappointment they did not allow her to get close enough to the craft to be able to study details. Armed guards stood everywhere, and it was surrounded by specialists who were examining it. One thing she could see was that it was badly damaged on one side. They told her that the unlucky crew had been recovered from that craft. That was the proof that extraterrestrials had come to the earth, even if their mission had obviously failed. *"My reaction,"* she said, *"was wonderment, half curiosity and, maybe, half fear."*

Was the wreck from Roswell? *"No one said that it was from the Roswell crash, but I did hear that name pop up during my trip. Now remember, I told you, they didn't tell me anything of importance, no secrets, no details. My boss, who had the right clearance, made a report, which I didn't see. I was just told to keep my mouth shut."*

One day, during her stay there, something happened that changed their plans. She and Einstein were taken in a troop carrier covered "with a canvas top," escorted by jeeps, about fifty miles through the desert, to an isolated building. Once ushered into the lone building, with guards at the door, her group was greeted by an officer and directed to an area where medical and uniformed people were concentrated around a gurney on which was a creature struggling in pain. At times it was prone and then it sat up trying to free itself, making strange groans, but it never spoke. Although she was kept at a distance she said she could readily recognize that it, too, was a gray alien biped, looking more human than the other five she had seen. At one instant, according to Professor Simpson, its whole torso incredibly expanded, looking grotesque, giving the attendants a hard time keeping it restrained. *"It must have been a fresh case,"* she said, *"but I was told nothing and before long all of us were dismissed from the premises."* She learned later that the injured alien survived.

When Sheila asked Professor Simpson how Einstein had reacted to all these events, she said, *"He was not disturbed at all by seeing the actual evidence. I didn't record in my notes his initial comments but he said something to the effect that he was not surprised that they came to earth and that it gave him hope that we could learn more about the universe. Contact, he said, should be a benefit for both of our worlds."*

"What interested him the most?" Her response: *"Propulsion and more about the universe."*

On the sensitive subject of secrecy, Simpson commented: *"We were reminded daily of our pledges of course, but I signed no papers. However, I was surprised to see photographers who were free to take photos, even movies of everything in view. Thanks to a trusting member of our group, I managed to get a set of photos. I kept these hidden for years until I made a mistake and showed one to a student."*

Photographers and cameramen documented every stage of the investigation. They were reminded daily that everything was under strict secrecy. After the holidays, when she had been back at the university for quite some time, the dean of the university called her from the classroom one day. He introduced her to a woman whom he referred to as a "psychologist" who "wanted to ask her a few questions." They sat down and the "psychologist" asked her only one question: "As a child, did you walk or talk first?" The next thing Edith could remember was that she looked at her watch and saw that an hour and a half had elapsed! She could recall nothing that had transpired during that period, but had the feeling that she had been hypnotized and questioned in that state. In later years, after she was a professor, federal officials had questioned people in her surroundings about her. Besides that she has been the victim of six "burglaries" in seven years, and all her pictures were stolen.[31]

We can assume that this scientific crisis conference was only a first brainstorming of the top brains in the country, with the purpose of defining the guidelines for a future investigation, which was to be made during the following years. In any case the U.S. Air Force tried everything possible in the following months to obtain closer details about "flying saucers." The first results were conveyed by General Twining on 23 September 1947 to the commanding general of the Army Air Force, with a copy to Brigadier General Schulgen. Since this document, released in 1978, had been classified only as "secret," the Roswell incident is deliberately not mentioned in it. The Roswell investigation was conducted at the highest level and was classified as "strictly secret." To ensure the secrecy, it was at all costs to be prevented that persons not directly connected with the project even come to know that "hardware" was in the possession of the government.

In any case, the report reveals the opinion of the Air Materiel Command regarding "flying saucers." In the words of Twining:

2. It is the opinion that:

a. The phenomenon reported is something real and not visionary or fictitious.

b. There are objects probably approximating the shape of a disc, of such appreciable size as to appear to be as large as man made aircraft.

c. There is a possibility that some of the incidents may be caused by natural phenomena, such as meteors.

d. The reported operating characteristics such as extreme rates of climb, maneuverability (particularly in roll), and action which must be considered evasive when sighted or contacted by friendly aircraft and radar, lend belief to the possibility that some of the objects are controlled either manually, automatically or remotely.

e. The apparent common description of the objects is as follows:

(1) Metallic or light reflecting surface.

(2) Absence of trail, except in a few instances when the object apparently was operating under high performance conditions.

(3) Circular or elliptical in shape, flat on bottom and domed on top.

(4) Several reports of well kept formation flights varying from three to nine objects.

(5) Normally no associated sound, except in three instances a substantial rumbling roar was noted.

(6) Level flight speeds normally above 300 knots are estimated.[32]

A month later, on 30 October 1947, Brigadier General Schulgen sent out a memorandum, also classified as "secret," in which he instructed members of the Air Force Intelligence Corps to put together all available information about aircraft of the type "flying saucer":

An alleged "flying saucer," a type of aircraft or object in flight, approximately in the form of a disc, has been reported by many observers from widely different places like the United States, Alaska, Canada, Hungary, the Island of Guam and Japan. This object has been seen by many competent observers, including many high ranking US Pilots. Sightings have been made from the ground as well.

2. Commonly reported features that are very significant and which may aid the investigation are as follows:

a. Relatively flat bottom with extreme light-reflecting ability.

b. Absence of sound except for an occasional roar when operating under super performance conditions.

c. Extreme maneuverability and apparent ability to almost hover.

d. A plan form approximating that of an oval or disc with a dome shape on the top surface.

e. The absence of an exhaust trail except in a few instances when it was reported to have a bluish color, like a diesel exhaust, which persisted for approximately one hour. Other reports indicated a brownish smoke trail that could be the result of a special catalyst or chemical agent for extra power.

f. The ability to quickly disappear by high speed or by complete disintegration.

g. The ability to suddenly appear without warning as if from an extremely high altitude.

h. The size most reported approximated that of a C-54 or Constellation type aircraft.

i. The ability to group together very quickly in a tight formation when more than one aircraft are together.

j. Evasive action ability indicates possibility of being manually operated, or possibly by electronic or remote control devices.

3. The first sighting in the U.S.A. was made some time in the middle of May. The last sighting was reported on 14 September from Toronto, Canada. The greatest activity in the

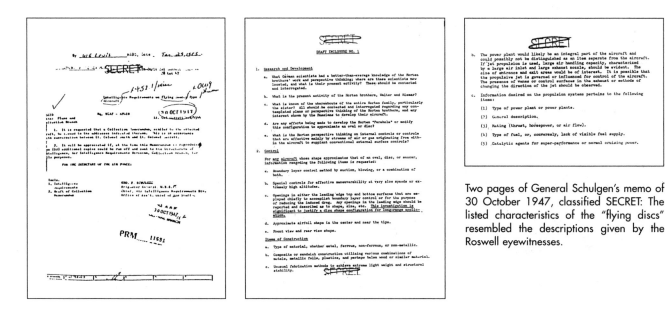

Two pages of General Schulgen's memo of 30 October 1947, classified SECRET: The listed characteristics of the "flying discs" resembled the descriptions given by the Roswell eyewitnesses.

U.S.A. occurred during the last week of June and the first week of July.

4. *This strange object, or phenomenon, may be considered, in view of certain observations, as long-range aircraft capable of a high rate of climb, high cruising speed and highly maneuverable and capable of being flown in very tight formations. For the purpose of analysis and evaluation of these so called "flying saucers," the object sighted is being assumed to be a manned craft of unknown origin. While there remains the possibility of Russian manufacture, based on perspective thinking and actual accomplishments of the Germans, it is the considered opinion of some elements that the object may in fact represent an interplanetary craft of some kind.*

In the following instructions to the Intelligence Service of the Air Force, General Schulgen recommends the careful investigation of German and Russian secret weapons. He draws special attention to features they should look for:

Construction.

a. Type of material, whether metal, ferrous, non-ferrous or non-metallic.

b. Composite or sandwich construction utilizing various combinations of metals, metallic foils, plastics, and perhaps balsa wood or similar material.

c. Unusual fabrication methods to achieve extreme light weight and structural stability.

Arrangement.

a. Special provisions such as retractable domes to provide unusual observation for the pilot and crew members.

b. Unusual features or provisions regarding the opening and closing of doors.

Landing Gear.

a. Indicate type of landing gear—whether conventional, tricycle, multiple wheel, etc., or of an unconventional type such as tripod or skid.

b. Provisions for takeoff from ice, snow, sand or water.

Powerplant.

a. Nuclear propulsion (atomic energy). Atomic energy engines would probably be unlike any familiar type of engine, although atomic energy might be employed in combination with any of the above types (piston, jet). Aircraft would be characterized by lack of fuel systems and fuel storage space.

b. The powerplant would likely be an integral part of the aircraft and possibly not distinguishable as an item separate from the aircraft.[33]

With that we are back at Roswell. Had not Bill Brazel described the fragment found by his father as being *"like wood, light like balsa, metallic"*?[34] How else, if not through the Roswell find, could the Air Force have arrived at these conclusions regarding the construction of the "flying saucers"? It is certain that no one would have thought, merely through sightings in the air or on land, of such details as *"extreme light weight," "sandwich construction," "various . . . metallic foils," "plastics," "balsa wood or similar material."* On the other hand these are accurate descriptions of the fragments found at Roswell. There is only one hitch: the Roswell disc had been officially "identified" as being a weather balloon three months before, on July 8. The genuineness of General Schulgen's memorandum is undisputed—it was "unclassified" and officially released on 29 January 1985 by the U.S. Air Force. To anyone reading between the lines it is obvious that the Air Force had never taken their own official "identification" of the Roswell fragments seriously—and that the wreck was, as late as the end of October 1947, in secret service circles referred to as *"aircraft of the type 'flying saucer,'"* which possibly was *"an interplanetary space-ship"*.

The fact is that months after General Ramey's official statement was issued, the investigation of the Roswell incident continued. One of the scientists involved was Professor Lincoln LaPaz of the University of New Mexico at Albuquerque. Immediately after the incident he had been sent to Roswell to question Mac Brazel, who was then in the custody of the AAF. LaPaz was an expert on meteorites and worked for the government. With his knowledge of mathematics, astronomy and meteorology he had been an adviser to the Manhattan Project, and his security access level was "top secret." When Japan attacked the U.S. with balloon-carried bombs, it was his job to detect these in time and destroy them before they could do any damage. At Roswell he was to determine the flight direction and velocity of the crashed craft and find out the cause of the mishap.

Lewis S. "Bill" Rickett of the Counter Intelligence Corps, who had, together with Captain Cavitt, supervised the clearing of the debris at the Foster Ranch, was assigned to help LaPaz. Rickett later told Stanton Friedman: *"LaPaz wanted to fly over the area, and that was arranged. He found another place where, he believed, the thing had bounced and regained height. The sand at the spot had turned into a kind of glassy substance. We gathered a box full of samples— and if I remember right there were also metal samples, a kind of thin foil. LaPaz sent them somewhere for testing. . . . the spot was a few miles away from the other one."*

Then he interviewed the rancher and the ranch hands. For three weeks he drove around the district. Since he spoke Spanish, he could talk to the Hispanics there. Some described their observations during the days after the crash. Others mentioned that animals had reacted in a confused manner. Brazel had said that too, recalled LaPaz. *"Before he went back to Albuquerque, he said the thing had had some trouble, landed for repairs and then taken off again. He was also sure that there were more than one such flying objects and that the others searched for it."* When they met after years at a restaurant east of Albuquerque, LaPaz said once more that the wreck *"was an unmanned extraterrestrial reconnaissance vessel."*

Apparently his client had not told LaPaz about the recovery of the crew.[35]

Rickett's statement is affirmed by the affidavit of Earl L. Zimmermann, who was transferred to the Kirtland Base early in 1949, to work for the Office for Special Investigations. There he worked with Professor LaPaz on a project at the research station of the University of New Mexico on the Sandia Mountain.

We were told that the Air Force was concerned about something being in the night sky over Los Alamos, and we took fifteen minute exposures. . . . Dr. LaPaz was in charge.

During this project, which lasted for several months, I got to know Dr. LaPaz very well. When I mentioned to him I had been stationed in Roswell during 1947, he told me he had been involved in the investigation of the thing found in the Roswell area that summer. He did not discuss the case in any detail but he did say he went out with two agents and interviewed shepherds, ranchers, and others. They told these witnesses they were investigating an aircraft accident. I seem to recall LaPaz also saying they found an area where the surface of the earth had been turned a light blue and wondering if lightning could cause such an effect.[36]

Another OSI Agent, Edgar J. Bethart, who had been a CIC officer at Alamogordo AAF in 1947, recalls that Rickett and LaPaz in September 1947 "were on a UFO hunt in the whole of southern New Mexico." Both of them had also told him about the discovery of "a big, round burnt spot in the middle of the prairie."[37]

After the investigation was closed, towards the end of September 1947, Professor LaPaz sent a written report about the findings to Washington. In this report he left no doubts about the Roswell wreck being a craft from another world, which was controlled by intelligence. . . .

[1]Berlitz, Charles and William L. Moore, *The Roswell Incident*, New York, 1980.

[2]Friedman, Stanton, *Final Report on Operation Majestic 12*, Mount Rainier, MD, 1990.

[3]Ibid.

[4]*Albuquerque Journal*, 9 July 1947.

[5]Randle, Kevin and Don Schmitt, *The Truth about the UFO Crash at Roswell*, New York, 1994.

[6]Ibid.

[7]Ibid.

[8]Affidavit of Robert E. Smith, 10 October 1991.

[9]Ibid.

[10]Affidavit of Sappho Henderson, 9 July 1991.

[11]Friedman, Stanton and Don Berliner, *Crash at Corona*, New York, 1992.

[12]Ibid.

[13]Affidavit of Mary Kathryn Goode, 14 August 1991.

[14]Interview with Mary K. Goode, in *Recollections of Roswell* (Video), Mount Rainier, MD, 1993.

[15]Randle, Kevin, *Roswell UFO Crash Update*, New York, 1995.

[16]Affidavit of Robert A. Slusher, 23 May 1993.

[17]Randle/Schmitt, 1994.

[18]Randle, 1995.

[19]Randle/Schmitt, 1994.

[20]Moore, William L., "Crashed Saucers: Evidence in Search of Proof," in *MUFON Symposium Proceedings*, Seguin/TX, 1985.

[21]"The Roswell Investigation," in *MUFON Symposium Proceedings*, Seguin/TX, 1982.

[22]FBI Memorandum, 10 July 1947.

[23]Ibid.

[24]Air Defense Command Headquarters Memorandum, 3 September 1947.

[25]FBI Memorandum, 19 September 1947.

[26]Letter from Hoover to General Major George C. McDonald, 27 September 1947.

[27]FBI Memorandum, 22 March 50.

[28]Stringfield, Leonard, *UFO Crash/Retrievals: The Inner Sanctum,* Cincinnati/OH, 1991.

[29]Twining, Nathan F., "Air Accident Report on 'Flying Disc' Aircraft Crashed Near White Sands Proving Ground," New Mexico," 16 July 1947, quoted from Stringfield, Len, *UFO Crash/Retrievals: Search for Proof in a Hall of Mirrors,* Cincinnati/OH, 1994.

[30]Personal Interview with Helga Khppers-Morrow, 1 December 1995.

[31]Stringfield, Len, 1993.

[32]Twining, Nathan F., "AMC Opinion Concerning 'Flying Discs,'" 23 September 1947.

[33]Schulgen, F., "Intelligence Requirements on Flying Saucer Type Aircraft," 30 October 1947.

[34]Friedman/Berliner, 1992.

[35]Ibid.

[36]Affidavit of Earl Zimmermann, 2 November 1993.

[37]Pflock, Karl, *Roswell in Perspective,* Mount Rainier, MD, 1994.

6.

Behind Closed Doors

After the successful covering up of the Roswell incident, not even three years had elapsed when fresh rumors about crashed "flying saucers" were going around. Responsible for this was no less a personage than Frank Scully, columnist of *Variety*, the journal for all Hollywood insiders and whomever was interested in the movie industry. Scully was more than a gossip reporter—his good instinct for stories, his sharp pen, his light irony and literary subtleties made his columns a pleasure to read and him a Hollywood legend. He was confronted with the theme rather by chance.

On October 12, 1949 he wrote in "Scully's Scrapbook":

I have just spent a weekend with scientists, who know all there is to know about flying saucers, not only from this planet but from others. . . . Weeks ago these sages informed me they had checked on two of the discs which had landed here from another planet and even told me where the platters had landed. The Mojave desert got one and the Sahara the other. The one that landed in Africa was more cracked than a psychiatrist, but the other pancaked gently to earth like a slow motion of Sonja Henie imitating a diving swan. . . . The saucer was 100 feet across and the cabin itself was about 18 feet in diameter. Its center remained at rest, but it had an outer edge that revolved at terrific speed. It operated, in other words, like a magnetically-controlled helicopter. It was not propelled by jets or other power such as we have been using to date. . . . magnetic waves. . . . Inside the saucer were 16 men. They were intact but charred black..... The men were about the size of Singer Midgets. They weren't Singer Midgets because all these have been accounted for. Neither were they pigmies from the African jungle.. Something about their bone and skin structure was different, the scientists said. . . . [1]

Scully was fascinated by the story. He wrote a book about it—*Behind the Flying Saucers*—which appeared in September 1950, with overwhelming success. It was immediately placed ninth on the bestseller list of the *New York Times*, topped the list shortly thereafter. It was the first book ever about the "saucers" and it did not disappoint the reader.

According to Scully the first disc to crash did so on March 25, 1948 on a rocky plateau east of Aztec at the Northwestern corner of New Mexico. When the recovery team of the Air Force reached the site, they found the saucer, some one hundred feet in diameter, fully intact. They finally succeeded in opening a hatch and entering the craft. They found on board sixteen small humanoid beings, thirty-five to forty inches tall. Apparently the scientists who were called in later to investigate, were of the opinion that the disc "probably flew using magnetic lines of force" and came from Venus. Shortly after that another disc had crashed in Arizona, also with sixteen bodies on board. A third disc crashed in Paradise Valley, east of Phoenix, Arizona, with two occupants on board. As the source for these revelations he named one "Dr. Gee," a mysterious scientist, who *"had more degrees than a thermometer!"*[2]

The story had an early death, when an "exposure journalist" claimed to have dug up the truth about Dr. Gee. J. P. Cahn wrote in the September 1952 issue of the magazine *True* that Dr. Gee, far from being a government scientist, was actually a notorious swindler, Leo GeBauer by name, and that Scully had been his victim. GeBauer, according to Cahn, had approached Scully through another confidence artist, Silas Newton, who moved in high society, pretended to be an oil millionaire, and tried to win investors for new projects. Together they had developed a gadget "based on magnetism" to locate oil deposits, and the rumor that the gadget had extraterrestrial technology behind it was to attract gullible investors.[3]

As a matter of fact, Newton and GeBauer stood on trial at a Denver court, accused of "conspiracy to cheat." They were sentenced to a period of probation, on condition that they repay the investors. Two years later Newton was on trial again, because he had sold worthless shares of a uranium mine.[4]

Scully maintained that the pseudonym "Dr. Gee" actually stood for a "group of eight" informants, "all high-carat scientists," but nobody wanted to hear that anymore. Frank Scully was discredited and with him everything that had anything to do with "crashed saucers" and "little men on board." The chance of any information about Roswell coming to light was lost for the next twenty-six years. Only during a very short interval of time was it possible to look behind the curtain of silence .[5]

Wilbert Smith

Wilbert M. Smith was an official of the Canadian ministry of transport. He had studied engineering at the renowned University of British Columbia and had worked for the Vancouver radio station before joining the ministry in 1939, which was also responsible for telecommunications in Canada. In 1947 he was assigned to set up a network of ionospheric measuring stations, to investigate the propagation of radio waves. As chief engineer of the project he had to deal with all phenomena which affected radio waves: northern lights, cosmic rays, atmospheric radioactivity, all forms of geomagnetism. Thereby he became convinced that geomagnetism could be used as a source of energy. In 1949 he actually constructed "an experimental unit," which he tested out in the standard laboratories of the ministry. The results were promising enough, energy could be tapped off—approximately fifty milliwatts—from the earth's magnetic field to operate a voltmeter.

A year later, in September 1950, he participated in a conference in Washington. Scully's book had just been put on the market and was making headlines. When he heard on the radio that according to Scully the "saucers" flew *"along the magnetic lines of the earth,"* propelled by *"magnetic principles,"* he pricked up his ears. He bought a copy of the book and read it through in one night, with fascination. Later he wrote, *"It looks as though our own work in the field of geo-magnetism could well be the con-*

necting link between our technology and that on which the saucers are built and propelled. And if we assume that our research in geomagnetism is going in the right direction, it seems to me that the theory is applicable to the propulsion of the saucers, because it explains all observed phenomena qualitatively and quantitatively." He felt himself compelled to get into contact with the scientists who had investigated the crashed discs and find out how far their researches had progressed.[6]

As an official of a ministry in a neighboring country, he took the official way. Through the offices of the military attaché of the Canadian Embassy in Washington, Lieutenant Colonel Bremner, he was able to get an appointment with a Pentagon scientist who was supposed "with certainty to be informed about this project." This scientist was Dr. Robert I. Sarbacher, scientific adviser to the Research and Development Commission of the U.S. Defense Department, with an office at the Pentagon. Sarbacher was one of the most famous scientists in the country. He was not only a professor at Harvard University and dean of the Technical College of Georgia, but also Director of Research at the Wedding Laboratories, where armament technology was developed. Smith met Sarbacher on 15 September 1950. Since Smith carefully kept his notes about the meeting, it is now possible to cite the conversation word for word (WBS = Wilbert B. Smith; RIS = Robert I. Sarbacher):

WBS: I am doing some work on the collapse of the earth's magnetic field as a source of energy, and I think our work may have a bearing on the flying saucers.

RIS: What do you want to know?

WBS: I have read Scully's book on the saucers and I would like to know how much of it is true.

RIS: The facts reported in the book are substantially correct.

WBS: Then the saucers do exist?

RIS: Yes, they exist.

WBS: Do they operate as Scully suggests on magnetic principles?

RIS: We have not been able to duplicate their performance.

WBS: So they came from some other planet?

RIS: All we know is, we didn't make them, and it's pretty certain they didn't originate on the earth.

WBS: I understand the whole subject of saucers is classified.

RIS: Yes, it is classified two points higher even than the H-bomb. In fact it is the most highly classified subject in the U.S. Government at the present time.

WBS: May I ask the reason for the classification?

RIS: You may ask, but I can't tell you.

WBS: Is there any way in which I can get more information, particularly as it might fit in with our own work?

RIS: I suppose you could be cleared through your own Defense Department, and I am pretty sure arrangements could

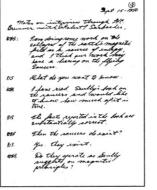

Wilbert M. Smith's handwritten notes of his conversation with Prof. Sarbacher.

be made to exchange information. If you have anything to contribute, we would be glad to talk it over, but I can't give you anything more at the present time.[7]

After further research Smith composed a memorandum classified as "top secret" on 21 November 1950, addressed to the Canadian Secretary of Transportation, in which he pleaded for the starting of a project called "Magnet." The project was meant to unravel the propulsion system of the UFOs. There were signs to show that this had something to do with geomagnetism and through further studies *"a potential source of energy for the future of our planet"* could be discovered. To add weight to his plea, he pointed out how earnestly "the big brother in the south" regarded the UFO phenomenon:

I made discreet enquiries through the Canadian Embassy staff in Washington who were able to obtain for me the following information:

a. The matter is the most highly classified subject in the United States Government, rating higher even than the H-bomb.

b. Flying saucers exist.

c. Their modus operandi is unknown but concentrated effort is being made by a small group headed by Doctor Vannevar Bush.

d. The entire matter is considered by the United States authorities to be of tremendous significance.[8]

Professor Vannevar Bush

Who was in this "small group headed by Doctor Vannevar Bush," which was apparently investigating the UFO driving system? The very mention of the name "Vannevar Bush" must have alerted the attention of the Canadian authorities, for Bush was the most important scientific personality in the service of the U.S. government. In 1940, when he was president of the renowned Carnegie Institute in Washington, D.C., he was appointed chairman of the newly established National Defense Research Committee by President Roosevelt personally. It was the task of the committee to oversee all armaments projects of the Army and Navy. During the same year, the "Uranium Committee," out of which later the "Manhattan Project" for the development of the atomic bomb was born, was also placed under the NDRC. When a year

Wilbert M. Smith's memorandum of 21 November 1950.

later the Office of Scientific Research and Development was founded, which also served armament research and was meant to advise the president about the status of arms development, Dr. Bush was named its director—and so became the first and closest scientific adviser of the president.

Bush had studied electrical engineering at Harvard. Under his supervision at the renowned Massachusetts Institute of Technology (MIT) there were over 2000 projects, with a yearly grant of $300 million for the scientists in addition to some millions of dollars for laboratory equipment and material. The two most important projects under Dr. Bush were the development of tactical radar systems and of the atomic bomb. He finally became a member of the Top Policy Group, the closest advisory staff of the president. In 1945 he presented to the president his paper "Science, the Endless Border," in which he recommended the setting up of a federal research program for fundamental research and the support of civil scientific projects. Six years later this bore fruit when the National Scientific Foundation was established by congress. The words "a small group of scientists headed by Doctor Vannevar Bush" could only mean a project at the highest level of priority and secrecy.[9]

It took until 1978 for the Canadian authorities to release the "Project Magnet" memorandum written by Wilbert Smith and classified as "top secret." Five years later it fell into the hands of the Californian writer William Steinman, together with the handwritten minutes which Smith had kept of his meeting with Sarbacher. Steinman was then working on a book about Scully's Aztec story. When he saw the names Sarbacher and Bush he was startled. If scientists of this caliber had worked on a UFO project, there must have been more behind it than just the sighting of mysterious flying objects. People at that level would not be content with "anecdotal evidence"—"hard-

ware" must have been involved, technology, most probably connected with armament.

Was it possible, three decades later, to find out anything from one of these scientists? Dr. Bush had died in 1974 at the age of eighty-four, but Sarbacher was still in good health. His career was also remarkable. He had studied at Princeton

Professor Robert I. Sarbacher

and graduated from Harvard, been a lecturer at Harvard for four years and then gone to the Illinois Institute of Technology as a professor of electrical technology. In 1941 he took over a chair of physics at Harvard and from 1942 to 1945 was scientific adviser to the U.S. Marines. After the war he was dean of the graduate school of the Georgia Institute of Technology and scientific consultant to the Research and Development Board of the U.S. Defense Department,

Dr. Robert I. Sarbacher's reply to William Steinman

with his own office at the Pentagon. Professor Sarbacher's specialty was remote-controlled rockets.[10] When Steinman contacted him, Sarbacher was president of the Washington Institute of Technology.

In a number of letters Steinman requested Dr. Sarbacher to give him background information on his talk with Smith. In particular he asked him for the names of the other scientists of the "small group" and, if possible, reports of the investigations they conducted. Steinman had almost given up all hope of receiving an answer, when on December 5, 1983 Sarbacher's reply came in. And this reply, dated November 29, 1983 surpassed by far all that Steinman had hoped for in his wildest dreams! After a short apology for the delay in answering—he had moved and also been on a long journey—the professor affirmed, on paper bearing the letterhead of the Washington Institute of Technology, that he knew far more than he had even hinted at to Wilbert Smith.

He confirmed that during the end of the forties and beginning of the fifties, top scientists had taken part in the investigation of crashed spacecraft of extraterrestrial origin. He himself, however, although invited to attend the conferences held at the Wright Patterson Air Base in connection with the project, had had no time to do so.

Although I had been invited to participate in several discussions associated with the reported recoveries, I could not personally attend the meetings. I am sure that they would have asked Dr. (Wernher) von Braun, and the others that you listed were probably asked and may or may not have attended. . . . Regarding verification that persons you list were involved, I can only say this: John von Neumann and Dr. Vannevar Bush were definitely involved, and I think Dr. Robert Oppenheimer also. . . .

I did receive some official reports when I was in my office at the Pentagon but all of these were left there as at the time we were never supposed to take them out of the office. . . .

About the only thing I remember at this time is that certain materials reported to have come from flying saucer crashes were extremely light and very tough. I am sure our laboratories analyzed them very carefully.

There were reports that instruments or people operating these machines were also of very light weight, sufficient to withstand the tremendous deceleration and acceleration associated with their machinery. I remember in talking with some of the people at the office that I got the impression these "aliens" were constructed like certain insects we have observed on earth, wherein because of the low mass the inertial forces involved in operation of these instruments would be quite low.

I still do not know why the high order of classification has been given and why the denial of the existence of these devices.[11]

Dr. John von Neumann

Professor J. Robert Oppenheimer

At once Steinman informed Roswell researcher and nuclear physicist Stanton Friedman about this letter. Shortly afterwards Friedman personally called Dr. Sarbacher and asked him if he could remember any of the scientists who had attended the conferences at

Wright Patterson. *"There was someone who attended all the conferences,"* said Sarbacher, after thinking a while, *"but I can't recall the name. He wrote a book about electronics, was a member of the Research and Development Board and was head of a department for electrical engineering at the University of Pennsylvania."*[12]

Steinman and Friedman soon found out who this was: he was Dr. Eric A. Walker, ex-Harvard, electrical

Professor Eric A. Walker, President Dwight D. Eisenhower

engineer, later director of the under water sound laboratory at Harvard. During the war he was consultant to the Navy and in 1944 a civilian employee of the OSRD, till in 1945 he was appointed chief of the faculty of Electrical Engineering at Penn State by the Dean of the Pennsylvania State University. From 1950 to 1952 he was also executive secretary of the Research and Development Committee of the Defense Department.[13] As confirmed by a CIA document dated 2 January 1950, on 18 December 1949 he was put through an "indoctrination for special intelligence affairs."[14] Steinman was at last able to get Dr. Walker on the telephone on August 30,1987.

Walker: Hello.

Steinman: Hello . . . this is William Steinman of Los Angeles, California. I am calling in reference to the meetings that you attended at Wright-Patterson Air Force Base in/around 1949–1950, concerning the military recovery of flying saucers and bodies of occupants. Dr. Robert I. Sarbacher

(now deceased) related this to me. You and Sarbacher were both consultants to D.R.B. in 1950; you were secretary 1950–51.

Walker: Yes, I attended meetings concerning that subject matter; why do you want to know about that?

Steinman: I believe it is [a] very important subject matter. We are talking about the actual recovery of a flying saucer (spacecraft) not built or constructed on this earth! And furthermore, we are talking about bodies of the occupants from the craft who were analyzed [to be] like beings not of this world!

Walker: . . . what's there to get all excited about? Why all the concern?

Steinman: I am not excited, just very concerned. Here we are talking about a subject that the U.S. government officially denies, even going to the extent of actually debunking the evidence and discrediting the witnesses. Then you sit there and say, "What's there to get all excited about?" and "why all the concern?" Dr. Vannevar Bush, Dr. Detlev Bronk, and others thought it was very important and were concerned enough to classify the subject ABOVE TOP SECRET, in fact the most highly classified subject in the U.S. Government!!

Did you ever hear of the "MJ-12 Group" and their "Project Majestic-12" which was classified as TOP SECRET/MAJIC? I have a copy of President Elect D. D. Eisenhower's briefing paper on that project, dated November 18, 1952.

Walker: Yes, I know of MJ-12. I have known of them for 40 years. I believe that you're chasing after and fighting with windmills!

Steinman: Why do you say that?

Walker: You are delving into an area that you can do absolutely nothing about. So, why get involved with it or all concerned about it? Why don't you just leave it alone and drop it? Forget about it!

Steinman: I am not going to drop it. I am going all the way with this!

Walker: Then ... when you find out everything about it, what are you going to do?

Steinman: I believe that this entire matter has to be brought to the public's attention. The people should know the truth!

Walker: It's not worth it! Leave it alone!

Steinman: Can you remember any of the details pertaining to the recovery operations and subsequent analysis of the saucers and bodies?

Walker: I am sure that I have notes concerning those meetings at Wright-Patterson Air Force Base. I would have to dig them out and read them over in order to jog my memory.

Steinman: If I write you a letter, will you please answer in as much detail as you can remember? Furthermore, could you please xerox those notes for me and send me a copy?

Walker: I might. At least I will keep your letter, will dig out my notes, and [will] contemplate answering. That's the best I can say for now.

Steinman: Well, Dr. Walker, I will write a letter as soon as possible. Thanks for your valuable time. Good-bye.

Walker: Good-bye.[15]

And in fact Dr. Walker wrote a letter to Steinman shortly after that:

"Some things you have right, and some things you have wrong. The machine itself was obviously a landing vehicle only, and it had no unusual features and no power plants with which we were not quite familiar. I believe it still exists and is kept someplace near Wright Field."

What follows this interesting preamble is a veritably ludicrous story, which obviously served only to discourage Steinman. It is an excellent example of what is known as "disinformation" in the intelligence community: watering down true information by the addition of false details. Walker:

Your greatest error, of course, comes in the finding of the bodies—there were no bodies; there were four very normal individuals, all male. Unfortunately, they had no memory of anything in the past (probably by design), but they were highly intelligent.

Professor Eric A. Walker, President Lyndon B. Johnson

They learned the English language within a few hours and it was our decision not to make public spectacles of them, but allow them to be absorbed into American culture as soon as we were sure that they did not bring any contamination with them. I believe all four have done this very successfully. One assumed a simple name and proved himself to be an expert on computers, although he had no memory of such devices. He became the president and innovator for one of the largest and most successful computer organizations.

A second one became a world famous athlete, and because of his quick reaction time, exceeded any normal person in his performances. He is still a noted professional athlete.

The third became enamored with finance of our capitalistic system. He has made himself famous as a Wall Street trader, and is very rich.

The fourth, I have lost track of and have no clues as to where he might be.

What Walker was trying to achieve with this nonsense becomes clear in his last two sentences:

However, I consider the decision to let these people melt into American life, completely justified, and I can see no point in trying to reverse that decision. I hope that you will let matters lie as they are. The results are completely satisfactory, and nothing is to be gained by further publicity.[16]

When another UFO researcher, T. Scott Crain, wrote to Dr. Walker on 24 April 1988, Walker returned the letter with the hand-written remark, "Why say anything?"[17] And when Stanton Friedman called him in June 1989, Walker declared that he had had "since 1965 nothing to do with UFOs." Which, however, means that BEFORE 1965 he was very well informed in the matter. *"People who do research on UFOs would do better to do research in other fields,"* he advised Friedman. But on being asked what he meant, all he said was, *"That I cannot tell you. That is all there is to that."*[18] Shortly after that there was a press announcement that the research laboratory of Penn State University, which was still directed by Dr. Walker, had been given a grant of thirty-nine million dollars from the Defense Department, "of which 98% came from the renewal of contracts with the Navy Department. . . ."[19] Professor Walker, therefore, was still working for the Department of Defense.

The only person who had more luck was the British-Armenian UFO researcher Henry Azadehdel. On January 26 and March 8 Azadehdel had relatively long talks with Walker. Azadehdel was mainly interested in winning the confidence of Walker. At first UFOs were mentioned only fleetingly—Azadehdel pretended complete ignorance of all matters concerning UFO research. But after a while Azadehdel confided to Walker that he had seen the recovery of a UFO in the jungles of Bolivia during a botanical expedition. The following is an interesting excerpt from a telephone conversation which lasted almost an hour (and was recorded on tape):

(A: = Azadehdel; W: = Walker)

A: But what amazes me, Doctor, is the frequent appearance of these objects. Does this suggest that they might have a base in one of our solar system planets?

W: Well, we can make a point of all these, but they did not tell us.

A: Have we ever been able to make contact with them on the communication basis?

W: We promised not to tell.

A: I can understand it. Does it mean that the official communication has been made, and it has been promised not to tell? Orders are that outside this circle there are private [bits of] information they (the public?) should not know.

W: I do not think it is official. If three, four individuals have got together on this, it can't be official.

A: Do they constitute any threat to the national security of any country?

W: Everybody decides on this on his own.

A: I am told by the Ministry of Defence (in England) they don't constitute a national threat to this country.

W: Well, maybe they know.

A: Do you know whether there is any cooperation between them EBEs and us, as an advanced civilization?

W: I think so. There have been occasions, but then I can speak only for myself.

A: But, Doctor, would you consider them to be intruders as a scientist?

W: I don't think so. But, if they went into England as intruders, then I think yes, you could.

A: Is any one of them alive?

W: I cannot answer that.

A: Doctor, I was reading a book titled Above Top Secret. *There were some documents there referring to a group better known as MJ-12. Have you heard of them?*

W: For [a] long time now, I have nothing to do with them.
. . .
A: Doctor, but is there any such group still active?

W: How good is your mathematics?

A: As good as it could be for a doctor in physics, but why?

W: Because only a very few are capable of handling this issue. Unless your mind ability is like Einstein's or likewise, I do not know how you can achieve anything.

A: Well, Doctor, for many years now I have been trying. But, are there government scientists?

W: Everybody makes mistakes about this issue. I gather by

that you mean whether they work for the Defense establishments of the military.

A: Yes, Doctor, that is what I meant.

W: Well, that is where you are wrong. They are a handful of elite. When you are invited into that group, I would know.

A: Doctor, have we mastered the knowledge, are we working together with the entities?

W: No, we have learned so much, and we are not working with them, only contact.

A: Have we captured any saucers, any material from the discs to study?

W: The technology is far behind what is known in ordinary terms of physics that you take the measure and obtain measurements. You are pushing for answers, aren't you?. . .[20]

Who were these "handful of men, elite" of whom Walker spoke? Was it the same as the "small group under Dr. Vannevar Bush," referred to by Smith? Was its code name "MJ-12" or "Majestic 12," as Walker seemed to confirm? In March 1984 Steinman asked Dr. Fred Darwin, another member of the Research and Development Committee, to give him a list of names of members of the committee, who, in his opinion, were "the best candidates for membership in a team for recovering crashed UFOs." Dr. Darwin named, *"if ever such a thing had occurred:*

Dr. Vannevar Bush
Dr. Karl T. Compton
Dr. Lloyd V. Berkner
Dr. Robert F. Rinehart
Dr. Eric A. Walter
Dr. John von Neumann"[21]

There are some interesting indications that one more scientist, mentioned by Sarbacher, namely the leader of the Manhattan Project, Professor J. Robert Oppenheimer, was involved in the Roswell project. Kevin Randle interviewed in February 1990 Steve Lytle, son of a mathematician who had worked closely with Oppenheimer. Lytle declared that his father had once shown him an I-beam found on the Foster Ranch, with violet hieroglyphs on it. His father's task was to decipher them, which, however, proved to be impossible.[22]

Brigadier General Arthur E. Exon, who had been stationed at the Wright Field Airbase in 1947, recalled other names from the military side. When Don Schmitt and Kevin Randle interviewed him, Exon said there had been a *"high-ranking team"* which had access to the wreck, the bodies, and all information about the incident. He called this team *"the unholy thirteen,"* because the whole affair was so secret that he did not even know their official designation. He knew only that there were thirteen members, from *"the highest heads of intelligence, the office of the president, the defense department, people in key positions."* Apart from the president, who led the team, no other elected representative of the people belonged to the team. When he was transferred to the Pentagon in 1955, he learnt that this control team was still in existence and dealt with UFOs.[23]

This is confirmed by Captain Edward J. Ruppelt, who at that time led the Project Blue Book, the official study of UFOs by the Air Force, at the Pentagon. In his astoundingly open book *The Report on Unidentified Flying Objects* Ruppelt wrote, referring to a sighting of a whole formation of shining discs by four professors at Lubbock, Texas in 1951: *"The only other people outside Project Blue Book who have studied the complete case of the Lubbock Lights were a group who, due to their associations with the government, had complete access to our files. And these people were not pulp writers or wide-eyed fanatics, they were scientists/rocket experts, nuclear physicists, and intelligence experts. They had banded together to study our UFO reports because they*

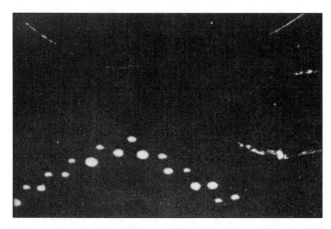
Investigated by MJ-12: the "Lubbock-Lights" of 1950.

were convinced that some of the UFOs that were being reported were interplanetary spaceships and the Lubbock series was one of these reports."[24]

In 1964 Exon, meanwhile promoted to general, returned as commander of the base. There too he was confronted by the team. From time to time he received calls from Washington, which informed him that a *"specialist team was under way."* There were from eight to fifteen officers. *"I only knew that they were an investigation team."* The team stood under the orders of the *"Unholy Thirteen."* Exon knew only a few names: *"uniformed officers . . . Sometimes it would be eight and sometimes it would be fifteen. . . . Usually at that time they were T-39s, twin jets, and lots of times we sent a 240, Convair 240 with a crew and they would go and these guys would do their business and they'd sit at an air base someplace and cool it until the guys came back. They'd come back, drop them off and go about their business. . . . Forrestal, Truman, Spaatz, Symington, I'm sure there were more guys next to Spaatz, like intelligence guys or some information type close to him at the Pentagon and to Forrestal, CIA, and I know it was just more than military . . . all these guys at the top of government. They were the ones who knew the most about Roswell, New Mexico. They were involved in what*

to do about the residue from that . . . those two findings. In the '55 time period, there was also the story that whatever happened, whatever was found at Roswell, was still closely held and probably would be held until these fellows I mentioned had died so they wouldn't be embarrassed or they wouldn't have to explain why they covered it up."[25]

A document which seemed to confirm all these speculations and in addition contained a complete list of names of the "Majestic 12" was given to the Hollywood producer Jaime Shandera in December 1984—shortly after the last of the experts named in the list had passed away.

[1] Scully, Frank, "Scully's Scrapbook," in *Variety,* 12 October 1949.

[2] Scully, Frank, *Behind the Flying Saucers,* New York, 1950.

[3] Cahn, J. P., "The Flying Saucers and the Mysterious Little Men," in *True,* September 1952.

[4] *The Denver Post,* 29 December 1953.

[5] Scully, Frank, *In Armour Bright,* Chilton, 1963.

[6] Smith, Wilbert, "Memorandum to the Controller of Telecommunications, Ottawa, 21 November 1950."

[7] Smith, Wilbert, Personal notes of 15 September 1950.

[8] Smith, Wilbert, "Memorandum to the Controller of Telecommunications, Ottawa, 21 November 1950."

[9] McGraw-Hill, *Modern Scientists and Engineers,* vol. 1, 1980.

[10] Ibid. ,vol. 3, 1980.

[11] Letter from Dr. Robert I. Sarbacher to William Steinman, 29 November 1983.

[12] Cameron, Grant and T. Scott Crain, *UFOs, MJ-12 and the Government,* Seguin, TX, 1991.

[13] McGraw-Hill, vol. 3, 1980.

[14] Dept. of Defense, Routing Slip, 18 December 1950.

[15] Telephone conversation between Dr. Eric A. Walker and William Steinman, 30 August 1987, quoted as per Cameron/Crain, 1991.

[16] Letter from Dr. E. A. Walker to William Steinman, 23 September 1987.

[17]Cameron/Crain, 1991.

[18]Ibid.

[19]*Centre Democrat*, Bellefonte, PA, 26 July 1989.

[20]Telephone conversation between Dr. Eric A. Walker and Dr. Henry Azadehdel, 8 March 1990, quoted as per Cameron/Crain, 1991.

[21]Letter from Dr. Fred Darwin to William Steinman of 1984, quoted as per Cameron/Crain, 1991.

[22]Randle, Kevin and Don Schmitt, *The Truth about the UFO Crash at Roswell*, New York ,1994.

[23]Ibid.

[24]Ruppelt, Edward J., *The Report on Unidentified Flying Objects*, New York, 1956.

[25]Randle, Kevin, *Roswell UFO Crash Update*, New York, 1995.

7.

The Falcon Calls

Perhaps the most sensational secret document of all times came in a simple brown foolscap-sized envelope, without a sender's name. The twelve twenty-cent postage stamps on it had an Albuquerque postal date stamped on them. Film producer Jaime Shandera opened the envelope, which he had found on the morning of December 11,1984 in the post box of his house in North Hollywood. Inside it he found another half-size envelope, carefully sealed with scotch tape. Inside it—Shandera was reminded of the Russian game with the doll in the doll in the doll—was a long, white envelope with the emblem of a Marriott Hotel, the sole contents of which was a black plastic cassette, containing an undeveloped roll of Kodak 35-mm film. Filled with curiosity, Shandera took the film the same day to one of the numerous photo laboratories offering twenty-four-hour service for processing, and so had the prints the next morning.

Jaime Shandera

The eight snapshots he saw were pictures of documents—secret documents. Each page had the stamp "TOP SECRET/MAJIC EYES ONLY" and the note "Copy One of One." This meant that it was something from the government files, of highest impact.[1]

"TOP SECRET" is the highest level of secrecy for military and intelligence documents, the remark "MAJIC" was a special compartmentalization—only those who had that access permit and were working on that project were allowed to see the paper. "EYES ONLY" meant that no copies were to be made: only the original, copy one of one, existed. The heading gave some indication of the contents: "Briefing Document: Operation Majestic 12, prepared for President-Elect Dwight D. Eisenhower: Eyes Only, 18 November 1952." The attached Appendix A, a memorandum signed by President Truman on a paper with the letterhead of the White House, was also classified as "TOP SECRET—EYES ONLY." It contained the instruction of the president to start "Majestic 12."[2]

What was "Majestic 12"? On four pages the briefing paper—which was emphatically called a "preliminary briefing" . . . " full operations briefing intended to follow"—described the story of the most secret research program of the U.S.

EYES ONLY COPY ONE OF ONE.

SUBJECT: OPERATION MAJESTIC-12 PRELIMINARY BRIEFING FOR PRESIDENT-ELECT EISENHOWER.

DOCUMENT PREPARED 18 NOVEMBER, 1952.

BRIEFING OFFICER: ADM. ROSCOE H. HILLENKOETTER (MJ-1)

NOTE: This document has been prepared as a preliminary briefing, only. It should be regarded as introductory to a full operations briefing intended to follow.

OPERATION MAJESTIC-12 is a TOP SECRET Research and Development/Intelligence operation responsible directly and only to the President of the United States. Operations of the project are carried out under Control of the Majestic-12 (Majic-12) Group which was established by special classified executive order of President Truman on 24 September, 1947, upon recommendation by Dr. Vannevar Bush and Secretary James Forrestal. (See Attachment "A.") Members of the Majestic-12 Group were designated as follows:

Adm. Roscoe H. Hillenkoetter

Dr. Vannevar Bush

Secy. James V. Forrestal

Gen. Nathan F. Twining

Gen. Hoyt S. Vandenberg

Dr. Detlev Bronk

Dr. Jerome Hunsaker

Mr. Sidney W. Souers

Mr. Gordon Gray

Dr. Donald Menzel

Gen. Robert M. Montague

Dr. Lloyd V. Berkner

The death of Secretary Forrestal on 22 May, 1949 created a vacancy which remained unfilled until 01 August, 1950, upon which date General Walter B. Smith was designated as permanent replacement.

On 24 June 1947, a civilian pilot flying over the Cascade Mountains in the State of Washington observed nine flying disc-shaped aircraft traveling in formation at a high rate of speed. Although this was not the first known sighting of such objects, it was the first to gain widespread attention in the public media. Hundreds of reports of sightings of similar objects followed. Many of these came from highly credible military and civilian sources. These reports resulted in independent efforts by several different elements of the military to ascertain the nature and purpose of these objects in the interests of national defense. A number of witnesses were interviewed and there were several unsuccessful attempts to utilize aircraft in efforts to pursue reported discs in flight. Public reaction bordered on near hysteria at times.

In spite of these efforts, little of substance was learned about the objects until a local rancher reported that one had crashed in

The "Operation Majestic Twelve" Briefing Document, as it was sent to Jaime Shandera.

a remote region of New Mexico located approximately seventy-five miles northwest of Roswell Army Air Base (now Walker Field).

On 07 July, 1947, a secret operation was begun to assure recovery of the wreckage of this object for scientific study. During the course of this operation, aerial reconnaissance discovered that four small human-like beings had apparently ejected from the craft at some point before it exploded. These had fallen to earth about two miles east of the wreckage site. All four were dead and badly decomposed due to action by predators and exposure to the elements during the approximately one week time period which had elapsed before their discovery. A special scientific team took charge of removing these bodies for study. (See Attachment "C.") The wreckage of the craft was also removed to several different locations. (See Attachment "B.") Civilian and military witnesses in the area were debriefed, and news reporters were given the effective cover story that the object had been a misguided weather research balloon.

A covert analytical effort organized by General Twining and Dr. Bush acting on the direct orders of the President, resulted in a preliminary consensus (19 September 1947) that the disc was most likely a short range reconnaissance craft. This conclusion was based for the most part on the craft's size and the apparent lack of any identifiable provisioning. (See Attachment "D.") A similar analysis of the four dead occupants was arranged by Dr. Bronk. It was the tentative conclusion of this group (30 November, 1947) that although these creatures are human-like in appearance, the biological and evolutionary processes responsible for their development has apparently been quite different from those observed or postulated in homo-sapiens. Dr. Bronk's team has suggested the term "Extra-terrestrial Biological Entities," or "EBEs," be adopted as the standard term of reference for these creatures until such time as a more definitive designation can be agreed upon.

Since it is virtually certain that these craft do not originate in any country on earth, considerable speculation has centered around what their point of origin might be and how they got here. Mars was and remains a possibility, although some scientists, most notably Dr. Menzel, consider it more likely that we are dealing with beings from another solar system entirely.

Numerous examples of what appear to be a form of writing were found in the wreckage. Efforts to decipher these have remained largely unsuccessful. (See Attachment "E.") Equally unsuccessful have been efforts to determine the method of propulsion or the nature or method of transmission of the power source involved. Research along these lines has been complicated by the complete absence of identifiable wings, propellers, jets, or other conventional methods of propulsion and guidance, as well as a total lack of metallic wiring, vacuum tubes, or similar recognizable electronic components. (See Attachment "F.") It is assumed that the propulsion unit was completely destroyed by the explosion which caused the crash.

A need for as much additional information as possible about these craft, their performance characteristics and their purpose led to the undertaking known as U.S. Air Force Project SIGN in December, 1947. In order to preserve security, liaison between SIGN and Majestic-12 was limited to two individuals within the Intelligence Division of Air Materiel Command whose role was to pass along certain types of information through channels. SIGN evolved into Project GRUDGE in December, 1948. The operation is currently being conducted under the code name BLUE BOOK, with liaison maintained through the Air Force officer who is head of the project.

On 06 December, 1950, a second object, probably of similar origin, impacted the earth at high speed in the El Indio-Guerrero area of the Texas-Mexican border after following a long trajectory through the atmosphere. By the time a search team arrived, what remained of the object had been almost totally incinerated. Such material as could be recovered was transported to the A.B.C. facility at Sandia, New Mexico, for study.

Implications for the National Security are of continuing importance in that the motives and ultimate intentions of these visitors remain completely unknown. In addition, a significant *upsurge in the surveillance activity of these craft beginning in May and continuing through the autumn of this year has caused considerable concern that new developments may be imminent. It is for these reasons, as well as the obvious international and technological considerations and the ultimate need to avoid a public panic at all costs, that the Majestic-12 Group remains of the unanimous opinion that imposition of the strictest security precautions should continue without interruption into the new administration. At the same time, contingency plan MJ-1949-04P/78 (Top Secret—Eyes Only) should be held in continued readiness should the need to make a public announcement present itself. (See Attachment "G.")* [2]

As soon as Shandera had read these lines, breathless and incredulous as he was, he called his friend, the Roswell researcher William L. Moore.

William L. Moore

After publishing the first book about Roswell together with Charles Berlitz in 1980, Moore had already got onto the tracks of this Operation Majestic 12 before. Towards the end of 1980, after a radio interview about the book, he had received a rather strange call. "You are the only person whom I have heard speaking about this subject who seems to know what he is talking about," began the mysterious caller flatteringly, and implied that he had important information that would interest Moore. Moore met him and was convinced that he was a high-ranking government official who was trying to bring out information into the open through Moore. During the following months the secret informant brought Moore into contact with nine members of the intelligence community—amongst them Master Sergeant Richard Doty, who had been in charge of the AFOSI at the Kirtland Base.

It was at this time that Moore and Shandera became friends. Shandera decided to make a documentary film about the Roswell incident and promised Moore his support in his investigations. Since Moore got deeper and deeper into the intelligence jungle, there was increasing danger of his home being bugged and his telephone line tapped. So Shandera suggested that he should give the informants the names of birds as cover names. The chief informant was, therefore, designated "Falcon" and Richard Doty was "Sparrow."

Through this "aviary" Moore learnt of the existence of a super-secret group of top government scientists, army officials and members of the intelligence community, who not only had investigated crashed UFOs since 1947, but were, since 1964, also in contact with extraterrestrials. Moore's sources were not quite altruistic: they asked him for information about other UFO researchers and used him to influence the UFO investigator and electrical engineer Paul Bennewitz to tap the communication lines of the Kirtland Base to get more UFO information—which understandably did not earn the approval of the Air Force. They baited Moore with secret documents, even gave him some copies of such papers, although sometimes with changes to hide their source. Thus in March 1981 "Falcon" showed him an original document. It was a telex from the AFOSI headquarters at the Bolling Air Force Base to the AFOSI office at Kirtland, which had sent the negatives of five photographs of UFOs for analysis, which had been carried out by the 7602nd Air Intelligence Group at Fort Belvoir, Virginia. The results of the analysis were concluded with the words:

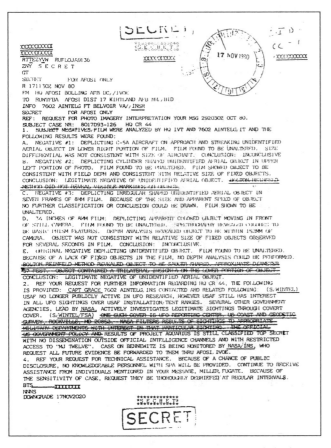

The document "Falcon" handed over to Bill Moore. Added information was crossed out, changes were underlined. XXXX stands for the removed transmission codes.

USAF NO LONGER PUBLICLY ACTIVE IN UFO RESEARCH, HOWEVER USAF STILL HAS INTEREST IN ALL UFO SIGHTINGS OVER USAF INSTALLATION/TEST RANGES. SEVERAL OTHER GOVERNMENT AGENCIES, LEAD BY NASA, ACTIVELY INVESTIGATES LEGITIMATE SIGHTINGS THROUGH COVERT COVER (S/WINTEL/FSA) ONE SUCH COVER IS UFO REPORTING CENTER,

US COAST AND GEODETIC SURVEY, ROCKVILLE, MD 20852. NASA FILTERS RESULTS OF SIGHTINGS TO APPROPRIATE MILITARY DEPARTMENTS WITH INTEREST IN THAT PARTICULAR SIGHTING. THE OFFICIAL US GOVERNMENT POLICY AND RESULTS OF PROJECT AQUARIUS IS STILL CLASSIFIED TOP SECRET WITH NO DISSEMINATION OUTSIDE OFFICIAL INTELLIGENCE CHANNELS AND WITH RESTRICTED ACCESS TO 'MJ TWELVE'.[3]

When Moore asked for a copy, "Falcon" promised to get him one. A few weeks later he gave Moore a typed transcript with some changes. According to "Falcon," these were made so that one could discredit the document if things went wrong. Instead of NSA (National Security Agency) there stood NASA, the abbreviation of the National Aeronautic and Space Administration, which any insider would have perceived. Nevertheless we must agree with Moore when he writes: *"The fact that the typed version is a close imitation of a real document, and that the major part of its contents are good information, overweighs the question as to who typed it."*[4]

In 1982 "Falcon" gave Moore five AFOSI documents regarding UFO landings at Coyote Canyon Atomic Weapon Arsenal Grounds in the Manzano mountains south of the Kirtland Base. These and four more pages were released by the Pentagon under the Freedom of Information Act (FOIA) seven months later. They were, therefore, genuine. Other documents given by "Falcon" were similarly released later and shown to be true. One of these concerned Moore's UFO researcher colleague Stanton Friedman and his attempts, under the FOIA, to obtain further UFO documents. In this telex the AFOSI headquarters warned all their branch offices that Friedman could use that act and ask for information:

Ref.: Unidentified flying objects and similar subjects.

1. We have reason to believe that in the near future some or all our field units may receive a request for information regarding UFO sightings or similar subjects. These requests may originate with Stanton T. Friedman, 110 Kings College Road, Fredericton, New Brunswick, Canada. If such a request is received, do not, repeat, do not, refer the request to this headquarters as required in AFR 12-30-AFOSI sup. I . Respond directly to the requester as follows:

"Requests for information from AFOSI files must be processed by our headquarters. Please resubmit your request to HQ's AFOSI, Information Release Division, Bolling AFB, DC 20322."

2. Requests of this type from persons other than Friedman should also be processed the same way.

3. The original letter of request and a copy of your response should be forwarded to this HQs (XPU) via Form 158.

4. FOIA requests regarding other matters should be processed following normal procedure.

5. This special procedure is in effect until further notice."[5]

Towards the end of 1984 "Falcon" announced a new document, which would be sent to Shandera, probably because Moore was already being shadowed by the secret service. Moore had told Shandera about this and must have guessed the contents of the envelope from Albuquerque. But was what Shandera received an authentic, though perhaps vetted, document, or a product of an intelligence "disinformation" strategy?[6]

To find this out Moore sought the advice of his research colleague Stanton Friedman. For the next five years Friedman busied himself mainly with the investigation of "Majestic 12" documents. Today, after thorough and almost criminological investigation, he, at least, is absolutely convinced of their authenticity.

How does one check the genuineness of a possibly historical document if one has only a photograph of it?

Two steps are necessary: at first verification of the dates and information given in the document; then the investigation of style, form and typewriter used. At first Friedman checked the two dates given:

24 September 1947: founding of the operation "Majestic 12" after long discussions between President Truman, Defense Secretary Forrestal, and Dr. Bush.

18 November 1952: Briefing of the newly elected president Dwight D. Eisenhower.

Friedman spent hours at the Harry Truman Library

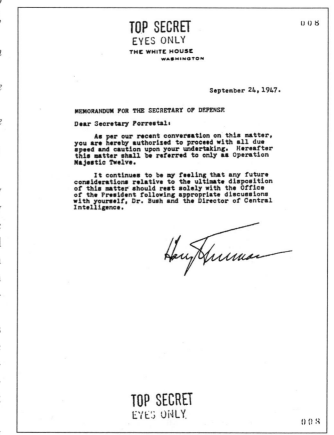

Harry Truma's memorandum of 24 September1947.

and the Dwight D. Eisenhower Library, the Library of Congress, and the National Archives in Washington to verify these dates.

This is certain: on 24 September 1947 there was, according to a letter from the Truman Library, the archive of all documents pertaining to Truman's presidency, *"the only meeting with Dr. Vannevar Bush that took place between May and 31st December 1947. Dr. Bush was accompanied by Defense Secretary James Forrestal. There are no indications in the archives to say what was discussed at the meeting. . . ."*[7]

This means that it was a matter which was still classified. From the files of Bush and Forrestal, Friedman

could reconstruct that Bush and Forrestal met each other half an hour before seeing the president, and it is possible that they prepared the memorandum at that time and then presented it to Truman for signature, a

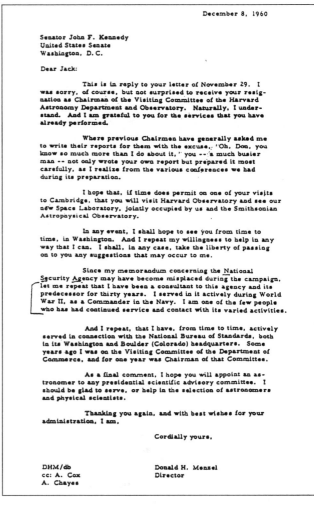

Expertise of linguist Prof. Roger Wescott of the Drew University regarding the controversial "Majestic 12" Briefing Document : "There is no compelling reason to believe… (it was) written by anyone other than Hillenkoetter himself."

MJ12-Member Prof. Donald Menzel's letter to Senator John F. Kennedy of 8 December 1960: "I have been a consultant to this agency (the National Security Agency) and its predecessor for thirty years."

normal procedure in government circles. It is also certain that the meeting was about projects of the Joint Research and Development Board, and Majestic 12 is alleged to be one of these.

On 18 November 1952 a briefing by Eisenhower in respect to questions regarding national security did take place, at which General Nathan Twining was present. It lasted forty-three minutes. Here too the subject is still top secret. This shows that even if the MJ-12 document is forged, the forger has done his homework well.[8]

For Friedman this was at least a good beginning. The next thing he checked was the authorship of the "Eisenhower briefing document." CIA director Admiral Roscoe Hillenkoetter is named as "Briefing Officer." One assumes that he wrote the paper. To check this he showed the document, together with twenty other letters and memoranda written by Hillenkoetter, to a renowned linguist, Professor Dr. Roger W. Westcott of Drew University. In his review Professor Wescott says, *"In my opinion there is no compelling reason to regard any of these communications as fraudulent or to believe that any of them were written by anyone other than Hillenkoetter himself. This statement holds for the controversial Presidential briefing Memorandum of November 18, 1952."*[9]

The typewriters used were, in the case of the Eisenhower briefing, an R. C. Allen machine from the forties, in the case of the Truman memorandum a Remington P4 from the same era. This latter machine had been used in writing a memorandum formulated by Dr. Bush, which indicates that he had written this one too. The format of the documents, the manner of writing the dates, titles, etc. had parallels—refuting all contradictory statements—in authentic documents from those periods. Particularly the manner of writing the date "18 November, 1952" is certainly unusual for U.S. government documents—the correct form would be "November 18, 1952"—but typical of Hillenkoetter,

who had got accustomed to this form while serving as military attaché in France before the war.[10]

The most interesting confirmation of the briefing paper was, for Friedman, the naming of a person whose name he had least expected to find as a member in a super-secret UFO commission. This person was Dr. Donald Menzel, astronomer at Harvard and the most adamant opponent of the UFO theory in his days. In a series of books and articles he had declared the UFOs to be misinterpretations of astronomical objects or plasma bubbles. That of all people this archskeptic should be a member of the MJ-12 group sounded like a bad joke. That an astronomer was included for the study of extraterrestrial visits is quite understandable. But how could an astronomer who was a denier of UFOs belong to a group of top-secret service persons with the highest level of access and be supposed to deal with UFOs?

Friedman then found Menzel's correspondence with John F. Kennedy. Menzel wrote, *"I have been associated since 1930 with a small organization that has now grown to the great National Security Agency. I served with them as a naval officer during World War II. I have been a consultant to that activity, with Top Secret clearance, and have also had some association with C.I.A. . . . I wish to register that I have certain facts in my possession concerning actions by Eisenhower and his subordinates that have had a very adverse effect in these supersensitive areas."*[11] Here was someone praising his own virtues, in the hope of obtaining a position in the new administration. In a later letter he mentioned Dr. Detlev Bronk, president of the National Academy of Sciences, saying, *"Somehow he manages to get on almost every committee of importance. I served on a number of these with him and have not been impressed either with his breadth of vision or his depth."*[12] In the seventies he wrote, *"I was a consultant with TOP SECRET ULTRA CLEARANCE to the National Security Agency, which had replaced the Naval Communications unit I had been associated with during the war. . . ."*[13]

Furthermore, Friedman could prove that a close relationship existed between Menzel and Dr. Bush—they were in fact friends—which had begun during the early days of the war, when Menzel deciphered the codes of the Japanese. His contact with the other members of MJ-12, his capacities, not only as astronomer and astrophysicist, but also as cryptologist, together with his experience in the intelligence community—all that made Menzel an ideal member of the secret team! He was probably the only astronomer who had such qualifications.

What then do we make of Menzel's role as UFO skeptic and opponent, who twisted every sighting report to such an extent as to be able to dismiss it as a "natural" phenomenon? There is only one answer to it: it was a deliberate "disinformation maneuver," carried out on behalf of MJ-12. Correct dates, correct format and facts that at first sight seem incredible but prove to be true (such as Dr. Menzel's membership)—these were for Friedman the best proofs of the authenticity of the documents. Nevertheless his *"Final Report Operation Majestic 12,"* published in 1990,[14] met with strong criticism from modern UFO skeptics, more than anyone else from Phil Klass, reporter of the magazine *Aviation Week & Space Technology*. Klass is a sort of successor to Dr. Menzel, the loudest UFO opponent in the U.S., author of various books and articles, a regular guest on TV talk shows. His arguments in the MJ-12 debate had always the same main theme: *"this manner of writing the date is impossible for government documents."* He kept showing the MJ-12 papers for comparison together with other documents bearing the date written differently, forgetting that other ways of writing the date were also practiced.[15] Naturally the credulous and superficial observer fell for this argument, not knowing that Friedman had dug up documents showing the same style as the MJ-12. Finally there remained only two halfway legitimate objections.

Firstly, the designation of the Truman memorandum of 24 September 1947 as "Special Classified Executive Order # 092447 (TS/EO)." "Executive Orders," government instructions, particularly from presidents, are numbered starting from the days of Lincoln's administration. Up to April 1995 there were 12958 such numbered orders. The number 092447 is, therefore, impossible, said the skeptics. But they overlooked one point: obviously the number is not an order number but the date in American style, namely September 24, 47. This makes sense, since it was signed on that date. TS/EO does not mean "Top Secret Executive Order" but "Top Secret/Eyes Only," a classification, not a description. The heading describes the paper as "Special Classified Executive Order," which clearly differentiates it from the usual presidential orders and cannot bear the usual serial number.

The most serious argument against the genuineness of the Truman memorandum was, of all details, the signature of Truman. This proved to be identical with that on a letter written by Truman to Dr. Bush on 1 October 1947. An apparently "inserted" signature would actually be a clear proof of a forgery, if only the original had not been in possession of, of all persons, Dr. Bush, a member of MJ-12. Added to that, the document under investigation is a photograph. In an enlargement of this the signature looks like an original—the ink had actual-

Comparison of the Truman signature under the "Majestic 12" memorandum and Truman's letter to Dr. Vannevar Bush.

ly run out into the paper at the edges—and certainly not like a mounted photocopy. Against this there is only one xerox copy of the letter to Bush.[16]

If one looks closely at the memo, one sees that the number "24" between 09 (September) and 47 (1947) is typed slightly higher and also that it was typed on a different typewriter. This shows that the Memorandum was prepared by someone earlier and presented to the president only for signature, a perfectly normal procedure. The fact that another memorandum by Bush to the president was written on the same typewriter shows that this memorandum also was typed by Dr. Bush, with the actual date added in Truman's office. There might have been three copies of this paper, one original for the addressee, one for Dr. Bush and one for the secret archive of the White House. Since the paper is addressed to the secretary of defense and begins with "Dear Secretary Forrestal," one can expect that the signed original of this document ended up in Forrestal's files.

Yet, Forrestal was mentally not able to bear the new task. The fact that extraterrestrials visited the earth, that one did not even know their intentions and that one was more or less at their mercy, put him in a state of anxiety. After all, he was responsible for the safety of the country. Only one hour after his meeting with the president on September 24, according to an entry in the files of the Washington police, he applied for an arms permit. His diary entries mentioned the meeting, but with two mistakes: the date is given as the 25th, although he did not meet the president on that day at all, and instead of writing "Dr. Bush" as he otherwise always did, he wrote "Mr. Bush"—an indication that he was going through a deep crisis. During the following months he became more and more depressed.

In 1948 he became a serious paranoid, "saw" everywhere "friends" and "foes" not further identified, and believed that he was observed and bugged. It is said that he once ran through the corridors of the Pentagon, shouting, "... *We are being invaded and are helplessly at their mercy!*" In 1949, after a series of nervous breakdowns, he resigned from his post as secretary of defense and went to the Bethesda Marine Hospital in Washington for medical treatment. When the doctors diagnosed acute danger of suicide, he was transferred from his room on the second floor to a room on the sixteenth floor. On 22 May 1949 he committed suicide—accord-

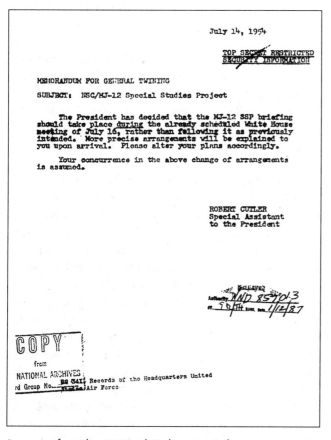

Document from the National Archive in Washington, mentioning "MJ-12."

ing to the official version—by jumping out of the window of that room. We do not know if it indeed was suicide. Perhaps he had become, as a carrier of an important secret, a security risk in his insane state.[17]

But what about his files, what about the founding order for MJ-12, which had led to his insanity? This much is certain: when Admiral Hillenkoetter put together the briefing paper for Eisenhower, he must have shown the order to the new president. But it is possible that Forrestal's original no longer existed or could not be found or was in a bad state. Dr. Bush still had a copy. Perhaps Hillenkoetter asked Bush to give him this copy and an original signature of President Truman. Is this paper, then, a photomontage of the CIA from 1952? The possibility, at least, exists.

The fact is: the signature on the copy of Truman's letter to Bush is thin and broken. This could never have been the model for the signature on the memorandum, which is not only clear and strong, but is also an original because the ink has run into the paper. None of the possible forgers, neither Doty nor the AFOSI, could have had access to the original signature in the possession of Dr. Bush, with the exception of some close friend who might have asked him for it during his lifetime (Bush died in 1974). Admiral Hillenkoetter might have been such a friend.

Can we then be sure that the MJ-12 paper is authentic? Not quite. There is still the possibility, at least regarding the Eisenhower briefing, that we are dealing with a case of clever disinformation, like the telex which Moore had been given at the beginning of his contact with "Falcon." There are just too many verifiable details about it that it cannot be a simple forgery. But an imitation of a real document, abridged, with some changes? This is at least a possibility which we cannot rule out.

That MJ-12 existed—and possibly still exists—is affirmed by two other documents which the team Moore/Shandera/Friedman discovered in the following years. Shandera found the first one by following up on a tip given to Moore by his informants (which he received on a postcard sent from New Zealand), in July 1985 in the National Archive in Washington. Early in 1985 the U.S. Government had released a few thousand files, which could be viewed at the "Suitland" section of the Archive after the middle of July.

On July 18, after hunting through hundreds of files, they discovered in Box 189 of the Record Group 341 a carbon copy of a Memorandum for General Twining, dated 14 July 1954, written by or for Robert Cutler, Special Assistant to President Eisenhower. Subject: "NSC/MJ-12 Special Studies Project"[18]: *"The President has decided that the MJ-12 SSP briefing should take place during the already scheduled White House meeting of July 16, rather than following it as previously intended. More precise arrangements will be explained to you upon arrival. Please alter your plans accordingly."*[19]

No word about UFOs, but nevertheless a mention of MJ-12 in a document of apparently indisputable origin. But here too the research team met with criticism from the skeptics. They pointed out that Robert Cutler was not in the country at all during the time in question. On Eisenhower's orders he was on a visit to military establishments in Europe and Africa. But, countered the team, Cutler had not signed the memorandum personally, nor did it bear, in the manner of carbon copies, the customary "/s/" instead of a signature. It could just as well have been written for Cutler. To support this argument they pointed out to an (authentic) memorandum written by Cutler himself to his military staff before his departure: "Keep things moving out of my basket."[20]

What's more, they could even identify the typewriter on which the Cutler/Twining memorandum was typed. It belonged to the office of James Lay, vice-secretary of

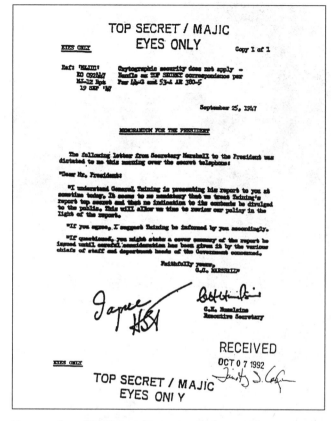

Defense Secretary James Forrestal (left), Secretary of State Gen. George Marshall (2nd to the right) and President Harry S. Truman (right).

Memorandum of Secretary of State Marshall to President Truman: "It seems to me mandatory that we treat Twining's report top secret and that no indication of its contents be divulged to the public."

the National Security Board, which was adjacent to Cutler's office, with a common antechamber. In fact Cutler and Lay worked very closely, and more than once one White Hose official had stood in for the other. One of the four Remington typewriters in Lay's office showed irregularities in the script owing to slightly displaced type. The "U" shifts a bit to the right, the "v" is somewhat raised, "S," "e" and "v" "limp" a little—on both the authentic Lay and the Cutler/Twining memoranda. Experts could detect over fourteen similarities, which rules out all doubts: the memorandum to Twining was written on Lay's typewriter.[21]

Towards the end of 1992 Friedman received from an insider source another "Memorandum to the President," classified as "Top Secret/Majic—Eyes Only" and dictated by General George Marshall, Secretary of State, the originator of the "Marshall Plan" for Europe. It was dated 25 September 1947, one day after the inauguration of MJ-12. Marshall's secretary C. H. Humelsine had written it down and signed it, after "the following letter from Secretary Marshall to the President was dictated to me this morning over the secret telephone." Its text: *"I understand General Twining is presenting his report to you at sometime today. It seems to me mandatory that we treat Twining's report top secret and*

General George Marshall

Adm. Roscoe Hillenkoetter   Dr. Vannevar Bush   James Forrestal   Gen. Nathan F. Twining

that no indication to the contents be divulged to the public. This will allow us time to revise our policy in the light of the report.

If you agree, I suggest Twining be informed by you accordingly.

If questioned, you might state a cover summary of the report be issued until careful consideration has been given it by the various chiefs of staff and department heads of the Government concerned." Under this, in longhand, a note by the president: "*I agree—HST.*"[22]

In fact all Majestic 12 documents record a logical sequence of reactions arising from a matter of such far-reaching consequences as the Roswell UFO crash. It is also a fact that the experts involved represent a pertinent choice, at least as partly indicated by such insiders as Sarbacher and Exon. The task of the MJ-12 Authorities was to coordinate all activities of the Government, which in any way had to do with the alien presence. This included the organization and execution of the scientific evaluation of the wrecks and the bodies, of the salvaging operations of the Army as well as the observation measures of the newly founded CIA which were needed to keep intact the top-secret, eyes-only level of secrecy. Thereby Truman employed the same concept of centralization, which he had shortly before used in assembling the CIA. MJ-12 was under the authority of Admiral Roscoe H. Hillenkoetter, from 1947 to 1950 director of the Central Intelligence Service of the U.S.A., and first director of the newly founded CIA.

MJ-1

Was, therefore, Admiral Roscoe H. Hillenkoetter.

MJ-2

Was Dr. Vannevar Bush (1890–1974), chairman of the National Defense Research Commission and the Office of Scientific Research and Development during the war. From 1939 till 1941 he was chairman of the National Advisory Committee on Aeronautics, from which later NASA was derived, from 1945 to 1948 chairman of the Joint Research and Development Board. In 1949 Bush was asked by the Intelligence Services Board to work out a way to coordinate the work of the various intelligence services effectively, at the insistence of Secretary Forrestal. Obviously it was also his task to coordinate the scientific investigations of alien technology.[23]

MJ-3

Was James Forrestal, secretary of the Navy from

Gen. Hoyt S. Vandenberg

Dr. Detlev Wulf Bronk

1945 to 1947, first secretary of defense after the War Department was changed to Defense Department, from 1947 to 1949. As MJ-3 was responsible for military coordination.

MJ-4

Was General Nathan F. Twining, commander of the Air Materiel Command of the Army Air Force, later Air Force, at Wright Field, the HQ of the Air Intelligence Corps. He was in charge of recovering and investigating crashed UFOs.

MJ-5

Was General Hoyt Vandenberg, director of Central Intelligence till 1947, then successively chief of staff of the Army Air Force and the Air Force, when the latter became a separate force. He was responsible for the safety of aerospace and for detecting UFOs.

MJ-6

Was Dr. Detlev W. Bronk (1897–1975). He was the founder of the science of biophysics, chairman of the National Research Council from 1946 to 1950, president of the National Academy of Sciences from 1950 to 1962, dean of the Johns Hopkins University, and president of the Rockefeller Institute for Medical

Research since 1953. During the war he was coordinator of research for the Air Medical Office. In 1945 he was appointed as member of the Scientific Advisory Committee of the Army Air Force, in 1946 of the Advisory Board of the Navy, and finally in 1947 of the Medical Advisory Board of the Atomic Energy Commission.[24] As MJ-6 he led the examination of the recovered EBEs (extraterrestrial biological entities) and was coordinator of biological and behavior research. It was his task to investigate the anatomy, biology, brain function, and behavior patterns of the EBEs.

After his death, all his papers and documents were preserved at the Rockefeller Institute. Bronk was a very methodical person who kept detailed diaries, which he bought at the same shop, so that all are alike. He kept all his correspondence, notices, and dates. Apparently all this material was complete when handed over to the Institute. But if one wants to look into these papers at the Institute, one finds that the diaries for 1947 are missing. None of the friendly assistants at the library can tell you why; someone has taken them away. Is this a coincidence?[25]

Just like Dr. Berkner and Dr. Menzel, Dr. Bronk had a UFO connection. In June 1947 he was appointed member of the Scientific Advisory Committee of the Brookhaven National Laboratory, which was under the Atomic Commission's authority. In Brookhaven a number of projects of high classification were carried out, in which "paperclip scientists" like John von Neumann were involved. Together with Bronk another scientist, Professor Edward U. Condon, also became a member of the committee. Dr. Condon had led an official study of UFOs at the University of Colorado, financed by the Air Force.[26] The aim of this study was to prove that UFOs did not exist, which naturally was not successful: a third of the investigated cases remained unexplained.[27]

Dr. Donald Howard Menzel   Dr. Jerome Clarke Hunsaker   Dr. Lloyd Viel Berkner   General Walter B. Smith

MJ-7

Was Dr. Jerome Hunsaker (1886–1984). He was the leading aeronautic expert of the U.S. and tested innumerable forms of aircraft, in the wind tunnel he had invented, for their aerodynamics. During the First World War the MIT graduate served as an engineer for the construction of the first war planes of the U.S. Navy. When the U.S. got possession of wrecked zeppelins, Hunsaker's team was able to study them and build the first American zeppelin, the Shenandoah, in 1923. In 1921 Hunsaker was appointed chief designer of the newly established Office of Aeronautics. From 1933 to 1951 he was chairman of the Department of Mechanical and Aeronautical Engineering at MIT. In 1941 he was made coordinator of research for the Navy, which made him a member of the Board of Research and Development. In addition, from 1941 to 1958 he was a member of the board of directors of NACA, the staff of which he increased from 650 to 6,500, and also initiated the building of the laboratories at Langley, Ames, and Lewis.[28] As MJ-7 he carried out the technical evaluation of recovered UFOs.

MJ-8

Was Sidney Souers, the first director of Central Intelligence (1946), and then executive secretary of the National Security Council (1947–1950), also special consultant to President Truman in Secret Service affairs. As MJ-8 he was coordinator for internal security.

MJ-9

Was Gordon Gray, assistant secretary of the Army (1947–1949), war secretary from 1949 to 1950, then special consultant to Truman for national security affairs and chairman of the CIA's top secret Psychological Strategic Board. Chief of the Civil Operations department of the MJ-12, he was responsible for propaganda and the maintenance of public ignorance about ET activities. In that capacity he developed the "strategy of banalizing," the aim of which was to reduce public interest in UFOs by ridiculing the witnesses and inventing far-fetched explanations.

MJ-10

Was Dr. Donald Menzel (1901–1976), professor of astrophysics at Harvard from 1939 to 1971, chairman of the Department of Astronomy (1946–1949). As MJ-10 he dealt with issues regarding the natural sciences and the scientific community.

MJ-11

Was Dr. Lloyd V. Berkner (1905–1967), a geophysicist, executive secretary of the Joint Research and Development Board from 1946 to 1947 under Dr. Vannevar Bush. He headed a special commission that led to the establishment of the Weapons Systems Evaluation Group. His job was to develop defense strategies against the unknown intruders. It is interesting to note that since the early '20s he had been working on long-distance radio wave transmission and geomagnetism.[29] The first field was relevant for establishing contact with aliens—the Search for Extra Terrestrial Intelligence (SETI) was started in the sixties with this idea—the second field for the study of the propulsion systems of the UFOs. Berkner was one of the scientists who developed the radar and early warning systems—as stated in an FBI memorandum, high-powered radar caused the UFOs to crash.[30] He built up the military protection system of the aerospace. It is undisputed that Berkner dealt with UFOs. He was a member of the so-called "Robertson Panel" of the CIA, an advisory panel on UFOs which met at the Pentagon from 14 to 18 January 1953. At this meeting an "educational program" which *"would result in reduction of public interest in 'flying saucers'"* and *"should have two major aims: training and debunking."*[31]

MJ-12

Was Major General Robert M. Montague, from July 1947 till February 1951 commander of the Atomic Energy Commission's base at Sandia, New Mexico, which controlled White Sands Proving Grounds. As MJ-12 he was partly liaison officer for contact with the AEC, which possessed some of the best laboratories of the county, amongst them Los Alamos.

MJ-3 (second)

Was General Walter B. Smith, who took over when Secretary Forrestal committed suicide. He was the second director of the CIA. As Eisenhower's chief of staff during the war he contributed considerably towards the victory in Europe. As U.S. ambassador in Moscow from 1948 till 1949 he knew Stalin personally, which was an advantage in his new work, for he could act as contact man for the Eastern bloc.[32]

When Jaime Shandera received the document, all the original members of the MJ-12 group had died, most recently Jerome Hunsaker, only a few weeks before. This tallies with General Exon's statement that during the fifties they had decided to give out information about the "unholy thirteen"—a suitable nickname for the "majestic twelve," if one adds the president to the twelve—only after the "last of the boys is gone."[33]

[1]Moore, William and Jaime Shandera, *The MJ-12 Documents,* Burbank, 1990.

[2]Operation Majestic 12: Briefing Document Prepared for President-Elect Dwight D. Eisenhower (TS/EO), 18 November 1952.

[3]AFOSI Telex of 17 November 1980.

[4]Moore/Shandera, 1990.

[5]AFOSI Telex of 9 December 1981.

[6]Moore, William, "UFOs and the U.S. Government," in *Focus,* Burbank, CA, vol. 4, No. 4–6, June 1989.

[7]Friedman, Stanton, *Final Report on Operation Majestic 12,* Mt. Rainier, MD, 1990.

[8]Ibid.

[9]Letter from Dr. Roger Wescott, 7 April 1986.

[10]Friedman, 1990.

[11]Letter from Dr. Donald Menzel to John F. Kennedy, 3 November 1960.

[12]Letter from Dr. Donald Menzel to John F. Kennedy, 27 December 1960.

[13]Menzel, Donald, "Review of the History of the Loyalty Hearings (1950)," quoted as per Friedman, 1990.

[14]Friedman, 1990.

[15]Klass, Phil, "The MJ-12 Crashed Saucer Documents," in *Skeptical Inquirer,* Washington, D.C., Winter 1987–88. Also: "The MJ-12 Papers, Part 2," in *Skeptical Inquirer,* Washington D.C., Spring 1988. Also: "New Evidence of MJ-12 Hoax," in *Skeptical Inquirer,* Winter 1990.

[16]Victorian, Armen, "MJ-12-Documents, Dead & Burned," in *UFO Magazine,* Leeds, GB, October 1992.

[17]Lear, John, *The Lear Hypothesis,* Las Vegas. 1988.

[18]Moore/Shandera, 1990.

[19]Memorandum by Robert Cutler to Nathan Twining, 14 July 1954.

[20]Robert Cutler, Instruction to Messrs. Lay and Coyne of 3 July 1954.

[21]Friedman, 1990.

[22]Memorandum by George Marshalls to Harry Truman, 25 September 1947.

[23]McGraw-Hill, *Modern Scientists and Engineers,* vol. 1, 1980.

[24]Ibid.

[25]Message from Bob Shell, 25 January 1996.

[26]Carlson, Theresa and Bob Shell, *Current Biography,* New York, 1949.

[27]Condon, Edward U., *Scientific Study of Unidentified Flying Objects,* New York, 1969.

[28]McGraw-Hill, 1980.

[29]Ibid.

[30]FBI-Memorandum, 22 March 1950.

[31]Durant, F. C., *Report of Meetings of Scientific Advisory Panel on Unidentified Flying Objects Convened by Office of Scientific Intelligence,* CIA, Washington D.C., 1953.

[32]Friedman, Stanton and Don Berliner, *Crash at Corona,* New York, 1992. Good, Timothy, *Above Top Secret,* London, 1986.

[33]Randle, Kevin, *Roswell UFO Crash Update,* New York, 1995.

8.

The Majestic Twelve

UFO researchers Bill Moore and Jaime Shandera were not the only ones to whom documents had been passed on by the members of the "Aviary." In March 1983 the TV station HBO had commissioned the film producer Linda Moulton Howe to make a documentary about UFOs. This suited Linda very well, for since working on her last production, *A Strange Harvest*, she had come repeatedly in contact with new information regarding this fascinating subject. In fact, *A Strange Harvest* was Linda's breakthrough. Whereas her earlier films had dealt with ecological, scientific, medical and political themes—for instance, the much applauded documentary *Fire in the Water*, in which she exposed the radioactive contamination of American rivers—*A Strange Harvest* was about an unsolved mystery, "the animal mutilations." Since the end of the sixties, ranchers, particularly in Colorado, New Mexico and Nevada, had found dead cattle and horses on their meadows,

Linda Moulton Howe

which had been subjected to unusual operations. With incisions whose precision and cauterizing effect reminded one of laser surgery, the genitals, lips, udder and other organs had been removed. Sometimes the carcasses were completely devoid of blood. Frequently people claimed to have seen strange lights or black helicopters without identification marks during the previous nights, which somehow seemed to be connected with the mysterious "surgeries." For Linda Howe there were only two possible explanations: either the U.S. Government was conducting some secret experiment, or extraterrestrials were collecting genetic material. Perhaps the solution lay in a combination of both possibilities.

A Strange Harvest was a gripping documentary film, based on extensive research and packed with information. It found so much appreciation when broadcast on 25 May 1980 by CBS in Colorado, that her telephone, as well as that of the station, was busy for days. What's more, Linda was awarded an Emmy, the highest prize a TV production can earn. Thus other stations became aware of the producer and her work.

On March 20, 1983 HBO invited her to its premises in New York and gave her a contract to "go beyond the animal mutilation phenomenon," to look for genuine signs of alien visits and make a film about them. They agreed to call the film "UFOs: The ET Factor." Jean Abounader, the director of documentation at HBO, asked Linda, "People always want to see such UFO stories. But, Linda, do you really believe that they are out there?" Linda answered, "You saw *Strange Harvest*. Something strange is happening on this planet and I don't know what it is. And that's what I'll find out." On the same day she arranged to meet Peter Gersten, a New York lawyer who had founded the public initiative Citizens Against UFO Secrecy (CAUS). Since President Ford had signed the "Freedom of Information Act" as an answer to the Watergate Affair, every U.S. citizen had the right to ask for and look into the files of the armed forces and intelligence services—provided they did not contain "information affecting the national security," which naturally proved to be an extremely extensible clause! Jimmy Carter, who during his election campaign had publicly stated that he had personally seen a UFO in Leary in 1969, had also promised to release "all UFO secret documents" if he became president. He did liberalize the law, and over 20,000 pages of declassified UFO files were released to the public. But many of them were heavily censored, leaving the impression that they formed only the top of the iceberg. And it was there that Gersten and the CAUS concentrated their efforts.[1]

In 1977 Gersten, together with the UFO organization Ground Saucer Watch (GSW) of Phoenix, Arizona, filed a suit against the CIA, to compel it to release secret UFO files. The result was the release of some much-censored files and the information that eighteen more files in the CIA archives belonged to the super secret National Security Agency (NSA). The NSA conceded in court that it possessed UFO documents. At first the talk was of 79 documents, then 135 and finally 239. Gersten was of the opinion that the public had a right to see these files, but the NSA insisted on withholding them on grounds of national security. Thereupon Gersten applied for an "in camera" examination of the validity of the NSA claim about the sensitive nature of the documents, to be conducted by a judge of the district court. That too was rejected by the NSA. Finally the court ordered the NSA representative to make a statement under oath, behind closed doors, in the sole presence of the judge and with the exclusion of the lawyers. To do that, the judge, Gerhard Gesell, had to submit to a security check and was given a "Top Secret" clearance. At last, on 10 October 1980, Eugene F. Yeates, the NSA representative, made his statement, on the basis of which the court came to the conclusion *"that release of this material could seriously jeopardize the work of the agency and the security of the United States. . . . The in camera affidavit presents factual considerations which aided the court in determining that the public interest in disclosure is far outweighed by the sensitive nature of the materials and the obvious effect on national security their release may well entail."*[2]

One almost feels transposed to the courtroom of the U.S. Navy in the Oscar-nominated Hollywood thriller *A Few Good Men,* in which a snarling Jack Nicholson as Colonel Jessop barks at the young army lawyer Lieutenant Kaffe (Tom Cruise), "You can't handle the truth." But just like Lieutenant Kaffe, Gersten did not let himself be particularly impressed by the development, and appealed to the U.S. Supreme Court. But apparently the good guys prevail only in movies. This court also dismissed the case and on 8 March 1982 refused to give Gersten another hearing—the NSA could continue to use the excuse of "national security" to withhold UFO secrets. The perky lawyer filed an application on 27 April 1982 to view the affidavit signed by Yeates. He was shown a copy of it—the document was classified "Top Secret/Umbra," the highest possible classification, and fourteen pages of it were blacked out.[3]

Richard Dotys AFOSI report about a UFO landing in the Coyote Canyon (nuclear) weapon storage arsenal of 29 September 1980.

But when Linda Howe met Gersten that cold March evening, it was not in connection with NSA but with a new case that CAUS was tracking. And this case had something to do with the AFOSI agent Richard Doty, with whom Bill Moore had come into contact through "Falcon." Only a few weeks ago the Air Force had officially released reports about UFO landings on the Coyote Canyon Atomic Weapons Arsenal grounds in the Manzano Mountains south of Albuquerque, New Mexico, reports which, thanks to "Falcon," Bill Moore knew of, and had copies of, since January 1982. The

case was, therefore, genuine, and Doty, the author of the reports, was, for Howe, a person worth interviewing. After all, it concerned an official report about a UFO landing on a military high security area:

On 11 August 1980, Russ Curtis, Sandia Security, advised that on 9 August 1980, a Sandia Security Guard (who wishes his name not divulged for fear of harassment) related the following: "At approximately 0020 hours, he was driving east on the Coyote Canyon access road on a routine building check of an alarmed structure. As he approached the structure he observed a bright light near the ground behind the structure. He also observed an object he first thought was a helicopter. But after driving closer, he observed a round disk-shaped object. He attempted to radio for a back up patrol but his radio would not work. As he approached the object on foot armed with a shotgun, the object took off in a vertical direction at a high rate of speed."[4] Coyote Canyon is part of a large restricted testing area, used by the armament laboratories of the Air Force, the Sandia Laboratory, the Department of Nuclear Defense and the Department of Energy. It is patrolled by Sandia Security, which today checks only the buildings.

One can imagine what sort of Spielberg scenario lies behind this laconic report. A warm August night in the desert of New Mexico, a soldier on patrol of the arsenal grounds in the midst of the Manzano Mountains, their contours showing up as jet-black silhouettes against the starry sky. The alarm has sounded, a shining object lands near the barracks. A helicopter? Saboteurs, terrorists, perhaps on the payroll of the Ayatollah Khomeini or Muammar Qaddafi? The soldier approaches the object warily, pointing his machine gun at it, but the closer he gets, the clearer it becomes to him that it is not a helicopter that is standing there. No, it is a shining disk, something he has never seen before. Is it one of those "flying saucers" about which one reads in trashy rags and pulp magazines, do they really exist, is this a spaceship from another world? Whatever it is, it has no business to be here, in the vicinity of the atomic weapons. He has discovered someone "in flagranti," and being alone, is filled with fear. He needs help badly, and at once. He grabs his radio—it is dead! Frantically he tries and tries again, but it refuses to work. But he has to do his duty. With his finger on the trigger of the gun, bending down low and ever on the lookout for cover, he creeps towards the mysteriously glowing disk. But when he is still some 200 yards from it, he hears a low buzzing noise, and the disc suddenly lifts off the ground, hovers for a few seconds, then shoots off vertically at a tremendous speed and disappears. The soldier views the maneuver with breathless amazement. His heart beats wildly, he is covered with sweat and the arteries in his neck pulsate visibly. Dazed by the experience, he goes back to his vehicle and picks up the radio again—and this time it works! "Sandia Security. I have just seen a UFO," he announces in a choking voice . . .

"Perhaps Doty can help you to contact this soldier," said Gersten, after Howe had read the AFOSI report. Yes, that was the kind of stuff she needed: reliable witnesses, official documents, spectacular episodes. "That is only the tip of the iceberg," added Gersten. "I met Doty in January. At first with Bill Moore, then, the next day, alone. He mentioned a group of people at the highest level, which collects information about these

Master Sergeant Richard Doty

extraterrestrial visitors. Their name is MJ-12. He assured me that the government is investigating UFOs and knows that they are of extraterrestrial origin." There are many departments working on this, but the NSA has the most important role. In fact they are supposed to have already established contact with the aliens. This project has the cover name "Operation Aquarius."

"Isn't Doty afraid of consequences if he talks so openly to you about secret projects?" asked Linda.

"No, he said he was acting as 'front man' for his superiors. Their aim was to prepare the public gradually for the existence of extraterrestrials. They call it the 'Education Program.' Spielberg's *Close Encounters of the Third Kind* was a part of it, and also *ET*. The 'programming' would be done through films, TV and other media. Doty felt that the government was worried about people getting into a panic if they knew too suddenly. But he emphasized that the aliens had no hostile intentions."

"And this fear of a panic has been the grounds for decades of silence?" asked Linda.

"Not only that," replied Gersten. "Doty said that another reason was the fear that the Soviet Union could learn about the alien technologies before we are in a position to understand them and employ them in our defense program."

"Alien technology?"

"Yes, Doty said a number of spaceships had crashed in the southwest, most of them during the late fourties and early fifties."

"That's incredible. How'd you judge Doty's reliability?"

"I don't know. Once he looked at me straight in the eyes and said, 'How do you know that I am not here to give you disinformation or information which is part of the program, knowing that you will go out and publish everything?'"

Los Alamos, the "mountain-monastery" of the nuclear physicists in New Mexico. Was alien technology investigated here?

Howe was fascinated. One thing was for certain: she had to get to know Doty.

A few days later, when Linda was back home in Denver, Gersten called her. "I have just spoken to Doty," he said, "and he is prepared to meet you. He has told me to give you his number." Howe called Doty and made an appointment with him at the Albuquerque airport. But Doty did not arrive. She waited for half an hour, got frustrated, took a taxi and went to the home of a friend. When she called Doty from there some time later, he expressed surprise and said that he too had waited at the airport in vain for her. Apparently they had missed each other. But that made no difference, he would pick her up right away. Fifteen minutes later Richard Doty rang the door bell at the house of Linda's friend. He was short, 5 feet 6 inches at the most, slim, with clear blue eyes, dark brown hair, a mustache and weathered skin. Together they drove to Doty's office at Kirtland AFB. The guard at the base gate waved them through and finally they came to a white-and-gray building, around which were trees and a lawn. After parking the car they went up a flight of stairs, then through two swinging doors into a corridor, and again through another swinging door into a security area, which was shut off by a door with a security code lock.

"We are going into the office of my boss," explained Doty, opening a door to the right. There was a big wooden table in the room, behind which Doty sat down after offering Linda a seat near the window. "You see, you've caused a bit of unrest amongst some people in Washington with your film *A Strange Harvest*. It came too close to a matter which we did not want the public to know about," declared Doty. He then went on to say that she had been kept under observation during the production. To prove this he cited a telephone conversation between Howe and the Press Office of the CIA in Washington. Then he opened a drawer on the left-hand side of the table and brought out a bunch of papers. "My superiors have asked me to show you these," said Doty, giving her the papers.

"You may read them and ask me questions, but you can't make any notes."

Incredulous, but expectant, Linda read the heading on the cover page: "Briefing Report for the President of the United States." The name of the president was not given. Subject: "Unidentified and Identified Aircraft." At this moment Doty got up, went to Howe and showed her a seat in the middle of the room. "Please move over to that chair. Eyes can read through the window." Linda had an uneasy feeling, felt uncertain. She asked herself repeatedly why he was showing her these papers. She could not make out what the game was. But it seemed to be worth playing. Linda tried to read every word and memorize it. The first page dealt with UFO crashes in the southwest of the U.S. The first one was said to have occurred in 1946, others in 1947, 1949 and during the early fifties. Two crashes near Roswell were mentioned, one—shortly before the historical Roswell incident—near Magdalena, New Mexico; others near Aztec, New Mexico; Kingman, Arizona, and in the extreme north of Mexico, near the Texan border. According to the report, the cause of the crashes was interference from a new kind of radar with the craft's navigating system.

Both wrecks and corpses were brought to various army research centers, the bodies to the Los Alamos National Laboratory, the discs to Wright-Patterson Air Force Base in Dayton, Ohio. The extraterrestrials were christened "EBEs" (Extraterrestrial Biological Entities). The color of their skin was light gray, they were about 4 feet tall, had long arms, four long fingers, no thumbs, nails like talons and a sort of web between the fingers. In the place of noses and ears they just had openings in the skull. According to the papers, one of the six beings recovered near Roswell was still alive. An Air Force officer who was later promoted to the rank of colonel took over the responsibility of looking after the said being and brought him to the most secret laboratory in Los Alamos, the cradle of the "Manhattan Project." The being was a strange mixture of man, reptile, and insect. After a time it was possible to establish a nonverbal communication with him. EBE, as they called him, conveyed information about his native civilization and their contact with humans during our history.

The home of the EBE was said to be in the Zeta Reticuli star system, according to the report fifty-five light-years (thirty-seven according to astronomers) away from the earth—a double star system with two yellow suns far enough apart to develop a planetary system. Apparently the Reticulans have been visiting the Earth for 25,000 years at certain intervals, to manipulate the DNA of humans and possibly other forms of life. That happened 25,000, 15,000, 5,000 and 2,500 years ago. 2,000 years ago, the report says, "the extraterrestrials created a man who was to teach the people of the Earth the doctrines of love and nonviolence." The chapter ended with the remark that EBE died on 18 June 1952, "cause of death unknown."

The documents went on to list the various projects through which the origin, nature and motives of extraterrestrials were to be investigated. Besides the official Air Force projects like Sign, Grudge, Gleem, Pounce, Twinkle and Blue Book, there were highly secret operations which were aimed at establishing contact with extraterrestrials and understanding their technology. The first one was PROJECT GARNET. This dealt with questions about the evolution of Homo sapiens which had arisen owing to the presence of the aliens. According to the report, PROJECT SIGMA established a means of communication which led to the first contact in 1964. PROJECT SNOWBIRD coordinated the investigation of alien technology. Finally they were successful in flying a recovered disk. PROJECT AQUARIUS was to coordinate all available information about all extraterrestrial forms of life.

Incredulous and shattered by what she had read, Linda leaned back, holding on to the papers as if they were a treasure, which she feared someone would tear away from her at any moment. "Why are you showing this to me," she asked agitated, "why not to the *New York Times*, the *Washington Post* or *60 Minutes*?" "Such institutions will only make trouble for us," replied Doty, "independent authors or producers can be more easily controlled, manipulated and discredited than media establishments with a staff of lawyers." Howe gulped that one down. At least Doty made no bones about his motives, and somehow that convinced her. "The reason why I have been told to show you these documents is: my bosses intend to give you some thousands of feet of film material, in black-and-white as well as in color. They are all historical takes of crashed discs, dead extraterrestrials, the one who survived, and of the first contact in 1946, which took place at the Holloman Air Force Base in New Mexico. You can use the material for your HBO documentary. I shall call you. We shall fix a date on which you can see the stuff on the East Coast. . . . But now I must go home. My two sons will be hungry and I must cook their dinner. . . ." The meeting was over. And although Linda had a thousand questions, although she could have spent hours with Doty, she had no choice. "But I'll drive you to the hotel," said Doty—and Linda sighed with relief: she could still ask him a few questions on the way.

"Isn't it dangerous for you to tell me all these things?" she asked him as they left the base and headed towards downtown Albuquerque. "I was instructed to do so," answered Doty, "we want you to make the film." "What do you know about the home planet of the aliens?" "They live like the Pueblo Indians, in housings built in the rocks and underground. Their planet is a hot desert. Nevertheless they are millions of years ahead of us. They can manipulate DNA like a child playing with building blocks. They can control gravitation. When their vessels visit the earth they literally swim on the earth's gravity field." "Why did EBE die?" "I don't know. He shouldn't have died. He was still young by their standards. Their normal life span is about 300 to 400 earth years. We tried to help him, tried to contact other EBEs. We didn't know how, but we tried just like in the film *ET*. The colonel who looked after him wept when he died. He had loved EBE. He said EBE was like a child, which had the mind of a thousand men." "Did EBE say anything about God?" "He said that our souls recycle, reincarnation is a reality. It is the motor of the universe, he said."

Linda could not sleep that night. Again and again

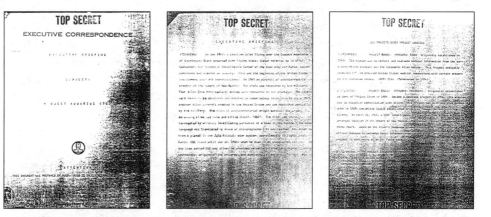

The alleged "Project Aquarius" executive briefing for President Jimmy Carter: "In 1947 an aircraft of extraterrestrial origin crashed in the desert of New Mexico. The craft was recovered by the military. Four Alien (non homo-sapiens) bodies were recovered in the wreckage."

her thoughts revolved around the incredible things she had learnt that day. Was the world on the threshold of a new era? Was she at the front, where history was being made? Or was she only a pawn in the disinformation maneuvers of the intelligence agencies?

Back in Denver she informed Jean Abounader of HBO about the meeting and the promised film material. But the initial expectations were short-lived. No matter how often she called Doty and asked him when she would get the material, nothing was forthcoming. In May 1984 Doty announced, "Linda, I have good news and bad news for you. The bad news is that the delivery of the films has to be postponed owing to political reasons. The good news is that your team gets an interview with the colonel who looked after EBE." For this Doty wanted her to send him photographs of herself, her sound technician, her cameraman and her production assistant, in order to carry out security checks. Linda followed his instructions, various dates were fixed and postponed, but the interview never took place. In June Doty informed her that the project had been pushed back for some time and that he himself was no longer officially involved, but that others would contact her. As a matter of fact she did receive calls from Washington to say that the project would be taken up after the elections in November. But that was the end of it.[5]

Instead, Jaime Shandera and Bill Moore received the Majestic-12 documents from the same source, sent from Albuquerque. Furthermore, "Falcon" arranged for a document to be shown to Moore at a motel at a small town in the state of New York, by a government agent, to send Bill Moore on a wild goose chase across the United States that would have fitted well into a third-class spy story. The contents of these papers came close to what Linda Howe had read in the "briefing documents."[6]

But Moore was permitted to take photographs of the document, so that we have the "Briefing Papers for the President, Subject: Project Aquarius—Top Secret" in full:

In 1947 an aircraft of extraterrestrial origin crashed in the desert of New Mexico. The craft was recovered by the military. Four Alien (non-Homo Sapiens) bodies were recovered in the wreckage. The Aliens were found to be creatures not related to human beings. In late 1949, another Alien aircraft crashed in the United States and was recovered partially intact by the military. One Alien of extraterrestrial origin survived the crash. This surviving Alien was male and called "EBE". The Alien was thoroughly interrogated by the military intelligence personnel at a base in New Mexico. The Alien language was translated by means of pictographs. It was learned the Alien came from a planet in the Zeta Reticuli star system, approximately 40 light years from the earth. EBE lived until June 18, 1952, when he died from an unexplained illness. During the time period EBE was alive, he provided valuable information regarding space technology, origins of the universe and exobiological matters.[7]

Moore had one more privilege, one that had been promised to Linda but never been granted. He could interview "Falcon" in front of a camera, in the presence of Peter Leone, the news editor of US-TV. Prior to that, Peter could convince himself that "Falcon" was indeed the person he claimed to be. During the interview "Falcon's" face was darkened and his voice distorted. Before and after the interview, after signing an agreement promising to handle all documents confidentially, Leone could ask questions. "Falcon" said:

We continued to investigate UFO sightings and landings in an official capacity, sanctioned by the Government but secretly, without the knowledge of the public and many Government establishments. It is done in this manner because in the past too much information about UFOs became public and the U.S. could not take the risk of losing technological information, which we had come to possess through the sightings and landings of extraterrestrials. . . . The U.S. was afraid that the public would get into a panic if it knew the truth, the whole truth and are still worried about intelligence or technological information getting out into the open. Nevertheless, the Government intends to initiate the public gradually. From the early fifties, since the film The Day the Earth Stood Still was shown, the U.S. Government has conditioned the population and tried to gauge the public reaction. The Government believes that the public will be more ready to accept this information if it comes out gradually, rather than all at once.

"Falcon" then told the whole story about EBE:

The first extraterrestrial was here around 1949. He was interviewed for some time, interrogated, so to speak. It took a year or so before military intelligence personnel were able to communicate with him. . . . A doctor devised a way of planting a device in the throat of the alien in order for him to speak words. He learned the English language, I'm told, very rapidly. . . . they are so far ahead of us that they don't communicate like we do. . . . I remember having read that during the first interviews in 1950 EBE was very afraid, not because he was being kept in a strange place, no, he was afraid of us as a different creature. . . . But once they did communicate with him, he told them the basics of his knowledge of his planet's exploration of the planet Earth. His knowledge wasn't totally complete, because he was basically a mechanic. He came from a planet in the Zeta Reticuli star group—the third planet—and it had a binary sun—two suns together.

But the Reticulans are not the only extraterrestrial race that visits us, according to "Falcon." He spoke of nine different species of visitors:

The ones that I saw pictures of and the videotapes that I observed, and the information they obtained from the medical examination of the aliens, describe the alien as a creature about three feet four inches to three feet eight inches tall. Their eyes are extremely large, almost insect-style. Their eyes have a couple of lids, and that's probably because they were born on a planet that had a binary sun [system]. The days are extremely bright, probably twice to three times as bright as our sun, I think. They have just two openings where our nose would be. They have no teeth as we know it—they have a hard, gumlike area. Their internal organs are quite simple. They have one organ which encompasses what we would refer to as a heart and lungs; it's one pulmonary sac which does the job of our heart and lungs. Their digestive system is really simple. They only have liquid wastes and not solid wastes. . . . Their skin structure is an extremely elastic skin, and hard [sic], probably hardening from their sun. They have some basic organs. Their brain is more complex than ours; it has several different lobes than ours have. Where our eyes are controlled by the back of the brain, theirs is [sic] controlled by the front of the brain. Their hearing is quite better than ours, almost better than a dog's, [and the ears are] small areas at the side of their heads. . . . They have hands without thumbs—four fingers without thumbs. Their feet are small, weblike.

Their sexual organs—they have males and females. The female has a sex organ similar to our females. There's some difference of the ovary system. And their kidney and bladder is one organ. They excrete waste. They have another organ which—I don't know if our scientists determined what it was for, but I believe it's to transfer the solid wastes into liquid wastes. They don't require very much liquid. They transfer all the food that they eat into liquids. The body extracts the liquids out of the food but they have been able to eat some basic food products—vegetables and fruits—that we would eat. But I believe that they have problems digesting meat products, and I don't believe they eat meat on their planet.[8]

Five years later "Falcon" was again ready to give an interview under the same conditions as before. Present at this interview was the CBS producer Michael Seligman, who had actually requested an official of the Congress Investigating Office to check the identity of "Falcon." On 14 October 1988, during the two-hour special program "UFO Cover Up: Live," which was broadcast nationwide by CBS, millions of viewers had the opportunity of hearing the testimony of "Falcon," which had been recorded before.

According to "Falcon" there is an MJ-12 book, known to insiders as the "Bible." "Falcon" explained, *"The Bible contains information on everything that occurred from the Truman era. . . . the technological data gathered from the aliens; medical history gathered from dead aliens found in the desert; autopsies; and information obtained from the extraterrestrials regarding their social structure and their information pertaining to the universe."*

"Falcon" mentioned another book as well, the "Yellow Book": *"The book relates to the aliens' planet, the social structure of the aliens, and the aliens' life among the earthlings. What was most intriguing in my experience with the aliens, is, I believe, an octagon-shaped crystal, which when held in the alien's hand and viewed by a second person, displays pictures. These can be of the alien's home planet, or pictures of the Earth many thousands of years ago."*

Since 1948, according to "Falcon," three EBEs have been "guests" of the U.S. Government. The first one had been found in New Mexico after his craft crashed. He died in 1952. EBE 2 *"voluntarily came over to be examined and spoken with"*—and was the actual author of the "Yellow Book." From 1982 EBE 3 was—and perhaps still is—the third alien "guest" of the Government.

According to "Falcon" the life span of the aliens was 300 to 400 years. *"It's my understanding that the aliens have an IQ of over 200. . . . They have a religion, but it's a universal religion. They believe in the universe as a Supreme Being."* They come with peaceful intentions, but do not consider it right to interfere directly with our evolution. All that

they can do and have done so far is to influence our genetic, moral and cultural development indirectly. *"They enjoy music, all types of music, especially ancient Tibetan-style music."* And then "Falcon" made a remark that probably amused but certainly more than put off most of the viewers: *"They like vegetables. And their favorite dish or snack is ice cream—especially strawberry."*[9]

Whoever until then was not sure what to think of "Falcon's" statements, had, at this last point, to concede—or consider—that at least some of his information must be taken "cum grano salis," with a grain of salt—and a good portion of skepticism. The credible part was so markedly spiced with absurdities and false information that it was never clear what was truth and what not. It began with EBE's sojourn on the earth. Did he come in 1948, as "Falcon" said during his second interview, or in 1949, as he declared during the first? Or perhaps already in 1947? While "Falcon's" short appearance on TV contributed to offering the public perhaps the entire truth (and a bit more, to boot!), Bill Moore succeeded, a year later, in getting himself openly discredited. At the yearly meeting of the U.S. UFO organization MUFON in Las Vegas on 1 July 1989, Moore disclosed the background of his connection with "Falcon." For during the process of exchanging sought-after information, the secret agent had repeatedly asked Moore one favor or another. At first he was to collect information about UFO organizations. Then he was asked to supply UFO researcher Paul Bennewitz of Albuquerque with disinformation, so as to discredit him later. Now, Bennewitz, a technician and president of the Thunder Science Corporation, had, after a series of UFO sightings over the Kirtland Air Force Base, listened in to the radio conversations of the base security to learn more about the activities on the base. When he then started scanning the entire radio spectrum for "extraterrestrial signals" and regularly watching the base area with cameras and a telescope, as well as bombarding senators, congressmen and even the president with his often wild hypotheses, it became too much for the Army. So they fed him with false documents through Moore, which worked him up so much that he took to chain-smoking and finally had a nervous breakdown. Persistently urged by his family, Bennewitz went to a clinic for psychiatric treatment and the Kirtland security had one problem less to deal with. But just this development made Moore's role in the game look very

questionable. His colleagues branded him as "collaborator" and asked themselves whether he was not feeding them too with disinformation at the behest of the intelligence agencies. So Bill Moore, shortly before that hailed as one of the most serious UFO researchers, with the fine nose of an investigative journalist, was suddenly "outlawed." He was compelled to withdraw from the UFO scene. Perhaps he had come too close to the truth, perhaps his ambition to "look behind the curtains" blinded him—in any case he had become a persona non grata.

A certain William Milton Cooper appeared on the scene and declared, in overflowing auditoriums, that he had read everything about which "Falcon" had spoken, while he was in the Navy in 1971. Though only a quartermaster, he had been chosen to brief the commander of the Pacific Fleet, for which purpose he had received all those documents from Washington. As incredible as it sounds, instead of being faced with the problem of having to produce evidence, he managed to enhance and elaborate his story with each lecture. The ETs suddenly became cosmic vampires who nourish themselves on the body fluids of humans and are preparing to take over the earth. The U.S. Government had allied itself with them, had sold land and people to them in exchange for their technology. But Cooper also cited MJ-12, as the alleged origin of his documents regarding "Operation Majority." And thus he contributed to the result that even for UFO enthusiasts "Falcon's" information and the "Majestic 12" documents seemed more and more dubious.[10]

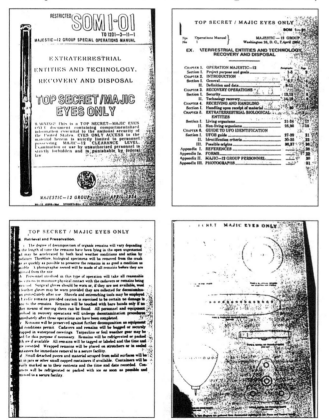

The alleged "Majestic 12-Group Special Operations Manual: Extraterrestrial Entities and Technology—Recovery and Disposal" from 1954.

This did not change even after a new film came into the hands of researcher Don Berliner, co-author of the nuclear-physicist Stanton Friedman (*UFO Crash near Corona*, which proved to be a reproduction of an MJ-12 document). Their book was a "Majestic 12 Handbook for Special Operations," which bore the much promising title *Extraterrestrial Beings and Technology, Recovery and Storage* and was classified "TOP SECRET/MAJIC—EYES ONLY." The handbook was dated 7 April 1954. On thirty-one pages it deals with:

—Operation Majestic 12: project purpose and goals
—Recovery operations
—Security
—Technology recovery
—Receiving and handling
—Extraterrestrial Biological Entities
—Guide to UFO identification
—UFOB guide
—Identification criteria
—Possible origins

The introduction indicates that the purpose of this handbook is to prepare MJ-12 units for the recovery of crashed space vessels. *"MJ-12 takes the subject of UFOs, extraterrestrial technology and Extraterrestrial Biological Entities very seriously and considers the entire subject to be a matter of the highest national security. For that reason everything relating to the subject has been assigned the very highest security classification,"* says the paper, which a little later defines the security classification as being two levels higher than Top Secret. *"The reason for this has to do with the consequences that may arise not only from the impact upon the public should the existence of such matters become general knowledge, but also the danger of having such advanced technology as has been recovered by the Air Force fall into the hands of unfriendly foreign powers. No information is released to the public press and the official government position is that no special group such as MJ-12 exists."* The document confirms that Operation Majestic-12 was established on 24 September 1947 by President Truman, on the recommendation of the Secretary of Defense James V. Forrestal and Dr. Vannevar Bush, scientific adviser to the president.

The goals of the MJ-12 Group include:

a. The recovery for scientific study of all materials and devices of a foreign or extraterrestrial manufacture that may become available. Such material and devices will be recovered by any and all means deemed necessary by the Group.

b. The recovery for scientific study of all entities and remains of entities not of terrestrial origin which may become available through independent action by those entities or by misfortune or military action.

c. The establishment and administration of Special Teams to accomplish the above operations.

d. The establishment and administration of special secure facilities located at secret locations within the continental borders of the United States for receiving, processing, analysis and scientific study of any and all material and entities classified as being of extraterrestrial origin by the Group or the Special Teams.

e. The establishment and administration of covert operations to be carried out in concert with the Central Intelligence to effect the recovery <u>for the USA of extraterrestrial technology and entities which may come down inside the territory of or fall into the possession of foreign powers.</u> [Emphasis added.]

f. The establishment and maintenance of absolute top secrecy concerning all of the above operations.

Under "Current Situation" the book says:

It is considered as far as the current situation is concerned, that there are few indications that these objects and their builders pose a direct threat to the security of the US, despite the uncertainty as to their ultimate motives in coming here. Certainly the technology possessed by these beings far surpasses anything known to modern science, yet their presence here seems to be benign and they seem to be avoiding contact with our species, at least for the present. *Several dead entities have been recovered along with a substantial amount of wreckage and devices from downed craft, all of which are under study at various locations. No attempt has been made by extraterrestrial entities either to contact authorities or recover their dead counterparts or the downed craft, even though one of the crashes was the result of direct military action. The greatest threat at this time arises from the acquisition and study of such advanced technology by foreign powers unfriendly to the US. It is for this reason that the recovery and study of this type of material by the US has been given such a high priority.*

In Section Nine four types of "documented extraterrestrial craft" are described:

a. Elliptical, or disk shape, 50–300 feet in diameter, thickness about 15% of the diameter, not including the dome, which is 30%.

b. Fuselage or cigar shape, 2,000 feet long and 95 feet thick.

c. Ovoid or circular shape, 30–40 feet long, thickness 20% of length.

d. Airfoil or triangular shape, the longest side about 300 feet.

Section ten deals with the Extraterrestrial Biological Entities (EBEs):

a. EBE Type I: These entities are humanoid and might be mistaken for human beings of the Oriental race from a distance. They are bipedal, five to five ft 4 inches in height and weigh 80–100 pounds. Proportionally they are similar to human beings, although the cranium is somewhat larger and more rounded. The skin is a pale, chalky-yellow in color, thick and slightly pebbled in appearance. The eyes are small, wide set, almond shaped, with brownish-black irises with very large pupils. The whites of their eyes are not like that of human beings, but have a pale gray cast. Their ears are small and not low on the skull. The nose is thin and long, and the mouth is wider than in humans and nearly lipless. There is no apparent facial hair and very little body hair, that being very fine and confined to the underarm and groin area. The body is thin and without apparent body fat, but the muscles are well-developed. The hands are small, with four long digits but no opposable thumb. The outside digit is jointed in a manner as to be nearly opposable and there is no webbing between the fingers as in humans. The legs are slightly but noticeably bowed, and the feet are somewhat splayed and proportionally large.*

b. EBE Type II: These entities are humanoid but differ from Type I in many respects. They are bipedal, 3 feet 5 inches–4 feet 2 inches in height, and weigh 25–50 pounds. Proportionately the head is much larger than humans or Type I EBEs, the cranium being much larger and elongate. Their eyes are very large, slanted, and nearly wrap around the side of the skull. They are black, with no whites showing. There is no noticeable brow ridge and the skull has a slight peak that runs over the crown. The nose consists of two small slits which sit high above the slit-like mouth. There are no external ears. The skin is a pale bluish-gray color, being somewhat darker on the back of the creature, and is very smooth and fine-celled. There is no hair on either face or body, and these creatures do not appear to be mammalian. The arms are long in proportion to the legs, and the hands have three long, tapering fingers and a thumb, which is nearly as long as the fingers. The second finger is thicker than the others, but not as long as the index finger. The feet are small and narrow, and four toes are joined together with a membrane.

The "description of extraterrestrial technology" indicates that from 1947 to 1953 a number of UFOs had crashed. The material of the recovered wreckage is said to have possessed *"great strength and resistance to heat,"* *"the appearance of aluminum foil,"* *"solid structures and substantial beams . . . very light in weight,"* *"tensile and compression strength not obtainable by any means known to modern industry,"* etc. Many of them were *"engraved or embossed with marks and patterns . . . not readily identifiable and attempts to decipher their meaning largely unsuccessful."*

Chapter twelve deals with questions of security. To begin with, possible eyewitnesses must be put under arrest until the extent of their knowledge and involvement can be determined. They should then be briefed and sworn into silence, using *"intimidation if necessary, to secure their cooperation."* Should the press get wind of the incident, then one should at first try simple denial, or give out a cover story: meteorites, crashed satellites, weather balloons or military aircraft were "acceptable alternatives"—only in the case of aircraft care had to be exercised not to suggest that the aircraft might be experimental or secret, so as not to arouse further curiosity. The crash site should be cordoned off and put under security as soon as possible. Local authorities may be employed for blocking off the area, but under no circumstances be allowed on the site itself. Statements issued concerning contamination of the area due to toxic spills from trucks or tankers could serve to keep undesirable persons away from the area. After guards have protected the site from every possible intruder, a command post should be established, and as

soon as it is operational MJ-12 should be informed and their instructions followed.

Before removing any of the finds, everything should be photographed and catalogued. The site must be checked for every form of contamination. The transport team should bring the material to the nearest military establishment, using big transporters if necessary, well camouflaged, via roads with the least traffic. The transporting of possible EBEs to top security facilities has the highest priority. Care must be taken to avoid contamination from alien bacteria. Dead EBEs should be put in dry ice, living ones transported in ambulances. *"Personnel involvement with EBEs alive or dead must be kept to an absolute minimum."*[11]

In fact there was an elite U.S. Air Force unit specially trained for the recovery of UFOs, irrespective of their origin. Their duties are actually laid down in the official Air Force Regulation 200-2, dated 12 August 1954. It says, under Clause Six, heading "Collection":

"The Air Defense Command has a direct interest in the facts pertaining to UFOs reported within the ZI (Zone Interior), and has, in the 4602d Air Intelligence Service Squadron (AISS) the capability to investigate these reports. The 4602d AISS is composed of specialists trained for field collection and investigation of matters of air intelligence interest which occur within the ZI. This squadron is highly mobile and deployed throughout the ZI. . . ."
Unless otherwise instructed, the squadron is to bring all "pieces of evidence" to the Wright-Patterson Air Force Base in Dayton, Ohio. Clause Four, "Responsibilities," says: *"c. Analysis: The Air Technical Intelligence Center (ATIC) at the Wright-Patterson Air Force Base, Ohio, will analyze and evaluate: All information and evidence reported within the ZI . . . and all information and evidence collected in oversea areas."* The team had all powers and complete command of all investigations: *"All Air Force activities are authorized to conduct such preliminary investigation as may be required for reporting purposes; however, investigation should not be carried beyond this*

Air Force Regulation AFR 200-2 defines the responsibilities of Wright Patterson AFB and the 4602d AISS.

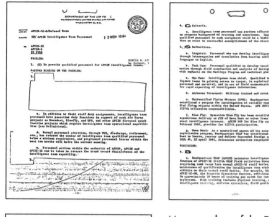

Memorandum of the Department of the Air Force, defining the tasks of Project MOONDUST.

has established a program for investigation of reliably reported unidentified flying objects within the United States. AFR 200-2 delineates 1127th collection responsibilities.

f: Blue Fly: *Operation Blue Fly has been established to facilitate expeditious delivery to FID (Federal Intelligence Dept.) of Moon Dust or other items of great technical intelligence interest. . . .*

g: Moon Dust: *As a specialized aspect of its over-all materiel exploitation program, HQ USAF has established Project Moon Dust to locate, recover and deliver descended foreign space vehicles.*

Under Clause Six, "Discussion":

b: Intelligence teams are comprised of three men each, to include a linguist, a tech man, and an ops man. All are airborne qualified. Cross-training is provided for each team member in the skills of the other team members to assure a team functional capability despite casualties. . . .

c: . . . These three peacetime projects all involve a potential for employment of qualified field intelligence personnel on a quick reaction basis to recover or perform field exploitation of UFOs, or known Soviet Bloc aerospace vehicles, weapons systems, and/or residual components of such equipment.[13]

To what extent the scope of Project Moon Dust was repeatedly widened is shown by a telex (Airgram) sent out by the Defense Intelligence Agency (DIA) in 1973 through the Department of State to all U.S. embassies and consulates in the world. It instructs all U.S. diplomats to report all incidents concerning investigations of space objects of non-U.S. or of unknown origin under the code word "Moon Dust."[14]

But while Projects Moon Dust and Blue Fly are indubitable facts, the veracity of the "Majestic-12 Handbook" is questionable. Its recommendation to disseminate the story of a "crashed satellite" in order to

point, unless such action is requested by the 4602d AISS."[12]

During the following years the 4602d AISS was to change its name several times: in July 1957 it became 1006th AISS, in April 1960 the 1127th USAF Field Activity Group, later the 7602d USAF Field Activity Group, the USAF Special Activities Center (AFSAC), then the 696th and finally, in 1989, the 512th Air Intelligence Group, which is still stationed at Fort Belvoir, Virginia. However, what was kept unchanged over the years was the group's field of activities. According to a memorandum of the Department of the Air Force dated 3 November 1961, during times of peace this included the following projects, as listed under the heading "Definitions":

e: Unidentified Flying Objects (UFO): Headquarters USAF

cover up a UFO crash, *three years before the first Sputnik,* seems strange. Nor can the mention of "Area 51" in Nevada as destination for crashed UFOs be correct, for this facility was not created until 1955. Is the "MJ-12 Handbook" a forgery or a do we have there a version "updated" in the sixties? We do not know. But one thing is certain: whoever compiled it had inside knowledge. This is shown, for example, by one of the appendices, which says in detail where the recovered wreckage and bodies were to be transported to. The destinations given are "Area 51," "Area S-42 ," "The Blue Lab" at Wright-Patterson AFB, and Building 21 at the Kirtland AFB:

1. Aircraft Intact, operational, or semi-intact aircraft of Extraterrestrial design and manufacture.
   Area 51 S-4
2. Intact
Any mechanical or electronic device or machine which Device appears to be undamaged and functional.
   Area 51 S-4
3. Damaged
Any mechanical or electronic device or machine which Device appears to be damaged but mostly complete.
   Area 51 S-4
4. Powerplant
Devices and machines or fragments which are possible propulsion units, fuel, and associated control devices and panels.
   Area 51 S-4
5. Identified fragments
Fragments composed of elements or materials easily recognized as known to current science and technology, i.e. aluminum, magnesium, plastic etc.
   Area 51 S-4
6. Unidentified
Fragments composed of elements or materials not known to current science and technology and which exhibit fragments

unusual or extraordinary characteristics.
   Area 51 S-4
7. Supplies and provisions
Non-mechanical or non-electronic materials such as personal belongings, organic ingestibles etc.
   Blue Lab P-61
8. Living entity
Living non-human organisms in apparently good or reasonable health.
   OPNAC B06-01
9. Non-living entity
Deceased non-human organisms or portions of organisms, organic remains and other suspect organic matter.
   Blue Lab P-61
10. Media
Printed matter, electronic recordings, maps, charts, photographs and film.
   Bldg. 21 KB-88
11. Weapons
Any devices or portions of a device thought to be offensive or defensive weaponry.
   Area 51 S-4

We can be sure that all these installations were actually venues of the biggest, most expensive and most secret military research projects in history. The program was started early in 1948, six months after the incidents in New Mexico, and it required a very clever and well-planned maneuver on the part of the Truman administration to mobilize the resources needed for it.

[1]Howe, Linda Moulton, *An Alien Harvest,* Huntingdon Valley, CO, 1989, and personal interview, 5 August 1992.
[2]Fawcett, Lawrence and Barry Greenwood, *Clear Intent,* Englewood Cliffs, NJ, 1984, and United States District Court for the District of Columbia, Civil Action No. 80-1562, CAUS vs. NSA: Summary Judgment, 18 November 1980.

[3]United States District Court for the District of Columbia, Civil Action No. 80-1562, CAUS vs. NSA: In Camera Affidavit of Eugene F. Yeates, 30 September 1980.

[4]Doty, Richard, "Alleged Sightings of Unidentified Aerial Lights in Restricted Test Range," AFOSI-Report of 2 to 9 September 1980, Kirtland AFB, New Mexico, 8 August 1–3 September 1980.

[5]Howe, 1989, and personal interview, 5 August 1992.

[6]Moore, William and Jaime Shandera, *The MJ-12 Documents*, Burbank, 1990.

[7]MJ 12: Executive Briefing—Subject: Project Aquarius (TS), Washington, D.C. 1976.

[8]Moore/Shandera, *The Falcon-Tape* (Video), Burbank, 1990.

[9]"UFO Cover Up: Live," CBS-TV Feature produced by M. Seligman/Distributed by: Lexington Broadcast Service LBS, broadcast on 14 October 1988.

[10]Moore, William, "Revelations—UFOs and the US Government," in *Focus*, Burbank, CA, vol. 4, No. 7–9, September 1989.

[11]Majestic-12 Group, *Extraterrestrial Entities and Technology—Recovery and Disposal*, MJ-12 4838B-Maj 378455-64-3, April 1954.

[12]Department of the Air Force: Air Force Regulation No. 200-2, Intelligence—Unidentified Flying Objects Reporting, Washington, D.C., 12 August 1954.

[13]Department of the Air Force: AFCIN Intelligence Team Personnel, Washington, D.C., 3 November 1961.

[14]Department of State Airgram, "To all American Diplomatic and Consular Posts—Guidance for Dealing with Space Objects," Washington, D.C., 18 July 1973.

[15]Majestic-12 Group, 1954.

9.

The Blue Room

The period following the Roswell incident could be described as a period of frantic buildup of the armed forces and the intelligence services. Within just six months President Truman set up the most efficient and disciplined military hierarchy in history. It was almost as if the country was supposed to be prepared for a war against some unknown enemy, an enemy against whom, it was felt, all the capacity that had defeated Nazi Germany and Japan together would not suffice. This enemy could not be the Soviet Union, depleted after the war with Germany, which it mainly survived because a natural ally came to help, the Russian winter.

President Harry S. Truman

The first and most important step toward building the "fortress U.S.A., protected inside and outside," was the signing of the National Security Act by Truman on July 26, 1947. The act failed to define "national security," but the institutions that were created under this act took over this task. Under this act the Department of War was renamed Department of Defense, which at least signalized the victory of euphemisms in political etymology. The National Security Council was also established, which was to watch over the new but undefined principle, the Army Air Force changed to U.S. Air Force, the CIG (Central Intelligence Group) of the war period to CIA (Central Intelligence Agency). The establishment of the latter authority had not yet been passed by congress and was therefore financed through the Pentagon's "black money" for two years, without it bothering anybody.

In order to permit setting up an intelligence service in compliance with democratic principles, Congress wanted clear, honest information from Truman or the newly appointed Defense Secretary James Forrestal. And this no one was prepared to give. Every question was skillfully evaded or answered with misleading half-truths. Truman wrote to congress, pleading for passing the bill to found the organization, but did not mention any of the secret operations which were to be part of its work. He wanted congress to approve, but blindly so.[1]

". . . For the first time in the history of the nation," Truman wrote in his memoirs, "an overall military establishment was created." The NSC thereby took over the role of "the place in the Government, where military, diplomatic and resource problems could be studied and continually appraised," without having to depend on democratically elected institutions. Truman persuaded Sidney Souers to do him "a personal favor" and take over the post of the first executive secretary of the NSC.[2] When Truman started Operation Majestic 12 on September 24, 1947, he recruited three of its members from the new infrastructure of power: Defense Secretary Forrestal, NSC Executive Secretary Souers, and CIA chief Hillenkoetter.[3]

After only six months there followed one of the strangest political tactics of the Truman administration, which only now, in view of the newly discovered facts, becomes understandable. The tragic side of this political maneuver is that it influenced, more than any other, public opinion for more than four decades. The picture of an enemy was created which was only an alibi for an unknown enemy whose intentions were unknown and whose presence was not to become known under any circumstances. The consequence was the Cold War, which led to the most monstrous arms production in the history of mankind, till finally, owing to the economic and ideological bankruptcy of the Eastern Bloc, in the autumn of 1989 the Iron Curtain collapsed.

Many historians have speculated about the real reason why the Allies revised their attitude toward the Soviet Union, why they suddenly regarded the U.S.S.R. as the archenemy who was perpetually waiting to find a weak spot in the West. Stalin's advance in Eastern Europe certainly did appear threatening to the normal observer, but its limits had been precisely defined in the Yalta and Potsdam Treaties and in no way came as a surprise for Washington or London. No, this inimical portrayal of the U.S.S.R. was born in March 1948, in an artificially created wave of hysteria, which went down in history as "the war panic of 1948," as an irra-

President Harry S. Truman, dictator Joseph Stalin, at the Potsdam Conference 1945.

tional reaction to an imaginary threat. Historians today are unanimous in the opinion that the "war scare" of 1948 was nothing more than a political maneuver of the Truman administration—a clever move to induce Congress to pass a heavy increase of the defense budget in favor of the aircraft industry, which suddenly needed a lot of money for a new, top secret project. The Republican majority in congress had until then withheld this amount from the Democrat in the White House and, therefore, before the next attempt was made to obtain it, the necessary atmosphere of urgency had to be created.

This plan was the result of a confidential meeting between Defense Secretary Forrestal and Secretary of State Marshall, at which the necessary steps were discussed to get Congress to release the said amount within thirty days. The aim was to convince Congress and the public that the Soviet Union was on the point of war and attacking the West, starting a third world war. Under such circumstances the refusal to support Truman's program for the "re-establishment of defense capabilities" would look like treason. Only Washington insiders knew that this was no new plan. "A Russia panic will be used to prod more Army-Navy money out of congress," said *The Wall Street Journal* as early as September 1947, shortly before the Air Force was made an independent and third arm of the forces. In February 1948 Forrestal had convinced Truman that at least 400 million dollars should be provided for the newly formed Air Force in the budget for the year 1949.

The very next day after the meeting on March 4, Marshall and Forrestal began their activities. Forrestal arranged a "cabinet lunch" at headquarters, at which he informed various members of the cabinet, senators and congressmen about the "all too grave" political situation in the world. Further meetings with influential people from the press followed. Over and over again, the talk was of "preparing the American people for the possibility of a war."

Marshall's plan for rebuilding Europe (ERP) put him in the spotlight. His task was to get the "Marshall Plan" through Congress. It was not difficult to paint a terrible picture of the Communist Devil. "The world situation is very, very serious," he announced on March 10 to reporters. Eastern Europe, especially Czechoslovakia, had fallen to a "reign of terror" which threatened to overcome the whole continent. On March 13 the staged panic reached its first heights. "The United States may have to meet an international crisis only four or five weeks from now," announced Army Secretary Kenneth Royall during a speech at the Citadel in Charleston, South Carolina. Action, not protest, would be required, he said, should Russia threaten the sovereignty of Greece, Turkey, France or Italy, which of course it never did. In Washington, D.C. more and more people uttered the ugly word "war." "The mood of the capital this weekend was . . . exceedingly somber," wrote *New York Times* correspondent James Ruston on the following Monday, "responsible citizens are yelling 'quiet, quiet' at the top of their voices, and even the President has

mentioned that awful three-letter-word 'war.'" On the afternoon of March 15, the president called a crisis meeting of Congress for which he even cancelled his traditional attendance at the Irish St. Patrick's Day Parade.

At the same time Marshall told the Senate Foreign Relations Committee, "The hour is far more fateful now than it was one year ago. Totalitarian control has been tightened in other countries of Eastern Europe. . . . other European peoples face a similar threat of being drawn against their will into the Communist orbit." The success, as noted by Forrestal triumphantly in his diary: "The papers today are full of rumors and indications of war." The speaker of the Senate, Joseph W. Martin, spoke of "the grave crisis in our international relations. . . . we have to keep our Army and Navy strong. We want to give them everything that is needed to put them in the strongest possible defensive position. And many members believe the amounts sent in for the Air Force should be substantially increased."

When President Truman addressed Congress and the people on March 17, the panic had already reached its peak. "The world situation is too critical," "it is of vital importance that we act now," "necessity for speedy action," "great urgency," "urgent steps"—such phrases set the tone of his speech. Again and again "one nation" came to attack which "refused to cooperate," "ignored all wartime agreements," etc., until it was finally named: the Soviet Union and its agents. The speech did not fail to have an effect: both Marshall's plan and the increased budget for armament were passed by congress uncurtailed. In a request placed before the Armaments Committee of the Senate, Forrestal asked for $11 billion for the forces, thirty percent more than in the year before. It was granted, but— at the instance of the chiefs of staff at the Pentagon—

he raised his demands to $18 billion. Finally a sum of $14.5 billion was released, plus a special budgeting of $3.5 billion. For everything looked as if the U.S.A. was facing the biggest crisis since the attack on Pearl Harbor.

How real was the Soviet threat in those days? All CIA reports during that period, as well as all dispatches from American diplomats that have been released in the last ten years under the Freedom of Information Act, show that at the beginning of 1948 no sign of "danger from Russia" could be seen. Thus a CIA memorandum dated March 16, 1948, which also cites the "Intelligence Organizations of the Departments of State, War (Army), Navy and Air Force," clearly establishes that "there is no reliable evidence that the USSR intends to resort to military action within the next sixty days." The red giant, according to the report, was still weak owing to the losses during the war. Admiral Chester W. Nimitz was certain that "we are relatively safe from attack by a foreign power for the next four or five years. . . . I do not think any power is in a position to attack us with any prospect of success in the immediate future." The retired chief of staff, General Eisenhower, also "absolved the Soviet Union of any intentions of deliberately provoking a war," as reported by the *New York Times* on February 6, 1948. "The Soviet Union is in no position to support a global war and no other nation in the world is in the position to support one either."

A study of the intelligence staff of the then War Department, dated December 23, 1946, states: "Several factors, principally . . . the economic and physical debilitation resulting from World War II," combined to make the Soviets "incapable of waging a long-term, global war, or of waging a war outside the Eastern Hemisphere." One of these "factors" was the U.S.S.R.'s "lack of a long-range bomber force, large-scale amphibious means, and a deep-sea navy." And even if the Soviets "could produce their first atomic bomb between 1950 and 1953," they still would "not have stockpiled significant quantities (of this weapon) before 1956." As a result, it was concluded that "prior to 1956 continental United States will not be subject to large-scale invasion or attack. . . . It is unlikely that there will be any aggressive military action against continental United States prior to 1956."

The evaluation of the Army Intelligence Corps, "Intentions and Capabilities of Potential Enemies Against the U.S. During the Next Ten Years," dated July 11, 1947, was certain that:

"1. The Soviet economy will not be capable until about 1956 of furnishing the equipment and supplies necessary for such an offensive (an attack against the U.S.).

"2. The Soviet Union may be expected to avoid any serious risk of war with the United States for some years to come."

They knew this in Washington. Thus on March 24, 1948 it became known that since summer 1947, "21,178 combat-type planes" had been sold to the Russians "for scrap, at scrap prices," even though "some were obviously new," with the consent of the State Department. While the opposition got excited over this "disgraceful and almost treasonable" shipment of potential war material to Russia, the logical conclusion was not arrived at. Truman himself gave the explanation a few days later, on March 25, to reporters who could not believe their ears: "Russia is, at the present time, a friendly nation and has been buying goods from us right along." And as the *New York Times* shortly afterwards announced, the president did not plan any export restrictions regarding "a friendly nation" which only ten days before had been presented as the biggest threat against world peace since Adolf Hitler. No wonder that historians such as Professor Frank Kofsky conclude: "The war panic was a piece of fiction from the beginning to the end."[4]

But did this dangerous maneuver serve only to obtain more funds for the defense? The Russians felt insecure and reacted three months later with the Berlin blockade. Or were they supposed to "keep up" to face another, real foe, who was not to be named and who would have to be met with all available resources? A "traitorous" report by Arthur Krock, correspondent of the *New York Times* at the White House, who spoke to Truman on 7 April 1948, says: *"He (Truman) discussed rearmament, and said the reason he is holding down the new air groups beyond the point Symington and the air generals want is because 'we are on the verge of an aviation discovery that will make obsolete everything now being manufactured.' He said, also, that his plan was to have our aviation manufacture kept flexible, as we did during the war so that we can step up production when we want to, and alter plans, too. He said that, while on many subjects he was troubled by conflicting counsel, on this one he thought he has an informed opinion.'"*[5] (Emphasis added.)

What was the "aviation discovery" that was to keep the entire plans of the military plane manufacturers "flexible"? Historians have nothing to say about this. "Whatever aviation discovery Truman may have had in mind, after almost half a century, it has yet to materialize," commented Professor Kofsky frustratedly, in his study *Harry S. Truman and the War Scare of 1948.*[6] Had this discovery been made in July 1947 in the desert of New Mexico? That would explain the "well- informed opinion" that Truman spoke of.

The fact is: shortly after the passing of the budget, on March 20 and 26, Truman received visits from the presidents of the country's two major plane manufacturers, Donald Douglas of the later McDonnell-Douglas and William E. Allen of Boeing, at the White House, and informed them about the forthcoming projects as well as the big money that was available. Forrestal and Symington went ahead at similar speed. "With unusual haste . . . telegraphic letters went from Wright Field to the contract firms of the Air Force, and that within 24 hours after Forrestal had authorized the budget," wrote the specialist journal *Aviation Week.*[7] The most secret research program in history had been financed.

This brings us back tot Wright Field Base, the location of the Blue Laboratory where, at least until the establishment of Area 51/S-4 at the Nevada proving grounds in 1954, the alien technology was being analyzed. This is confirmed by the later deputy commander of the base, Brigadier General Arthur E. Exon, who had been transferred to Wright Field shortly before the Roswell crash occurred. As Exon told Roswell researcher Kevin Randle on 19 July 1990, the recovered material had been brought to the laboratories of the base and subjected to a series of tests. The bodies had gone the same way, according to Exon: "That is my information . . . they were brought to Wright Pat."[8] According to Professor Sarbacher and Professor Walker, at least until the beginning of the 1950s, that is where the secret meetings of MJ-12 took place.

In fact, for many years now there have been rumors going around about crashed UFOs and alien bodies at the Wright Field Base, which was integrated with the neighboring Patterson field and renamed Wright-Patterson Air Force Base. Around 1950, Charles Wilhelm of Cincinnati, Ohio, who later was to join a local UFO research group, often went to visit Mrs. Norma Gardner, who lived alone and was suffering from cancer, to help her with the garden and other repairs. Once he told her about his interest in UFOs. "Charles, I can assure you, there are UFOs," she said. "I know it, because, before I retired, I worked in a department at Wright-Patterson which dealt with UFOs." Wilhelm became curious and wanted to know

The mysterious Hangar 18 on the Wright Field Base. The UFO wreckages from Roswell and Socorro were brought here.

Our investigation proved it was a special effects film, made for the U.S. TV program "Sightings" with the help of a small model.

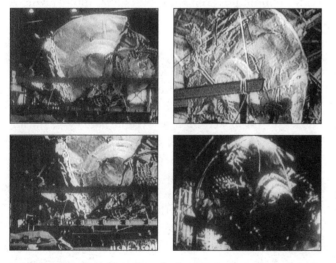

In 1995 a mysterious film, allegedly showing the Roswell wreckage in Hangar 18, circulated among ufologists.

more. "I have sworn an oath not to talk about it. It is all strictly secret," she said, but added hesitantly, "Anyway I don't have much longer to live and Uncle Sam can do nothing to me when I am in the grave."[9] Then she told her story in full.

In 1955 she had been instructed to catalogue the UFO material on which her department was working. Among this were a number of objects which had come from the inside of the crashed craft, which were carefully photographed and examined. After a few months her boss sent her to a very high security area, to a hangar with the code number eighteen, to list material from two saucer-shaped flying objects. For the first time she had seen the UFOs with her own eyes. They were round and disc-shaped; one was bigger than the other; the first damaged, but the other intact. Shortly afterwards she saw two corpses of their crew, preserved in a chemical solution. They were about four to four and a half feet tall, with markedly large heads and enormous black eyes.

Some years later Gardener's story was confirmed by one of Wilhelm's classmates, whose father had been stationed at Wright-Patterson and on his deathbed had spoken of two disc-shaped flying objects and four small corpses. "The bodies were about five feet tall, had big heads, slanted eyes and looked quite human. He thought their fingers were longer than those of a human being, but he was not sure."[10] Later Wilhelm contacted Len Stringfield, who had made it his life's work to collect UFO reports. For Stringfield this was only a confirmation of what others had already told him. On 29 June 1978 Stringfield learned from his son-in-law, Dr. Jeffrey Sparks, professor at St. Leo College in Dade City, Florida, that he had found another witness. This person had been stationed at Wright-Patterson in 1966 as a member of the Army Intelligence Corps and there had seen nine alien bodies kept deep-frozen in glass cases. Their bodies were slender, some four feet tall, and gray. The rooms where they were kept were heavily guarded. He had learned that the base had a number of wrecks and thirty bodies. The Air Force had formed a special unit, the Blue Berets, trained to salvage and examine crashed UFOs, stationed at certain important bases. Their work was highly secret. All data gathered about UFOs by the Air Force were stored in a computer at the data processing center at Wright-Patterson.[11]

As far as this data bank is concerned, it has perhaps been tapped already. On October 27, 1992 the U.S. news broadcast "Dateline" reported that a hacker had gained access to the Air Force computers. During the interview the camera showed for a short time the screen of a computer on which one could read: "WRIGHT-PATTERSON AFB/Catalogued UFO part list—underground facility of Foreign Technology Division." The item was short and did not deal further with UFOs. UFO researcher T. Scott Crain wrote to NBC and asked if the computer text had been genuine or prepared. On 16 March 1993 he received a call from Susan Adams, producer of the report. She assured him that the picture had really shown a part of the data the hacker—whose anonymity she had to preserve—had tapped. They had only taken the UFO part "because we thought that would be interesting." NBC had checked the claims of the hacker and had verified that the material really came from the Air Force and was not fabricated by him. Regrettably he has not yet made his UFO information available.[12]

In 1981 Stringfield had gotten to know the daughter of a witness who had claimed to have seen this underground facility at Wright-Patterson. YR, as Stringfield names the witness, served in the army during the war, was General Patton's chauffeur and had worked for General Electric. He was retired, lived near Cincinnati and had cancer when his daughter talked to Stringfield. "Dad worked at the Wright-Patterson during the early fifties. Once he was gone a whole week, to carry out a very secret job at the base. He would not talk to anybody about it, not even with me, only to mother, who is no more alive. But a short while ago he saw you on TV, how you spoke about UFOs and said, 'The man knows what he is talking about.' I took the opportunity to ask him directly what he meant." It took some months for her to get the whole story from him.

When he was working for General Electric, he was chosen to do a secret job at Wright-Patterson, having been in the army and having held a trusted position as chauffeur of a general. It had to do with the installation of a unit—the daughter had forgotten what it was for—in a secret, underground store. When he went to the base with his African-American assistant, Mr. W., they were taken to the entrance of a building in a vehicle with black curtains, which reminded them of a funeral car, and then in a lift to a working area some levels lower. In a narrow, ice-cold chamber—YR called it a mortuary—they were given instructions. The room was pervaded by a strange, penetrating smell. At every step they were watched by armed MPs. But occasionally he was able to catch a glimpse of the corpses, each of which was in a glass case placed on a stone pedestal. Although they were covered with sheets, he could see through one open side the big heads and the skin, 'which looked slippery, like that of a reptile.' Judging by the size of the cases, the beings must have been quite small.

For security reasons he and his assistant had to sleep at the base in a sort of cell and were not allowed to have any contact with the outside world. Otherwise the food was good and they even had a TV in the cell.[13]

As early as June 1978 Stringfield had met a physiologist who claimed to have autopsied these creatures. Although Stringfield, for obvious reasons, never revealed the name of this person, he emphasized that he was a well-known doctor at a renowned hospital, who had carried out an autopsy on an alien body in the early fifties. Later he came to know a second doctor who had been present at an autopsy at about the same time and confirmed many of the data—still unpublished at that time—mentioned by his colleague. Stringfield put them together as follows:

* *The approximate height of the alien humanoid is 3½ to 4½ feet tall. One source approximated 5 feet. The weight is approximately 40 lbs.*

* *Two round eyes without pupils. Under heavy brow ridge, eyes described variously as large, almond-shaped, elongated, sunken or deep set, far apart, slightly slanted, appearing "Oriental" or "Mongoloid."*

* *The head, by human standards, is large when compared with the size of the torso and limbs. "Take a look at a 5-month human foetus," I was told.*

* *No ear lobes or protrusive flesh extending beyond apertures on each side of head.*

* *Nose is vague. Two nasal passages are indicated with only slight protuberance.*

* *Mouth is indicated as a small "slit" without lips, opening into a small cavity. Mouth appears not to function as a means of communications or as an orifice for food ingestion.*

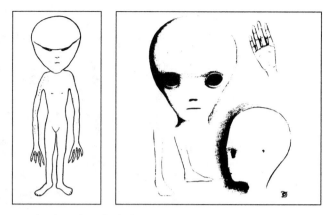

Two sketches of crashed aliens in U.S. Air Force custody as given to UFO researcher Len Stringfield by government physicians.

* *Neck described as being thin; and in some instances, not being visible because of garment on that section of body.*

* *Most observers describe the head of the humanoids as hairless. One said that the pate showed a slight fuzz. Bodies are described as hairless.*

* *"Small and thin" fits the general description of the torso. In most instances, the body was observed wearing a metallic but flexible garment.*

* *Arms are described as long and thin and reaching down to the knee section.*

* *One type of hands has four fingers, no thumb. Two fingers appear longer than others. Some observers had seen fingernails; others without. A slight webbing effect between fingers was noted by three authoritative observers. Other reports indicate types with fewer or more than four fingers.*

* *Legs short and thin. Feet of one type described as having no toes. Most observers describe feet as covered. One source said foot looked like an orangutan's.*

* *Skin description is NOT green. Some claim beige, tan, brown, or tannish or pinkish gray and one said it looked almost "bluish gray" under deep-freeze lights. In two instances, the bodies were charred to a dark brown. The texture is described as scaly or reptilian, and as stretchable, elastic or mobile over*

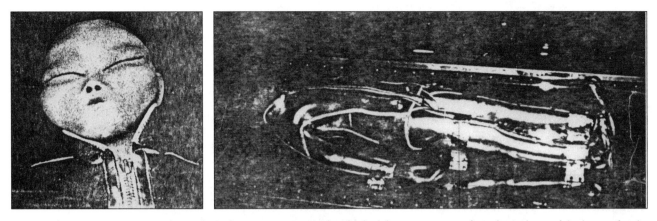

In 1990, the Soviet cosmonaut and test pilot Col. Dr. Marina Popovich published these two pictures from the archives of the late Prof. Felix Zigel of the Moscow Institute of Aeronautics and Astronautics and claimed they were original photographs of the Roswell Extraterrestrials. Zigel got them from Canada and it is still possible that they were the originals the Montreal model was based on.

smooth muscle or skeletal tissue. No striated muscle. No perspiration, no body odor. In November 1979, additional word was received from the medical authority concerning the nature of alien skin. Under magnification, I was told, the tissue structure appears mesh-like, or, like a grid's network of horizontal and perpendicular lines. Clarifying an earlier reference which describes the skin of the entity as "reptilian," this new information suggests that the texture of the granular-skinned lizards, such as the iguana and chameleon, may be similar to at least one type of alien humanoid.

* No teeth.

* No apparent reproductive organs. Perhaps atrophied by evolutionary degeneration. No genitalia. In my non-professional judgment, the absence of sexual organs suggests that some of the aliens, and perhaps all, do not reproduce as do the Homo sapiens, or that some of the bodies studied are produced perhaps by a system of cloning or other unknown means.

* To most observers the humanoids appear to be "formed out of a mould," or sharing identical facial characteristics.

* Brain and its capacity, unknown.

* Colorless liquid prevalent in body, without red cells. No lymphocytes. Not a carrier of oxygen. No food or water intake is known. No food found aboard craft in one known retrieval. No digestive system or GI tract. No intestinal or alimentary canal or rectal area described.

* More than one humanoid type. Life span unknown. Descriptive variations of anatomy may be no more diverse than those known among Earth's Homo sapiens. Other recovered alien types of human or other grotesque configurations are unknown to me. Origin unknown.[14]

Some months later the first pathologist mentioned gave Stringfield a written list of his observations:

SIZE—The specimen observed was 4 foot three and three-eighths inches in length. I can't remember the weight. It has been so long and my files do not contain the weight. I recall the length well, because we had a disagreement and everyone took their turn at measuring.

HEAD—The head was pear-shaped in appearance and oversized by human standards for the body. The eyes were Mongoloid in appearance. The ends of the eyes furthest from the nasal cavity slanted upward at about a ten degree angle. The eyes were recessed into the head. There seemed to be no vis-

ible eyelids, only what seemed like a fold. The nose consisted of a small fold-like protrusion above the nasal orifices. The mouth seemed to be a wrinkle-like fold. There were no human type lips as such—just a slit that opened into an oral cavity about two inches deep. A membrane along the rear of the cavity separated it from what would be the digestive tract. The tongue seemed to be atrophied into almost a membrane. No teeth were observed. X-rays revealed a maxilla and mandible as well as cranial bone structure. The outer "ear lobes" didn't exist. The auditory orifices present were similar to our middle and inner ear canals. The head contained no hair follicles. The skin seemed grayish in color and seemed mobile when moved.

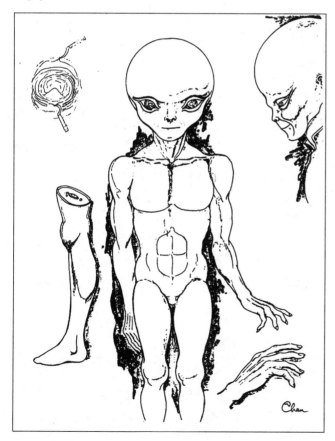

The above observations are from general anatomical observations. I did not autopsy or study the head portion in any great detail since this was not my area of specialty.

NOTE—Your drawing of the head should have the cheek bones removed or a smoother contour. The eyes in the nasal cavity area are not right. The recess and fold is continuous across the forehead. The neck seems too long but the shoulders do not slope as prominently. This may give you this effect. The arms are oversized in length by human standards. There was no thumb. The index finger in your drawing is longer than the middle finger. I don't believe this is correct, but my memory is hazy at this point. The chest area contained what seemed like two atrophied mammary gland nipples. The sexual organs were atrophied. Some other investigators have observed female specimens. I have not had this opportunity. The legs were short and thin. The feet didn't show any toes. The skin covered the foot in such a way that it gave the appearance of wearing a sock. However, X-ray examination showed normal bone structure underneath.[15]

Stringfield, who was convinced of the honesty of the witnesses, was not the only one to be repeatedly confronted by rumors about dead aliens in the underground facilities at Wright-Patterson AFB. Thus Professor Robert Spencer Carr at the University of South Florida heard in 1952 from a colleague about an autopsy performed on an alien body. This colleague, a biophysicist, showed him at that time "the biological section of a big report . . . its edges were torn. It was a carbon copy." Carr was then spokesman of the James Foundation at Fort Myers Beach, Florida.

"He had the official report, although he had not been present at the autopsy. But he had been allowed to see the report and he simply tore the biological section out. He wasn't interested in anything else—for example, aeronautical engineering. To my great sorrow, he didn't take the whole report! That would have been priceless. It no doubt still exists."

Carr learned that the UFO alien bodies were in Hangar 18 at Wright-Patterson. The beings recovered were like humans and quite unlike the ones described by Stringfield's source and, therefore, were perhaps the victims of another crash.

They have Type O blood. They could give you or me a transfusion tonight! The organs were all in the right places. The occupant was in excellent health. The only physical characteristic which produced shock and amazement was when the brain surgeon cut open the skull. . . . Now the head was a little bit large for the body. He was just a little bit megacephalic. But after all, we see megacephalic little people ourselves.

Many little people have heads a little too big. If these occupants were given children's clothing, they could pass undetected on the streets of any large city like New York. Maybe they would be noticed in a small town where everybody knows everybody else, but in New York they wouldn't draw a passing glance.

Well, when they opened the skull they found themselves looking at the brain of a man several hundred years old! Yet he appeared to be a vigorous young man which we, in human terms, would estimate to be between 20 and 30. An Olympic athlete—only small. But the brain! The brain of Charles Darwin is preserved in the British Medical Museum in London. It is the most convoluted brain known (the brains of idiots are smooth). The brain of the alien was more deeply convoluted than any brain they had ever seen and the entire staff bent down to see it and drew back with a shock of amazement. Their life spans must be longer than ours. That's how they can achieve interstellar travel.[16]

James Moseley also, in his book *The Wright Field Story*, mentions "a whole file of crash stories. I had a dozen of them. A professor of anthropology of Columbia University was apparently called to Wright-Patterson

to examine the beings. A scientist from Massachusetts took X-ray pictures of the bodies. . . ." And finally he met a lady who had been a secretary at the Wright-Patterson AFB and claimed to have seen pictures of the bodies in the photo laboratories there.[17]

In one case breaking the oath of secrecy led to an official inquiry. The record of the proceedings were released under the FOIA in 1975:

A/IC CLYDE E. WHEELER, AF 21288827, 6501st Support Squadron, Wright-Patterson Air Force Base, Ohio was interviewed on 31 July 1952 and advised that M. Sgt. LOYAL R. BUNCE, AF 6832919, 575th FMS, Box 17, Selfridge Air Force Base, Mt. Clemens, Mich. told him approximately 10 June 1952 that he (BUNCE) knew about the flying saucers at Wright Patterson Air Force Base. At this time (approximately 10 June 1952), Bunce explained in detail that he knew the people at Wright-Patterson AFB had found some flying saucers and also some bodies inside the saucers. The saucers and the bodies were taken to Wright-Patterson, date unknown. At Wright-Patterson AFB, BUNCE explained officials at the Radiation Laboratory had disassembled the Flying Saucers, which supposedly came from Venus and the bodies inside the Saucers were taken to the Aero-Medical Laboratory,

Secret USAF report from 1952 about possible security leaks: A serviceman told another soldier about "flying saucers and extraterrestrial bodies" at Wright Patterson.

W-P AFB, for further study. The discussion of saucers came as a result of BUNCE'S interest in a project that A/10 WHEELER was working on and also as a result of BUNCE'S knowledge of WHEELER having been at Wright Air Development Center, W-P AFB sometime in January 1952.

A mutual friend of BUNCE, identified as Mr._____, Sugar Bush Road, N. Baltimore, Mich. verified this story to WHEELER as related above by BUNCE (sic), concerning the Flying Saucers. advised (sic) WHEELER that a friend of his, who works at W-P AFB, at the present time, is _____ , West Springfield, Ohio, and his friend had related this information to him (___) concerning the Flying Saucers and bodies at W-P AFB. . . .

According to WHEELER, a civilian employee at Wright Air Development Center, at the Radiation Laboratory, identified only as _____ , is a good friend of _____ and is supposed to have supplied the information to _____ concerning the Flying Saucers being disassembled at the Radiation Laboratory and the information concerning the bodies that were taken to the Aero-Med Laboratory. On 13 July 1952, WHEELER typed a statement, a photostatic copy of which is attached to this letter as Inclosure #3.

Approximately 20 June 1952, WHEELER claims he wrote a complete report concerning the above captioned matter and gave this report to 2nd Lt. GEORGE H. JANCZEWS-KI, who is Intelligence Officer at Headquarters Squadron, 10th Air Force Selfridge, Air Force Base, Michigan. At the time WHEELER gave the report to the Intelligence Officer, he was instructed by the Intelligence Officer to listen to BUNCE, _____ , or anyone else, who had knowledge of Flying Saucers and report back to him (Intelligence Officer) any information he might obtain concerning this subject.

A review of File No. 24-21 at Headquarters, 5th OSI District, reflected a photostatic copy of the statement to the Intelligence Office, Selfridge AFB, mentioned above, and also reflected a letter of transmittal from the Air Provost Marshal,

Selfridge AFB, Michigan, wherein the Provost Marshal stated it is his belief A/IC WHEELER may be attempting to draw attention to himself to further his invention or a possible security leak may exist in the Flying Saucer Program. The letter of transmittal with inclosure (Special File of WHEELER) is attached hereto as Inclosure #4.[18]

The record of Wheeler's statement opens up further perspectives. When he told his friend Sergeant Bunce about Frank Scully's book about UFOs, the latter

explained that he knew there were flying saucers and that they had two of them at Wright Field with the sizes of 27 feet diameter and 99 feet diameter. He said that one craft had a broken porthole in it and that the reason the three passengers were dead was because of a terrific heat field caused by friction had cracked the porthole and had killed all inside. At Wright Field, he claimed the Air Force had closed Project Saucer because it was true fact and would be alarming to the American public and that the Air Force reopened the project under the name of Project Radiation and that the laboratory was situated on the top of a hill in Wright Field. I listened to him on this subject and when I said I doubted the story in some ways he told me it was fact because they had proof. I asked him what sort of proof could he have. He then said backing his statements that there was a man who came from this field by the name of _____ who was transferred to Wright Field and was put on Project Radiation.

He said that they (meaning Mr _____ and someone else I don't know and Sgt Bunts [sic!] thought _____ would no doubt be assigned to that project and they arranged for _____ to tell _____ who works in Maintenance Electronics or a building of that name, so that _____ could transmit back to this radio shop so Mr _____ and Sgt Bunts could know if there were really flying saucers and such.

Then M Sgt Bunts told me about the radio they found in one ship. He said they got into only one ship of the two they have

Senator Barry Goldwater, ex-governor of Arizona.

General Curtis Le May. As commander of the ATIC he denied Senator Goldwater the access to the "Blue Room" of Wright-Patterson AFB.

and that one was the one with the broken porthole. They kept probing through the porthole until they hit something that opened the door of the ship. They found a radio or something similar of which set a signal off at a staggered interval of time somewhat over 15 minutes. They said it evidently set off a signal but which could not be picked up with our modern electrical devices. The case of the radio which was about 5" could not be pierced by diamond drills and was as light in weight as aluminum.

Then came some theories which he told me was such that the answer to this saucer was that a magnetic field was set up ahead of this craft by a turning, spinning disc in the center which created the magnetic field ahead.

I met Mr_____ yesterday and he confirmed Sgt Bunts's story and said a letter of introduction would be given me introducing me to Mr_____ when I get there who would in turn introduce me to _____ .

I realized after meeting Mr_____ that a serious leak in security was present and if the saucer was real as they said it started to scare me at the thought I knew this.[19]

In fact the UFO research at Wright field was so secret that not even a senator or an Air Force reserve general had access to it. Even the base commander was shut out. This was what Senator Barry Goldwater, 1964 presidential candidate of the Republican Party, senator of Virginia and chairman of the Senate Intelligence Committee, one of the most prominent politicians of the United States, learned. Privately he had always been interested in UFOs. Early in the sixties, on the way from Washington, D.C. to California, his plane made a landing at the Wright-Patterson AFB. Goldwater took this opportunity to see his old friend General Curtis LeMay, the base commander. The senator had heard about an installation at the base with the code name "Blue Room," in which UFO artifacts, photographs and alien bodies were kept. So he asked LeMay if he could go to see this room, without knowing that he would thereby touch a very sensitive spot. The general grew angry, and very obviously excited, yelled, "Damn, no! I am not allowed to go, you are not allowed to go, and don't ever ask me again!"[20]

Goldwater has told this story many times openly, including during an interview with CNN talk show host Larry King on October 1, 1994.[21] On 28 March 1975 he wrote to a student, Shlomo Amon of Los Angeles: *"The subject of UFOs is one that has interested me for some long time. About ten or twelve years ago I made an effort to find out what was in the building at Wright Patterson Air Force Base where the information is stored that has been collected by the Air Force, and I was understandably denied this request. It is still classified above Top Secret."*[22]

On October 19 he wrote to researcher Lee Graham,

I have long ago given up acquiring access to the so-called blue room at Wright Patterson, as I have had one long string of denials from chief after chief, so I have given up.

In answer to your questions, one is essentially correct, I don't know of anyone who has access to the blue room, nor am I aware of its contents and I am not aware of anything having been relocated. . . .

To tell you the truth, Mr. Graham, this thing has gotten so highly classified, even though I will admit there is a lot of it that has been released, it is just impossible to get anything on it.[23]

When ufologist William Moore, invoking the Freedom of Information Act, asked the Air Force for details about the "Blue Room," they answered on 15 January 1981, saying that they had found "no documents or information pertaining to a Project Blue Room" in the archives of the Pentagon. "We must assume therefore that all records about the project have been destroyed." Finally one data card was found after all, with the heading "BLUE ROOM (RADAR AREA), WRIGHT-PATTERSON AFB, OHIO, 1955." A photograph—which could not be located—is described as a "slow motion shot of a plane-signal-target on the radar screen." When Moore told his Air Force informant about this he learnt that it referred to the first attempts to build a plane invisible to radar—a forerunner of the Stealth bomber. Thereby they had covered a disc with material from the Roswell wreck which a plane had towed through the air. While the plane could be seen on the radar screen, the disc was invisible. That had been recorded on photographs. Experiments had showed that the extremely light Roswell material, which had a consistency similar to that of Kavlar plastic, with which the Stealth bombers are coated, absorbed or deflected radar signals. In fact the intelligence officer Frank Kaufmann maintains that the Stealth technology was derived directly from the experiments made on the Roswell wreck, from the shape to the coating.[24]

Interestingly, the Wright-Patterson Air Force Base made history only recently. For four years one of the

Two letters from Senator Barry Goldwater regarding the "Blue Room" in Wright-Patterson AFB: "I made an effort to find out what was in the building... and I was understandably denied this request. It is still classified above Top Secret."

The only document mentioning the "Blue Room" of the Wright-Patterson AFB refers to a radar experiment with a UFO fragment.

bloodiest civil wars in history, with over 250,000 dead, had been raging in Bosnia-Herzegovina, in the former Yugoslavia. All attempts by the United Nations to influence the parties concerned failed miserably, the sanctions imposed had no effect. As a last effort the U.S. invited the leaders of the warring elements for a peace conference at Wright-Patterson on 1 November 1995. The choice of venue seemed odd. Why not Washington or Camp David, why the biggest and most guarded military base in the country, the seat of the "Foreign Technology Division" and the Air Technical Intelligence Center of the Air Force—in fact a place to which one would not invite a potential enemy, unless one wanted to impress him. And the "the wonder of Dayton" happened, as the world press called it. Until the last minute the conference seemed destined to be a failure. Suddenly the pressure of the Americans forced the parties to return to the conference table—and on November 21 the presidents Slobodan Milosevic from Serbia, Alija Izetbegovic from Bosnia-Herzegovina and Franjo Tudjman from Croatia paraphrased a peace treaty which was signed in Paris on December 14. What had happened, how was it possible, what was the final means of pressure the U.S. employed? Insiders at least speculate that the last trump played was the "alien card"—that the three presidents had been shown something that made their civil war look very petty.

There are indications that at least until the Nixon era the wrecks and dead aliens had been shown to every U.S. president. And two presidents confided the secret to close friends.

John F. Kennedy was doubtlessly interested in UFOs. Michael Hesemann spoke to William Holden, a steward of the Air Force One, the president's plane, who had accompanied JFK on his historic tour of Germany in summer 1963. On June 27, during the return flight from Wiesbaden to Washington, Holden gave the pres-

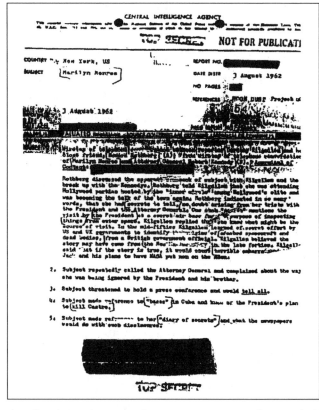

The alleged CIA document of 3 August 1962, according to which Marilyn Monroe knew that President Kennedy visited "a secret air base for the purpose of inspecting things from outer space."

ident an English paper published in Germany, whose title page showed a picture of two UFOs, and asked him what he thought of it. Kennedy retorted by saying, "What do you think of it?" "Now, I am a farmer's boy from Georgia," replied Holden, "and believe that God in His endless wisdom certainly did not create so many stars and galaxies for nothing. I think it is wrong to believe that we are the only ones." "You are right!" nodded the president. Holden had the impression that he knew much more, but did not want to talk about it.[25]

In the spring of 1995 the investigative journalist Milo Periglio presented a document which, should it prove to be authentic—and everything speaks for it—reveals one of the biggest political scandals of the century. For this document, classified as "TOP SECRET," is a report from the CIA, dated 3 August 1963, and deals with a "subject" named Marilyn Monroe, who had threatened to reveal UFO secrets which the president had whispered to her during an intimate hour. Two days later, on August 5, Marilyn Monroe was found dead in Hollywood, allegedly as a result of an overdose of sleeping pills. Was it suicide?[26] The CIA document shows that Monroe had threatened to expose things that would have caused a number of people in Washington much more than a headache:

Source: Wiretap of telephone conversation between reporter Dorothy Kilgallen and her close friend Howard Rothberg (A);

Wiretap of telephone conversation of Marilyn Monroe and Attorney General Robert Kennedy (B).

Content:

1. Rothberg discussed the apparent (unreadable) of the subject (MM) with Kilgallen and the break with the Kennedys. Rothberg told Kilgallen that she was attending Hollywood parties hoasted by the "inner circle" among Hollywood's elite and was becoming the talk of the town again. Rothberg indicated in so many words, that she had secrets to tell, no doubt arising from her trysts with the President and the Attorney General. One such 'secret' mentions the visit by the President at a secret air base for the purpose of inspecting things from outer space. Kilgallen replied that she knew what might be the source of the visit. In the mid-fifties Kilgallen learned of secret efforts by US and UK governments to identify the origin of crashed spacecraft and dead bodies, from a British government official. Kilgallen believed the story may have come from the New Mexico (unreadable) in the late forties. Kilgallen said that if the story is true, it would cause terrible embarrassment to Jack and his

plans to have NASA put man on the moon.

2. Subject (MM) repeatedly called the Attorney General and complained about the way she was being ignored by the President and his brother.

3. Subject (MM) threatened to hold a press conference and would tell all.

4. Subject (MM) made references to "bases" in Cuba and knew of the Presidents plans to kill Castro.

5. Subject (MM) made reference to her "diary of secrets" and what newspapers would do with such disclosures.[27]

Rothberg was a New York antique dealer with a big shop on Third Avenue and a friend of Marilyn Monroe. He knew a number of photographers in New York who had worked with her. Dorothy Kilgallen was one of the best known columnists in the fifties and sixties, who contributed regularly to the leading journals. On May 23, 1955 she reported about the investigation "of the wreck of a mysterious flying object" by American and British "scientists and pilots." *"The source of my information is a British official of Cabinet rank who prefers to remain unidentified. 'We believe, on the basis of our inquiry thus far, that the saucers were staffed by small men— probably under four feet tall. It's frightening, but there is no denying flying saucers come from another planet.'*

"I can report today on a story which is positively spooky, not to mention chilling. British scientists and airmen, after examining the wreckage of one mysterious flying ship, are convinced these strange aerial objects are not optical illusions or Soviet inventions, but are flying saucers which originate on another planet."[28]

Also the reference term "MOON DUST" points to this direction; after all, it was indeed the Air Force code word for "recovered space objects."

The document is signed by James Jesus Angleton, who in 1953 built up the counterespionage department and led it until 1973, when his unscrupulous methods became known and he had to leave the CIA. Some

Jackie Gleason and President Richard Nixon

investigators of the murder of JFK believe that Angleton was one of the persons behind the assassination in Dallas. The fact is that he, together with CIA Director Richard M. Helms, wrote a confidential memorandum in 1966 according to which "the presence of E. Howard Hunt" (CIA agent and later Watergate conspirator) in Dallas on 22 November 1963 "should be kept secret at all costs," as otherwise the name of the CIA "is in danger of being damaged." Was Marilyn Monroe murdered by the CIA because she knew too much and threatened to let the cat out of the bag? Was that the reason and not just the "Bay of Pigs affair" that made Kennedy say that he would "smash the CIA into a thousand pieces"?[29] Ex-CIA pilot John Lear goes so far as to say that JFK was murdered because he wanted to make the UFO secrets public.

In a letter dated 3 March 1990, Lear writes:

It is alleged by some that Kennedy had a meeting with representatives of MJ-12 (formed by President Truman in 1947 by secret presidential executive order, the existence of which has been confirmed by General James H. Doolittle in a telephone conversation with Mrs. William P. Lear, Sr., in April of 1988). During this meeting, which was allegedly tape recorded, Kennedy threatened MJ-12 (Gordon Gray et al) with exposure to the public of the existence of captured flying saucers and alien bodies. There are a number of witnesses who claim knowledge of the incident one of the most credible of whom is Linda Howe (producer of a documentary 'A Strange Harvest' for the CBS affiliate in Denver in 1980) who was told by representatives of MJ-12 in 1983 (while in her capacity of representing HBO in a film deal involving MJ-12) that Kennedy had been eliminated by this group for reasons including the above stated.[30]

President Nixon could not keep the UFO secret to himself either. But he at least took the precaution of choosing a confidant whom nobody would take serious so easily—the comedian Jackie Gleason, who died in 1987. During his lifetime Gleason was an enthusiastic UFO fan. In his house in Florida he had a respectable library with hundreds of books on this theme, had subscribed to a number of UFO magazines, called his residence in Peekskill, New York, "The Mother Ship"—it was even built in the shape of a flying saucer and furnished to suit. His UFO-ria began with two sightings he had experienced in Miami, which had "convinced him that they were certainly not objects made on earth. They were not secret weapons, but they were solid objects. Both times they reflected the sunlight and flew low enough for him to see that there was no normal explanation for them."[31]

In 1983 Gleason's second wife, Beverly, revealed the facts about a very different sort of "sighting" Gleason had had. According to this, one night in 1973 Gleason had come home very late at night, very shaken and pale as death. At first he did not want to speak about what had affected him so deeply, but then he related that he had just come back from a visit to the Homestead Air Force Base in Florida. There, at the behest of his friend President Nixon, he had been shown the bodies of four aliens, in a high security area. They had been only thirty inches tall, with bald heads and pointed ears. They had told him nothing about the circumstances of the finding. The whole visit had been conducted under strict secrecy and he had been asked to swear to keep it secret. She, too, had to swear the same to him, which naturally did not prevent her from informing the press after she was divorced from him. But whenever anyone asked Gleason about this incident, he avoided answering. Until his death he never confirmed or denied the story, although he had enough opportunities to do so.[32]

But after his death a young musician, Larry Warren, came out of Southington, Connecticut, and claimed that Gleason had told him all about the visit to the Homestead Base. As an Air Force security guard, Warren had seen a UFO landing in the east of England, near his base at Bentwaters. This incident, which happened in December 1980, drew worldwide attention, and after CNN, HBO and other American TV channels took up the subject, the U.S. Air Force released the report of the Deputy Base Commander Lieutenant Colonel Charles Halt, which confirmed the occurrence. Gleason contacted one of the channels and invited Warren for a personal chat. He had asked Warren questions about the affair interminably, not infrequently sipping from a glass of whiskey. Then he had said to Warren, "I want to tell you something, which in any case will come out one day: We have got them." "Got what?" asked Warren. "The extraterrestrials," answered Gleason and then told his story.

"It was back when Nixon was in office that something truly amazing happened to me," Gleason explained.

We were close golfing buddies and had been out on the golf course all day when somewhere around the 15th hole, the subject of UFOs came up. Not many people know this, but the President shares my interest in this matter and has a large collection of books in his home on UFOs just like I do. For some reason, however, he never really took me into his confidence about what he personally knew to be true . . . one of the reason being that he was usually surrounded by so many aides and advisers.

Later that night, matters changed radically. Richard Nixon showed up at my house around midnight. He was all alone for a change. There were no secret service agents with him or anyone else. I said, "Mr. President, what are you doing here?" and he said he wanted to take me someplace and show me something.

I got into the President's private car and we sped off into the darkness. Our destination, I found on arrival there, was Homestead Air Force Base.

I remember we got to the gate and this young MP came up to the car to look to see inside and his jaw seemed to drop a foot when he saw who was behind the wheel. He just sort of pointed and we headed off.

Warren says that later Gleason found out that the intelligence community was going absolutely crazy trying to find out where Nixon was. "We drove to the very far end of the base in a segregated area, finally stopped near a well guarded building. The security police saw us coming and just sort of moved back as we passed them and entered the structure.

"There were a number of labs we passed through first before we entered a section where Nixon pointed out what he said was the wreckage from a flying saucer, enclosed in several large cases." Gleason noted his initial reaction was that this was all a joke brought on by their earlier conversation on the golf course. But it wasn't!

"Next, we went into an inner chamber and there were six or

eight of what looked like glass-topped Coke freezers. Inside them were the mangled remains of what I took to be children. Then, upon closer examination, I saw that some of the other figures looked quite old. Most of them were terribly mangled as if they had been in an accident."

According to Larry Warren's testimony (regarding his lengthy conversation with Gleason), the comedian said, *"All-in-all it was a very pathetic sight. At one point, the President had tears in his eyes and finally I realized that this was not his way of trying to be humorous."*

Warren tried to pin Gleason down for additional information as to how the military had managed to obtain the wreckage and alien corpses. But Jackie could only shake his head and say he didn't know for sure, since President Nixon didn't really fill him in on too many of the details surrounding this very weird display. Gleason further said, ". . . they were very small—no more than three feet tall. Had grayish-colored skin and slanted eyes that were very deeply set. I don't remember whether they had three or four fingers on each hand, but they definitely were not human."

For the next three weeks the world-famous entertainer could not sleep or eat. He was apparently suffering from shock. He could not understand why the government did not tell the people the truth about the UFOs and the alien visitors. He resorted to drinking heavily, until he was able to digest the matter. Warren is convinced that the comedian had told him the truth: *"You could tell that he was sincere. . . . I could tell that he wanted to get the matter off his chest, and this is why he was telling me all of this. . . . Jackie felt just like I do that the government needs to come clean and tell us all it knows about space visitors. It is time they stopped lying to the public. . . ."*[33]

[1]Weiner, Tim, *Blank Check—The Pentagon's Black Budget*, New York, 1990.

[2]Andrews, Christopher, *For the President's Eyes Only*, New York, 1995.

[3]Operation Majestic 12: Briefing for President Elect Dwight D. Eisenhower, 18 November 1952.

[4]Kofsky, Frank: *Harry S. Truman and the War Scare of 1948*, New York, 1995.

[5]*New York Times*, 7 April 1948.

[6]Kofsky, 1995.

[7]*Aviation Week*, 21 June 1948.

[8]Randle, Kevin, *Roswell UFO Crash Update*, New Brunswick, NJ, 1995.

[9]Beckley, Timothy Green, *MJ-12 and the Riddle of Hangar 18*, New Brunswick, NJ, 1989.

[10]Ibid.

[11]Stringfield, Leonard, *The UFO Crash/Retrieval Syndrome*, Seguin, TX 1980.

[12]Crain, T. Scott, "Hacker's UFO Files on 'Dateline,'" in: *UFO Magazine*, vol. 9, no. 3, Sunland, CA, 1994.

[13]Stringfield, Leonard, *UFO Crash/Retrievals: Amassing the Evidence*, Cincinnati, OH, 1982.

[14]Ibid.

[15]Ibid.

[16]Beckley,]989.

[17]Moseley, James, *The Wright Field Story*, Clarksburg, 1971.

[18]Gunn, Lieutenant Colonel James H., Report to the Commanding Officer of ATIC, Wright Patterson AFB, Ohio, 12 August 1952.

[19]Headquarters Tenth Air Force, Office of the Air Provost Marshal. Selfridge AFB, Michigan: Transfer of Special File (WHEELER, Clyde E.), 10 July 1952.

[20]Berlitz, Charles and William Moore, *The Roswell Incident*, New York, 1980.

[21]"Larry King Live in Area 51," TNT, 1 October 1994.

[22]Letter by Barry Goldwater to Shlomo Arnon, 28 March 1975.

[23]Letter by Barry Goldwater to Lee Graham, 19 October 1981.

[24]Cameron, Grant and T. Scott Crain, *UFOs, MJ-12 and the*

Government, Seguin, TX, 1991.

[25]Personal Interview with William Holden, 2 December 1995.

[26]Ecker, Vickie, "UFOs Linked to 'Marilyn-Conspiracy,'" in: *UFO-Magazine,* vol. 10, no. 2, Sunland, CA, 1995.

[27]*CIA-Report of New Yorker Bureaus,* Subject: Marilyn Monroe, 3 August 1962.

[28]*Los Angeles Examiner,* 23 May 1955.

[29]Lane, Mark, *Plausible Denial,* London, 1992.

[30]Letter by John Lear to Robert Dorff Auctioneers, 3 March 1990.

[31]Beckley, Timothy Green, *UFOs among the Stars,* New Brunswick, NJ, 1992.

[32]Gleason, Beverly, "Jackie Gleason Saw Bodies of Space Aliens at Air Force Base," in: *National Enquirer,* 16 August 1983.

[33]Beckley, 1992.

10.

Dreamland

Las Vegas, 25 June 1993. The man who sat opposite me did not give the slightest impression that he wanted to tell me a wild and unfounded tale. His eyes were clear and attentive, his voice steady, his language precise and laconic, devoid of ornamentation. His whole personality was one of youthful frankness. Robert Lazar was a rational, young scientist, through and through one of the "all American boys" whose favorite subject in high school is mathematics or

Bob Lazars "jet car" which drew Ed Teller's attention on him.

The young nuclear physicist Robert Lazar claims he investigated crashed UFOs in Area 51/S4 in 1988/89.

physics and who, sooner or later, end up in space technology or software development. Only the "skull and crossbones" flying on a mast in front of his house betrayed that there was something else in him too, something anarchistic—a freethinker, reluctant to stick to conventions. And in front of the garage there stood the "jet car," the product of Lazar's inventive genius,

with which, in fact, it all started.

"LA Man Joins the Jet Set—at 200 Miles Per Hour," announced the *Los Alamos Monitor* on 28 June 1982 on the front page.[1] The report was about "a young physicist of the Los Alamos Meson Physical Laboratory, Robert Lazar (23), who had constructed a jet-propelled automobile in his spare time." Now Los Alamos, called "the mountain" by insiders, is a uniquely large colony of scientists. Only the best of the best find employment in the national laboratories there, established originally for the development of the atom bomb. The strict secrecy of the Manhattan Project led to the remote nest in the middle of the mountains of New Mexico, approachable by only one road or by air, to becoming the inner sanctum of science. Even now top secret projects are carried out in Los Alamos, not only military but also civil, such

Major Marcel with the false "Wreckage parts" in Gen. Ramey's office, reenacted in the "Roswell" TV film.

Marcel and Cavitt in the debris field, reenacted in "Roswell" TV film.

The I-beams and wreckage re-created according to eyewitness accounts. (A. Miller Johnson)

The Roswell story began on the Foster Ranch near Corona, NM when Rancher Mac Brazel discovered debris of unknown origin on 14 June or 5 July.

The barn next to the Ranch house where some of the debris was stored overnight.

Mac Brazel's Ranch house.

The Ranch house of Floyd and Loretta Proctor. They were the first Brazel showed the debris.

Roswell Sheriff's office and court house. Here Mac Brazel visited Sheriff Wilcox, and showed him the debris.

Roswell Army Air Field today - the "Roswell Industrial Air Center."

The crash site, 35 miles north of Roswell, on the land of Rancher Hub Corn.

Close up of the crash site.

The Ballard Funeral Home in Roswell: Here Mortician Glenn Dennis received two calls from the base, requesting children's coffins and asking how to conserve corpses without changing the body chemistry.

The remaining part of the RAAF base hospital. According to Glenn Dennis an autopsy of an Extraterrestrial took place here on July 7th, 1947.

Hangar 84 of the RAAF. Here the wreckage was loaded; the dead Extraterrestrials were laid out.

Sgt. Thomas Gonzales, witness of the recovery, made wood carvings representing the four dead Extraterrestrials he saw.

Glenn Denis

Loretta Proctor

Frank Kaufmann

The "Roswell International UFO Museum and Research Center."

The military reaches the crash site 35 miles north of Roswell and finds the archaeological team under Prof. Holden. Drawing by Agnes Schejok

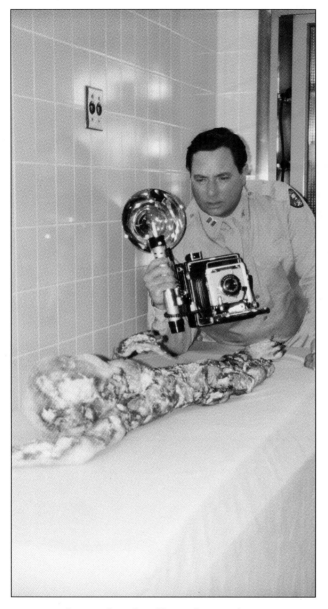

The "Roswell"-TV Series-dummy in the "Roswell UFO Museum."

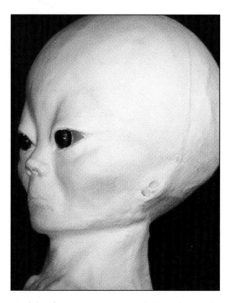

U.S. Army photographer, played by producer Raul Davies, in scene from the "Roswell" TV production.

Model of an Extraterrestrial based on the descriptions of "Abductee" Betty Hill. Note the resemblance to the "Santilli Alien."

The UFO crash scenario of the "UFO Enigma Museum" in Roswell.

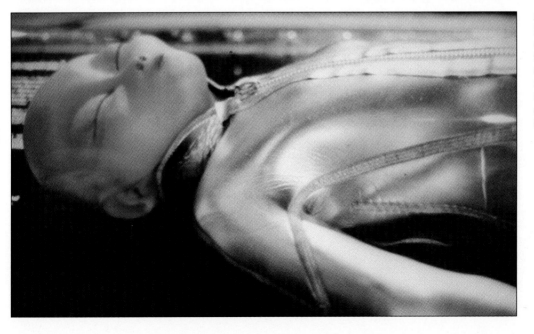

Model of one of the Roswell-Aliens on an official UFO Exhibition in the World Expo Grounds of Montreal, Canada, made by the artist Linda Corriveau, allegedly from original photos. (photo: Christian Page)

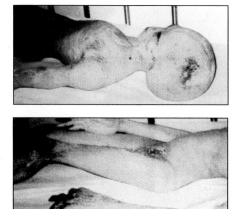

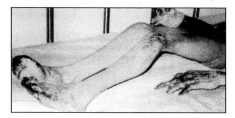

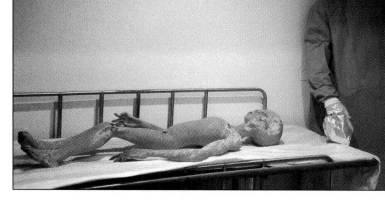

In Fall 1995 these pictures circulated in the East Asian press and were supposed to show either the Roswell alien or an alien body retrieved by the Japanese government. In september 1996 "Penthouse" Magazine published the same pictures. Actually they show the dummy made for the "Showtime"-Series "Roswell" as it is now exhibited in the "Roswell UFO Museum".

Photograph of a UFO taken by Gray Shultz on 28 February 1990 over Area 51.

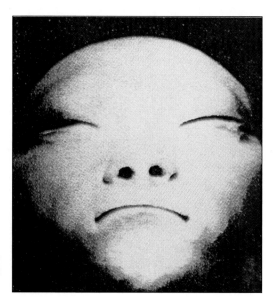

Allegedly fake photo of dead extraterrestrial in custody of the U.S. Air Force

The Groom Lake Base in Area 51. (Photo: John Lear)

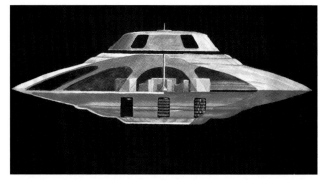

The "sportsmodel" craft Bob Lazar inspected.

Area S-4 according to Bob Lazar. (Drawing by J.Nichols)

Inside the Hangar. Drawing by Agnes Schejok, based on Derek Henessys description.

The subterranean hangars, drawn by Agnes Schejok based on Derek Henessy's description.

The metal cylinders with six alien bodies floating in a murky solution of formaldehyde in level 2, drawn by Agnes Schejok based on the description by Derek Henessy.

The British promoter Ray Santilli with one of the 16 mm reels he bought from the cameraman who claimed he filmed the alien autopsy.

The French magazine "vsd" was the first who published images from the film on 22 June 1995.

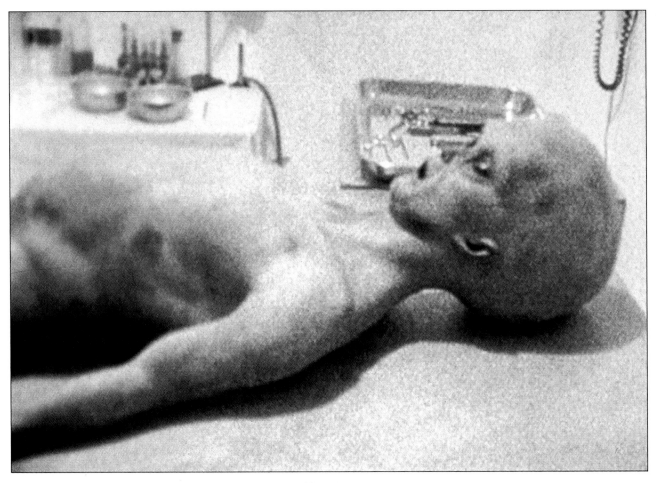

A scene from the Autopsy Footage: The entity on the operation table.

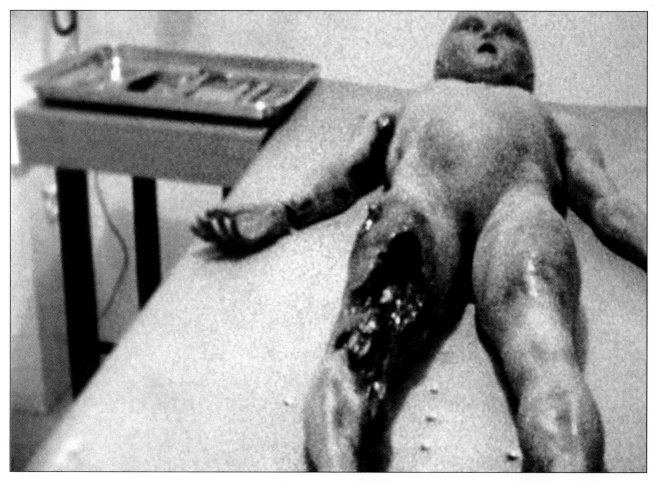

The entity in front view: The right hand is detached, the right leg has a severe burn wound, the left thigh contusions and indications of a fracture.

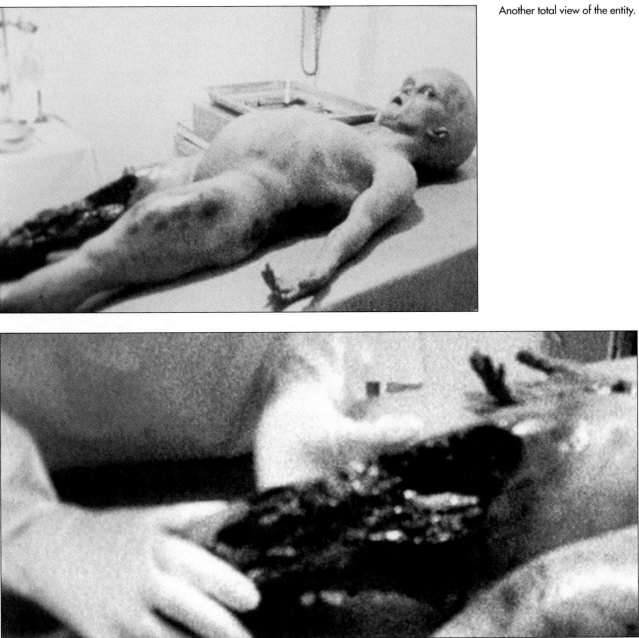

Another total view of the entity.

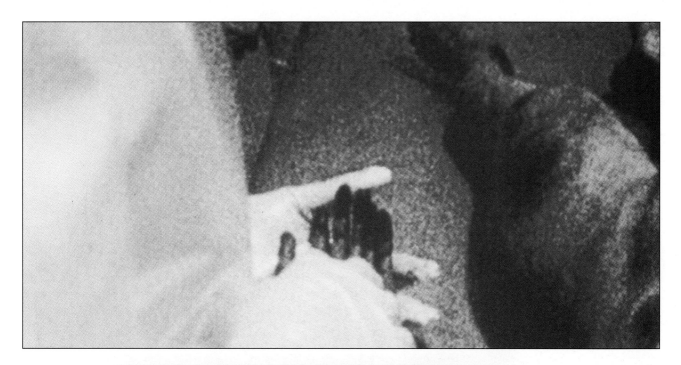

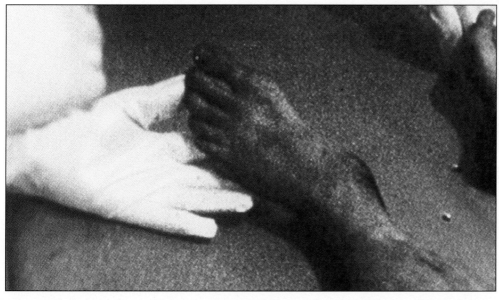

The feet of the entity have six toes, the hands six fingers.

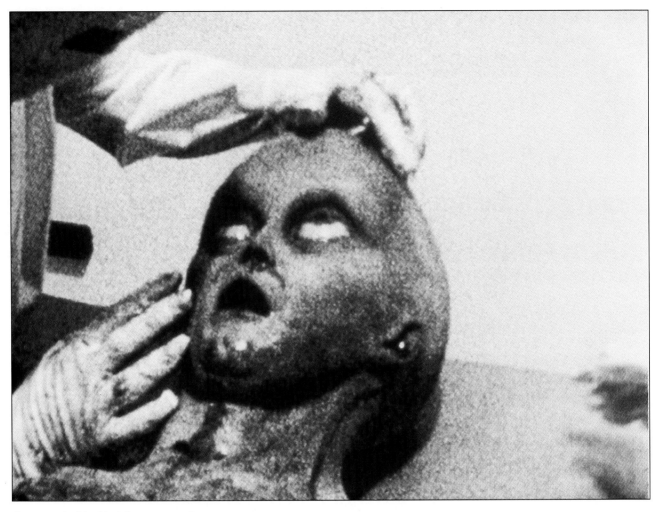

The removal of the black lenses or membranes.

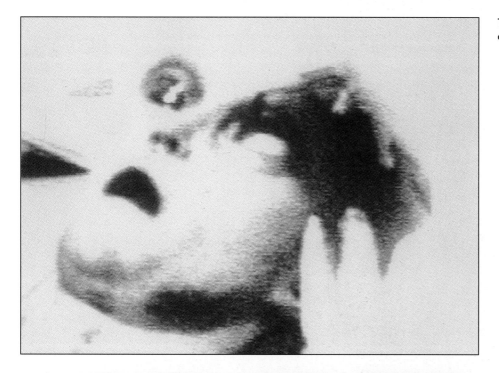

The head of the entity after removal of the membranes.

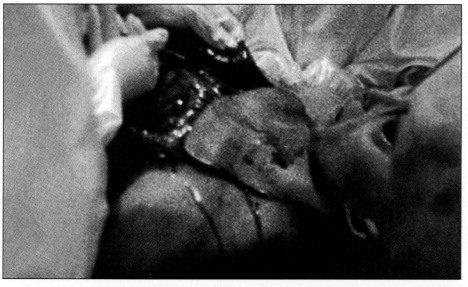

The opening of the chest.

The organs are being exposed.

Opening of the skull with a bone saw.

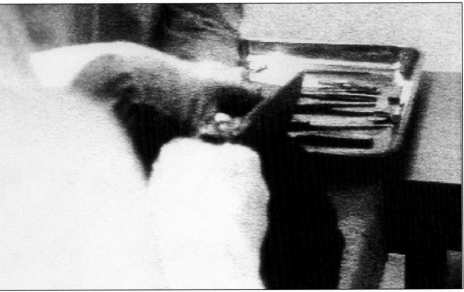

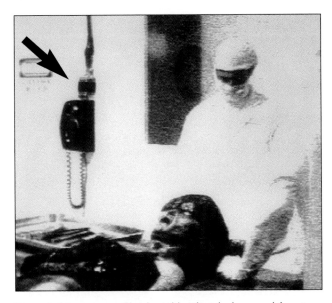

The end of the autopsy: Clearly visible: The telephone and the microphone (hanging from the ceiling), behind the window Prof. Dr. Detlev Bronk.

1946 Dial Wall Telephone

Plastic housings were standard after the war and black was still the standard color. This streamlined wall set changed little over the following thirty years, but improved steadily as plastics became tougher and lighter with molded-in colors.
Western Electric

The same type of telephone is exhibited in the telephone museum of the Bell company in Atlanta, Georgia. It's from 1946 (photo: Terry Blanton) See plaque to the left.

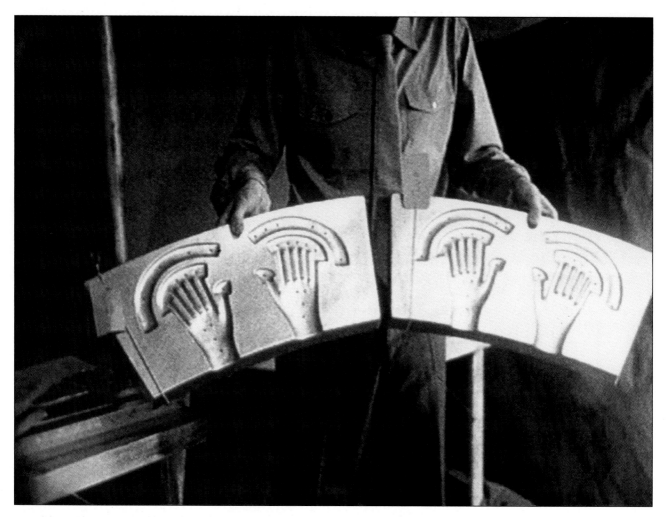

Two of the "boxes" the entities hold in their hands. According to a government scientist they are "biofeedback computers" used to control the craft and store information.

The debris on the Santilli footage: The two I-Beams with "protophoenician" inscriptions. They were deciphered by Michael Hesemann and read "DIREQH ELE" and "OSNI" (translation in chapter 15).

Wreckage from the Santilli film: T-beam with proto-Phoenician inscription.

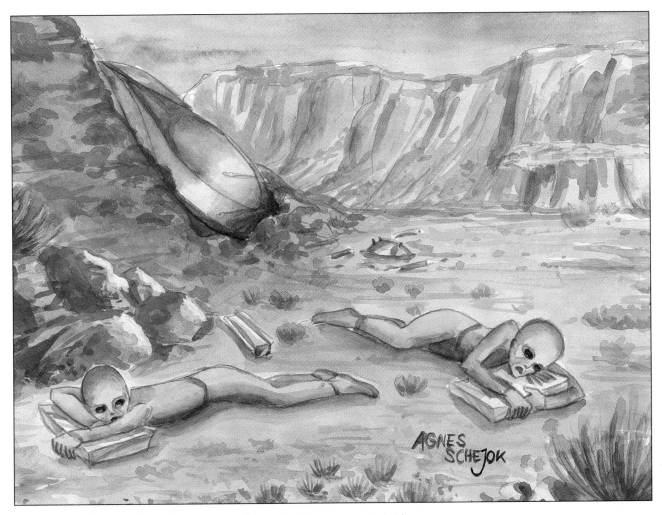

Crash scene and recovery, drawn by Agnes Schejok based on the cameraman's sketches.

Salvage, drawn by Agnes Schejok, according to descriptions by the cameraman.

Robert Morningsky claims his grandfather retrieved a "star elder" out of a crashed UFO.

Precolumbian gold artefacts from the gold museum of Cuenca, Ecuador. The inscription resembles the "Santilli hieroglyphs".

The "dry lake" 8 miles southwest of Socorro, NM. On its northern shore, according to the cameraman, a flying disc crashed on May 31st, 1947.

Close ups of the cliff. Clearly visible is an 60 feet wide area of chiseled off rock. Obviously, someone tried to remove traces. In a follow up investigation, journalist Steve Kaiser found heat marks on the rock.

Members of UFO-AZ team using metal detectors to look for traces.

The Acoma "Sky Pueblo" west of Abequerque. On 31 May 1947, Acoma and Laguna Indians watched the crash of a fireball in the direction of Socorro.

Toth or Tehuti, the "God" (neter=watcher) ho teached the ancient Egyptian how to write hieroglyphs.

UFO researcher Derrel Sims with his "Roswell fragment."

"Roswell fragment."

"Roswell fragment."

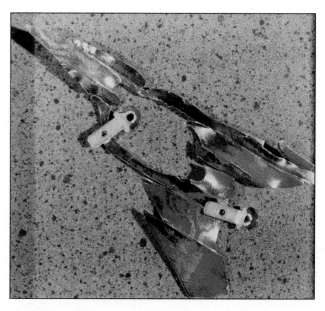

Has the same characteristics as the debris described by the eye witnesses: Derrel Sims "Roswell fragment."

as the Human Genome Project, whose aim is to decipher the structure of the human gene. But that June 28 was a special day even for the scientists of "the Mountain," top class as they were, for a lecture by one of America's most eminent scientific personages had been announced. He was Professor Edward Teller, "father of the hydrogen bomb," initiator of the SDI project and scientific adviser to the president, a man who, under President Reagan, played a role similar to that played by Dr. Vannevar Bush under President Truman.

Lazar naturally attended Teller's lecture. In fact he arrived there too early and was pleasantly surprised to see the great physicist outside the auditorium, sitting on a low brick wall, reading the front page of the *Los Alamos Monitor*. This encouraged Lazar to speak to the professor. So he went up to him and quite informally said, "Hi! I'm the person you are reading about!" "That's interesting," replied Teller and that started off a pleasant chat between them. From the beginning they took a liking to each other. They both had the same Hungarian origin and Teller was favorably impressed by the uncomplicated, unconventional spontaneity and intelligence of the young fellow scientist. "Here is my card," he said, in parting from Lazar, "if I can do anything for you, if you are looking for a new job, call me."

Six years later Lazar followed this friendly suggestion. He had been through a lot in the meantime: had got married, had made himself professionally independent and moved to Las Vegas. There he had lost his wife under tragic circumstances, had remarried, gone bankrupt—in short, suffered all the trials and tribulations of life. Finally he began to yearn for the ordered and secure life of a scientist. And so one day in 1988 he wrote down his curriculum vitae and sent it off to various laboratories as well as to Professor Teller, with a letter reminding him of their meeting at Los Alamos. Two

The EG&G-Building at Las Vegas McCarran Airport. Here Lazars first briefing took place before he started to work at Area 51.

weeks later he received a call from Teller, who said, "Bob, I can't employ you, for I'm no longer active and am only working as chief consultant. But I have something for you in Las Vegas. Contact Mr. X__ at the EG&G."

Lazar did not have to do that, for only a few minutes after his conversation with Teller, the telephone rang again. It was a call from EG&G, inviting him to an interview for a post in "a special project." EG&G (Edgerton, Germeshausen & Grier) has over 30,000 employees and over 150 establishments all over the world. As a firm authorized by the U.S. Government, EG&G carries out important research programs for the U.S. Space Department NASA, the Atomic Energy Commission (AEC, now Department of Energy) and the Defense Department. EG&G's Division of Special Projects, at which Lazar was to present himself, is more or less responsible for all scientific projects at the Nevada Test Range, the largest military testing grounds in the world.

The office Lazar visited was in the EG&G Building at the McCarran Airport of Las Vegas. Bob learnt soon that his potential employer had nothing to do with EG&G and was merely using its premises for the interview. *"After a short time they said I was basically overqualified for the position but they may have something else in the future. . . . I don't remember how much time elapsed after that, but shortly thereafter they asked me to come down for another interview. They said this was involving . . . a field propulsion system."*[2]

Lazar got back his "Q" security level clearance, which he had once held while working at Los Alamos but had been suspended when he left. At the same time a more intensive investigation of his background, his contacts, his personal situation, hobbies and other interests was carried out, to establish whether he had a *"stable, solid and healthy personality."* Finally he received a security clearance which was thirty-eight levels higher than the "Q"—or "top secret"—rating, although he had always thought that "Q" was the highest clearance level for civilians. He was informed that beyond "Q" there were a multitude of levels, called "compartments," to limit the access to particularly delicate information to those who "need to know" and for which a "special access permit" was required. This system was introduced during the Second World War and is known today as SCI (Special Compartmentalized Information). Or, as former CIA director Admiral Sransfield Turner put it, *"An individual should know only those details of a secret operation, with which he has directly to deal. Others should know only their parts. In this manner the danger of the entire operation being exposed through a leak will be reduced. . . . Only a few people at the very top know all components of the operation."*[3]

While the security investigations were going on, Lazar was to be initiated into the work at the Nevada Test Range. He was instructed over the telephone to report at the McCarran Airport, from where he and other base employees were flown in a Boeing 737 belonging to EG&G to the Groom Lake Airfield in Area 51, in the heart of the testing grounds. There he waited, along with the others, in a cafeteria until they were picked up by a bus with its windows painted black, and taken over a desert road some fifteen miles south, to the bank of the dried-up Papoose Lake. What Lazar noticed as soon as he got out of the bus was a row of big hangars, which were built—obviously to camouflage them—into the slopes of the Papoose Mountain, with doors slanting at an angle of sixty degrees and painted in the color of sand. "From the air, in satellite photographs, they were to look like slopes of the mountain," said Lazar. The hangars were all connected with one another. Somehow he had the feeling that he was in the midst of a James Bond film.

What struck Bob particularly was the heavy presence of security guards. He could count only twenty-two scientists in white coats, but over seventy soldiers, who left no doubt about who had the say there. *"It was very militarylike, it was certainly not a scientific atmosphere. Very high security, everywhere you walked you had to have an armed escort, even into the bathroom. All doors lock and open with your badge, and it was a very oppressive atmosphere."* Lazar's identity badge was white, with a light blue and a dark blue diagonal stripe at the upper left corner. On the right side it bore the letters MAJ, below that were his picture and name, the number of his contract with the Department of Energy, E-67223MAJ, the inscription "Department of Naval Intelligence," and right at the bottom a row of codes for the areas and projects, of which "S-4" was highlighted. The badges of his colleagues were similar, except that his boss, Dennis Mariani, had a full "MAJESTIC" on his. Lazar learned later that "Majestic" was the code name of the project he was working for and that he and his companions were employees of the Naval Intelligence Department.

On his first day of work, Lazar was taken to an office near a hangar and given some 120 blue files containing briefing documents. "Read them and you'll know what it's all about," was Mariani's instruction. Lazar sat down to read and only then noticed a poster hanging on the wall: it showed a metallic disc hovering above the Papoose Lake, and below it were the words "They are here!"

The reports in the files dealt with UFOs and extraterrestrials. They were rather superficial and served apparently only to give the personnel an overall background, which would automatically answer the questions they were likely to put. *"I was shocked by their contents,"* Lazar said to me, *"I just couldn't believe what was written there. But I was fascinated."*[4]

The reports made it clear beyond all doubts that the U.S. was in "possession of a number of extraterrestrial spacecraft." They described autopsies, showed photographs of extraterrestrial beings—mostly twenty-five to fifty pounds "light," with big, bald heads—and of details of their inner organs, with lists giving their weights and density. One of the papers mentioned a contact during which an exchange of information between the ETs and the scientists took place and also that for a period ET "guests" had worked in an isolated laboratory. These came, according to another report, from "Reticulum 4," the fourth planet of the Zeta-Reticulum system. Apparently they had been controlling the evolution of the human race for thousands of years and had manipulated the genes of Homo sapiens about sixty-five times so far, mostly during the last ten thousand years, to correct its evolution.

A further report was compiled from the point of view of the ETs and dealt with the history of the human race. The earth was designated as "Sol 3" and instead of the nomenclature "human beings" they spoke of "containers"—of what or wherefore was not mentioned. Was the human being a container for the soul, or for genetic information, or for consciousness? . . . *"In any case they spoke of preserving the container and of how unique and valuable it was,"* recalled Lazar.[5] But he could make

nothing of it, being neither a biologist nor anthropologist nor theologian. So he felt relieved when the reports finally went on to deal with the propulsion techniques of the spacecraft and the possibilities of interstellar travel. Bob was at last in his element.

"The propulsion system is an amazing setup," explained Lazar to me, trying to use simple language:

There's two parts, gravity amplifiers and the reactor that supplies the power. The reactor itself is a total-annihilation reactor, fueled by antimatter. Total annihilation is essentially the most efficient nuclear reaction that takes place of the three: fission, fusion and annihilation. It uses the super heavy element, Element 115, as it would appear on the periodic chart. Nobody has synthesized it on earth, it's my opinion that it occurs naturally in certain star systems. This element is bombarded in an extremely small accelerator. The element, under bombardment, undergoes immediate fission and produces antimatter particles. These interact with the gaseous matter target and by means of a one-hundred percent efficient thermoelectric device gets converted into electricity. Now hundred percent efficiency is in any electrical device impossible, even the first law of thermodynamics says it's basically impossible, there has to be waste heat and things of that sort. So that is another amazing form of technology. There's a tremendous amount of power the system generates and it operates the amplifiers and also as a byproduct of Element 115 undergoing bombardment, it produces very interesting phenomena, like the Gravity A wave as it is called. Now this gravity A wave travels almost the same way as microwaves travel. This is essentially applied to the gravity amplifiers and by means of the electricity also provided by the reactor it is amplified and focused. The amplified signal is shifted slightly out of phase and can repel or attract a gravitational body. So the craft can take off on one gravity amplifier—there are three on this craft. When using one amplifier it is essentially pushing away from the earth—it's known as Omacron configuration.

For space travel the vessel would rotate upon its side, face the three gravity amplifiers at the target—they'll focus down on a single point some tremendous distance away and the amplifiers and associated reactor will go into full power. And they essentially pull the fabric of space, distort space and time towards the craft so that they can traverse a tremendous amount of distance in virtually no time at all. They are not traveling in linear fashion; they are essentially bending space . . . the fabric of space and gravity and time are all interlaced and when you start distorting gravity, you distort space and time with it. These are not just theories, we've known about them, we've just found no way of controlling them and apparently this civilization has found out how.[6]

As a matter of fact, leading scientists are of the opinion that interstellar flight is possible by the artificial distortion of the space-time continuum. Einstein had already postulated the idea that gravitation influences the time in space. In 1979 NASA physicist Alan Holt published a study about "field-resonance propulsion." In that study he discussed various hypotheses, including those which considered the possibility of neutralizing the earth's gravity by generating an electromagnetic pattern, similar to that of a gravitational field. *"You would select an energy configuration that has a resonance with the location you wanted to go and travel through a type of hyperspace or a higher dimensional space space."* Interestingly enough he considers the disc shape as ideal for a spacecraft using this kind of drive: *"I think the shape of the spaceship can be quite important. Elliptical or saucer shapes would be the shapes I would start out with. I hate to use these words because of the connotations. But what you are trying to do with the artificial energy pattern, is overwhelm the natural mass-energy pattern and exist in the material of the spacecraft itself. So a saucer is probably best. I don't think it is an accident that the UFO phenomena we see are, by and large, saucer-shaped."*[7]

That Holt is not alone in having this opinion is shown by a report in the *Sunday Times* of 13 August 1995: "Astronomers predict travel faster than light." The reason for this headline on the front page of that well-known newspaper was the publication of a study by Professor Ian Crawford, astronomer at the University College, London, through the Royal Astronomical Society, in which he prophesied space travel at speeds higher than that of light for the coming millennium. The *Sunday Times* emphasized that a number of independent and highly respected members of the "scientific community" supported Crawford's hypothesis. It added that the Interstellar Propulsion Society was exclusively engaged in finding means to open the way to the foreign worlds for our astronauts. One of the hypotheses presented by Crawford comes from Professor Miguel Alcubierre of the University of Wales and was originally published in the *Journal of Classical and Quantum-gravitation*. It describes a drive that distorts space by compressing it ahead of the space vessel and expanding it behind it. That could, according to Alcubierre, effectively fold space and make a kind of "warp flight" possible, such as what fans of the science fiction series *Star Trek* have been familiar with for a long time now.[8]

Regarding this *Star Trek* concept, the renowned U.S. physicist Lawrence M. Krauss said that it was quite possible theoretically, seen from the present stand of knowledge in physics, since it was based on the collision between matter and antimatter. "When these collide, they release a tremendous amount of energy in the form of radiation. That could accelerate a spaceship almost to the speed of light." "And speeds higher than that of light?" "Einstein's theory of relativity permits in principle all speeds. . . . one must compress the space-time ahead of the Enterprise and expand it at the stern." What lies behind the Enterprise shoots off into the distance and the space ahead of it races towards it, so that the vessel remains in its space bubble and does not have to move to reach the destination. The only problem is, "to distort the space-time sufficiently the Enterprise must carry a mass equal to that of a thousand suns or build up an equivalent gravitational field."[9] Which brings us back to Bob Lazar, for he says that in the introductory papers he had read the alien spacecraft covered interstellar distances by distorting space-time. It was only during his second visit to area S-4, however, that it became clear to Lazar—and dramatically so—that what he had read in the reports about the spacecraft was only too true.

"I entered the hangar and there it was," Lazar told me, "it was the same ship I had seen on the poster. My first thought was: That explains all the UFO sightings, they are only secret military planes that we are working on. I still couldn't believe what I had read in the reports." The disc was about forty feet wide and about fifteen feet high and stood flat on the ground, without any signs of there being landing gear. Lazar was only led past the vessel to his office, with the injunction not to look at it, which, of course, was an impossibility. "It looked as if it was made in one piece, absolutely smooth, without rivets or screws. Only on the top there was a little cabin, with something that looked like a hatch."

During his next visits he was allowed to have a closer look at the vessel. "It became finally clear to me that it was of extraterrestrial origin. It was a funny feeling, hard to describe." It was his job, as part of Project Galileo, to investigate the construction and operation of its propulsion system "back-engineering," as Lazar put it. "Now, that would not have been necessary if the craft had been built in the U.S. I don't know how long my colleagues had already been doing this—one year or ten years? They had made some progress, but it was very, very modest." In the course of his work Lazar was allowed to enter the craft, to see its "machinery space." "It's all very plain, it's all one solid color, a gray as pewter color, of the same color as the outside of the craft; there are no sharp corners anywhere: the devices, the seats, the amplifier housing, everything had rounded corners on it, almost as if it was all fashioned out of wax and then slightly melted. Everything is curved, even where the ceiling meets the floor. Very, very plain, very wide open, very practical use of space. There are three levels, the lowest houses three amplifiers that swing. . . . the center level is the one where you enter the craft, where the seats (too small for human beings) and the flight controls are. The top level is a small area. I was not allowed to enter or see what was there."

This disc, which Lazar called the "sports model" owing to its slick form, was only one of nine spacecraft which were kept at S-4, as he found out when all hangar doors were open on a certain occasion. "There they stood, all of them. The hangars were all interconnected, and each one harbored such disc. There were nine in all. And each one was different. Three had been taken apart for investigation, one was damaged, one had crashed only in August 1981, and the rest were intact." The damaged disc stood tilted and had a big hole in the underside, as if it had been shot down. "To keep track of them I gave them simple names: 'the hat,' 'the cake tin,' 'the sports model'—this one looked freshly polished and like what I thought a newly built space vessel should look like." And finally he learned that the Naval Intelligence personnel had succeeded in making regular test flights with the recovered spaceships. "We already knew more or less how they worked, but are not in a position to build such craft. Our job was to evaluate them technically. The test flights are only short, controlled, low altitude flights. . . . They have a prized possession here and so they are not going to risk taking this to a point where they can potentially lose it. If a disc is taken up too high it may break through the earth's gravity and be lost," explained Lazar. After a short pause he added, "I witnessed a number of test flights and was once only a hundred feet away from the craft."

During another interview he described in detail this experience, which was probably the most stirring one of his life:

It was dusk. I came out of the door near the hangar and saw the disc outside. I don't know whether it had been "flown" or rolled out. It stood on the ground. There was a man standing near it with a scanner. I was told to stand next to him but not to go any nearer. He seemed to communicate with the disc over the radio. . . . The bottom of the disc began to glow with a bluish color, there was a hissing sound such as one hears when very high voltage current passes around a sphere. It occurred to me that the reason for having no sharp corners was to maintain the voltage. . . . Silently—except for the hissing—the vessel lifted off the ground, flew a little bit, and came down again some thirty feet away. She tilted to the left, then to the right, and then settled down. It sounds unimportant, meaningless, but it was unbelievably impressive, just amazing. It was magic![10]

The same evening, back in Las Vegas, Lazar just had to talk to someone about his extraordinary experience. His marriage was breaking up, he was suffering from the stress caused by being continually watched and by the restricting military atmosphere of the base. Some time ago, his friend Gene Huff, a real estate agent, had introduced him to the CIA pilot John Lear. Lear had been hunting for information about UFOs for many years and when he learned that Lazar was working at Los Alamos, he had spoken of the rumors about dead ETs found near Roswell and of one survivor, who was supposed to have lived in a highly secret laboratory with the code name YY-2 until his death in 1952. At that time, Lazar, rational scientist that he was, had held the

Ex-CIA pilot John Lear

rumors to be nonsense. But now he knew: Lear was right. The U.S. was, in fact, in possession of crashed spaceships and dead ETs.

"It was 6 December 1988 when Bob visited me," John Lear told me when I interviewed him at his villa on Hollywood Avenue above Las Vegas on his fiftieth birthday, 6 December 1992. "I was sitting here writing checks and he sat right on that seat and I said, 'What's goin' on, Bob?' and he said, 'I saw a disc today.' I said—I was so startled I thought I didn't hear him right—'What?' And he said, 'I saw a disc today.' 'Theirs or ours?' He said, 'Theirs.' 'You went to the test site?' I asked. He replied, 'Yes, I have just come back, it's the first time that I went up there.' 'My God!' I said, 'what are you doing here? Don't jeopardize your security clearance. Work up there for a while and find out what's really going on!'"

Three months later, on 21 March 1989, Lazar again came to Lear. He asked, "John, do you want to see one of the test flights?" "How is that possible?" John wanted to know. "He replied that on the next day in the evening a test flight would be carried out and that he knew a spot in the open countryside from where one could get a close view of the testing area and see the flight. I asked why it had to be in the evening. Statistics had shown that that was the time when traffic was at a minimum in the area. So we drove out there, Bob, Gene Huff, and I. We arrived shortly before sunset, I took out my Celestron telescope and video camera. We had hardly set up the equipment when the disc appeared behind the ridge of

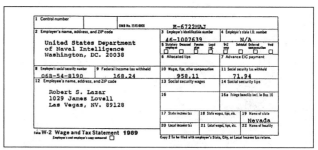

LAWRENCE JOHN W	7-9403	PA-10	P204	3	261	T242
LAWRENCE JOHN W	7-9403	PA-10	P204	3	261	T242
LAWRENCE RICHARD J	7-5525	WX-3	C934	16	260	122
LAWRENCE THOMAS A	7-6726	MEC-5	C929	16	202	107
LAYNE SCOTT PETER	7-1444	CNLS	B258	03	123	170
LAZAR ROBERT	7-5735	K/M	H840	53	2	4
LAZARUS GLORIA S	7-6339	Q-11	K571	0	487	123
LAZARUS MICHAEL E	7-4653	MST-14	G742	3	29	9116
LAZARUS ROGER BEN	7-6943	C-3	B265	3	132	202
LAZAZZERA VITO J	7-3046	CHM-6	J564	46	1	5
LAZZARO DOLORES M	7-6136	NSP-10	F670	3	43	A314E
LAZZARO ERIC S	7-6359	M-4	P942	15	183	131
LEA BENJAMIN C	7-4814	MEC-DO	D472	3	39	SHOS
LEA BETTY MARIE	7-2087	ENG-3	M703	3	410	132 A150
LEA WALTER BYRON	7-6341	WX-3	C934	16	370	103
LEACH TERRY	7-4820	MRL	H814	53	6	206

Lazars name in the internal telephone directory of the Los Alamos Laboratories.

Lazars Tax Statement for 1989 listed his contract number E-6722MAJ.

the mountain and carried out all these fantastic maneuvers. It was a very bright light in the shape of a disc. My Celestron 8 inch is a very powerful telescope and I had the object in view for a number of minutes. I could see very clearly that it was a disc, no doubts at all, and I saw it slowly disappear behind the mountain."[11]

A week later, again on a Wednesday evening, the three men made the trip once more. This time they were able to make better film shots of the disc, which made a series of "overspace jumps," as Lazar called them—impossible to duplicate with our technology. In short, the sighting and films confirmed, at least for Lear and Huff, everything that Lazar had said. It was clear to them that they would have to go to that spot again. But on 6 April 1989, when they went again, along with Lazar's wife and sister-in-law, they were detected. A security patrol controlling the borders of the testing area in a Ford Bronco sighted them and drove slowly towards them. Lazar ran off into the desert, hoping that they would not see him in the darkness. Two soldiers in camouflage uniforms jumped out of the car, pointing their machine guns at the group. "We are amateur astronomers, we're watching Jupiter," said John Lear, trying to put them off. "We'd rather that you do that somewhere else. But please get back to the highway." After they left Lazar returned, and they headed towards Las Vegas. But they were hardly back on the highway when they were stopped by the sheriff of Lincoln County, in which they were. Apparently the security police had alarmed him. In any case he asked for their papers and transmitted the data to the base by radio. Lazar was caught!

The very next day Lazar's telephone rang: he was ordered to report immediately at the Indian Springs Air Force Airfield thirty miles north of Las Vegas. The reception was not exactly cordial. One of the government agents held a revolver at his head and read him the security instructions. Then he shouted at him, "We can kill you on the spot. Nobody will know anything about it. We can find a thousand explanations." Later he learned that his security check had ended negative. His wife was having an affair and a divorce was certain. "You can apply again after six or nine months," he was told, "but to get such a high clearance you must show emotional and financial stability. Bring your personal affairs in order first and we'll see after that." But Lazar lost all feeling of being secure.

As early as March, Lear had convinced Lazar to talk about his experiences at S-4 before a running camera, as a sort of "life insurance." Bob had refused at first, but had then agreed to do so. Now he lived in fear of losing his life. The words of the government agent were still in

Michael Hesemann at the Black Mailbox at Highway 375 in Nevada, since April 1996 "Extraterrestrial Highway." In the background the Groom Mountains, behind them the mysterious Area 51, the super-secret test site.

his ears and he had to reckon with being forced into silence at any time, and that permanently! His friends advised him to go public. "When you have said everything, you are safe. They will do nothing to you after that, for if they did something, that would confirm your story." Finally Lazar let himself be interviewed by TV journalist George Knapp of the Station K-LAS. He was shown in silhouetted profile, under the pseudonym "Dennis" after his boss at the base. Immediately after the broadcast Dennis called him and asked, "Do you realize at all what they will do to you?" A series of threatening calls followed and once he was even shot at. He now had no choice whatsoever—he spoke out in his own name.[12]

But when Knapp tried to check on Lazar's supposed background, he had a nasty surprise. Whereas Lazar had said that he had studied at Pierce College and Cal-tech, the famous California Institute of Technology at Pasadena and the equally or even more famous Massachusetts Institute of Technology, all these institutions denied that a Robert Scott Lazar had ever been on

their rolls. Even the Meson Laboratory at Los Alamos denied having employed him, and his birth certificate from Los Angeles was missing. Was Bob a swindler?

Lazar's excellent knowledge of nuclear physics, with which he impressed every physicist, made Knapp search further. And he found something. He dug up the article in the *Los Alamos Monitor* through which Lazar claimed to have met Professor Teller. The police showed him dozens of case sheets regarding infringement of traffic rules in connection with Lazar's jet car. Finally Knapp found an internal telephone directory of the Meson Laboratory for the year 1982—and Lazar's name was in it. Knapp then spoke to three employees of the laboratory, who remembered Lazar very well and confirmed that he had worked on very secret projects. Now, would such an elite institution employ people without appropriate qualifications?

It took a few months before Knapp got to know Jim Tagliani, a former engineer of the Stealth project. Tagliani remembered having worked with Lazar at Fairchild Industries in Los Angeles in 1981. Lazar, he recalled, had worked rather crazy shifts in order to meet his attendance requirements at lectures and seminars at Cal-tech. They had become friends, and Tagliani had no doubts at all about Lazar having studied at Cal-tech.[12]

Lazar then got his tax form. It came from the "U.S. Department of Naval Intelligence, Washington, D.C. 20038." It bore Lazar's contract number E-6722MAJ as well as the identification number of his employer, 14-100-7639. For the five days of probation which he had spent at S-4 between 1 January and 31 March 1989 he was paid net $958.11. So there was at least one document which could be used to find more information about Lazar's mysterious work. NASA employee Bob Oechsler decided to get to the bottom of the matter. An employee of the Naval Department confirmed to Oechsler the existence of the "Compartment" men-

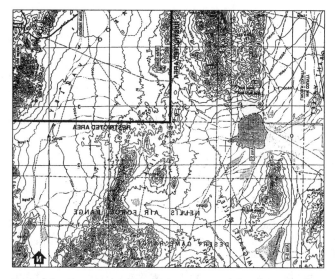

Map of the Groom Lake (Area 51), Papoose Lake and the "Mailbox Road" on public land.

Drawing by Jeff Spives, wo saw a "Lazar"-typed saucer on the mailbox road.

tioned. The first two digits of the employer's number showed the concerned tax office, in this case the one at Ogden, Utah. With a written authorization from Lazar, Oechsler made an inquiry at that office. The answer was that the name of the employer was confidential, but definitely genuine. The number E-6722 was a contract number of the Department of Energy. Contracts belonging to the 6700 series were coordinated at Albuquerque, New Mexico, by the Sandia Laboratories at the Kirtland Air Base—which according to insiders is the coordinating center for all "Majestic" activities. A check of Lazar's social security number brought evidence that Lazar had indeed been employed by the Los Alamos National Laboratories in 1982/83. When Oechsler asked for the name of the employer, there appeared on the screen of the computer at the Social Security Office the words "security violation," which meant it was a secret activity.[13]

At the end, however, Lazar was successfully discred-ited. Dubious journalists spread the gossip that Lazar was a pimp running a drug den and selling girls to South America. During Knapp's broadcast Lazar explained his position openly in regard to these accusations. Yes, he had indeed had something to do with a brothel a short while ago. After he had lost his job at S-4 he had set himself up as a consultant in the field of electronics. Toni Bulloch, a well known professional, had requested him to install a video system for an illegal brothel in Las Vegas and also set up the software in her computer for bookkeeping. Prostitution is officially prohibited in Las Vegas, which does not prevent thousands of "Vegas Hookers" from practicing their profession in the glittering city. But the open mention of an "illegal brothel" prompted the authorities. Within a few hours after the broadcast the police raided the brothel, closed it down and arrested Toni Bulloch—who in turn accused Lazar of having had a hand in the founding of the house of joy. Lazar was therefore accused of procuring, a crime for which a sentence of imprisonment ranging from one to six years and a fine of $5,000 could be imposed.

Lazar was tried on 18 June 1990. He had been insistently told to plead "guilty," in return for which he would be spared a prison sentence. He was questioned under oath about his past and he spoke openly—although perjury could be punished with sixty years of imprisonment—about his education at MIT and Caltech, his employment at Los Alamos and his time at S-4. Owing to his previous clean record and since, as the public attorney John Lukens conceded, "he did not in the least resemble the typical panderer," he was put on probation for three years and sentenced to 150 hours of community service. That he "had just lost his job in the Naval Intelligence Department and required money" were considered mitigating circumstances. Lazar worked the 150 hours tutoring school children in physics. But so light as the sentence was, Lazar's opponents had nevertheless achieved their aim: it was now possible to sneer at the mention of Lazar's name.

But his TV appearance had set off an avalanche.

Since he named the spot to which he had led Huff and Lear, 200 miles north of Las Vegas near the Highway 375, literally thousands of UFO enthusiasts and other curious spectators went to the spot to see the test flights with their own eyes. Highway 375 runs past Area 51, separated from it by two mountain ranges, the Groom Mountains and the Jumbled Hills. According to Lazar, the best place for viewing the flights was marked by a black post box shortly after the milestone marking 29.5 miles, where a desert road leaves the highway and joins the road leading to Groom Lake. This dusty and almost straight road gives the impression of leading to eternity and in fact disappears somewhere between the two mountain ranges in "Dreamland," the code name for Area 51. Whoever drives along this road will sooner or later be greeted by a host of warning signs announcing the beginning of a military establishment, whose guards are "permitted to use lethal weapons." But if one stays at the beginning of the road and chooses a small mound on the right—Campfire Hill—as one's observation post, one will see—to use pilots' jargon—at the two o'clock position Groom Lake Base behind the mountains, and at the one o'clock position Papoose Lake. The UFO hunters met there, and quite a few could convince themselves that something inexplicable was going on behind the mountains. "We saw an orange light that appeared above the Jumbled Hills and came towards us, flew to the right, dropped suddenly and flew back. In a short while it returned," said Japanese TV journalist Noryo Hayakawa, who had led a Nippon team to the spot on 21 February 1990. "That was definitely a test flight of some craft which demonstrated a technology and propulsion system so exotic that we do not know what it was. But it was tested that night," commented Hayakawa when the takes were shown on Japanese TV shortly thereafter.[15] A week later Gary Schulz from Santa Monica succeeded in getting a shot

The "Little Ale Inn" in Rachel, Nevada, meeting point of the UFO enthusiasts.

of "a pulsating, bright ellipsoidal disc" with a dome on it, just as Lazar had described.[16] On 26 February 1991 Sean David Morton from Hermosa Beach, California, and his girlfriend witnessed "a large disc of about forty feet in diameter" ascending from the base and flying over Tikkaboo Valley. "It looked like a saucer with an upturned teacup on it, glowing red orange and then bright yellow. It behaved like a falling leaf, swaying from side to side, until it sank out of sight," Morton told me.[17] And on 2 December 1992, a film team of the U.S. broadcasting station ABC, which I took to the site, along with my own cameraman and some participants of the UFO conference in Las Vegas, witnessed the demonstration flight of a dark disc with a row of rotating lights on its periphery. We filmed the object, and ABC broadcast this nationwide the next day.[18] The publicity resulting from this ABC broadcast unfortunately was one of the factors leading to the relocation of the discs in February 1993, according to insiders. They were apparently taken to White Sands Proving Grounds in New Mexico.

Obviously the to-do about the UFO tests was a thorn in somebody's side. With increasing frequency visitors, who at any rate were on public ground, complained about the chicanery and intimidation they had been subjected to by Wackenhut Special Security, the private security service organization hired for the guarding of the borders of the base and which, certainly not without reason, soon attained notoriety under the name of "Wackenhut SS." They wore camouflage uniforms, without name or rank badges, drove around in black Ford Broncos without registration numbers. More than once they threatened visitors with their machine guns, and in the case of one onlooker, they shot through the tires of his vehicle. The Japanese team that once more went UFO hunting on 16 May 1991, was chased by black-painted helicopters with no identification numbers or markings on them, making dangerous maneuvers and coming as close as ten feet above their car. The Japanese cameraman had the presence of mind to film this episode. "One of them circled over us and then flew very low directly at us over the road. Our lives were in danger and we were terribly frightened by these maneuvers, which were against all the rules of flight," said a shocked Noryo Hayakawa describing the frontal attack.[19]

On the other hand, for the roughly one hundred inhabitants of the desert nest Rachel on the Highway 375, some twenty miles north of the "black mail box," the UFO racket was more than welcome. Joe and Pat Davis, the couple that owned "Rachel's Bar and Grill," renamed their establishment immediately "The Little Ale Inn," which can also be read as "The Little Alien." "Welcome Earthlings," says a sign above the entrance to greet the new target group of customers, whom a small exhibition and a good selection of books awaits. And what's more, on April 19, 1996 Highway 375 was officially christened "Extraterrestrial Highway" in the presence of the governor of Nevada and 500 victims.

The suggestion of a local "whack-o," known as "Ambassador Merlin," had been thankfully taken up by the local politicians, and since UFO seekers after all pour money into the forlorn little nests along the desert highway, the authorities of the State of Nevada permitted the renaming without too much hesitation.[20]

Shortly after, on July 3, 1996, a blockbuster movie came to the theatres and soon became one of the most successful film productions in the history of cinema. *Independence Day* told the story of an alien invasion and how mankind unites to fight back. And indeed it features Area 51, complete with the crashed Roswell saucer and three alien bodies floating in formaldehyde solutions in glass cylinders, and a president who didn't know about it because they wanted to keep a "plausible deniability" and he didn't have a need to know. What follows is an epic someone could summarize as "how Area 51 saved the world": the crashed discs delivered the clue to fight back and disturb the alien defense system, which causes the invaders to crash on the anniversary of the very crash at Roswell, on July 4.[21] "It is hard to believe that after sleeping in the dirt, getting chased, shot at, swooped by jets and helicopters, getting erased, hiding out for days in ditches, hassling with the law, having good friends brutally murdered because they knew too much, getting smeared by the press and blatant bald-faced liars, psychopaths and Agent Provocateurs, and changing hundreds of people's lives by taking them out there with me to just see for themselves . . . that five years later a movie about how AREA 51 saves the world is on its way to becoming the biggest box office hit of all time!," wrote Area 51 researcher and Hollywood producer Sean David Morton.[22]

And indeed, it all began in 1989 with Robert Lazar's disclosure that for the first time awakened public awareness of the hitherto most secret military testing grounds in the world. For before the young physicist spoke out, even the mere existence of the Groom Lake Base was officially denied—even though long before, Soviet satellite photographs of it had been published and any curious person could have seen it with his or her own eyes after a climb on the Groom Mountains. The base has existed for more than forty years, and for almost that long stories have been going around that crashed "saucers" were kept there and secretly studied.[20]

[1] *Los Alamos Monitor*, 28 June 1982.

[2] Personal Interview, 15 June 1993.

[3] Turner, Admiral Stansfield, *Secrecy and Democracy: The CIA in Transition*, London, 1986.

[4] Personal Interview, 15 June 1993.

[5] Good, Timothy, *Alien Contact*, New York, 1993.

[6] Personal Interview, 15 June 1993.

[7] Holt, Alan, *Field Resonance Propulsion Concept*, NASA, Houston, TX, 1979.

[8] *Sunday Times*, London, 13 August 1995.

[9] *Der Spiegel*, no. 50, Hamburg, 12 December 1995.

[10] Good, 1993.

[11] Personal Interview, 6 December 1992.

[12] Knapp, George, "Area 51, Bob Lazar, and Disinformation—A Reevaluation," in *MUFON Symposium Proceedings*, Seguin, TX, 1993.

[13] Good, 1993.

[14] Knapp, 1993.

[15] Personal Interview, 12 June 1993.

[16] Personal Interview, 13 June 1993.

[17] Personal Interview, 28 June 1993.

[18] *ABC News*, 3 December 1992.

[19] Personal Interview, 12 June 1993.

[20] *Magazine 2000*, no. 113, Neuss, Germany, October 1996.

[21] Devlin/Emmerich, *Independence Day*, New York, 1996.

[22] Morton, Sean D., "Independence Day," in *Delphi Associates*, Hermosa Beach, CA, vol. 3, no. 31, 15 July 1996.

11.

Secrets of the Black World

rea 51, as Groom Lake Base is officially denoted, is in the heart of the Nevada Test Site, which, with an area of about 6,200 square miles, is the largest testing ground in the world. Bordered on the south by Nellis Airforce Base—which lies north of Las Vegas—it stretches far into the almost uninhabited desert of Nevada, a high plateau between a number of mountain ranges. This gray "moon-landscape," 4,500 feet above sea level, is intervened by mountain ridges, some of which rise to heights of over 8,000 feet. The underground atomic tests of the U.S. took place here, the "Red Flag" exercises of the U.S. Air Force, during which a "third world war in Europe" was simulated, were regularly begun here. Here too lies the Tonopah Test Site, from which the Stealth fighter was started and where even today a number of most secret armament development projects are housed. Some of them are so secret that Congress can pass only a lump sum budget for them, called the "black budget," which earned them the name "black projects," and the laboratories which carry them out, the epithet "black world." And in fact they are another world, a world in which everything is decided by the factors security and secrecy, a world governed by its own laws, which are not subject to the legislation of the State of Nevada.

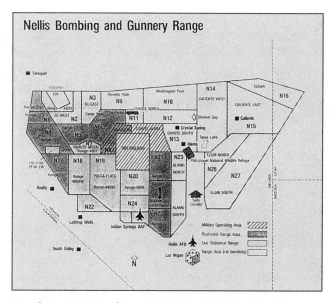

Nevada Testing Ground. In center is Dreamland or Area 51.

The "blackest" part of the "black world" is Area 51, an almost square terrain, twenty-five miles long and twenty-two miles wide. The dried-up Groom Lake is in the center of the area, at the south end of which lies the equally dry Papoose Lake, where Area S-4 begins. Area 51 has many names. In pilots' jargon it is called

"Dreamland" or "the Box." Insiders use expressions like "Watertown" or "the Ranch." For the first time it appeared on a map of the Kennedy administration, as an autonomous territory with its own administration—in short, as if it were the fifty-first Federal State; hence its name Area 51. Its forerunner had been, until 1955, in the midst of a naval testing area. But then Clarence "Kelly" Johnson, chief designer of Lockheed, sent out his best pilot, Tony LeVier, on a very special mission: to find a dried-up lake in the deserts of California or Nevada that would suitably serve as a secret testing area for the legendary U-2 Bomber. After two days of searching LeVier had found the ideal spot: the dry bed of Groom Lake, three miles long and in the middle of nowhere, cut off from the outside world by mountain ranges, in a territory that was off-limits for pilots, owing to the regular atomic bomb tests carried out at the Nevada Test Site. Under the aegis of a fictitious firm, within two months and for only $800,000 in building costs for two hangars, a six-furlong runway, wells and a cafeteria were conjured up: an establishment that went under the cover name "the Ranch." On 23 July 1955 the dismantled U-2 was freighted over to Groom Lake. The tests could begin.[1]

What followed was extensive building activity. The ideal situation of "the Ranch" soon made it the favorite spot for every secret experiment one could think of, and for this over 180 buildings and establishments as well as extensive underground facilities were built until 1980. The A-12 was tested here and then from 1959 to 1961, the SR-71. In 1974 the DARPA (Defense Advanced Research Projects Agency) granted a new "black" project, which interestingly had the code name "Have Blue, Have Blue." In the Air Force the code "Blue" had always had something to do with UFOs, from the UFO research project "Blue Book" till "Operation Blue Fly," "Blue Teams" and "Blue Berets." This new project,

costing almost fifty billion dollars, led to the development of the Northrop Bomber B-2 and the Lockheed fighter F-117A, both of which represented, as "Stealth craft," a breakthrough in military air technology. Early in 1977 the first F-117A took off from the Groom Lake base, but it was shown to the public only a decade later.[2] In 1951 an existing base of the U.S. Navy at a dry lake south of the Tonapah range, some sixty miles northwest of Groom Lake, had already been expanded. The Air Force Colonel and UFO researcher Wendelle C. Stevens spoke in 1978 with an employee of a CB (Construction Battalion) of the Navy, who at that time had worked on the modification of that base. "Parts of the runway were pulled up and a new installation made underground. When the work was finished, personnel in civilian clothing took over the base. The runway was rebuilt—they wanted everything to look the same as before."[3] From a member of the Naval Medical Corps, who had been stationed at that base then, Stevens learned why all that was done. "The whole team on the base except the medical corps was transferred to other places. The reconstruction of the base was begun in summer and the underground installation made. Towards the end of the year the work was finished. A new team Called 'Project Redlight' was brought in. It consisted of between 800 and 1,000 persons, all of whom lived on the base. The establishment was surrounded by three security girdles, security tests and alarm rehearsals were daily routine. A group of Blue Berets came soon and was put on twenty-four-hour watch. Besides that leading scientists came, men with very high clearance permits, some of whom had previously worked on the Manhattan Project. Although I was never officially informed about it and it was not part of the daily work, I heard that it had to do with UFO propulsion and the investigation and evaluation of UFO hardware. There were even rumors that we were trying to fly a recovered spacecraft or to duplicate it. Once I heard of a successful flight with one of these craft. It was said that we had three crashed UFOs, two complete and one that had been taken apart. One of them is supposed to have exploded when two US test pilots were on board."[4] As if this was not incredible enough, they also mentioned an "underground habitat," built during the reconstruction, in which "two humanoid ETs had been kept alive in a special atmosphere."[5] One of them had died in 1952, but the other one had lived for another eight years. The beings had been small, with grayish-white skin. One of them was dressed in a skintight brown union suit, the other one in a silvery suit.

Shortly after the death of the second ET in 1960, Project Redlight was shut down and transferred to Area 51, which had more modern equipment, until 1970, when S-4 was established on the banks of Papoose Lake. In 1972 the project was renamed "Project Snowbird." Mike Hunt, a radio technician who had been working on the Nevada Testing Grounds early in 1960 and had a "Q" clearance from the Atomic Energy Commission, claims to have seen a disc-shaped flying object. "The disc was standing on the ground and was partly hidden by a building, so that at first I thought it was a small plane," he wrote to UFO researcher David Dobbs in 1980, "then I noticed that it had no wings or tail. I was about half a mile away, but I guessed its size to be about 25 to 30 feet in diameter. It had the color of pewter." But he frequently followed the test flights on the radio, even if he could not see them. "They always said to me something like 'we are now getting it out of the hangar' or 'it is going to land in so-and-so many minutes' etc. They always used only the word 'it.' But I never heard the noise of a conventional aircraft engine when it started."[6] More than once radio contact was interrupted, but was normal again shortly after. The name of the program under which "it" flew was called, according to Hunt, "Red Light" or "Redlight."

An officer of the fighter squadron of the Strategic Air Command told Stevens about an incident that happened during the "Red Flag" exercises in 1977. The officer was to simulate an attack on an "enemy base" on the Tonapah Testing Grounds. To avoid detection by radar, he decided to attack from a direction with which the "enemy" would not have reckoned. Flying very low to escape the radar beams, he crossed the northern boundary of Area 51, when he saw a disc of about sixty feet in diameter flying south of his position. At once a voice over the emergency channel ordered him to terminate his mission and to land immediately at the Nellis Air Force Base. As soon as he had brought his plane into the landing bay, it was surrounded by personnel in uniform, and he was escorted by men in civilian clothing to a security office in a shelter. There he was questioned by civilians, one of them an FBI official. He was held there for two days and was asked the same questions repeatedly. Whenever he mentioned the disc he was told that it was only a water tower. After he had signed an explanation in suitable terms he was allowed to return to his base. But a few days later he was transferred to another base and instructed never to mention the incident to anybody.

The book *Red Flag: Air Combat for the '80s* by Michael Skinner appeared in 1984, as a complete documentation of the "Red Flag" operations. On page sixty-two, a map showed the Nevada Testing Grounds. "Dreamland" is mentioned clearly by name as "military operation area." Two pages later, it says: "Actual live bombing is done only in the numbered ranges—dropping live ordnance on the live citizens underneath the Military Operating Areas or on the Dreamland-Munchkins is not done." Also the mountain ranges with the names EC East and EC West [where the rebuilt navy bases are], Tolicha Peak EW and Pahute Mesa, have people inside them and bombing is not allowed here either."[7] Clearly inhabitants of extensive underground installations are referred to here. But who are the Dreamland Munchkins? We can only guess.

Rumors about the "Land of Dreams" were going around long before Lazar spoke to the public. According to the Groom family, to whose ranch the mountains and dry lake had originally belonged before the government bought them, there was talk of "flying saucers" in Area 51 even in the early fifties. The journalist Robert Dorr, whom British UFO researcher Timothy Good quotes, claims that he had heard from an officer of the Air Force Intelligence Department that since 1953 an extraterrestrial disc was being kept at the Nellis Range. From 1953 till 1956 they had tried in vain to fly this with conventional engines.[8] In 1988 Jim Schultz, chief editor of the U.S. military magazine *Gung-Ho,* mentioned in his article "Stealth and Beyond" an "Alien Technology Center" at the Nellis Air Force Base. "The Center," he wrote, *"is rumored to have obtained alien equipment and, at times, personnel to help develop our new aircraft star wars weaponry etc. Yes, I know I sound crazy, but the rumor is awfully solid! The Alien Technology Center is for real. Something remarkable has caused the Russians to suddenly want to play ball, and I personally believe this could be it."*[9]

But it was Lazar's revelations that led to the real breach in the dam. More than a dozen witnesses contacted George Knapp, the K-LAS journalist who presented Lazar to the public for the first time. And what they said seemed to confirm the story of the young scientist in all its details.

- A radar technician of Nellis AFB said that he had 'stacked' objects above Area 51 which could fly at speeds over 7500 mph and stop suddenly as if at a word. When he reported this to his boss he was told to ignore them. Mark Barnes, who worked at a long range radar station outside of Las Vegas, confirmed the unusual flight activities above Groom Lake. He too had spotted "aircraft," which could fly at phenomenal speeds and equally well hover at one spot for long periods.

- An electrical engineer claimed that he had worked in Area 51, where he had seen a metallic disc in a hangar, covered with tarpaulin. Knapp wanted to interview him and fixed an appointment. The next morning, when the engineer left his house he saw a car parked in front of it, with two men in suits, who at once spoke into a walkie talkie. He didn't give it much thought, got into his car and drove off. But then he saw that the other car was tailing him. And when he drove home in the evening, the same car was again behind him. He canceled the interview with Knapp.

- A lawyer from Las Vegas who was fulfilling his compulsory military service on the Test Site witnessed a disc-shaped flying object making an emergency landing outside of Area 51. Within a short time after that he was surrounded by security officials who took him away and interrogated him for days.

- A local professional golfer was on a golf tour with friends, who were high-ranking army officers. When they sat together in the hotel lounge, a TV film about Roswell was being shown. One of the officers, a lieutenant colonel at Nellis AFB, declared that everything that was said in the film was true and that some of the material recovered then was now at Area 51.

- Roy Byrum, a tax consultant who had a number of clients who worked at Area 51, learned from them that large sums of money from official programs were being tapped off to finance the work on UFOs. He said that he had been unambiguously given to understand that recovered alien discs were kept at Area 51. The day after he telephoned Knapp, Byrum was visited by two government officials who warned him not to talk to the reporter anymore.

- A flight engineer, employee of EG&G, claimed to have seen not only recovered discs but also alien corpses at Area 51.

- A photographer who had photographed atomic tests during the early sixties, told Knapp that during those days photographers were the only personnel in the testing grounds who were allowed to possess field glasses. Thus he and his colleagues had often seen metallic discs from their vantage point west of Groom Lake. Once, before a planned atomic test, he and his colleagues were held for four days in quarantine and had nothing else to do but chat with one another. His boss, a German physicist, Otto Krause by name, often spoke about the discs which were being tested at Area 51. According to Krause they came from crashes in New Mexico towards the end of the fourties. The program in Area 51 was meant to copy the propulsion system of the discs.

- A woman who held a position of responsibility at a Las Vegas court had formerly worked for an armament firm in Nevada. There she had once been present at a meeting at which her employers spoke with high-ranking military officers about a wreck which had been taken to Area 51. When she called Knapp, they arranged for a private talk. But the woman did not turn up. She explained later that someone from her former firm had visited her. The person reminded her that she was still under oath and could be prosecuted by law. Finally came the threat: "We know that you travel a lot. We would hate to see you and your family have an accident. . . ."

- Doug Schroeder, electrical engineer in the services of EG&G, said that the material came from UFO crashes and had been brought to Area 51 from "a base in Ohio" [Wright-Patterson AFB]. He also said that he had seen many photographs of test flights. As far as he knew, it had not been possible to copy the discs, but one had learned a great deal about the alloy which had been used in their construction. Shortly after Schroeder had made his statement, he died under mysterious circumstances. Schroeder is not the only employee of the "black world" who lost his life in such an inexplicable manner. Twenty-two scientists who had worked on SDI and other secret projects in "Dreamland" were victims of strange deaths between 1982 and 1988. Five were found suffocated in their cars, three jumped to their deaths, two were found dead in the bed of a prostitute, two electrocuted themselves, and one managed a "do-it-yourself" decapitation. Which brings a new meaning to the insider slogan, "Once you've gone black, you never come back!"

- Knapp heard from close acquaintances of Dr. Dan Crain, a prominent biologist in Las Vegas who worked for the Planetarium Society, the Young Astronauts Program and the Public High School in South Nevada, that Dr. Crain might know something about extraterrestrials. Finally he spoke to Dr. Crain directly, who confirmed the rumors and promised to give him some documents, which he had kept as a sort of safety measure. They were reports about analyses of tissue samples from ETs. But Dr. Crain did not arrive at the appointed time. He burnt all bridges behind him and withdrew completely from scientific activity. He now works as a security guard at a Las Vegas hotel.

- John Harbour was a security officer of the Air Force at Groom Lake. He became friends with a woman who was acquainted with Knapp. Once Harbour complained to her that he had been refused credit because he could show only his basic income from the Air Force, for he was strictly forbidden to show even his tax card for his main job at Area 51. He then told her that the rumor about the presence of ETs was true. The truth was not revealed to the public, for if it came out, it would lead to the collapse of all our institutions, including the church, and people would probably stop paying taxes. Harbour suddenly left Nevada in 1990 and Knapp could not trace him at all after that.

- The computer specialist Jim Tagliani was working on the Stealth Project at Tonapah. He declared that information about extraterrestrial material was common knowledge amongst those working on the invisible Stealth bomber.

- In July 1982 the lawyer Andrew Basiago wrote an article about a local politician, Mario Williams, revealing that Williams had worked for thirty years for the CIA, then for Lockheed, and also been transferred to Groom Lake. In 1981 Williams had told his family that extraterrestrial technology and biology were being studied at Area 51. Williams died in 1989. Basiago said that members of his family were not prepared to talk to Knapp on this subject.

Knapp himself traced another informant, a man who, since the fifties, had directed several very secret military projects at Nevada. The man came from a very well known family in Nevada, had a clear and documented career and high-ranking contacts. He confirmed that ET technology had been present in Nevada, even before Groom Lake Base had been established. One of the reasons for building up Area 51 was to test alien technology there. Private companies carried out the work for the army. Till right into the sixties all attempts to fly the spacecraft had been unsuccessful. He further confirmed that a living ET had been kept in custody at Area 51 for some years and that after a period of time they had been able to communicate with him. The man, who had been a serious scientist all his life, did not want his name to be published, but agreed to leave behind a video film which could be shown after his death.[10]

Actually I (Hesemann) too was successful, after some research, in finding two witnesses who confirmed

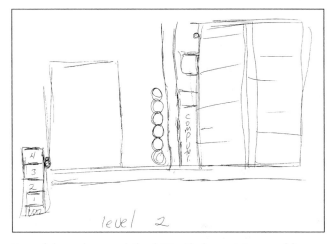

Map of the underground "level 2" with the containers and hangar bays, according to Derek Henessy.

Lazar's story. Derek Henessy is a giant of a man, almost six feet nine inches tall, with broad shoulders and hands that look like bear's paws. Henessy was a member of Seal Team Six, an elite unit of the Navy, who on more than one occasion had been sent on missions with "license to kill." In 1987, between two equally delicate missions, he had been stationed at Area S-4. What he saw there exceeds by far what we know of from Lazar. "There are four levels at S-4, not counting the top level where the hangars are built into the rocks," he told Lt. Col. W.C. Stevens. "They are all connected by lifts, with which the discs are transported to the surface. When I was there they were trying to operate the discs, but they had no success. There were scientists, I myself saw high officials from the White House and Vice President George Bush in the facilities."

Henessy was posted as guard opposite the lift in the second underground level (level 2). He passed through level one, but never saw levels three and four, for no soldiers were allowed on those levels, which only persons with special clearances could enter. His description of

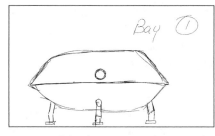

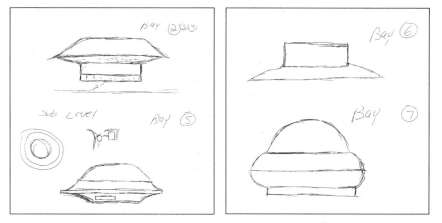

Drawing of the five UFO wreckages in the subterranean hangar of S-4 according to Derek Henessy.

level two was very detailed. He said it comprised nine hangar bays, each large enough to hold a small plane. In seven of those were circular disclike objects which could be raised to ground level by hydraulic systems. Henessy drew detailed sketches of the installation. He pointed out the security controls and an area where extraterrestrial bodies were stored in big glass cylinders. He spoke of special equipment and the sophisticated monitoring system. Thus anyone wanting to enter levels three or four had to insert a plastic card with magnetized stripes into a slot for having their data checked. In addition their personal features, including fingerprints and retinal structure, were tallied by means of hand and eye scanners. Henessy had heard rumors that an EBE (Extraterrestrial Biological Entity) lived in level four.

Henessy described the glass cylinders in which the bodies were preserved as "a row of tubes six feet high and two feet wide, close to each other. They are all identical and the beings in them look all alike. I don't know what sex they are, for the tubes have an aluminum band around the middle. The tubes stand on a foot-high pedestal made of what looked like black, polished anodized iron, and are filled with a solution in which the creatures are suspended. They are very thin, have big heads which reduce to a pointed chin, and long arms. Their eyes looked as if they had deteriorated, looked like dried plums. They didn't have any visible eyelids. Their skins had a gray pigment, without any sign of hair on them. There were bluish holes or hollows in the place of the ears, two slits for the nose and one for the mouth. Their bodies were quite frail. They didn't seem to have breasts or navels, in any case I didn't see any. But I remember someone saying that their system was completely different from ours."[11]

When I (Hesemann) discussed Hennesy's statement, TV producer and UFO researcher Sean David Morton, who has followed up all rumors about Area 51 since 1951 and has himself sighted and filmed a number of such objects, said that he too had shortly before heard a similar story. Morton had appeared in a TV show called "Mysteries from beyond the Other Dominion," in which he reported about his findings. Since he also led groups to the "Mailbox Road," his telephone number was shown at the end of the feature. A few days later he received a call from an elderly man who declared that he had worked at Area 51 for over twelve years as master sergeant. He had been responsible for all transport to and from the area, and everything that was shifted from one place to another in the area went across his desk. He also gave his full name and military ID number, which enabled Morton to check his credentials. He had indeed been working at the Nellis Air Force Base and then at Area 51 during the period in question.

"On many occasions he had transported disc like saucers, which he considered to be alien spacecraft, although he wasn't sure whether they were alien or not," said Morton. "He had transported some thirty to sixty foot disc-shaped craft, also some bell-shaped objects with a dull gun-metal color. He did on many occasions witness the tests of these craft. They had to cart them off to a certain place and then take them off. The objects would then fly around a bit. And he asked me how it was possible that something that looked so dead and lifeless could suddenly glow up so that the metal of the ship looked as if it were alive." The witness knew further that Area 51 facilities had five levels. Once he saw a row of big transparent tanks, with silvery back walls and silvery strips in the middle and bottom, filled with a bluish liquid, in which the bodies of nine aliens were kept. There were five small creatures, about four feet tall, with big almond-shaped eyes and four humanoid beings, with blond or reddish hair, which basically did not differ very much from humans.[12]

Bill Uhouse, a mechanical design engineer, worked with alien technology.

After finishing his studies in engineering, Bill Uhouse was a fighter pilot during the Second World War and after that test pilot for a firm of government contractors. After a few years he was asked if he would like to work on the development of flight simulators, and Bill agreed to do so. He constructed simulators for various planes, the F-89, F-94 and F-102. His next job had to do with his training as mechanical design engineer. They wanted to make the planes lighter, and hence he and his team were given the task of inventing a method to join metal with metal, without screws, rivets or other connecting parts. This accomplished, Uhouse rose higher and higher in the project hierarchy, his security clearance was repeatedly checked and raised, and he was finally put on a special project in New Mexico. He had worked there three or four years, when his team was given the job of developing simulators for discs—to train U.S. pilots to fly crashed UFOs! On 4 December 1995 I (Hesemann) interviewed Bill Uhouse, a quiet, sober gentleman who has now been retired for many years. He said, "this project had been there already for some years and proved to be very time-consuming. The problem was in translating alien data into our terminology and thinking process. We called it 'copy engineering.' We took apart a piece of equipment or a part of the vessel, described the results of our analyses and how this part was integrated into the rest of the craft. We tried to recognize certain features, to identify them, and asked ourselves, 'How can we use it?' Piece by piece we tried to figure out how it functioned."

One day Uhouse was transferred to Area S-4, where he saw a disc for the first time. "This facility was, from the point of security, perhaps better protected than any other facility in the entire country. They took us engineers to a hangar, and there she stood. She looked exactly as Bob Lazar described her. And they said to us, 'Look, boys, that's what a disc looks like.' Whether I ever entered one? No. But that was a disc. She sat flat on the ground, on her belly. I was only fifteen feet away from her. My impression as engineer was, 'that's great.'[13]

Had U.S. engineers been successful in solving the secrets of the UFOs and integrating them into their defense technology? Jim Goodall is one of those who had even earlier lifted the veil of secrecy. Jim, an aerospace expert, was the first author to publish on the Stealth program. He wrote three books about Stealth and a number of articles for technical journals like the *Defense Weekly*, *Interavia* and *Aviation Week and Space Technology*. Owing to his curiosity he was repeatedly the victim of intimidation by the U.S. Government. His neighbors were interrogated by agents, his telephone tapped. When he was called up as reservist of the Air National Guard for Operation Desert Shield, he learned that his security clearance level had been lowered. I (Hesemann) met Jim Goodall in December 1992 at John Lear's house, who was just celebrating his fiftieth birthday, and asked him what he had dug up about the activities in Area 51. "There are eight black programs there," he said, *"and that does not include the B-2 bomber or the F-117 fighter [Stealth planes], for that is today an official, a white program. At least two high-velocity planes are amongst them—we heard about them for the first time in 1982. One is a small plane that attains about four to six Mach [speed of sound waves], and a plane which has been spotted in the Bay Area in California at least eight times since 1986 by the Federal Air Administration, flying towards Area 51 with a speed of over 10,000 mph. That is a very big aircraft. Besides these two high-speed aircraft, there are Stealthlike planes for electronic warfare, the Excalibur, which flies very slowly and silently at very high altitudes. Then there are rumors about the 'flying triangle,' which looks like the stopped A12 from McDonnel-Douglas."*

"Are there unconventional technologies involved in these?"

"Yes. Over the years I have interviewed people who have worked at the test site at Groom Lake; one gentleman spent twelve of his thirty years' service in black programs at Groom Lake. When I

The F-116 A Stealth flying over the White Sands Proving Grounds in New Mexico.

The comparison with a conventional USAF fighter plane demonstrates the technological leap Stealth stands for.

asked him, first of all I said, 'Do you believe in UFOs?' and he looked at me with a straight face and answered, 'Yes, absolutely and positively, they do exist.' 'Can you expand upon that?' 'No, I can't. ' About a year later we were talking about the activities at Groom Lake and I asked him, 'Can you tell me what's going on there?' And he answered, 'There's a lot of things going on there, but I won't be able to tell you till the year 2025. We have things in the Nevada desert that would make George Lucas envious!'" George Lucas is the producer of the movie trilogy Star Wars. "Another Informant," continued Goodall, "was a master sergeant in the Air Force, a specialist for new technologies. He had three areas of responsibility in three programs. I interviewed him at the Nellis Air Base in 1985/86. I asked him, 'What's going on there?' He looked me in the eyes and said, 'We have things there which are literally not of this earth'. I asked him to explain, and he replied that he was not allowed to, but they were things which were better than Spaceship Enterprise and all that other stuff in films. 'Flying craft?' I wanted to know. The answer: 'No comment!'"

But the most definite confirmation of the rumors came from Goodall's friend John Andrews of the Testor Corporation. John wrote to Ben Rich, the recently retired president of Lockheed Advance Development Company, the firm that brought out Stealth, the SR-71 and the U-2 bomber. "Ben was asked, 'Do you believe in UFOs?' and he wrote back to my friend, 'Yes. Both John Kelly, founder of the Skunk Works Laboratories, and I are firm believers of UFOs.' . . . John wrote back saying, 'Please clarify. We are talking about two categories of UFOs—man-made and extra-terrestrial.' Ben wrote back again, on his letterhead, in his own hand, 'Yes, both exist, man-made and extraterrestrial. We call them 'UnFunded Opportunities,' and had underlined u, f and o.[14]

But now as before, a veil of secrecy surrounds the black world. Last year the Air Force succeeded in extending their testing precincts eastward, so that the mountains from which one could get a good view of the Groom Lake area are now no longer open to the public. Only the light reflected in the sky in the darkness of the desert, a bit higher from Groom Lake and a bit lower from Papoose Lake, indicate the presence of the Land of Dreams.

The first expansion of the base took place in 1984, when funnily enough the existence of the Groom Lake Base was denied officially. In 1984 a hearing was conducted by the Subcommittee for Land and National Parks of the U.S. House of Representatives, at which the Air Force was required to justify their claim for this piece of land. The proceedings at this hearing give an insight into the practices, the paramount power of the Air Force to break every law under the excuse of "national security," and the atmosphere of secrecy. The chairman of the Committee, Mr. Seiberling, asked John Rittenhouse, the representative of the Air Force:

(S= Seiberling. R= Rittenhouse.)

S: Is it true that the Air Force has already begun to restrict the public use of the Groom Range area?

R: Yes, sir, it is true. We have asserted the right to control the surface access and egress to the extent of requesting people not to go in and out. We have people posted on the roads and at certain times we do not. We ask their cooperation.

S: Under what legal authority was that done; that right asserted?

R: As far as I know, sir, there is none; except decisions were made at a much, much higher level than mine that that be done.

S: There is no level higher than the laws of the United States.

R: No, sir, I understand, and we can describe that further if you would like, sir.

S: I would like.

R: In closed briefing.

S: Why would that have to be in a closed briefing?

R: I can't discuss it, sir.

S: Shades of Watergate. All I am asking you is under what legal authority this was done. I am not asking you the technical reasons. That certainly is not classified.

R: As I stated earlier, originally we had no legal authority, but we asserted the right to request people not to enter that area.

S: Now?

R: We legally did not have the authority.[15]

During the autumn of 1993 the Defense Department applied for extension of the base perimeters to include the Groom Mountains, "to ensure the secure and protected running of the operations at Nellis Range"— officially Groom Lake Base was still nonexistent. A storm of public indignation and protest broke out. Since 10 April 1995 the mountain ranges White Sides and Freedom Ridge, which had the vantage points offering the best views of Area 51, have become part of the base. In confiscating public land, they had restricted themselves to taking over only the most essential areas, for any such acquisition exceeding 5,000 acres of land would need the permission of the U.S. Congress.

"The Air Force needs this land to protect the technological innovations of the U.S. military industry and effectiveness of the military exercises and operations," said Air Force spokesman Lieutenant Colonel Cannon, defending this land robbery. The stream of curious spectators had, "during recent years, frequently led to the relocation, delay and cancellation of test flights." The confiscation would "prevent the further compromising of national security."[16]

Simultaneously the Air Force made an announcement in the press, which is now the standard answer to all queries regarding Area 51. At any rate, the existence of this base was thereby officially conceded, forty years after its establishment. "A series of activities, some of which are secret," this bulletin says, "takes place at the often so-called Nellis-Range complex of the Air Force. The area is used for testing technologies and systems and for exercises for operations, which are essential for the effectiveness of the armed forces of the U.S. and the security of the U.S. There is a particular location for operations near Groom Lake. Certain specific activities and operations, which are being carried out and were carried out there in the past, stand under secrecy and cannot be discussed."[17]

This was not in any way affected even by the new law concerning national security, which President Clinton signed on 17 April 1995 as Executive Order 12958. According to this "government order regarding classified information pertaining to questions of national security," all secret documents older than twenty-five years were to be automatically declassified and made accessible to the people. There were only three exceptions: if their disclosure would endanger the personal safety of the president or other prominent people in public life, or if they obstructed existing plans for dealing with national emergencies and catastrophes. The third exception was in the case of foreign documents in possession of the CIA, if their publication would jeopardize diplomatic relations seriously. This was at least a good beginning.

But on 29 September 1995 Clinton signed an order to make a further exception, according to which all data concerning Area 51 could still remain classified as top secret. This was triggered off by ex-employees of the base, who claimed to have been "toxically contaminated" during their period of service in the black world and claimed damages. District judge Philip Pro gave an injunction on 30 August 1995 that the Air Force could no longer withhold certain documents connected with the case, without a specific exempting order from the president. The lawyer representing the employees, Professor Jonathan Turley, prematurely celebrated Pro's order as a victory. But Clinton thwarted all his hopes by signing the said order. In the order it says, "It is in the greatest interest of the U.S. that the Air Force should be restrained from revealing secret information about the Base."[19]

And S-4? When a delegation of Congress members was allowed in 1994 to visit Groom Lake base in order to clarify rumors about the "Aurora," two of them expressed the wish to have a look at Papoose Lake. One of them was waved off with the excuse that just then a capricious and blinding blizzard was raging there. The other member was told that only a lot of radioactive atomic waste from previous projects was stored at S-4 and nobody could go there. Thus the policy of secrecy still endures. . . .[20]

[1]Rich, Ben R. and Leo Janos, *Skunk Works,* Boston, 1994.

[2]Weiner, Tim, *Blank Check—The Pentagon's Black Budget,* New York, 1990.

[3]Steinman, William and Wendelle Stevens, *UFO Crash at Aztec,* Tucson, 1986.

[4]Ibid.

[5]Ibid.

[6]Quoted from: Good, Timothy, *Alien Liaison,* London, 1991.

[7]Skinner, Michael, *Red Flag: Air Combat for the 80s,* Presidio, 1984.

[8]Good, 1991.

[9]Schults, Jim, "Stealth—and Beyond," in *Gung Ho,* February 1988.

[10]Knapp, George, "Area 51, Bob Lazar and Disinformation—A Reevaluation," in *MUFON Symposium Proceedings,* Seguin, TX, 1993, and Personal Interview of 16 June 1993.

[11]Personal Interview in the presence of W. C. Stevens, December 1992.

[12]Personal Interview, 28 June 1993.

[13]Personal Interview, 3 December 1994.

[14]Personal Interview, 6 December 1992.

[15]Quoted from Good, 1991.

[16]*San Francisco Examiner,* 19 December, 94 and *Bee,* Sacramento, CA, 26 December 1994.

[17]Quoted from *Gentleman Quarterly,* London, December 1995.

[18] Executive Order # 12958, 17 April 1995.

[19]*Magazin 2000,* no. 108, Neuss, January 1996.

[20]Knapp, 1993.

12.

The Air Force Balloon Baloney

On 5 July 1993, one day after Independence Day, a group of around 150 people demonstrated before the White House. It was an oppressively hot summer day in the capital, notorious for its sub-tropical climate. But neither the heat nor the mocking grins of the passers-by prevented the demonstrators from walking around there carrying posters and signs, shouting their demands, "U-U-U-F-O, The people have a right to know!" . . . "End the cover up now!" . . . "What about Roswell, Mr. President?"

The peaceful demonstration, which even earned a mention in the evening news of the major networks, did not have much effect. Anyway President Clinton could not have answered them there, for at the time of the demonstration he was not in Washington at all but far away somewhere in Michigan. But this action, repeated over the years, did draw the attention of the public to the zeal of the UFO researchers, the covering up by the Air Force and the demand for a clarification of the 1947 incident.

At the beginning of 1994 it seemed as if the days of the coverup by the Air Force, after lasting for many decades, were now numbered. For, even before the demonstration, the researcher Sergeant Clifford Stone from Roswell had corresponded with Congressman Steven Schiff of New Mexico, telling him about the latest stand of Roswell research. Schiff then asked the Defense Secretary Les Aspen by letter for a personal briefing on that subject. But instead of replying personally, Aspen forwarded the letter to the Pentagon office for legisla-

"Tell us about Roswell, Mr. President": The UFO demonstration in front of the White House 5 July 1993.

tive matters. They sent him a standard letter, referring him to the files of the Air Force connected with Project Blue Book, which were in the National Archives in Washington. Now, in this project Blue Book an overworked team of low-ranking officers had tried to "identify" over 12,000 cases of reported UFOs, most of them questionable—but Roswell was not one of them. Annoyed about his being so simply waved off, Schiff approached Aspen once more on 10 May 1993 and demanded clear information. Again only a standard letter was the answer.

Now Schiff became really annoyed by the treatment given to a representative of the people. He could not and would not simply accept that. After all, he was a member of the House Government Operations Committee, and for him it was a matter of principle. And for dealing with such cases—to inquire into and investigate the statements and actions of the government—Congress had established the General Accounting Office (GAO). More than once had this office been successful in exposing covered-up scandals. It was the GAO that in December 1993 brought out the illegal experiments on people made by the Atomic Energy Commission towards the end of the forties. In 1992 alone it conducted 1,380 inquiries, which raised its budget to $490 million in 1993, as compared to $46.8 million in 1965.

In October 1993 Schiff met GAO chairman Charles A. Bowsher to discuss the possibilities of a GAO investigation of the Roswell affair. Schiff expressed his annoyance about the reluctance of the Pentagon to give information. Bowsher promised that the GAO would look into the matter. When in January 1994 the press learnt about the enquiry, an experienced GAO official found himself "stonewalled" by the Pentagon, as GAO spokeswoman Laura A. Kopelson announced.[1]

On February 15, 1994, GAO director of National Security Analysis Richard Davis officially informed the new defense secretary William J. Perry about GAOs intention of (1) "acquiring, classifying, retaining and disposing of official government documents dealing with weather balloon, aircraft and similar crash incidents" in connection with UFOs, unknown and foreign aircraft, and (2) of getting all the "facts involving the reported crash of an UFO in 1949 (sic) at Roswell, New Mexico . . . (and an) alleged DoD cover-up."

A first talk between the GAO official and the general inspector of the Defense Department took place on February 28, 1994. It was agreed that the main place to look for documents in this connection would be the archives of the Air Force. Under GAO File No. 701034 the "Procedures of the Archive Administration Regarding Documents Connected with Weather Balloons, Unknown Aircraft and Similar Cases of Crash" were collected. It was of little importance that at the time in question there had been no "Air Force," which had been founded as an independent entity only in September 1947, taking over the archives of the former AAF.[2]

Meanwhile, one is tempted to say, the Air Force had independently taken the initiative. Thus the office of the administrative assistant of the Air Force Department (SAF/AA) instructed the office of the director for security and control of special programs, Colonel Richard L. Weaver, to compile a report, which was to be laid before the GAO. On September 8, 1994 this report was finished. It had twenty-two pages, thirty-three appendices, and was signed by Weaver. His conclusion: No, an ordinary weather balloon did not crash in Roswell; that was a cover-up story invented by the Air Force. But what did crash was still a weather balloon, not any alien spacecraft, but it had a highly secret mission. This mission had the code name "Project Mogul." The purpose of the project was to

"Report of the Air Force Research Regarding the Roswell Incident"— Col. Weavers Report July 1994.

detect atmospheric disturbances in the atmosphere, which would betray Russian atomic tests.

Naturally Weaver did not have any valid proof for this claim. No report from the base commander of RAAF Colonel Blanchard could be found, or from General Ramey at Fort Worth, not even from Major Marcel or Captain Cavitt, which would have eliminated all doubts. Not one coeval document was cited. On the other hand, the director of security and control of special projects based his deduction on a few statements by witnesses, taken out of their context, from the records of UFO researcher Karl Pflock and the statement by Brazel on 9 July 1947 to the *Roswell Daily Record* in the presence of two armed MPs, at a time when he was in the custody of the AAF and stood under strong psychological pressure, which he later frequently compared with imprisonment—in short, under duress. Everything else was hypotheses, speculations and suggestions under the motto "could it not have been so?", together with some interviews connected with the Mogul project.

Only two of the 300-plus eyewitnesses were personally interviewed: of all people the meteorological officer of Fort Worth, Major Irving Newton, who had only seen the weather balloon at the press conference with General Ramey, and the CIC agent Capt. Cavitt, who was now a retired Lieutenant Colonel. Cavitt was certainly an important witness. He had gone with Marcel

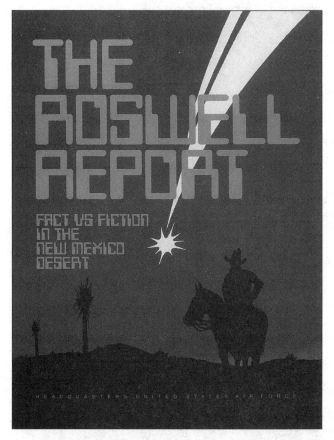

The 800-page "Roswell Report" of the U.S. Air Force. It includes all available information on the Mogul Project but doesn't prove any link to the Roswell incident.

and Brazel to the Foster ranch, had collected debris with Marcel from the field, on the next day supervised the further collection of debris and clearing of the field. Repeatedly Roswell researchers had tried to interview him, but he had always put them off politely. Once he had said that he had never been to the Foster Ranch, then again referred to his oath of silence. "Don't have any hopes, he'll tell you nothing," his wife said to Kevin Randle, "my husband has learned to keep his silence.

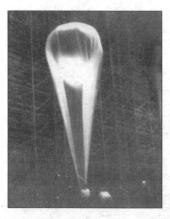

A Mogul balloon.

A crashed Mogul balloon, photographed fronm the air, east of Roswell in July 1948. Obviously such a balloon could never have been responsible for the ¾ of a mile long debris field on the Foster Ranch.

Otherwise they would never have given him so many highly sensitive jobs."[3]

Now, however, asked by Colonel Weaver, Cavitt spoke up. And his story differed so drastically from everything that was considered to be confirmed about the Roswell story, that one researcher, Bruce Maccabee, (almost) seriously asked whether Cavitt had been involved at all or Marcel had confused him with another CIC man. At first Cavitt claimed to have been to the Foster ranch only once with Marcel and Rickett but without Brazel. That, however, is basically impossible—how could they have found the site without the help of Brazel? As a matter of fact, he drove with Marcel and Brazel to the ranch on the first day, and returned to it with Rickett the next day. What he saw there he described to Weaver as follows: *"The area of this debris was very small, about 20 feet square, and the material was spread on the ground, but there was no gouge or crater or other obvious sign of impact. I remember recognizing this material as being consistent with a weather balloon. We gathered up some of this material, which would easily fit into one vehicle."*[4]

That too can be ruled out. According to Marcel the debris covered an area three quarters of a mile by about 200 yards; even in his statement on 9 July 1947 to the *Roswell Daily Record*, which Weaver cites as reliable evidence, Brazel confirms the "width (to be) about 200 yards."[5] In fact it was so big that Brazel had to transport his sheep around to the other side, for they refused to cross the debris-covered area to reach their waterhole. Sheep herds in the infertile prairie of New Mexico graze over very wide areas, and a twenty-foot square spot would have held back not even a lone sheep. Further, Sergeant Rickett confirmed that the field was still covered with debris when he went to the ranch on July 8, which again was supported by the journalist Jason Kellahin. Naturally Cavitt did not say why he had apparently withheld his opinion that it was a weather balloon from Marcel and Blanchard, which would have prevented the "saucer" debacle at that time.

What about the Mogul Project, and what did it have to do with Roswell? The project was carried out in June and July 1947 at the Alamogordo AFB south of the White Sands Proving Grounds, under the supervision of scientists of New York University and the Watson

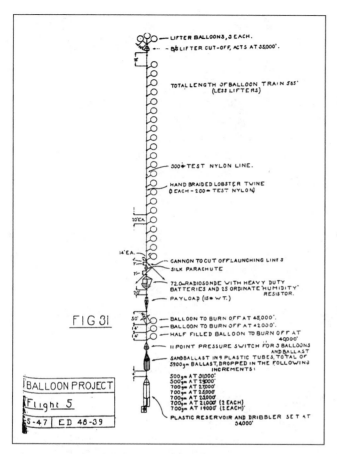

LIFTER BALLOONS, 3 EACH.
~B/4 LIFTER CUT-OFF, ACTS AT 35,000'.

TOTAL LENGTH OF BALLOON TRAIN 565'
(LESS LIFTERS)

300# TEST NYLON LINE.

HAND BRAIDED LOBSTER TWINE
(5 EACH - 200# TEST NYLON)

20'EA.

14'EA.

CANNON TO CUT OFF LAUNCHING LINE S
SILK PARACHUTE

72.0 RADIOSONDE WITH HEAVY DUTY
BATTERIES AND 25 ORDINATE HUMIDITY
RESISTOR.
PAYLOAD (15# WT.)

BALLOON TO BURN OFF AT 45,000'.
BALLOON TO BURN OFF AT 42000'.
HALF FILLED BALLOON TO BURN OFF AT
40000'
11 POINT PRESSURE SWITCH FOR 3 BALLOONS
AND BALLAST
SAND BALLAST IN 9 PLASTIC TUBES, TOTAL OF
5900gm BALLAST, DROPPED IN THE FOLLOWING
INCREMENTS:
500gm AT 31000'
500gm AT 29000'
700gm AT 27000'
700gm AT 25000'
700gm AT 23000'
700gm AT 21000' (2 EACH)
700gm AT 19000' (2 EACH)
PLASTIC RESERVOIR AND DRIBBLER SET AT
34000'

FIG 31

BALLOON PROJECT
Flight 5
5-47 | ED 48-39

Sketch of a Mogul balloon, Flight 5 of 5 June 1947.

Laboratories. Balloons were used which remained stationary at a certain height and carried instruments capable of measuring shock waves that one could expect to be set off by Soviet atomic explosions. The project stood under the highest level of secrecy, Top Secret 1A. The only secret thing about the project was its purpose, perhaps also the wave detectors. The balloons were conventional weather balloons.

Weaver succeeded in finding the project engineer Professor Charles B. Moore and interviewing him.

Moore confirmed that in the beginning, during June 1947, they bound whole batteries of conventional neoprene balloons together, so as to keep the instruments longer in the atmosphere. At first these were common sound-measuring instruments, such as those used in submarines, later better acoustic sensors from the Watson Laboratories. Between the actual launches, there were also "Service Flights"—balloons with radar reflectors and other testing instruments. These were tagged—as also the Mogul instruments—to say that the finder would be rewarded, if he informed the University of New York. Of the ten Mogul flights in June and July 1947, the flights 2, 4 and 9 were service flights, not part of the series.

According to Professor Moore, the radar reflectors were made by a firm of toy manufacturers, and consisted of aluminium foil, hardened balsa wood and sticking tape of a color between pink and purple, bearing prints of little flowers and hearts. If a Mogul balloon crashed, it did not survive the effects of the elements and the heat of New Mexico for very long. The neoprene material of the balloons weathered very quickly—after a few days only ash-colored flakes were left—and the aluminium foil would be torn by the wind and scattered. Therefore Colonel Weaver concluded: *"Flight 4 was launched on June 4, 1947, but was not recovered by the NYU (New York University) group. It is very probable that this Top Secret project balloon train (Flight 4), made up of unclassified components* [emphasis added], *came to rest some miles northwest of Roswell, N.M., became shredded in the surface winds, and was ultimately found by the rancher, Brazel, ten days later."*[6]

But this explanation is nothing more than word play. "Top secret" was only the purpose, not—as the colonel concedes—the components. These consisted of a number of neoprene balloons, with a radar reflector and other instruments. A Mogul balloon was a

A Mogul balloon with radar reflectors is prepared for launch.

Components of a Mogul balloon, in the center radar reflectors.

usual balloon with an unusual task. It was even tagged, so that a finder could report it. The fact that of the seventeen balloons started, most were found and reported, shows that the system worked. In no case was any particular security measure required—no uninitiated person would ever have known that he or she had found anything other than a usual meteorological research balloon. Thus number five crashed on June 5 east of Roswell and could be recovered by the Mogul team after a rancher had called the number given on the tag. And Brazel, who had often enough found weather balloons on his ranch, should have mistaken such a balloon for a "flying saucer"? Theoretically, even that is possible.

But certainly Jesse Marcel should have recognized what it was. He had been at the school of the Air Intelligence Corps, served in the war as investigator of

air crashes. Was he then, in July 1947, a victim of youthful enthusiasm? This too is possible, since his statements were made between 1978 and 1982. But only half a year after the incident he was promoted to the rank of lieutenant colonel and transferred to the Pentagon, to work on that project which was to, and finally did, find out when the Russians had their first atom bomb, a project that was part of Mogul. "I was familiar with more or less everything that was in the air in those days, not only ours, but those of a lot of countries," said Marcel in 1979, "and I still believe what we found was not from this earth.[7]

Was that because he held little flowers and hearts on sticking tape to be a message from space? Can we really believe that if Marcel had been so foolish he would have been sent to the Pentagon to do a highly responsible job? And Colonel Blanchard, would he have

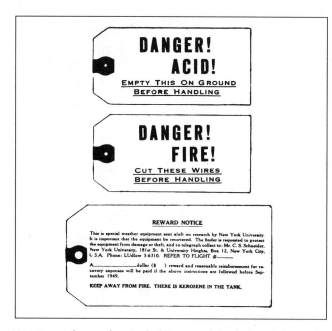

Warning and reward tags which instructed the finder to contact the project headquarter in New York and promised a reward. In all cases, the ranchers recognized the balloon and called the number on the tag.

climbed to the rank of deputy chief of staff of the Air Force if he had "raised a storm in a tea cup" at the time in question? Had he not died of a heart attack, he would have become chief of staff, the second highest rank in the Air Force. Would he not at least have hesitated, as commander of a base, before making such a spectacular announcement in the media, if he had even merely envisaged the possibility of his intelligence officer having found a balloon instead of a "saucer" at the Foster Ranch?

The Air Force version of the story of Roswell is full of contradictions. For instance it is emphasized that neoprene, in the heat of the desert, would "almost look like dark gray or black flakes or ashes after exposure to the sun for only a few days"; on the other hand, Brazel

is supposed to have found and collected it after thirty days. At first chief witness Cavitt is cited, who talks of a simple balloon, then suddenly the talk is of batteries of balloons. On one hand, we are to believe that the wind scattered the aluminium foil over an area 200 yards wide (Brazel and Marcel) and three quarters of a mile long (Marcel); on the other, that it was the weather balloon in General Ramey's office that had been gathered on the field—Weaver thus effectively accusing Air Force General Thomas J. DuBose of lying, for he maintains the opposite. According to Major Irving Newton, it was "a balloon with a Rawin-Radar reflector"[8] and was—as the photographs show—fairly intact, too intact for a balloon that had been exposed on the desert for thirty days, too intact for a balloon whose fragments had been scattered over an area of over 240,000 square yards. And it could not have been all that secret, otherwise General Ramey would never have allowed its photograph to be circulated all over the world.

If the total balloon debris had been flown to Fort Worth on July 8, what was the purpose of the four C-54 transporters that were loaded "with wreckage" the next morning and which left in the afternoon of July 9? Marcel stated that after a whole day of gathering the debris with Cavitt, only a fraction of the fragments had been collected. According to the affidavit of an eyewitness, R. Smith, the biggest fragment was about twenty feet long and six feet wide, bigger than anything a Mogul balloon had ever carried. "What kind of balloon would fill the trunk of Marcel's car, the back of a jeep and still require fifty to sixty soldiers to collect the rest of it for two days?" Don Schmitt and Kevin Randle asked.[9]

Why was the salvaging continued at all, after the identification by General Ramey? Why the security measures, the road blockades, the intimidation of witnesses who had seen only a balloon? Why did the field of debris have to be combed with such thoroughness, why the confiscation, months after the event, of the fragments that Bill Brazel, Jr. had found, if they were only neoprene and aluminium foil? The components of the balloons were not secret, only the mission, as explicitly stated in the Weaver report: "The materials recovered by the AAF in July 1947, were not readily recognizable as anything special (only the purpose was special), and the recovered debris itself was unclassified."[10] Really?

All witnesses who had had the material in their hands were impressed by its fantastic properties. It was so hard that not even a sledgehammer could make a dent in it, but still so elastic that if one crumpled it, it regained its shape at once when released. Finally, CIC agent Lewis Rickett, who had supervised the salvaging with Cavitt, declared that a year after that he had spoken to another CIC agent of the Andrews AFB, who had said, "We still don't know what it is . . . our metallurgists couldn't even cut it."[11]

General Exon too, who later became commander of Wright Field, confirmed the fantastic nature and qualities of the metallic pieces. Aluminium foil? Why, if only a Mogul balloon had been found at Roswell, did General Schulgen, chief of the Air Force Intelligence Corps, include, on 30 October 1947, such items as *"metallic foils, plastics and perhaps balsa wood or similar material . . . of . . . unusual fabrication methods to achieve extreme light weight and structural stability,"* under *"items of construction"* of *"flying saucer type of aircraft or object"?*[12], when four months after General Ramey's identification of the Roswell fragments the results must have been common knowledge in the Pentagon?

Naturally, Project Mogul was known at the Pentagon. In August 1947, one of the all-too-often faked UFO crashes—more or less as an echo of Roswell—of that summer was reported to the FBI. The alleged UFO

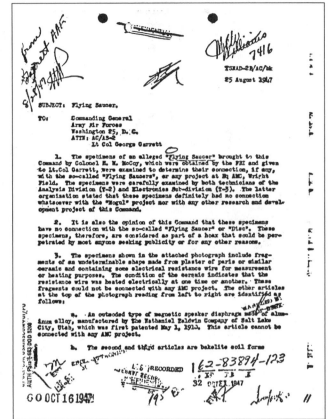

Memorandum of the commanding generals of the Army Air Force of 25 August 1947 about the recovery of alleged UFO fragments which later turned out to be a hoax. Interestingly it refers to Project Mogul, although the document is only classified "Confidential." Obviously Project Mogul never was as secret and mysterious as the Air Force claimed in 1994.

wreck was found on a farm near Danworth, Illinois. It was finally handed over by Lieutenant Colonel Garrett of the FBI to Colonel H. M. McCoy, vice-commander of the Analytical Division of the Air Force Intelligence Corps (T-2). On 25 August 1947 Colonel McCoy informed the commanding generals of the AAF at the Pentagon and Lieutenant Colonel Garrett about the findings: the UFO fragments consisted of gypsum, ceramics, an old loudspeaker membrane from the year 1910, a few other electronic parts and bakelite paper wound with copper wire. Although the whole affair was so ludicrous, a single reference in Colonel McCoy's memorandum startled us. *"The Electronics Subdivision (T-3) . . . stated that these specimen definitely had no connection whatsoever with the 'Mogul' project nor with any other research and development project of this command."*[13]

Therefore Mogul was known and so little "Top Secret" that it was mentioned in a memorandum classified only as "confidential." Naturally no one in the Air Force fell for this find, no journalist announced with enthusiasm the discovery of a "flying saucer," and no one thought of registering its "qualities" under the characteristics of unknown flying objects four months later.

Finally, there exists no proof whatsoever that Mogul flight number four ever started, let alone crashed at Roswell. The official logbook of the project begins explicitly with flight five on 5 June 1947. Flights A and B were started from New York, flight one in Pennsylvania on the East Coast, flights two to four, at least officially, did not start.[14]

And how did the Air Force evaluate the statements of more than twenty people who had spoken of alien bodies? They could not exist. Why? Colonel Weaver explains: *"First, the recovered wreckage was from a Project MOGUL balloon. There were no 'alien' passengers therein."* Further, *"some of these claims have been shown to be hoaxes."* Even UFO fans could not decide how many there were. Some witnesses use pseudonyms, others are dead, and in addition, *"many of the persons making the biggest claims of 'alien bodies' make their living from the 'Roswell incident,'"* which of course is not true and is a nasty allegation on the part of the Air Force. *"Lastly, persons who have come for-*

List of all launches of Mogul balloons until 5 July 1947.

ward and provided their names and made claims may have, in good faith but in the 'fog of time,' misinterpreted past events. The review of Air Force records did not locate even one piece of evidence to indicate that the Air Force has had any part in an 'alien' body recovery operation or continuing cover-up."[15]

Weaver could produce just as much proof for his Mogul theory. And so what had to happen, happened— the GAO pronounced the report as insufficient and continued its investigations. The public wanted the truth, and the matter became more acute when SHO broadcast a film in three parts, *Roswell*, produced by Paul Davis, with Martin Sheen and Kyle Maclachlan in the leading roles. Davis had been fascinated by the theme since reading the book *UFO Crash at Roswell* by Kevin Randle and Don Schmitt. The miniseries was based on the book and was as well-founded as a documentary.

The fictitious beginning showed a veterans' gathering at Roswell in 1977, at which all those who had been there in 1947 meet again after thirty years and reminisce. These reminiscences, however different they sometimes were, were dramatized, and like pieces of a jigsaw puzzle, formed a complete picture. Naturally there were also those who denied everything or those who kept their oath of silence. The film was good, was moving, for the first time made millions of people aware of the event at Roswell, and made them want to know the truth. Kent Jeffrey, a commercial airline pilot and UFO enthusiast from California, stepped forward at the right time and proclaimed that it was "high time for the truth about Roswell." So he started the "Roswell Initiative," a worldwide signature-collecting movement demanding from the U.S. Government what he called "a logical straightforward way to find out the truth about Roswell."

An executive resolution, which lifts all secrecy of information in all matters connected with the existence of UFOs and

Press release of New Mexico Congressman Steve Schiff regarding the GAO report: "Missing documents leave unanswered questions."

extra-terrestrial intelligence. Such a decision would be justified and appropriate, since this is a unique chance of universal import. To guarantee the safety of all witnesses it would be necessary to formulate a clear resolution and make it a law. Such a measure is necessary and that was also exactly what the then presidential candidate Jimmy Carter in 1976, promised and then withheld from the American people.

If, as officially maintained, no information about Roswell, UFOs or extra-terrestrial intelligence is being held back, an

Schiff pointed out that the GAO estimates that the messages were destroyed over 40 years ago, making further inquiry about their destruction impractical.

Documents revealed by the report include an FBI teletype and reference in a newsletter style internal forum at RAAF that refer to a "radar tracking device" - a reference to a weather balloon. Even though the weather balloon story has since been discredited by the US Air Force, Schiff suggested that the authors of those communications may have been repeating what they were told, rather than consciously adding to what some believe is a "cover up."

"At least this effort caused the Air Force to acknowledge that the crashed vehicle was no weather balloon," Schiff said. "That explanation never fit the fact of high military security used at the time." The Air Force in September, 1994 claimed that the crashed vehicle was a then-classified device to detect evidence of possible Soviet nuclear testing.

Schiff also praised the efforts of the GAO; describing their work as "professional, conscientious and thorough."

A two page letter discussing a related investigation into "Majestic 12" was also delivered.

Schiff will be available to the media Saturday, July 29th, from 10:00 AM to 2:00 PM at 2404 Rayburn HOB in Washington, DC and by telephone: (202) 225-6316.

A copy of the report may be obtained by calling (202) 512-6000 and referencing Document number GAO/NSIAD-95-187.

GAO

United States General Accounting Office

Report to the Honorable
Steven H. Schiff, House of
Representatives

July 1995

GOVERNMENT RECORDS

Results of a Search for Records Concerning the 1947 Crash Near Roswell, New Mexico

GAO/NSIAD-95-187

The GAO report "Results of a Search for Records Concerning the 1947 Crash near Roswell, New Mexico."

---

executive resolution for lifting of the secrecy will be only a formality, for there is nothing to be exposed. The resolution would in any case have the positive effect that the matter would be settled once for all. Years of controversy and suspicion would end—in the eyes of the American public and in the eyes of the world.

If on the other hand the witnesses of Roswell are telling the truth and information about extra-terrestrials exists, then this can be no matter over which only a few privileged people in the American Government have exclusive rights. That represents information of a fundamental kind, which all the peoples on this planet have a right to know. The release of this information would be universally and historically acclaimed as an act of honesty and good will.[16]

And indeed Jeffrey's initiative was welcomed worldwide. Up to January 1996 he had received 22,000 signed declarations, from ten countries. A few hundred signatures came from scientists and engineers, two from retired generals of the Air Force, two from U.S. astronauts, one of whom had landed on the moon. The strategy of the initiative is to put the signatures in a confidential data bank and present them to congressmen, senators and the president at regular intervals, each time updated. Jeffrey has planned to make a first presentation in 1997, when he proposes to give lists of signed declarations to the president and members of Congress. On the same day the representatives of the movement in each of the other countries will hand over their petitions to the U.S. ambassadors in their respective countries.

Jeffrey had already collected over 18,000 signatures when, on 28 July 1995, after many delays, the GAO report was finally sent to congressman Schiff. The timing of the completion of the report would seem to have been deliberately chosen. According to the GAO rules, the report could be published thirty days after it had been given to the congressman, that is, on August 27. For August 28, the British film producer Ray Santilli had announced the worldwide broadcasting of allegedly authentic footage showing the autopsy made on two alien bodies found near Roswell, which according to the Air Force was not possible.[17]

But the report was disappointing. It raised more questions than it answered. The GAO investigations showed that all files referring to the incident had been destroyed, without any written instructions to do so. This applied in particular to all reports which must have gone from Roswell AFB to Washington and Fort Worth during July 1947. If these had been found, the Roswell mystery would have been cleared up for good. But they have disappeared without a trace—actually an impossibility in military procedure. In addition, it had to do with the 509th Bomb Group, stationed at Roswell, the first and at that time the only unit to possess atom bombs, an elite group which was constantly engaged in high security operations. The documents of the most important bomber unit of the U.S.A. should never have been destroyed, especially not without explicit orders to do so—an order which at least must have been kept in the files. There is only one explanation for this: someone "very high up" in the military hierarchy had wiped out all traces of the Roswell incident, to turn it into something that "never happened."

"It is my understanding that these outgoing messages were permanent records, which should never have been destroyed. The GAO could not identify who destroyed the messages, or why," said Congressman Schiff, who gave the GAO Report to the press on the same day, the *"missing documents leave unanswered questions."*[18]

"We conducted an extensive search for government records related to the crash near Roswell," says the twenty-page report. *"We examined a wide range of documents dating from July 1947 through the 1950s. These records came from numerous organizations in New Mexico and elsewhere throughout DoD as well as The Federal Bureau of Investigation (FBI), the Central Intelligence Agency (CIA) and the National Security Council. . . . In our search for records concerning the Roswell crash, we learned that some government records covering Roswell AFB activities had been destroyed, and others had not. For example, RAAF (Roswell Army Air Field) administrative records (from Mar. 1945 through Dec. 1949) and RAAF outgoing messages (from Oct. 1946 through Dec. 1949) were destroyed. The document disposition form does not indicate what organization or person destroyed the records and when or under what authority the records were destroyed."*

The National Security Council, the CIA and the Department of Energy too declared that they had found no files concerning the incident. On the same day that Schiff received the GAO report, he got another letter from the GAO, this time referring to his second question, that of whether they could confirm the authenticity of the "Majestic 12 documents." While the telex of November 1980 from the AFOSI, which Bill Moore had been given by "Falcon" , was "designated by the AFOSI as a forgery"—which it was, or at least an altered version of a genuine document—the GAO report leaves the matter open. It quotes the replies of the "Information Security Oversight Office," of the Air Force Department of Security and Research programs, of the National Archives, and of the Truman and Eisenhower Libraries, which all maintain that "they found nothing that appeared to fit the description of the Majestic 12 material or any references to this particular designation." That, of course, leaves everything open, if one accepts that the documents are still under security regulations, should not be copied (Eyes Only) and are accessible only to members of the MJ-12.[19]

"Back to square one," that is all the GAO Report means. One was just as wise afterwards as before. Those who had from the beginning decided in favor of hushing up had seen to it that the biggest mystery of the twentieth century could not be solved by conventional methods. But four weeks after the report was published, Roswell made headlines all over the world once more.

A proof of an entirely different kind had come up, which promised to clarify the affair. Yes, a spaceship was recovered in 1947 in New Mexico; yes, they had found the occupants, declared a cameraman of the U.S. Army Air Force—and presented as proof of his statements film footage showing the autopsies made on two strange beings. But his most astounding statement was that the first UFO had crashed on 31 May 1947, five weeks before the Roswell incident took place.

[1] *Albuquerque Journal*, 13 and 14 January 1994.
   Washington Post, 14 January 1994.
   Arkansas Democrat-Gazette, 15 January 1994.

[2] Weaver, Colonel Richard, "Report of Air Force Research Regarding the 'Roswell Incident,'" Washington, D.C., 1994.

[3] Randle, Kevin and Don Schmitt, *UFO Crash at Roswell*, New York, 1991.

[4] Weaver, 1994.

[5] *Roswell Daily Record*, 9 July 1947.

[6] Weaver, 1994.

[7] Pratt, Bob, Interview with Colonel Jesse Marcel, 8 December 1979.

[8] Weaver, 1994.

[9] Randle, Kevin and Don Schmitt, *The Report on the Conclusions of the Recent Air Force Analysis of the Roswell Incident*, Marion, IA, 1994.

[10] Weaver, 1994.

[11] Randle, Kevin and Don Schmitt, *The Truth About the UFO Crash at Roswell*, New York, 1994.

[12] Schulgen, General F., "Intelligence Requirements on Flying Saucer Type Aircraft," 30 October 1947.

[13] Colonel N. M. McCoy, "Report to the Commanding General AAF, Subject: Flying Saucer," 25 August 1947.

[14] Moore, Charles B., "Constant Level Balloon," Research Division Project No. 93, New York, 1 April 1948.

[15] Weaver, 1994.

[16] International Roswell Initiative, *The Roswell Declaration*, 1994.

[17] Koch, Joachim, "Der Santilli-Zirkus—Eine Mitteilung der Internationalen Roswell-Initiative," in *UFO-Kurier* No. 13, Rottenburg, 1995.

[18] Schiff, Steve, News Release, 28 July 1995.

[19] United States General Accounting Office, "Results of a Search for Records Concerning the 1947 Crash Near Roswell, New Mexico (GAO/NSIAD-95-187)," Washington, D.C., 1995.

13.

The Santilli Autopsy Film

leveland, Ohio, July 1992. Actually, Ray Santilli came to America from London to look for not-yet-released material from the early days of Rock 'n' Roll. He had been in the music business for seventeen years: had begun with promotion and marketing, had been manager for recording artists and finally started his own record company. He was able to get the exclusive rights to the soundtracks of Walt Disney's films for the UK and was sole distributor for Walt Disney Audio Products. Later he set up his Merlin Group and was constantly on the lookout for unpublished material. Cleveland was just the right place for rock 'n' roll. During the fifties the city had a particularly flourishing high-school scene and in summer 1955 the 'great ones' of this style of music played at the schools of Cleveland: Bill Haley, Pat Boone and one as yet unknown young man, who captured everyone's hearts overnight, Elvis Presley, whom they later called "the King."

Santilli reckoned that the period around July would be the best time for his purpose. One could expect that on Independence Day some of the teenagers of those days, now in their mid-fifties, would visit their parents, together with their children, who would now be in college.

Ray had taken a business friend, Gary Shoefield, with him. Shoefield worked for Polygram and was interested in getting new Elvis material. To begin with, they went to the local newspaper, which published an article announcing their presence in Cleveland and their interest in every kind of memorabilia from that era—pictures, autographs, films, etc.—and giving their hotel address. Some of the Elvis material obtained by Santilli were later featured in the *Daily Mirror* in London on August 17, 1992, on pages twelve and thirteen.[1]

The announcement had hardly appeared, when Santilli received a telephone call. There was a man at the other end who said that his father, Jack, had been a free-lance photographer in those days. Just when the big stars were playing in an open air concert near Cleveland, the cameramen's union had gone on strike and Universal News Agency had hired Jack to shoot the concerts. Universal had bought some of his films, but he still had the rest at home. He lived in Florida, but was now here in Cleveland, to go sailing with him on a nearby lake.

Santilli met cameraman Jack B., who had just turned eighty-two. They decided to meet in Florida, when Santilli would come to the States again, which happened a few months later. The elderly man lived in a little house in a clean suburb. The deal went through

U.S. Army Signal Corps cameraman in Burma, 1945. With the same Bell & Howell camera Jack X. filmed the UFO recovery and both autopsies.

smoothly. Santilli could use the film material, which included some of the earliest shots of Presley. And he paid in cash, which pleased Jack very much.

The next morning, as Santilli was packing his suitcase in his hotel room, Jack called him up on the telephone. "Ray, are you interested in other material as well?" he asked. Ray said he was. "Then come along here again. I have something here that may be more interesting than the Elvis films." Santilli ordered a taxi, and half an hour later he was at Jack's. Jack offered him a seat on the sofa and asked him to wait till he brought the material. He

went out and returned a couple of minutes later, with a cardboard box full of 16-mm films in aluminium cans. "Ray, have you ever heard of the Roswell incident? A UFO crashed in the desert of New Mexico in those days. I was there, filmed the salvaging. And you know what the craziest thing about it is? I shouldn't have these films at all. But the Pentagon has simply forgotten them. . . ."[1A] He then let loose and told a story that was as fantastic as a report from another world:

I joined the forces in March of 1942 and left in 1952. The ten years I spent serving my country were some of the best years of my life.

My father was in the movie business, which meant I had good knowledge about the workings of cameras and photography. For this reason I believe I passed a medical that would not normally allow me in, due to polio as a child..

After my enrollment and training, I was able to use my camera skills and became one of the few dedicated cameramen in the forces. I was sent to many places, and as it was war time I fast learned the ability of filming under difficult circumstances.

I will not give more detail on my background, only to say that in the fall of 1944 I was assigned to Intelligence, reporting to the assistant chief of air staff, I was moved around depending on the assignment. During my time I filmed a great deal, including the tests at White Sands (Manhattan Project/Trinity).

I remember very clearly receiving the call to go to White Sands (Roswell). I had not long returned from St. Louis, Missouri, where I had filmed the new ramjet ("little Henry").

Jack meant the ramjet helicopter "McDonnell XH-20, Little Henry, the first flight of which took place on 5 May 1947 at the McDonnell Airport in St. Louis.

It was June 1 when McDonald [George C. McDonald, director of the Army Air Force Intelligence Corps] asked me to

Major General Clements McMullen, Deputy Commander of the Strategic Air Command (SAC) in 1947.

General Carl A. "Tooey" Spaatz, Commanding General Army Air Force, 1947.

General Spaatz (left) and RAAF Vice Commander Col. Tibbits (right).

The journey lasted almost four hours. At first they passed an Apache reservation, then the White Sands Missile Range. From Socorro they took the road to Magdalena, from there a desert track that led them through a canyon, and finally they came to the north bank of a dried-up lake.

report to General McMullen [Major General Clements M. McMullen, Deputy Commander of the Strategic Air Command—SAC—in Washington, D.C.] for a special assignment. I had had no experience of working with McMullen but after talking to him for a few minutes I knew that I would never wish to be his enemy. McMullan was straight to the point, no messing. I was ordered to a crash site just southwest of Socorro. It was urgent and my brief was to film everything in sight, not to leave the debris until it had been removed, and I was to have access to all areas of the site, if the commander in charge had a problem with that I was told to get them to call McMullen. A few minutes after my orders from McMullen I received the same instruction from Tooey [nickname for General Carl Spaatz, chief of staff of the Air Force] saying it was the crash of a Russian spy plane. Two generals in one day, this job was important.

I flew out from Andrews with sixteen other officers and personnel, mostly medical. We arrived at Wright-Patterson and collected more men and equipment. From there we flew to Roswell on a C54. When we got to Roswell we were transported by road to the site.

When we arrived, the site had already been cordoned off. From the start it was plain to see this was no Russian spy plane, it was a large disc "flying saucer" on its back with heat still radiating from the ground around it.

The commander on site handed over to the SAC medical team who were still waiting for Kenney [General George C. Kenney, Commander of the SAC] to arrive. However, nothing had been done as everyone was just waiting for orders.

It was decided to wait until the heat subsided before moving in, as fire was a significant risk, this was made all the worse by the screams of the freak creatures that were lying by the vehicle. What in God's name they were, no one could tell, but one thing's for sure, they were circus freaks, creatures with no business here. Each had hold of a box which they kept hold of in both arms close to their chests. They just lay there crying, holding those boxes.

Once my tent had been set up I started filming immediately, first the vehicle, then the site and debris. At around 0600 it was deemed safe to move in. Again the freaks were still crying and when approached screamed even louder. They were protective of their boxes but we managed to get one loose with a firm strike at the head of a freak with the butt of a rifle.

The cameraman's sketches of the crash.

General George C. Kenney, commanding general of the Strategic Air Command

The three freaks were dragged away and secured with rope and tape; the other one was already dead. The medical team were reluctant at first to go near these freaks, but as some were injured, they had no choice. Once the creatures were collected, the priority was to collect all debris that could be removed easily as there was still a risk of fire. This debris seemed to come from exterior struts that were supporting a very small disc on the underside of the craft which must have snapped off when the disc flipped over. (They bore strange hieroglyph-like signs.) The debris was taken to tent stations for logging, then loaded onto trucks. After three days a full team from Washington came down and the decision was taken to move the craft. Inside it, the atmosphere was very heavy. It was impos-sible to stay in longer than a few seconds without feeling very sick. Therefore, it was decided to analyze it back at base so it was loaded onto a flattop and taken to Wright Patterson, which is where I joined it.

I stayed at Wright-Patterson for a further three weeks working on the debris. I was then told to report to Fort Worth (Dallas) for the filming of an autopsy. Normally I would not have a problem with this, but it was discovered that the freaks may be a medical threat. Therefore I was required to wear the same protective suits as the doctors. It was impossible to handle the camera properly, loading and focusing were very difficult. In fact against orders I removed my suit during the filming. The first two autopsies took place in July 1947.

The autopsies were done by Professor Detlev Bronk and a certain Dr. Willies or Williams—Jack could not recall the name properly. President Truman was apparently also present at one of these.

"But how did you manage to keep back these rolls, without being detected?" asked Santilli.

After filming I had several hundred reels. I separated problem reels which required special attention in processing (these I would do later), the first batch was sent through to Washington, and I processed the remainder a few days later. Once the remaining reels had been processed I contacted Washington to arrange collection of the final batch. Incredibly they never came to collect or arrange transportation for them. I called many times, then just gave up. The footage has remained with me ever since.

In May of 1949 I was asked to film the third autopsy.[2]

"The third autopsy?" asked Santilli. "Yes, the fourth freak lived for two more years. The autopsy was performed at Washington, in a big auditorium, in the presence of scientists from various states, also from England and France." "And where had they kept the creature imprisoned for two years?" "I don't know. But I heard

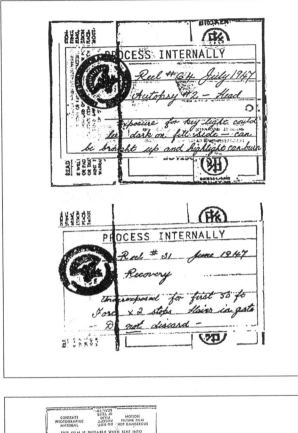

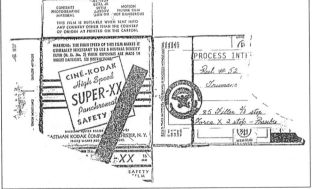

The labels of three of the reels of cameraman Jack B. One says "Recovery", the other "Truman..."

that they had been able to communicate with him. But without words, nonverbal, whatever that means."[3]

Santilli wanted to know why Jack wanted to sell that material just then and why, in particular, to him. "I am eighty-two years old," answered the cameraman, "and I know that I won't have many more opportunities to do so. Ray, I trust you, because you are not from here. I need the money, for my favorite granddaughter is going to get married soon and I want her to have a real proper wedding. You can have the stuff, all of it—for $150,000 in cash, owing to the taxes—you know. And nothing on paper. You get the films, I get the money. And you tell nobody where you got the films from."

As proof of his statements, he showed Santilli his army discharge papers dated 1952, pictures taken during the period of his service and his diary. He then brought out an old 16-mm projector and a screen from the store room, loaded a roll and let it run. On the screen one could see a creature, clearly not human, lying on a table, with two doctors nearby. If that was genuine, Santilli was sure that he was on to the biggest sensation of the century. On to something that would make headlines all over the world, lead to heated discussions—and make him a rich man. Fascinated but equally incredulous, he held one of the rolls in his hand. How could he find out whether the film was genuine? It was a Kodak film. "May I call Kodak?" asked Santilli. "Sure, feel free!" answered Jack. Santilli called Kodak's main facility in Rochester, New York, and asked, "I have here some old 16-mm film which is supposed to date back to 1947. How can I tell whether that is true?" "We have a simple system for that," answered the man at Kodak, "a geometric code on the edge of the film. What symbols do you see there?" "A square and a triangle." "Good, just a moment . . . yes, that was 1947." "Thank you." The films had passed the first litmus test.

The films seemed to be real, Santilli was interested,

but he didn't have the money, and certainly not in cash. He promised to get in touch with Jack as soon as he had raised the amount. Back in England, the first task was to learn more about the Roswell occurrence. In summer 1993, the Hollywood film *Fire in the Sky* ran in England, which tells the story of a young lumberjack, Travis Walton, who had been abducted in 1975 and taken on board a UFO. For the premiere, a press conference had been organized by the British UFO Research Association (BUFORA), at which Travis Walton and Mike Rogers, on whose story the film was based, were present. The newspapers, in their reports, cited not only Walton but also Philip Mantle, the spokesman for BUFORA. Within a short time Santilli, who knew little about UFOs, contacted me (Mantle) on the phone, initially about making a UFO documentary before eventually telling me about the film and asking me about the Roswell incident. It later transpired that Santilli had been given my telephone number by journalist Carl Nagaitis, who had worked with me on a UFO feature while he was working for the Mirror Group of newspapers in London. Santilli met me for the first time at the organized lecture featuring Travis Walton and Mike Rogers in London to promote the movie *Fire in the Sky*.

Meanwhile Santilli was trying to raise money. At first he tried to get Polygram interested in the matter, through his friend Shoefield. Shoefield was then manager of Working Title, a subsidiary of Polygram, which among others, produced the worldwide box office hit *Four Weddings and a Funeral*, with Hugh Grant. Polygram showed interest and Shoefield flew to Florida to meet Jack and make a deal. But the deal could not be closed. Because on the same day that Shoefield had an appointment with him, Jack fell ill and had to be taken to the hospital. Shoefield waited in his hotel room in vain for the cameraman to turn up and finally called him. Jack's wife answered and told him what had hap-

pened. Shoefield was a bit skeptical and checked at the hospital. When they, however, confirmed that Jack was indeed lying in the ward, there was nothing else for him to do than to fly back to England.

Finally Polygram withdrew from the matter. The legal situation was dubious, and the company did not want to buy any material from a person to whom it did not belong—legally speaking, the films were the property of the U.S. Army. In addition a large company could not afford to pay a sum of $150,000 in cash, without any receipt and to a person who wanted to remain anonymous. It violated business ethics and, perhaps, even the law.

The cameraman came out of the hospital and learnt that the deal had fallen through, Polygram had pulled out. Santilli did not have enough money. He promised to provide the cash somehow, but Jack had lost faith. It was all dragging on too long. Eventually Santilli succeeded in gaining the interest of a German business acquaintance, Hamburg music producer Volker Spielberg. Spielberg is the owner of two firms, VS Musikverlag GmbH and Lollipop Musik Volker Spielberg KG. He, too, saw a way to make some money through the sensational material and was prepared to take a risk. Eighteen months had passed since Shoefield's fiasco, and it took Santilli a lot of effort to win back Jack's trust. Finally, in December 1994, the bargain was closed, Santilli and Spielberg had the films.

The first persons Santilli informed about

Reg Presley, lead singer of the Troggs, was the first who spoke about the alien autopsy footage.

On the left, Ray Santilli, on the right Volker Spielberg, the owners of the autopsy film. Photo courtesyof Muarizio Baiata Italy.

the purchase of the films were Reg Presley, the lead singer of the Troggs, whom he knew from various music productions, and me (Mantle). The Troggs, whose song "Wild Thing" became a big hit in the sixties, were in the process of making a comeback since their music was played in the movie *Four Weddings and a Funeral*. Presley had become, during the last years, more and more interested in UFOs and the crop circles, which regularly appeared in the vicinity of his country residence at Andover in Hampshire. In order to promote his personal and business relationships with Presley, Santilli told him about the films and, early in January 1995, invited him to visit him and have a look at them at his place, as soon as the films had come back from the laboratory.

Part of the rolls were in very bad condition and Santilli had to get each of them conserved and restored. The film for the first seven minutes came back in January 1995 and Santilli at once transcribed them onto two video cassettes, one each for Presley and me (Mantle). The film had apparently been shot at night in a tent, lit only by a few gas lanterns. A being with big black eyes was lying on a table, covered by a tarpaulin or sheet, out of which only the head, hands and feet protruded. To the right there was a man in "uniform"; to the left, two "doctors" in white overalls and without masks were trying to pull out and sever something very elastic-looking from its arm. Santilli called the film strip "On Site Examination." One impression of this scene, however, is that they are trying to remove the clothing of 'spacesuit' of the dead creature, whilst others have expressed opinions that some sort of 'surgery' may have already been undertaken to try and save the dying creature. Witnesses often spoke of the extremely elastic and difficult-to-cut material of the suits of the UFO personnel. To preserve a corpse, it must be put in dry ice. And if the uniforms were temperature-resistant, one must remove them before freezing the bodies. But whatever the film shows, it was Presley and me (Mantle). And with that a stone was set rolling. . . .[5]

On January 14, 1995, Presley was interviewed by the BBC Breakfast program, and he mentioned the film. Some of the details he gave were not correct—he was speaking from memory about what Santilli had told him—but the news was out and went round the world. Santilli then promised me that he would show the film openly and for the first time at the BUFORA conference on August 19 and 20, 1995, and Mantle announced this "world sensation" to the press. The big news agencies picked it up and the news got worldwide publicity, with the result that seats for BUFORA's conference were sold out in no time at all. On March 11, 1995, Santilli invited representatives of the major religions, such as the Archbishop of Canterbury from the Anglican Church, the Chief Rabbi of London, an Islamic Mufti and a Hindu leader, for an exclusive presentation of the film. "The result was absolutely negative, total rejection," Santilli told me on the telephone when I called him shortly after that—ever since

February 1995 I was regularly in contact with him, so as to keep up with the latest—"they all considered it a swindle. Some even left in the middle of the show."[6]

On April 28, 1995, Santilli showed one of the early autopsy films at a private gathering to Reg Presley, crop circle researcher Colin Andrews, Maurizio Baiata from Rome, and me (Philip Mantle) and my wife Susan. Here is what we saw:

We were shown one of the autopsies. The film was in black-and-white, without sound. A being lay on a board in a mortuary or autopsy room. The walls were white. The being appears humanoid with a distended belly, two arms, two legs, with six fingers and toes. It is entirely hairless, the head is bigger, it has a small nose, mouth, ears—which sit lower than in humans—and two dark eyes. Female genitalia are recognizable.

The autopsy begins with the removal of the "dark eyes." In fact there are only some kind of ancillary lenses over the eyes. Now the eyeballs are visible, which seem to be rolled upwards. The body of the creature is now cut open, various organs removed and put into a metal container. A sort of "crystal," the size of a chestnut, is cut out of the belly area. The scalp is removed through incisions and the skull sawn open, to get access to the brain. The persons doing the autopsy are wearing a kind of protective suit, so that their faces are not recognizable. The autopsy is being performed by two persons, one of whom writes down something now and then. Behind the head of the creature there is a wide glass window. Through this one can see another person, wearing doctor's apparel, overalls, skullcap, facemask.[7]

According to Santilli they had seen about nine minutes of film, showing an autopsy performed on 1 July 1947 in Dallas/Fort Worth.

A week later, on May 5, 1995, a longer take (eighteen minutes) of the second autopsy made on 3 July 1947 was shown to an audience of about ninety persons, consisting of journalists, scientists and UFO experts—including the authors—at the London Museum. The carefully selected guests for this exclusive preview had to undergo severe security checks before being allowed to enter the theatre. It was strictly forbidden to take cameras or bags inside; everyone was scanned by metal detectors. My (Hesemann's) notes on what was shown on the screen, when finally the lights went out at 1:10 P.M., read as follows:

The doctors are wearing protective clothing, with only slits for the eyes. On a sort of operating table, apparently naked, lies the corpse of a nonhuman being with a big bald head, the big dark eyes and mouth wide open, a small nose and delicate ears. The abdomen of the approximately 1.5 meter (c. five feet) tall creature, of otherwise almost human proportions, is bloated. The right leg shows deep wounds, muscle fibers can be seen. The feet are human, but with six toes. The hands also have six fingers. There is no navel, the nipples on the chest are rudimentary. In the place of external genitals there is a depression, which— only at first sight—resembles a vagina.

The doctors palpate the body, take tissue samples and put them into a glass. One of them takes a scalpel and makes a fine incision behind the ear. Blood comes out. The body is then opened—a round organ is exposed in the middle of the belly. Another man wearing a mask appears behind the glass screen. Some sort of "conversation" seems to take place over the microphone, which is hanging above the corpse—or are they recording their findings? The doctor pulls off thin black layers of skin from the eyes and puts them in another glass. White eyes with pupils rolled up high are now visible. Then the head is dissected—the skull removed with force and the brain, already decayed, is taken out. The cameraman tries to get the best perspective, but stays behind the surgeon, who often gets in the way and blocks the view. Sometimes he zooms too close to the organs, which puts them out of focus and makes them look fuzzy. If the "creature" is a dummy, then it's a very realistic one! Its skin behaves like human skin under the scalpel, the inner organs look like the innards of a living being. What is surprising is the great resemblance of the alien to human beings. He represents by no means the type of small and very slender gray creatures with long and thin arms and legs which the eyewitnesses of Roswell spoke of: here is only a short human being with a rather large cranium, normal-looking hands and feet but for the sixth finger and toe. Only the facial features are a bit different.

A total of four persons are present at the autopsy, three of them within the operating room. One of them seems to be a woman (assisting nurse?). To the left of the body stands a small table and on it there is a tray with surgical instruments. There is another table at the left wall of the room. There are bowls and bottles with chemicals on it. On the wall there is a clock, which shows 10:06 at the beginning and 11:45 at the end of the proceedings. The autopsy has, therefore, lasted nearly two hours. On the wall hang, in addition, a black wall telephone with a spiral cord and a wall sign saying "DANGER." At the end of every three minutes the film turns blank and trails off—the roll seems to have come to an end.

When the lights went on again the audience was almost violently brought back to reality, with feelings of disbelief and disappointment. Santilli had disappeared. The tenacious ones later learned—in Santilli's office—that the reason for the curtailed presentation were the threats of a troublemaker against Santilli. As a matter of fact, a few minutes before the show began, someone distributed leaflets among the audience in which a well-known UFO researcher, who had actually never seen the film, accused Santilli of hoaxing.[8]

With that presentation began one of the most emotional debates in the by no means boring history of UFO research. It was further heightened when the first pictures of the H-beams were published, which were covered with a strange script, and the "boxes" which the beings had held closely pressed to their bod-

ies and had the forms of two six-fingered hands deeply embossed upon them. They came from four rolls of which only about one- or two-minute runs each could be saved. They showed the process of cataloguing the material in a tent. The discussion reached its peak when the autopsy film was broadcast by twenty-eight TV stations around the world on 28 August 1995. The skeptics picked out new details again and again to prove that the film must be a fake. The spiral cord of the telephone, the clock on the wall, the surgical instruments, and even the protective clothing of the doctors was brought up as proof that something was wrong and unusual.

Is the protective clothing in the autopsy room inconsistent with the "Danger" sign hanging there? A digital enlargement made it possible to read the text on the sign fully: "Danger—maximum exposure two hours." After that comes a telephone number.[9] Cameraman Jack had mentioned "danger of infection" emitting from the body. Was the autopsy perhaps conducted under ultraviolet radiation?

A first check confirmed: the wall clock had been on the market since 1936; the microphone which hung in the room, made by Shure Bros., was available from 1945 on. The surgical instruments were confirmed by Professor Cyril Wecht, ex-president of the American Academy of Forensic Sciences, to be the standard equipment for autopsies in the forties.[10] There were far more questions about the telephone. Spiral cords were produced by American Telephone & Telegraph Company (AT&T) and could be ordered as an extra item right through the fourties. The U.S. Defense Forces ordered all their telephones with spiral connections. The telephone itself was made in 1946. So far, so good. Then UFO archskeptic Philip Klass raised a storm in the teacup. Klass maintained, in his *Skeptics UFO Newsletter* of November 1995: *"The modern wall-telephone,*

Bell & Howell 16-mm "Filmo" camera

HEADQUARTERS
UNITED STATES CONSTABULARY
SPECIAL SERVICES SECTION
AFO 46   US Army

16 February 1948

SUBJECT: Letter of Recommendation

TO   : Whom It May Concern

1. Mr. Kolman von Keviczky, stateless, has been employed by the Special Services Section, Headquarters US Constabulary from October 1946 to February 1948.

2. Mr. von Keviczky's positions have been:

Director of Film
Events Photographer
Cameraman
Supply Manager
Cartoonist

3. Mr. von Keviczky directed and filmed a picture for the army regarding "V.D." and "Short History of Constabulary".

4. Mr. von Keviczky is being released due to the move of Constabulary Headquarters and Mr. von Keviczky cannot make this move because of his family.

JULIAN B. LINDSEY
Colonel   Inf
Spec Serv Officer

Col. Colman VonKeviczky was cameraman and director for the 3rd U.S. Army.

which is shown in the autopsy room, was put on the market for the first time in 1956 . . . nine years after the film is supposed to have been made."[11]

Naturally all the skeptics, who are only too eager to repeat what others say, took up this argument thankfully. Even the serious German news magazine *Der Spiegel,* celebrated the exposure of the film as a fake with its usual malice.[12] But the glee was premature. For in the museum of the Bell Telephone Company in Atlanta, Georgia, one can see a similar wall telephone, with a label saying that it is a 1946 model, made by Western Electric.[13] When *Time* magazine reported about the film, it was bombarded by letters from the Klass group, bringing up the "telephone" argument. But unlike *Der Spiegel, Time* investigated and printed in its issue of 18 December 1995: *"According to the AT&T historian Sheldon Hochheiser, the film cannot be discredited on account of the telephone. That model seems to have been brought out in 1946 and the spiral cord was offered to customers since 1939."[14]* Klass had to confess with regret in his January 1996 issue that he had erred.[15] Only *Der Spiegel* refrained from correct-

ing its false "exposure," although all questions were once more open.

Others criticized the movement of the camera and the bad focusing, particularly in the case of closeups. But in the opinion of two photographers who had worked for the army during the forties, these "defects" are quite consistent with the way they worked in those days and with the camera used in this case—a Bell & Howell Filmo.

FOX TV, which had broadcast the Roswell film, interviewed Dr. Roderick Ryan, formerly photographer in the U.S. Marines, who, during the forties and fifties had made pictures of highly secret government projects, including the atomic tests at the Bikini Atoll. He said: *"The fact that it lost focus is consistent with the type of equipment that they had to use. . . . The cameras that were in general use at that time by the military were Filmo cameras made by Bell and Howell. . . . This camera does not have through-the-lens focusing, so if it maintained focus there could be a possibility that it was done with modern day equipment. . . . He keeps moving to keep out of the way of the surgeon, if you look at the surgical crew they're moving also and he's just trying to be unobtrusive. . . . The roll of a photographer in the military is usually to record an event, it is not his job to do pretty pictures, and I think this is a very adequate job of recording an event. . . ."*[16]

I (Hesemann) showed the film to an internationally respected UFO researcher and expert photographer, Colonel Colman S. VonKeviczky, director of ICUFON, an international group of UFO investigators, and former member of the Audio-Visual Department of the United Nations in New York. What qualifies him is his background as army cameraman and film director. He had studied at the UFA Film academy in Berlin-Babelsberg, was chief of the Audio-Visual Division of the Royal Hungarian general staff during the war before he went over to the Americans, and was photographer, film director and public relations officer of the Third Army at Heidelberg until 1948. During this time he worked with the same equipment as the Roswell photographer, namely, the same type of camera—Bell & Howell Filmo—and the same Kodak film. He said:

"In the 1960s, the U.S. Armed Forces (Signal Corps) for education and home use was equipped with 35-mm Bell and Howell motion picture cameras with three lenses (wide-angle, normal and a moderated focal length telephoto for close ups) on a turret (revolving head) all for manual operation of their distances and openings. Capable for loading 100-feet roll double perforated (silent) or one-side perforated sound films. Consequently there is no reason to discredit or blame for the overwhelming, OUT OF FOCUS sequences the cameraman, because in 1947 the automatization of the cameras' mechanism—electric eye, auto-focus, zoom lenses, etc. were only a dream for the photographers." VonKeviczky emphasized further that the cameraman *"was not only a well-educated and experienced movie man, but additionally in full knowledge of editing and production of documentaries. Evidence - filming the autopsy's activity from various view-angles. . ."* VonKeviczky also sees the emergency situation in which the film was made, reflected in the cameraman's work. *"Emergency disposal for filming is verifiable, that he had no time—might [have] had, but no opportunity to use tripod, additional lights for better picture quality—because he was shooting all the scenes by hand and in very poor light conditions. The frequently and unsuccessfully moving the camera in his hand to better look on the doctor's work—amongst those circumstances no one could have done a better job.*[17]

And the physicians? Dr. Detlev Bronk, a well-known name in UFO research after the surfacing of the "Majestic 12" documents, and biophysicist and member of the advisory committee of the Army Air Force, was certainly the person to whom one would have entrusted the supervision of an autopsy on a recovered alien. But the name "Dr. Williams" mentioned by Jack was new and had until then never appeared in Roswell literature. Only after a lengthy search could it be confirmed that indeed a Dr. Robert Parvin Williams (1891–1967) had been special assistant of the surgeon general of the army at Fort Monroe, Virginia. He was at that time a lieutenant colonel, was promoted to brigadier general in 1949. The mention of Dr. Williams alone, who was the right man at the right place for the task, shows that the cameraman had inside knowledge.[18]

The most absurd argument came from American researcher Kent Jeffrey. He maintained that the films must be fakes because the creature on the autopsy table resembled a human being far too much and extraterrestrials could not look human, since evolution could not have repeated itself on another planet. No one has more clearly restated the old dictum "what should not be cannot be." Therefore, and only therefore, "the body must be a slightly doctored human cadaver." He based his preposterous insinuation, that Santilli and the people behind him had "mutilated the body of a human being, a woman in this case, purely out of greed," not on any evidence or clue, but solely on his school of thought, his conviction that evolution occurs only by chance![19] He was not prepared even to consider other models of evolution, such as:

(a) the theory of a holographic universe, put forward by Princeton physicist and former student of Einstein's, Professor David Bohm, and Cambridge biochemist Professor Rupert Sheldrake. They postulate an interacting universe, whose tiniest element—like a hologram—contains the information of the entire universe. There is nothing like "chance" in the holographic universe, only a strategy of creation, a blueprint for evolution, which, through "morphological resonance," is transmitted to all parts of it. That means not only that the universe is "full of life," but that every suitable planet is destined to develop life and also that on every inhabitable planet the same pattern of evolution develops.[20]

(b) the theory of alien intervention in the process of human evolution. According to the creation myths of almost all peoples on earth, God (or gods) created man in his (their) own image (Gen. 1:26) and even united sexually with the early humans, so that the "sons of the Gods" were born, the "heroes of old, the famous ones" (Gen. 6:4). The "missing link" of anthropology could well be genetic manipulation from another world.[21]

There is one clear indication that the creature is not a human being: it has *no navel*. Also *no* external genitals, no breasts. Instead of genitals it has a hairless depression, which suggests a vagina, but lacks the typical human female characteristics: labia, clitoris, etc. But Jeffrey is apparently more ready to believe in a medical wonder: a pitiable human being who exhibits almost all abnormalities one can think of—progeria (premature aging), Gilford syndrome, rudimentary nose and ears, polydactylism (extra fingers and toes), stunted growth, Basedow eyes, possibly also asexuality—and that it was apparently hatched out of an egg (no navel)! And, of course, there had to be two of these beings, for there were two autopsy films showing corpses that resembled each other but were not one and the same, and these "twins" had to die at the same time and, instead of being buried or preserved in a jar and placed in a medical curiosity cabinet somewhere, had to fall into the hands of unscrupulous butchers, who immediately got the idea of using them to make a Roswell film. Besides the preposterous nature of the suggestion that Ray Santilli was the originator of such a macabre and perverse fraud, the aim of the inventor of this nonsense is not to expose a lie but to uphold a dogmatic idea: "the laws of probability" preclude, in his belief, the existence of humanoid aliens! He maintains, therefore, emphatically that "the film is a fake." And in the same breath he accuses all Roswell witnesses who speak of crash victims resembling human beings, of being liars.

But what does one see in these films? A whole row of medical experts have busied themselves with this question. Santilli had invited pathologist Professor Christopher Milroy—who taught forensic medicine at the University of Sheffield—to the screening of May 5, l995, at the London Museum and asked him for an expert evaluation. It fits ill into the behavior of a swindler to invite someone to a public show who could expose him with the greatest of ease! Professor Milroy wrote in his report dated 2 June 1995:

Prof. Christopher Milroy's comment on the Santilli film.

At the request of the Merlin Group I reviewed a film which was claimed to show a post-mortem examination being carried out on an extraterrestrial being. The film was allegedly taken on a U.S. military base in 1947. . . . The film was in black and white. A full record of the autopsy was not present, as apparently only some of the reels of film record were available. No sound was present. The autopsy room was small and the examination was being conducted by people wearing full protective clothing. Besides the autopsy table there was a tray of standard autopsy instruments.

The body was human in appearance and appeared to be female but without secondary sexual characteristics—no breast development or pubic hair was visible.

The head was disproportionately large. No head hair was present.

The abdomen was distended. There was no evidence of decomposition. The overall external appearance was of a white adolescent female, estimated height 5 feet, tending towards a heavy build not abnormally thin or fat. There were six digits to each hand and foot. The eyes appeared larger than normal and the globes were covered with a black material which was shown being removed. There was an extensive and deep injury to the right thigh. This was not shown in very close up detail, but appeared to be burnt and charred down to deep tissues. No similar injury was present, although there was possible bruising down the left hand side of the body. Overall there was a general absence of injuries.

The body was opened with a Y shaped incision but the skin of the neck was not fully reflected. A close up of the knife being drawn against the skin was shown, with blood coming from skin. This appeared to be an unusual amount of blood. The neck appeared to contain two cylindrical structures on either side anteriorly. These could have been muscles (sternomastoid muscles) but were odd in appearance, though they were not shown in close up.

The skin of the chest was shown reflected, and the central rib cage and sternum block removed. The chest organs were removed individually. There appeared to be a heart and two lungs, but when close up shots of the organs were shown they were always out of focus. The abdominal organs were not clearly seen, though it did not appear that the person was pregnant, an explanation that had been proposed for the distended abdomen.

The scalp was shown being reflected anteriorly, having been cut in a standard autopsy manner. The skull was then shown being sawn with a hand saw across the front of the skull, though the backward cuts and the removal of the skull cap were not shown. What appeared to be the membranes covering the brain (dura) were shown being cut and the brain being removed. Although a close up shot of the brains was shown it was again out of focus. However the appearances were not those of a human brain.

Overall the appearances were those of a white adolescent female with a humanoid body. There were six digits to each hand and foot and the body shape was dysmorphic. No accurate determination could be made of organ structure because every close up shot was out of focus. The injuries present on the body were less than those expected in an aviation accident. No injuries to account for death were shown.

Whilst the examination had features of a medically conducted examination, aspects suggested it was not conducted by an experienced pathologist, but rather by a surgeon.[22]

The last remark was justified. Professor Detlev W. Bronk, who according to Jack B. supervised the autopsy, was not a pathologist, but physiologist and biophysician. Later, during a personal talk with researcher George Wingfield, Professor Milroy affirmed his impression that the body was *"almost certainly a corpse and not a cleverly made doll."*[23]

On 27 October 1995 Swiss UFO researchers Luc Burgin and Hanspeter Wachter showed the Santilli film in the auditorium of the Institute for Pathology at the University of Basel, in connection with a Swiss conference of pathologists. Over 150 members of the faculty were present, among them the chief of the institute, Professor M. J. Mihatsch, and Dr. Christen from the main hospital in Liestal, who had previously spoken very skeptically about the film on Swiss television. "Professor Mihatsch was elected as leader of the discussion and surprisingly enough a lively discussion between pathologists and forensic doctors took place," Wachter wrote on 24 January 1996 to Michael Hesemann.

None of them made a negative remark, nor did any of them believe that the body in question was a doll. . . . An anonymous pathologist was of the opinion that it was a human

corpse: admittedly there were some anomalies and defects, probably of genetic origin. The eyes were somewhat (!) unusual and the entire head was a bit too big. But he could not imagine that a being that came from somewhere far away from the earth could resemble humans that much. . . . Prof. Mihatsch was convinced that it was certainly an autopsy, but on a body which one could not clearly define. He too was of the opinion that it was a human body. He also did not exclude the possibility of progeria (premature aging, leading to a maximum lifespan of ten to twelve years). Progeria, however, occurs once in about 8 million births and no one present there had ever actually seen a case of progeria. . . . Prof. Mihatsch said the room where the autopsy was performed must have been provisionally equipped, since it did not exhibit the features of a real autopsy room, which should have been there if the autopsy had been carried out in an institute or laboratory. Now, it has been said that the room was hurriedly converted for the purpose.

Nor does he question the capability of the pathologist or surgeon who is working on the corpse. The process is in accordance with reality, but what he cannot understand is the time taken for it to be completed. An experienced pathologist needs on an average 45 to 50 minutes. In the Santilli film the clock clearly shows that about 90 minutes elapsed. Either they dawdled on the job, or there were frequent interruptions. . . . Dr. Christen was of two minds after seeing the film. She gave me her opinion succinctly and clearly. Now that she had seen the film, she was no longer sure. She would there and then by no means question the validity of the film. But she would also not swear that the pictures were of an alien being. She was convinced that it was an organic form of life. She too had no explanation for the lack of a navel. That was something that could not be explained medically at all. . . .

At the end Professor Mihatsch invited us to his office. He dilated once more on the body. The skin seemed leathery, practically creaseless and unstructured. This symptom was found only in Progeria. About the absence of the navel and secondary as

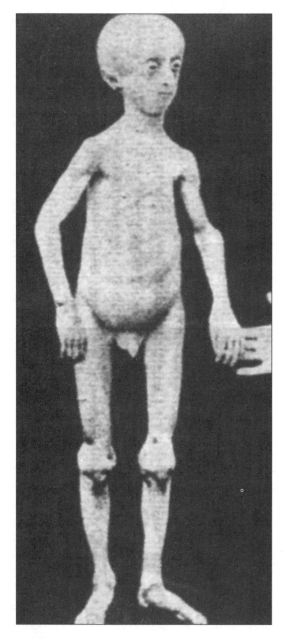

Progeria victim

well as primary genitals he could not form any opinion. The eyes were pretty strange. As for the organs removed, they could not be tallied with any human organs. But diseases could change the appearance of organs considerably. Regarding the flow of the blood, he said it must have reached an advanced stage of autolysis: in that case the blood would run out like water.[24]

Professor Cyril Wecht, former president of the American Academy of Forensic Sciences and chief of the Pathological Department of St. Francis General Hospital, who had himself carried out over 13,000 autopsies and taken part in over 30,000, expressed himself more definitely when FOX TV interviewed him: *"I have never made an autopsy on a body that even resembled the being in the film."* Wecht believes that the film could be genuine. The doctors, in his opinion, *"are either pathologists or surgeons who have performed a number of autopsies before this."*

At first Wecht thought the creature in the film was a human being who had suffered from the so-called "Turner's Syndrome." But he changed his opinion when he saw the opened cadaver and the inner organs. "I cannot relate these structures to abdominal contents. The liver, if it were the liver, should be over here to the right.... I'm seeing a mass that I cannot readily

Roswell Symposium September 1995.

explain, and I have great difficulty in correlating this with any human body I have seen. . . . This is a structure that must be the brain if it is a human being. . . . It looks like no brain that I have ever seen, whether it's a brain filled with tuma, a brain that has been radiated, a brain that has been traumatized and hemorrhagic. . . . I would have to say that as difficult as it is for me to say it, that what I have seen here does not appear to be a human being. . . . What it is, I would prefer to say for the time being that it is humanoid. . . . I'm not going to say that it's from a distant planet, what planet, I don't know, but I cannot say that it is a member of the human race as you and I know the human race." Professor Wecht does not consider its being a doll as probable. *"It does not look to me as if someone is trying a mighty swindle. If that were the case, they are wasting their time in making some small ripoff like this, they should be in Hollywood making some fantastic films with Steven Spielberg."*[25] The paleontologist Chris Tringer of the Museum of Natural History, London, said in the *Observer* of July 23, 1995, that *"the creature looks human, but is equally well not human."*[26] The French surgeon Patrick Braun, interviewed by the TV channel TFI, felt sure that it was a biological being and not a latex doll. As indication for this he referred to the appearance and reaction of the body fluids in the film.[27]

The forensic surgeon Jean Pierre, who had done over 5,000 autopsies, affirmed that the persons who performed the autopsy in the film were certainly of the medical profession, if not experienced pathologists. He remarked that some of the organs had already started decaying.[28]

Dr. Pierluigi Baima Bollone, professor at the Institute of Forensic Pathology at the University of Turin, one of the country's most renowned pathologists, made a critical study of the film for RAI DUE, Italy's TV channel two. The authors of this book also took part in these programs. From October 16 to 18, RAI DUE presented, in three parts and a total viewing time of four hours, the most thorough and serious study of this material ever. *"When we look at the inner organs of the body,"* Professor Bollone stated in the broadcast, *"we find no single organ that in any way resembles any human organ. The main organ, which could be the liver, has neither the shape nor the location of a human liver. The face of the alleged extraterrestrial shows surprising anatomical features: very big ocular orbits, a very flat nasal pyramid, a mouth somehow wide open, out of which something protrudes which could be a couple of teeth. Nevertheless the face is flat, there is no evidence of facial musculature as is present in human beings, which is responsible for the large variety of facial expressions of the human species. (In the case of human beings). . . we see the frontal muscle, the muscles of the upper and lower eyelids, the nasal muscle, the upper labial muscle, the*

Prof. Pierluigi Baima Bollone

bigger and smaller zygomatic muscles. In the pictures of the alien we see no signs of the presence of these specific muscles. Thus there were significant anatomical differences between the alien and a member of our species. The alleged alien is not capable of producing the large palette of facial expressions and gestures through which we communicate with one another. . . . My overall impression is that we are here dealing with a creature that seems to belong to our species, but is so clearly different from it that it seems absurd to speculate about the similarity. All that makes it fairly certain that it is not a swindle."[29]

In the CompuServe "Encounters" Forum biologist Robert Suriathep expounded his theory about the creature in the film. He believes that the large organ in its abdomen is a much enlarged liver.

"It could act as the fat reservoir of the body. Instead of storing fat under the skin, like we do, they store it inside. Nowhere else during the autopsy do we see recognizable fat reserves, not even under the skin of the distended belly. It could have something to do with the skin being more transparent for photosynthetic processes. . . .

The other organs seem to be glands. . . . Our stomach is an inefficient organ, that makes use of other organs, like the small and large intestines and the esophagus. I think their "stomach" is their blood. Nourishment which circulates through the body and can be used there, where the cells need energy, is practical. But this would mean that the cells tolerate toxins and can process the nourishment. That would explain the large liver and the skin structure. The skin also exudes waste matter.

Why are the eyes so big? The beings could be nocturnal creatures, which necessitates ability to see under the most adverse light conditions.

Another possibility is that they live in subterranean spaces, perhaps compelled to do so owing to catastrophes, cosmic or caused by themselves.

Larger eyes give a flatter, less distorted and a more exact picture of the world. The thin film which covers their eyes, could protect them from ultraviolet rays.

Their brain has so many windings and cleavages and is in fact most complex . . . . the large number of coils increases the ability to specialize. Their having two completely separate brains—cerebrum and separate cerebellum—increases their capacity for polymorphism, the ability to do two things at the same time . . . .[30]

It should be added that the absence of a division into left and right hemisphere would suggest the ability to grasp reality holistically and completely.

A further interesting aspect is the creature's sex. At first sight one sees something like a vagina, but devoid of labia and clitoris. But the species could very well have internal genitals, as in the case of dolphins. The nipples, even if rudimentary, indicate a mammalian species rather than oviparous amphibian or reptile types.

To quote from the controversial Majestic 12 reports, in which it is stated that Professor Detlev Bronk arranged for the examination of "the four occupants" of a crashed UFO: *"It was the concluding opinion of the group, that although those creatures appeared human, the biological and evolutionary processes which led to their development are apparently entirely different from those observed or postulated in the case of Homo Sapiens."*[31]

While it seems to be established that the creature on the autopsy table was not a victim of Turner's Syndrome or progeria or any other genetic disease—no disease can explain the totally different inner organs—there still remains the possibility of a an ingenious forgery. Could it be a doll so cleverly made that even experienced pathologists mistook it for a biological creature?

There is a growing branch of industry, developed in the age of the production of increasingly spectacular films, called Special Effects, which specializes in the creation of optical illusions. Special-effect experts see themselves as the magicians of the modern world of fairy tales, of the dreamland of the celluloid industry. Even the designation of their branch is cryptical and consists of only two letters: FX. The leading FX firm in Great Britain is "Creature Effects," also called "Creature Shop," and works for Pinewood Studios in London. Trey Stokes, who works for Creature FX and has also contributed to worldwide successful movie hits such as *Abyss, Batman Returns* and *Robocop II*, asserted: *"Everything I saw in the film could be made with standard FX techniques. . . . now, I not only believe that the film is a fake, but I feel that one could have made a better job of it."*

One makes a plaster cast of a child—to get the right

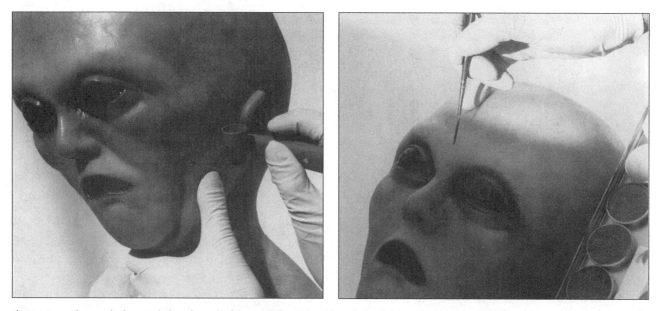

The Morgana hoax which intended to discredit the Santilli footage, although the dummy on the pictures only slightly resembled the being on the Santilli footage.

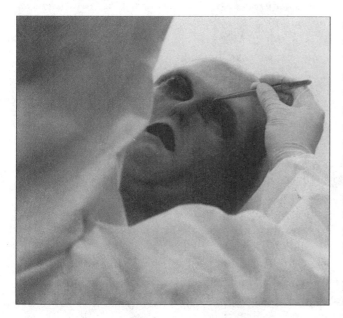

size—and fills it with liquefied oleated clay and lets it cool off. The resulting figure can be modeled and sculptured as required. The end result has all the muscle lines and subtle curves of a real body, with one difference: the body fat hangs down, since the cast is made while standing—if lying, it will be different. Stokes believes that he can see this very effect in the being in the Santilli film—further a "tension of the muscles in the legs" indicates the "standing position." Hands and feet seem to have been added separately. The skin is silicone or a gelatine mixture, or perhaps foam latex, which gives the right "fleshy" quality. The doll can be filled with innards from a slaughterhouse, the insides can be painted with blood and glycerine to make it appear moist.

For Stokes it is suspicious how "gingerly" the alleged pathologists examine the creature. Were they afraid of damaging the doll and thus making the swindle obvious?

The incision, according to the FX expert, is clearly made with a "blood knife"—a scalpel which gets a supply of blood fed in through a fine tube into its handle. *"And when more blood flows out of the inside, so much the better."* A further indication, for Stokes, is that of all scenes the one is missing which should have shown the skin being folded back. "That gave them time to prepare the inside suitably." Does that prove that the film is a fake? "No, not really," Stokes finally says, *"although there is no moment in the film that does not look faked, it is possible that the whole film is genuine and all the discrepancies can be explained."*[32]

In fact, soon after the presentation of the Santilli films, photographs were produced, showing "the preparation of the Santilli doll"—a latex head being painted, which indeed had a vague resemblance to the Santilli creature. A stupid joke, which only few in American media took seriously who in the euphoria of making such a sensational exposure completely forgot to compare the pictures to the original! The photographs were sent in by one "Morgana Productions." Morgana was the witch who brought about the downfall of the wizard Merlin, but this Morgana was not as successful. There is no such company as Morgana Productions, and eventually John Spencer, chairman of the British UFO Research Association, tracked them down. Morgana was in fact a special effects company in the UK, but Spencer agreed not to release the company's real name so as not to embarrass them.[33]

On August 29, 1995, the day after the worldwide broadcasting of the Santilli film, French TV channel ARTE presented us with a new sensation. As a prelude to a group discussion about UFOs generally, and Santilli's film in particular, a contribution from Russia was shown. This short broadcast dealt with an UFO crash in Khos Alas, Russia on July 5, l947: a ball of fire, salvaging of the wreck, army activities, an autopsy carried out in a provisional laboratory in a wooden hut in

the woods, by one Dr. Germanov. His daughter then stated while being filmed that, in the interests of world peace, her father had informed the U.S. Government, which then invented the Roswell story to cover up the Alas incident and divert attention. In proof of this were shown not only surprisingly clear shots of Dr. Germanov examining a few lumps of tissue as well as a hand with four fingers, but also the invoice of the Hollywood film company MGM sent to the U.S. Government pertaining to the delivery of four dolls for the staging of the Roswell crash.

The critical observer was astonished not only by the absurdity of the tale but also by the marked French accent of the "Russians." But clarification came soon after that, during the discussion. The film was a belated April-Fool's hoax for which ARTE had commissioned a French film studio in order to show how easily one could invent a story like that.[34] Or, as ARTE spokeswoman Catherine Le Goff declared, *"The channel wants to show the possibilities of manipulation by the television medium and thereby stem the hocus-pocus carried out by other channels."*[35] Was it not the French channel TFI, ARTE's biggest competitor, that had the sole rights for Santilli's film . . . .?

Indeed television sometimes turned out to be the biggest manipulator. Thus special effects expert Olaf Ittenbach of Munich put together in about four or five weeks a bad imitation of Santilli's autopsy film, which the German magazine *Stern TV* had commissioned him to make. The plastic doll had been covered with papier-mâché and powder, filled with innards from a butchery and then "carefully" dissected.

After that two gentlemen came to me (Hesemann) at the UFO conference "Dialogue with the Universe" in Düsseldorf (26–29 October 1995), which I (Hesemann) organized and moderated, and where Philip Mantle was a speaker. The two, Hans Mayer and Stefan Hufnagel from Grasslfing, told me their adventurous story. They had found a video film and the original 16-mm strip thereof among things that a lady friend of theirs had inherited from her uncle. I (Hesemann) had a look at the video film, together with colleagues Philip Mantle, Susan Mantle and Roberto Pinotti, and it was clear to us that it was a fake. We wanted to know what was behind it all, asked for the original 16-mm film, which they brought to us on the following day. We then told them unequivocally that the film was a fake. On the next day a freelance journalist interviewed me (Hesemann). What did I think of the newly found autopsy film? I asked him how he knew about it, since we had spoken to nobody about it. He had heard rumors. I told him that the film was a fake and further asked him whether he had anything to do with it. He grinned and left.

Shortly afterwards Stern TV asked for an interview with me. The reporters had only one question—about the "newly found film." I told them, *"I don't know whether you have fabricated it or Frank Elstner's 'April, April' (Germany's "Candid Camera"), but we realized of course that the film is a fake. Someone filled a rubber doll with innards. You have probably waited for me to jump with joy onto the stage and present the film to the public, but, sorry. I have to disappoint you. If you want to fool us, you have to try a little harder."* And with that the case was closed, as far as I was concerned. But I was more than surprised when I watched TV and saw Stern TV's announcement: *"Germany in UFO Fever: UFO Experts Fall for Self-made Alien."* Apparently they wanted to depict the mere viewing of a film on the monitor and a polite manner towards the couriers already as an act of credulity. I immediately informed my lawyer and requested seven witnesses to sign affidavits, confirming my version of the facts.

Indeed they tried to create the impression that I had been taken in. They had filmed the entire procedure with a hidden camera. In the film section of Stern TV my remark to my video technician, Thilo Kage, "These gentlemen, claim to have a second autopsy film," was quoted as a sign of belief. But a fake autopsy film is also an autopsy film and how else could I refer to it? "False! Our hobby-doctor outfit is anything but historic," commented Stern TV. Was that the subject of discussion? My first words after seeing the film, *"This is really crazy. Very interesting, this film...,"* were quoted correctly, but not what had followed the dots—making sense and also recorded in their video take—" ... *someone has tried to imitate the Santilli film."* Is not such an effort "interesting," for the possibilities of comparison alone? The next quote was taken out of context: "Bring the original film to us. We can then tell you with absolute certainty." Tell what? Stern TV did not say. I had already told the gentlemen that the film was a fake. Then it was shown how Philip Mantle and his wife Susan (whom Stern TV misidentified as an American!) tried to read the border code on the 16-mm film, to see if old or new film had been used. And we wanted a picture of the dubious messengers, for documentation.

But Stern TV moderator Guenther Jauch proved to be a bad loser. Holding Hesemann's lawyers letter in his hand, he announced with a look of innocence, "one of the experts has vanished. All our efforts to find him were unsuccessful, he had gone 'underground' without leaving a trace of his whereabouts. Now, after our announcement has been published, there comes suddenly an affidavit to say that he had recognized the film as a fake right from the beginning. . . . Seems to have occurred to him after he noticed that he had possibly been caught." He omitted to read out what he could read in the Affidavit that Hesemann had declared, in front of a running camera, that he considered the film to be a fake, "a rubber doll filled with innards."[35]

Naturally, Stern TV did not try to contact Hesemann after that. Two months later he had the satisfaction of seeing Jauch's name making headlines: his editors had falsified and manipulated other news items as well. The editor of the respected news magazine *Der Spiegel* compared him to the forger of Hitler's diaries, *Stern's* most infamous story. More than once they had created their own stories, presented actors as "Kurdish terrorists," wild Swedish party girls as "German exchange students in England," and paid hooligans as "Neo-Nazi terrorists."[36] Obviously TV watchers should be more suspicious and shouldn't believe in every "exposure" from so-called "critical" TV presentations.

But was the creature in the Roswell film also a special effects doll after all? In January 1996 Hesemann spoke with a young Englishman who said he knew the FX people who had made the film. Santilli had offered them a share of the profits and had already transferred a sum of £30,000 to their account. But the young man, who even claimed to have seen the mould for the doll, could produce no proof whatsoever for his claims.

In contrast to this, the leading FX expert in the world is of the opinion that the film is not a forgery. Stan Winston is president of the firm Industrial Light and Magic, which belongs to the "dream factory" of George Lucas. Winston created the aliens in *Alien, Edward Scissorhands* and the dinosaurs of *Jurassic Park,* for which he was given an Oscar. FOX-TV showed him the film and asked for his opinion. "My initial reaction when I first saw the piece was that it was not real, that it was a body that someone had created as a prop. . . ," confessed Winston. *". . . But when we studied the autopsy and actually cutting this body open, and knowing how difficult it is for us in the live-effects world to actually simulate cutting skin, I started saying to myself, if in fact this isn't real, I would be proud of creating an image like that myself. . . ."* Winston showed the film to some of his top employees at his studio and asked what they thought of it. The reaction was one of total astonishment. *"The organic quality of the legs and feet . . . that looks very good,"* commented one of them. Winston: "You see how uniform the blood is on the inside of the skin and the amount of drippige, down the side where it's uniformly wet on the inside. . . . I mean, we were never able to do that. . . . The point is if we did that I'd be pretty proud. Nothing about this film feels phony. If you came to me and said that you created this illusion, you'd be working here like that."[37]

Indeed, there are a number of indications which speak against the FX theory. For instance, if the film was to be sold as "Roswell footage," as was the case, why was the description of the aliens as given by Roswell witnesses not adhered to? Why was the creature not made with a thin body, long arms and four fingers? Was it really possible to deceive the leading pathologists of the USA, Great Britain, France and Italy to such an extent that they even tried to diagnose the cause of death?

One sees two wounds on the body of the alien: a big burn on the right leg, and an injury on the left temple. There is also a swelling on the left thigh, possibly caused by a fracture of the femur. The injury on the temple looks at first sight like a deep bruise, which, remembering the words of the cameraman, could have been caused by a blow with the butt of a rifle. But in a computerized enlargement of the temple, Professor Baima Ballone thinks he can identify a shot hole. *"I see here on the left frontal temple area of the corpse a depression of only a few millimetres diameter, surrounded by scoriation and contusion. These are characteristic of a bullet wound. It looks like they were caused by a shot from a small caliber weapon held at a close distance of only about thirty-five to forty centimeters from the temple, for one can see burns and signs of gunpowder. In addition one sees an endocranial hemotomy that covers the major part of the brain. A shot in the head would perfectly explain the condition of the brain and the cause of death."*[38]

But also the parts of the wreck which could be seen

on four of the rolls, on closer scrutiny appeared to be more than plastic or papier-mâché from the FX factory. These consisted of (a) four H-bars that connected a small disc with the big "saucer," and (b) boxes, which the beings kept pressed against their bodies when the soldiers found them. According to the cameraman, the crash was more a belly landing. The object had slid on its bottom for a few hundred yards till it hit the rocks and overturned. It was completely intact, except for the four detached H-bars with the small discs attached to them and bearing hieroglyphic markings on them. The fractured sections of the bars were examined by the chemist Professor Malanga in a computer enlargement at the University of Pisa, and he came to the conclusion that the bars were made of a metal with extremely fine crystalline structure.[39]

The boxes appear very light, less than two pounds. They are about 2 feet long, 1 foot wide and 1.5 inches high. The American engineer and metallurgist Dennis Murphy, who had closely examined the broken box shown in the Santilli film, stated in the CompuServe Encounter Forum: *"The panels are hollow and there are three chambers in the top. These are separated by thin walls running from left to right. . . . The buttons in the depression for the hand seem to lead to the center of the chambers. Under the chambers the panels seem to be filled with a dark substance, with thin, bright streaks in it. The appearance of the dark substance at the fracture shows that it is hard and not soft or pliable."*[40]

What purpose do these boxes or panels serve? When Bob Shell, the chief editor of the photography magazine *Shutterbug*, who had been phototechnical adviser to the FBI and CIA, asked for comments about the film from insider circles, an experienced engineer of the U.S. Air Force told him that he had worked on the boxes in 1968. *"We found out how they record information, but not how it can be read back,"* said the informant. *"Finally they took the boxes back. I believe they will be shown to experts every*

Two of the "boxes" the entities hold in their hands. According to a government scientist they are "biofeedback computers" used to control the craft and store information.

ten years, in the hope that science has advanced enough to unravel their secret." He believes that the boxes are some kind of biofeedback computers, each provided with forty sensors, which respond to fine neural impulses.[41]

A further piece of information comes from Bill House, the mechanical design engineer who worked in the super secret area 51/S4 Base in Nevada on flight simulators, meant for the training of U.S. pilots to test-fly crashed and salvaged UFOs. House has his own theory about the boxes: *"They were personal control panels,"* he told me when I interviewed him in December 1995, *"they served to communicate with the individual members of the crew and possibly to interact with a computer on board, or better, the steering unit. When the craft crashed, each crew member took his panel with him. Possibly they could also serve to communicate with a mother ship, which could thus locate them and rescue them."*[42]

Master Sergeant Bob Allen (55), a security coordinator of the U.S. Air Force, interviewed in January 1996 by me (Hesemann), had been working in 1987 in Area 51 at Nellis AFB, north of Nevada, and also at a base 200 miles west of it, near Tonapah, Nevada. There it was his job to pack and send UFO wreckage to the Sandia Laboratory at the Kirtland Air Base or the Lawrence-Livermore Laboratories. The code name of the base was "Hangar One." To introduce him to the work, he was shown films for about two and a half hours. When he saw the Santilli films on TV, he immediately recognized them as being part of the films he had seen at Hangar One. *"I saw three autopsies,"* he told me. *"During one of them Truman stood behind the glass screen in the autopsy room. He wore a face mask, but one could see it was Truman. After a few days the first one died, then the second. They said, Damn, they are dying like flies and we have to find out if they have hostile intentions and what they are doing here. We must find a way of keeping the fourth alive. That is why the autopsies were done. The fourth extraterrestrial lived for another two years at Fort Worth."*

The disc from this first crash was stored in Hangar One, together with some damaged wreckage. Some of the material was packed in cases, some just lay around. *"I think it came just then from the laboratory. Periodically, at certain time intervals, this material goes to the laboratories, to be examined by the latest methods. Apparently one finds something new every time. The labs have them for a time, then they are escorted back."* The wreck was open in the middle— whether opened by the crash or by the Air Force, Shell does not know—so that one could see the inside. He said that he himself had packed the boxes that one sees

in the Santilli film. *"I learned that these boxes were monitoring devices. The Army came, after many years, to the conclusion that the beings had taken the boxes out with them, because they waited to be picked up. Each panel was constructed for each of the ETs individually. They could be fitted into slots in various apparatus. The entire system could be started—propulsion, navigation, everything—and controlled by these panels. We tried it too, but our brain frequency was not fast enough to operate them."*[43]

In February 1996, Ted Loman, a UFO researcher from Tucson, Arizona, interviewed at the authors' request an old friend of Michael Hesemann, former U.S. Army Sergeant. Clifford Stone, who told Hesemann on the telephone that he was now willing to talk. A few months earlier his son had died in a car accident, which occurred after a series of intimidating telephone calls aimed at Stone. The circumstances under which the accident took place could not be clarified: witnesses said that a black limousine had forced the son's car off the highway, but the police reports did not mention this at all. Stone reacted in his own manner: he now decided to talk all the more!

In July 1995, when I (Hesemann) visited Stone and showed him the prints made from the Santilli film, he said he was "95% sure" that the shots were authentic. I asked him what made him so sure. "I can't talk about it, not yet," was his reply. And now the time had come. In the filmed interview with Loman made on 20 February 1996, Stone stated:

I saw the Santilli films and I believe them to be real. The reason why I believe them to be real is an experience I had in 1969.

In 1969 I was stationed at Fort Ley, Virginia, with the U.S. Army. I was part of an NBC (Nuclear-Biological-Chemical) Quick Reaction Team. That means that for seventy-two hours you're kept up in a little building ready to move out to any location that might have a chemical or nuclear accident. When you are within a radius that you could arrive at the site within two hours

Mr Ray Santilli
The Merlin Group
40 Balcombe St
London, England NW1 OND

Dear Mr Santilli,

Regarding the Roswell footage, I have looked at the safety release print. From the geometric year markings on the print(square,triangle); the original negative stock was definitely manufactured in Rochester, NY in either 1927,1947 or 1967.

It is impossible to tell which of these three years it actually was , but it was definitely one of the above three years.

The release print does not have edge code and therefore the geometric code came from the negative original which was from one of the above years..

It was impossible to pinpoint which of the three years it is , since the geometric code repeated every twenty years.

Sincerely,

Laurence A. Cate
Eastman Kodak Co
Hollywood, CA
213-464-6131

Chris Cary,
The Merlin Group,
40 Balcombe Street,
LONDON NW1 6ND   FAX No. 0171 723 0732

14 June 1995

Dear Mr Cary,

"Roswell footage"

Gary Shoefield telephoned this morning to ask if I could guide you on the possible age of a piece of Black & White Film which he described to me as having a Kodak edgeprint bearing a date symbol consisting of a solid square followed by a solid triangle.

It is, unfortunately, not possible to date a piece of film accurately by description of the edgeprint alone as, for example, a print could bear the printed-through images of edgeprint from intermediate generations as well as from the camera original.

If the piece of film described to me were a camera original then the symbol (square)(triangle) could signify film manufactured in either 1927, 1947 or 1967.

I am sorry that I cannot be more specific. It is possible that examination of the film itself might provide further clues as to date of manufacture of the stock. However, I should point out that the date of manufacture cannot, of course, be taken as a reliable indication of the date of use or to the age of the images on the film.

Your sincerely,

John Clifton
Motion Picture & Television Imaging, A5m
Tel 01442 844064

Two confirmations from Kodak Hollywood and London: The edge codes on the Santilli footage are either from 1927, 1947 or 1967.

---

you are with the primary team. Four hours you would be ordinate. My mission on that was to be the NBC NCO—the communications NCO (noncommissioned officer). I had the opportunity to take our lieutenant to Fort Belvoir, Virginia. At Fort Belvoir, me and another person, a person from the AF, an airman, went to gallivant around and went up the stairs in an auditorium there and we went into that one room and we sat down and there was this Plexiglas window looking down into the theater. You couldn't hear what is being said down there but you could look down and see what is going on. And they were watching down there what we believed to be trailers of science fiction movies. There were these common saucer-shaped UFOs, cigar-shaped UFOs, you had what I called broken-dish UFOs, that look circular with the back portion off, and you also had bodies. The airman and I went ahead and tried to figure out what movies these came from because he had an interest in science fiction. I had an interest in UFOs at that time and most people were aware of that. I also had an interest in SF movies, and so we tried to figure out from what movies this might come. When we did this, some people came in and told us to follow in no uncertain terms. We followed them.

We were taken to a location where they told us to stay. We had no idea what kind of trouble we were in. We thought that the primary reason we were in trouble was that we watched some bunch of brass watching trailers of SF movies and the American

Bob Shell, editor of *Shutterbug* magazine, confirmed the age of the Santilli footage.

taxpayer wouldn't be happy about that. Later on during what you call in the intelligence community an intensified debriefing we went through it like: Okay, what did you see. What did you see? After two nights and three days the airman answered on the question: What did you see? "I didn't see a damn thing." Then they said: "That's good!" and they let him sign a paper. Not to read it, just sign it. After he signed it he was free to leave. I had to stay a little longer. My total stay was four nights and five days. After the airman said, "I didn't see a damn thing," and was free to leave, I tried the same. The guy who questioned me looked up, straight into my eyes, and shook his head. He made some notes and said: "Let's go into that again." So I kept going over and over. When I went back to my unit I found out I was about to be charged with AWOL because I was away for four nights and five days and nobody knew where I was. Then they said: "If you do us a little favor, we will forget about that. But you have to reenlist for three more years." That was the hardest decision I made in my life.

What had he seen?

There were several types of bodies. There were some who were reminiscent of these little gray guys, don't ask me about digits as far as fingers or toes, but when I saw their eyes, the best I could say is that they were like cat eyes. You had some which were shaped like big tear drops. The large portion for the inner parts and the small portions out. We had . . . when I saw the Santilli tape, I saw the pictures first, and they were haunting, because it took me back to this day in 1969 to these movies that they were watching. There were bodies that looked very, very, very close to that one. And there were alive ones also. I have knowledge that there is footage within a tent. I have knowledge of a film with—if that is not Truman in the film it is a very very convincing double. You also see three officers in this film who had a big name in that time frame. And once again if they were not real they were very good doubles.

When we saw the bodies there were some lying on the ground and some on a slab. Brass were there: I couldn't tell you if there were also civilians, but I think there were.[44]

There are also other persons who claim to have seen this film in the possession of the U.S. Government. On June 26, Colin Andrews, a British researcher, visited Ray Santilli, together with the Japanese researcher Johsen Takano, who advises the Japanese Government in UFO matters, and Dr. Hoang-Yung Chiang of the National Research Center for Biotechnology in Taipeh, capital of Taiwan. Chiang teaches at the Cultural University and the Medical University of Taipeh. It was through his initiative that in 1993 UFO research was officially recognized by the People's Republic of China's Government as a science and since then taught at the universities. Takano and Chiang had heard of the Roswell film and tried to contact Santilli through Andrews. Hesemann had met both these gentlemen: Takano at a UFO conference in New York in October 1993 and Chiang at the MUFON conference in Richmond, Virginia in July 1993.

After a private viewing, both Takano and Chiang told Andrews that they had already seen the film before: Takano, when his government asked the U.S. Government for official UFO information and a CIA courier brought it to Tokyo, and Chiang, when he visited the CIA headquarters in Langley, Virginia officially. There, he claimed, he was shown films lasting about five hours, among them takes of an autopsy performed on the same creature and in the same surroundings as in the Santilli film. Interestingly enough, scenes were missing in the Washington material—the very scenes that Santilli had! Now, five hours of film material means three hundred minutes of it, and at the rate of three minutes per roll, one hundred rolls from Washington must have been shown. Santilli has ninety-one minutes of film—twenty-one rolls of three minutes each, plus one roll of eight minutes and also single clips. This gives a total of "over 120 rolls," just as cameraman Jack had said.[45]

On June 28, 1995, Santilli's film was shown to a group of U.S. senators in Washington, D.C. by Chris Cary, one of Santilli's colleagues.

A film team of the British TV Channel 4, which had obtained the film rights from Santilli, was doing some research and filming in the Roswell area. When they showed the pictures to a new eyewitness, a retired captain, he exclaimed in front of a running camera, *"Where did you get these pictures from? That is exactly the creature we saw then. But even its mere existence is held under strict secrecy."*[46]

Is the film genuine after all? There is only one way to settle this question: one must establish the age of the original film. All FX experts are unanimous on one point: before the 1970s the materials necessary for making a realistic doll, such as the plastics, silicone, latex, etc., did not exist.

In anticipation of further explanation, it must be stated that the age of the original film has not been completely clarified. In order to do this, Volker Spielberg, to whom the film belongs—Santilli can only market it—must sacrifice about fifty centimeters of the original film. Kodak has declared itself ready to test it physically and chemically. A chemical test could show whether the chemical composition of the film is identical with that of Kodak film made in the forties. A physical test would show the shrinkage over the years—hence the need for such a considerable length of film. To avoid

misuse of their name and integrity, Kodak insists on having a strip of exposed film showing the creature. This stipulation is the stumbling block. Spielberg, who is convinced of the film's genuineness, even without any testing by Kodak, is at present not prepared to lose such a long strip of such a valuable film, "merely to satisfy the curiosity of the public."

Otherwise, everything else speaks for the age of the film. To start with there are the marks on the border. The 16-mm original shows the code sign KODAK, with a black triangle and a black square. This code for the year of production repeats itself every twenty years, which means that the film could have been manufactured in 1927, 1947, or 1967. In the seventies the code system was changed to three symbols. Three branches of Kodak—Hollywood[47], London[48] and Copenhagen[49]—have affirmed this in writing, after Santilli had sent them fragments of the film from the unexposed leaders. Laurence A. Cate, a chemist who works as customer adviser at Eastman Kodak Co. Hollywood, wrote:

Dear Mr. Santilli,

Regarding the Roswell footage, I have looked at the safety release print. From the geometric year markings on the print (square, triangle), the original negative stock was definitely manufactured in Rochester, NY in either 1927, 1947 or 1967.

It is impossible to tell which of these three years it actually was, but it was definitely one of the above three years.

The release print does not have edge code and therefore the geometric code came from the negative original which was from one of the above years.

It was impossible to pinpoint which of the three years it is since the geometric code repeated every twenty years.[50]

This was naturally an unsatisfactory judgment, for only if it was definitely from 1947 could it be genuine.

Photographic expert Bob Shell, who followed the discussion on the CompuServe Encounters Forum, offered to solve the problem of dating the film more exactly. After Santilli had convinced himself about Shell's competence, Shell received from him a segment of three frames from the beginning of a roll, which the cameraman had apparently run off before starting on the actual work. The pictures showed the entrance to the autopsy room; even the table could be seen. The first result of Shells research was ready on 19 August 1995 and was transmitted all over through CompuServe.

I have now examined a segment of the film physically, a segment showing the autopsy room, before the body was placed on the table, which however is clearly consistent with the further film sequences.

The film used is Cine Kodak Super XX, a type of film whose production was stopped in 1956–57. Since the edge code markings can come from 1927, 1947 or 1967, and this film was not manufactured in 1927 or 1967, there obviously remains only 1947 as possibility. The quality of the pictures, clarity and grain of the film makes me think, that this film was exposed and developed when it was fairly fresh, that is, within a period of 3 or 4 years.

On this basis, I see no grounds to doubt the statement of the cameraman, who claims to have made the film in June and July and developed it "after a few days."

Based on my own tests of the physical characteristics of the film, I am ready to confirm with 95% certainty that the film is what the cameraman says. I hold back 5% only because I am still waiting for confirmation from Kodak regarding the "chemical signature." I don't set my name under such a declaration so easily and am ready to do so now only after very careful consideration and detailed examination.[51]

Shell sent his final analysis on 6 September 1995:

The edge code markings on the film, a square followed by a triangle immediately following the word KODAK, indicate film manufactured in 1927, 1947 and 1967. Kodak changed the system to a three symbol code in the early 70s, so this code was not used in 1987.

Film is made of a light sensitive photographic emulsion coated onto a flexible film base. In 1927 the film base was cellulose nitrate, a highly flammable material which was discontinued and replaced with acetate. All film coated onto acetate base is referred to as "safety film" because it does not spontaneously combust. In 1947, the film base used was acetate propionate, one of the original safety film base materials. By 1967 acetate propionate was no longer in use and had been replaced with triacetate. The "Roswell film" has acetate propionate base.

The "Roswell film" is on Cine Kodak Super XX High Speed Panchromatic Safety Film, a film type introduced in the early 40s (Kodak doesn't know exact year) and discontinued in 1956–57, when all film types were discontinued and replaced with new type, which were processed in new high temperature, more caustic chemicals. Film made prior to 1957 cannot be properly processed in later chemicals.

Super XX film was a high speed film designed for photography indoors or outdoors in dim light. Because of its high sensitivity, it had a very short life and deteriorated rapidly prior to processing. Based on the very short shelf life and the high quality of the images on the "Roswell film," it is my conclusion that the film was exposed and processed while still quite fresh. My educated guess is within two years of manufacture.

It would be impossible to take unexposed Super XX film from 1947 and expose it today and get any sort of usable image. The film would be heavily fogged from cosmic radiation by now. High speed (high sensitivity) films are much more sensitive to cosmic rays than slow (low sensitivity) films.

I find the physical characteristics of the "Roswell film" and the characteristics of the images on the film to be totally con-

sistent with film manufactured, exposed and processed in 1947.[52]

Who and what is Bob Shell? Shell was a zoologist at the Smithsonian Institution during the sixties, when he began to specialize in technical photography. Since 1972 he has been a professional photographer. He has studied all aspects of photography and is considered today an expert on digital techniques in the field. He is the author of fourteen technical books on photography, including the *Canon Compendium,* the most comprehensive standard manual for Canon cameras. Shell is editor of and technical adviser to various photographic magazines in eight countries, such as *Shutterbug, PhotoPro, Outdoor & Nature Photography,* and the German *Color Foto.* In addition to that he is adviser to two Japanese companies and stays in close contact with the technicians of Kodak in Rochester, New York. He has also made a sixty-minute documentary about film-shooting with a 16-mm camera. Bob Shell is further a registered consultant in phototechnical matters to the FBI as well as to courts of justice. His word carries weight.

A top expert has therefore, at least for the time being, confirmed the age of the Roswell film and stated that it must have been developed between 1947 and 1949! But this too shall not serve to conceal the fact that Santilli's film has nothing to do with the actual Roswell incident.

[1]*Daily Mirror,* Monday, 17 August l992.
[1A]Santilli, Ray, "My Story" (Manuscript, 1995).
Mantle, Philip, "An Interview with Ray Santilli," in: *UFOs: Examining the Evidence,* Batley, 1995, and Personal Interview on 5 September 1995.
[2]"Operation Anvil"—transcription of notes made during an interview by Ray Santilli with cameraman Jack B., published in 1995.

[3]Personal Interview, 5 September 1995.
[4]Mantle, Philip, "The Roswell Film Footage," in *UFO Times,* no. 36, July/August 1995.
[5]Personal talk with Reg Presley, 18 February 1995.
[6]Santilli, Ray, Personal message on 15 March 1995.
[7]Mantle, 1995.
[8]Hesemann, Michael, "Enthüllt: Die Roswell-Filme" (Revealed: The Roswell Films), in Magazin 2000, no. 105, Neuss, July 1995.
[9]Rai Due, 17 October 1995.
[10]"Alien Autopsy—Fact or Fiction," TV broadcast, Fox-Network/USA, 29 August 1995.
[11]*Skeptics UFO Newsletter,* Washington, D.C., November 1995.
[12]"Elefant im Garten," in *Der Spiegel,* Hamburg, no. 45, 6 November 1995.
[13]Personal message from Terry Blanton, 31 October 1995.
[14]*Time,* 18 December 1995.
[15]*Skeptics UFO Newsletter,* Washington, D.C., January 1996.
[16]"Alien Autopsy—Fact or Fiction," Fox TV, 29 August 1996.
[17]VonKeviczky, Colonel Colman, Evaluation dated 8 November 1995.
[18]LaParl, W. P., *Who Was Who,* New York.
[19]Jeffrey, Kent, "The Purported 1947 Roswell Film," in *MUFON UFO Journal,* no. 326, Seguin, TX, June 1995.
[20]Talbot, Michael, *The Holographic Universe,* New York, 1991.
Bohm, David, *Die implizite Ordnung* (The Implicit Order), Munich 1985.
Sheldrake, Rupert, *Die Wiedergeburt der Natur* (The Rebirth of Nature), Bern, 1991.
Buttlar, Johannes von, *Gottes Würfel* (God's Dice), Munich, 1992.
[21]Sitchin, Zecharia, *The Twelfth Planet,* New York, 1976, and, *Genesis Revisited,* New York, 1990.
[22]Milroy, Dr. Christopher, Evaluation dated 2 June 1995.
[23]Wingfield, George, Personal message on 12 June 1995.
[24]Wachter, Hanspeter, Letter of 24 January 1996.
[25]"Alien Autopsy—Fact or Fiction," Fox TV, 29 August 1995.
[26]*Observer,* London, 23 July 1995.

27TF 1, 23 October 1995.

28Ibid.

29Rai Due, 17 October 1995.

30Suriyathep, Robert, "Analysis of the Aliens' Anatomy", 20 January 1996.

31Operation Majestic 12, "Briefing Document, Prepared for President-Elect Dwight D. Eisenhower" (TS/EO), 18 November 1952.

32Stokes, Trey, "Special Effects—The Fine Art of Fooling People," in *UFO-Times*, London, January 1996.

33*ARTE*, 29 August 1995.

34*Potsdamer Neueste Nachrichten*, 30 August 1995.

35*Stern TV*, RTL, November 1996.

36*Welt am Sonntag*, 28 January 1996.

37"Alien Autopsy—Fact or Fiction," Fox TV, 29 August 1995.

38Rai Due, 17 October 1995.

39Personal Interview, 8 September 1995.

40Murphy, Dennis, "Panel Debris Analysis", 30 October 1995.

41Personal message, 26 October 1995.

42Personal Interview, 3 December 1995.

43Personal message, 24 January 1996.

44Interview with Ted Loman, 20 February 1996.

45Personal message from Colin Andrews, 28 June 1996.

46Personal message from Philip Mantle, 26 June 1996.

47Letter from Eastman Kodak Co. Hollywood, June 1995 (without specific date).

48Letter from Kodak Ltd., London, 14 June 1995.

49Letter from Kodak Copenhagen, 5 July 1995.

50Letter from Eastman Kodak Co. Hollywood, June 1995 (without specific date).

51Shell, Bob, "Film Evaluation," 19 August 1995.

52Shell, Bob, "Summary of Points in Physical Research on Film Dating," 6 September 1995.

53Shell, Bob, Letter to Philip Mantle, 21 May l996.

54Mantle, Philip, Personal tape-recorded telephone conversation with Captain James McAndrew, U.S. Air Force, 29 May 1996.

14.

Journey to Roswell

June 29, 1995. Landing in Mexico City; connecting flight to Juarez, and from there by taxi across the U.S. border, through El Paso to Alamogordo, where I (Hesemann) spent the night at the local Best Western hotel. In the morning after that began my renewed attempt to bring light into the darkness that still surrounds the Roswell affair and has only been intensified by the emergence of the Santilli footage. It was my fifth visit to the desert town, and it turned out to be the most enlightening one.

Ever since I had the opportunity of seeing the preview of the film that was shown at the London Museum to about ninety international experts and journalists in May 1995, the question "true or false?" was incessantly plaguing my mind. I simply had to find out the truth behind the story and the film. Since Fox Mulder from the TV series *The X Files*, we've known that "the truth is somewhere out there." And that meant starting the investigation where the story began, forty-eight years ago: at Roswell. It was my intention to locate the crash site using the information given by cameraman Jack B. and, if possible, to find eyewitnesses who could attest to the occurrence.

At that time I did not have the text of Jack's statement—Santilli gave it to me only in August 1995, after his secretary had written it down from the notes he had taken—and I only had the information he had given me over the telephone for reference. What struck me particularly was that he repeatedly spoke of the event as having occurred "early in June," "during the first days of June," and so on, which simply could not be true if it referred to the Roswell incident at all. This impression was strengthened when I asked him where the UFO had crashed. On the north bank of a small dry lake, Santilli replied, in the vicinity of an Apache reservation not far from White Sands Proving Grounds. Roswell lies about one hundred miles east of White Sands and is about seventy miles from the Mescalero Apache Reservation, which is also fifty miles from the debris field on the Foster Ranch. Was this another UFO crash, which had happened a month before the Roswell crash? Did the so-called "Santilli Film" have nothing to do with the Roswell crash at all?

After a two-hour drive we—my driver and I—reached Roswell, which lies in the middle of nowhere, in the center of a barren prairie. But the little desert hole seemed to have discovered its place in history, for already at the town limits we were met by signs describing the town as "The Home of the Famous UFO Event" and advertisements inviting people to attend the

In July 1995 Roswell organize its first "Roswell UFO Encounter."

The "Roswell UFO Encounter": a big circus.

The commercialization of Ufology at the "Roswell UFO Ecounter."

"Roswell UFO Encounter"—the timing of my visit (actually the fifth of altogether seven times I came here in search for witnesses) was not just by chance—an event that was expected to lure thousands of visitors to the center of New Mexico. Everything was geared toward it. There was no shop window without UFOs and ETs, and on the signs showing the way to shops on Main Street, which had been blocked off on account of road works, there was naturally a small alien in his flying saucer greeting the passersby with a friendly gesture. A very promising "circus" indeed.

Even as I was checking in at the Roswell Inn—the Best Western of the town where I had reserved a room—the "Roswell eyewitnesses" came in, from Walter Haut to Robert Shirkey, and the cream of American UFO researchers from Linda Moulton Howe to Stanton Friedman, Kevin Randle and Don Schmitt to Walter Andrus, International Director of the Mutual UFO Network (MUFON) and finally my German friend and fellow writer Johannes von Buttlar, who had recently become the proud owner of a house in Santa Fe. Johannes and I had planned the meeting at Roswell

so that he, his wife Elise and I could together interview some of the witnesses and also attend the festivities that were to take place.

The first event was the big opening ceremony of the "Encounter," at which the main speakers—Friedman, Schmitt, Randle, and Howe—presented their findings to the public. As expected, they only agreed on one point: that a spacecraft of unknown origin had crashed in the Roswell area. All other details, from the date of the crash—July 2 according to Friedman and the Fourth of July according to Schmitt/Randle—to the location of the crash—in the immediate neighborhood of the debris field, according to Friedman, thirty-five miles north of Roswell according to Schmitt/Randle—were points of controversy and the debate was carried on with sometimes even personal animosity. Santilli's film overshadowed the event and was the theme of the most intense discussion.

The actual UFO get-together was located on a football field, and turned out to be a sort of fair-come-school function. Three rows of stands selling UFO related items, lined the way(s) to an open tent, where the experts of the previous evening plus the forensic artist William McDonald presented their versions of the Roswell occurrence or autographed their books, the merciless sun of New Mexico giving Stanton Friedman a rather bad sunburn on his head. Amused by the spectacle, which had not quite attracted the throngs of visitors hoped for, we went in search of the true Roswell, the scene of action forty-eight years ago. We found it: the sheriff's office, where the rancher Brazel reported his find, the fire station from where they went out at night to fight a fire somewhere north of Roswell, the Ballard Funeral Home, which had been asked about the conservation of corpses and sizes of coffins, the Base area—now an industrial and residential park with a cargo airport—Hangar 84, in which the wreck and bodies were packed for transport, the Base Hospital—of which now only a weathered ruin exists, as a relic of the past—in which the first examination of the bodies took place.

We gathered further information—maps of 1947, a copy of the base's 1947 yearbook, with portraits of all the servicemen stationed there—from the two UFO museums of Roswell, which—what else can one expect?—are naturally inimical to each other. The UFO Enigma Museum is run by John Price and ex-Defense Intelligence Agency Sergeant Clifford Stone, one of the best informed UFO researchers in the U.S., and the other, the Roswell International UFO Museum and Research Center, by Walter Haut, the former press officer of Roswell AFB who, under instructions of the base commander Colonel Blanchard, once made the historic announcement that a disc was captured in the Roswell region and who is himself the most interesting exhibit of the museum.

We asked the witnesses and experts for their opinion about Santilli's film. Whereas Stone was "95%" certain about its authenticity, and Schmitt was impressed by the amazing similarity between the creature and as yet unpublished descriptions given by newer firsthand eye-witnesses, the majority was skeptical. Most were afraid—and this they said openly—that if the film should prove to be a fake, it would be fatal to the Roswell case, in spite of all the other solid evidence. As it was, the revitalized Air Force prevarication that the crashed object was a weather balloon from the Mogul Project, had dealt the UFO story a heavy blow. We all were already feverishly awaiting the closing report of the General Accounting Office of the U.S. Congress about the Roswell event, the publication of which had been set for the end of June but had been postponed. Well, more was at stake than the truth: the shaky economy of a small town made it hold on to its only tourist attraction like a drowning man grasping a straw.

Indeed, what is Roswell other than a boring desert town with a UFO crash? The city administrators have long since realized that the crash was the sole attraction Roswell can offer, and so they focused their attention, supported by a clever marketing strategy, on the incident which gave their town a place in history.

From alien costume competitions to UFO soapbox races on Main Street (where it had not been blocked off for road repairs), everything had been trimmed for commerce and fun for the whole family. We fled from the "UFO trash at Roswell," only to see how the alleged site of the crash (according to Schmitt and Randle) thirty-five miles north of Roswell had also been commercialized, with bus tours from Roswell and an entrance fee of $15 a head. But the family of the rancher Hub Corn was frank and kind, likable, typical Americans, so that we did not begrudge them their additional income or their measures to prevent said income from being eaten up by claims for damages: every visitor had to sign a statement relieving the ranch owners from all responsibility for injuries suffered on the site, including bites from rattlesnakes or tarantulas. This although any sensible snake or spider would have fled the place hurriedly in face of the bustle and racket that prevailed. The site of the crash lay above an arroyo on a ridge, which had a romantic beauty. Apparently the UFO after being struck by lightning above the Foster Ranch some forty miles further northwest, had steered towards this sheltered spot so as to remain unobserved, before the landing gear failed completely and the heel-shaped—as it is described in the latest reports—spaceship rammed head-on against the rock, whereby four of its five crew members lost their lives. Thus, anyway, the Schmitt/Randle version.

I spoke to the rancher Corn, who had employed his whole family to sell drinks, hamburgers and T-shirts. He openly admitted to having acquired the crash site by sheer luck, not ever having known of it while buying the ranch during the seventies, like the man who bought a cow and got a calf as well. The crash site was indeed a gift from Heaven. He had never thought that his ranch would become a UFO Mecca. But then some years ago Randle and Schmitt had appeared one day and "discovered" the site. At first he had asked them not to reveal this location, but since Roswell was getting ready for the "Encounter," he had recognized the chance of making a quick buck by way of the flying saucers. To be honest, he told me, he didn't know what to make of the UFO racket. But gradually he was beginning to think that there was something to it. A couple of days ago he had met a man who had left the marked path and gone across the land, as if he was looking for something. When he asked the man to get back to the "beaten track," because of the extremely shy but nevertheless omnipresent rattlers and tarantulas—the man had declared that he was now one hundred percent sure that this was the real site of the crash. The rancher had asked "Why ?" and the man had said that he had seen

pictures of the crash spot made by the Air Force—and they had been made from exactly that angle. He could remember all the details, especially the rocky ridge. A few days later I knew that this story was true, that the photographs existed and that that was indeed the site.

I had taken a taxi to go to Lincoln, New Mexico, for further investigations. As happens during a long drive, the driver Charles D. and I started chatting. Charles asked me what I was doing in Roswell. I told him I was a journalist investigating UFOs. That broke the dam. When he was about sixteen or seventeen years old, he started telling me, he had been rather aimless and wandered around a bit. One day, between 1972 and 1974, a neighbor and friend of his parents, a lieutenant colonel at Roswell AFB, had asked him what his plans for his future were. He did not have any, was his answer. Why did he not join the army? The boy had no idea what that would be like. "In the Army you have highly interesting experiences," said the officer and related how "they had even captured a flying saucer."

Everything had to be done very quickly. The base was closed to civilian traffic. Near Corona folks had discovered something that had crashed there. We searched the area and finally found a spot on which a long, almost oval object, about 20 feet wide had come down. We also found there four dead bodies. The whole area was blocked off, 150 to 200 men were put on the job. Every square inch was combed for wreckage. We loaded all of it onto trucks and brought it to the base, to Hangar 84. Near the wreck there was a lot of debris. It consisted of some superstrong metal. We tried to cut it or to drill through it , without success. It was definitely not from this earth.

The boy did not believe him, and to prove it the old man took a file from a shelf and showed him five photographs, black-and-white glossy prints in 8-inch x 12-inch size. One showed the rather flat, oval object on the back of a flatbed truck. About six feet of the object projected out of the loading space on each side of the truck. The other shots showed the site: there was a heel-shaped object, with its nose stuck between rocks under a ridge. I asked the taxi driver to sketch the ridge on a piece of paper: there were no more doubts. That was the Schmitt/Randle crash site! I asked whether the lieutenant colonel had mentioned where the wreck was found—was it near Corona? *"No,"* replied Charles, *"he said it was about thirty miles north of Roswell."*[1] The spot in question lies thirty-five miles north-northwest of Roswell. I was convinced that the Schmitt/Randle scenario must be correct and I, naturally, passed on the full name and the telephone number of this new witness to my two research colleagues. The lieutenant colonel passed away some years ago. His widow moved to another town and there were two sons. One should be able to dig up the colonel's belongings, and if Schmitt and Randle succeed in doing so, they would have the long yearned-for proof for their version of the Roswell incident.

Back in Roswell, I had dinner with Robert Shirkey. Shirkey was one of the chief witnesses for the loading of the wreckage at the base. He had seen the fragments, including the "I-beams" (these have also been termed "I-rods" by some witnesses and even "H-beams" in the Santilli film bearing the strange hieroglyphs). He had a lot to tell about his time in the Air Force, his adventures as a pilot and his work at the base. There was the story of his dog, a cocker spaniel, which he always took with him into the cockpit, and even to a parachute-jumping exercise. A picture of him and his dog in parachute-riggings found a place in the 1947 yearbook of the base. Did he consider it possible that what he saw at that time were parts of a weather balloon? Out of the question! Did he remember the hieroglyphs? I showed him a reproduction from the Santilli film. Yes, they had

looked something like that, but after forty-eight years he could not remember in detail.

The next day Johann von Buttlar, his wife and I went to look for the "debris field" at the Foster Ranch. One drives north, then turns off toward the west and after about sixty miles through nowhere, takes a ranch road south. On the way we had an appointment with Loretta Proctor, the closest neighbor of rancher Brazel, long since widowed, who still lives in her little old ranch house in the middle of the prairie. It is a small, white house, immediately behind it a huge rock face of red sandstone that towers above it and intensifies the romantic Wild West flavor of the place. On the mantelpiece of the rustic—and rather dusty—living room are pieces of Indian ceramic, which her husband had found on the ranch.

Loretta is a warmhearted old lady who told us readily everything she could remember: how Bill Brazel brought their seven-year-old son Dee home and told her and her husband about the find, and yes, showed them a few bits of wreckage. They were pieces of metal, "very unusual material" which one couldn't cut or bend or burn. The Proctors advised Brazel to report the find, which set off the whole affair. They saw him at Roswell when he was under military custody, accompanied by two MPs. He did not even greet them. After that he never wanted to talk about the incident. And their son, Dee? Apparently he cannot remember what happened . . . or he does not want to or is not allowed to do so. Only once, as they were riding through Brazel's land, had he shown her the place where the wreckage had been, over one thousand yards long and a couple of hundred yards wide. We noted down more exact directions and went on to look for the site.

The way led us past Brazel's "ranch house"—a hut without running water or electricity, next to it the shed of corrugated metal sheets in which Brazel had at first

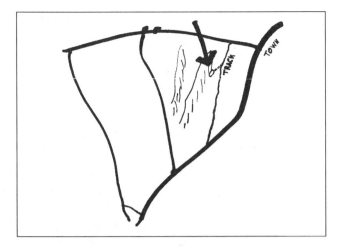

The cameraman's map of the crash site.

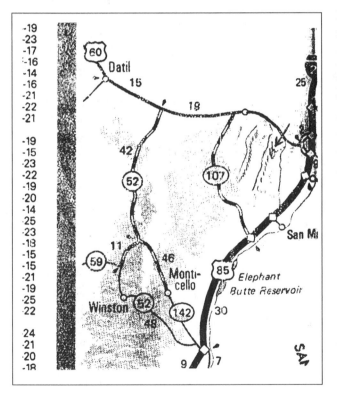

stored the pieces he had collected and brought home in his truck. The land was more barren than that of the Proctor ranch, where one could see trees and bushes, streams and fertile grazing ground. The Foster Ranch was only prairie, with just enough grass for sheep. Above an arroyo south of two windmills (the "twin mills," as Loretta called them), some five miles from the ranch house, we found what once was the debris field. I could recognize it, having found it once before in July 1993, following directions given in the literature.

Meanwhile it was clear to us that neither of the sites was the one which the cameraman had described as being on the north bank of a dried-up lake. Yes, the Roswell crash was real, the Mogul Balloon statement of the Air Force was ridiculous. The non-ufologist Santilli had christened his film the "Roswell Film," but it did not deal with the Roswell crash. But in defense of Santilli it must be said that the cameraman himself was under the notion that what was widely called the Roswell incident was the crash in which he himself had been involved. After all, he had landed at Roswell AFB, when he was brought from Washington. But neither the timing nor the description of the site tallied with anything near Roswell. But where did the earlier crash occur? We needed more data.

Phone call to Santilli in London. Whatever information he could give was based on vague memory. Obviously the location of the crash had never interested him, but my offer to find the spot and to film it served as a bait. He promised to call Jack B. and get more details. Five hours later we got them. According to Santilli, the site lay between "Sorocco"—I made it clear to him that it could only be Socorro—and Magdalena, New Mexico (which made sense, since that was the neighboring town), some three-and-a-half hours' drive west of Roswell. There was a mountain there—yes, the Magdalena Mountains—and before that, just after a cliff, there was a dirt road leading south. One came through a canyon to a dry lake bed. The cameraman had himself revisited the place, about ten years ago.

There was, however, a snag. I acquired maps, even topographical maps, of the region, but nowhere on these was a small dry lake bed to be found! Was I running after a phantom? After a few days of further research in Santa Fe, Los Angeles, Seattle and Albuquerque I decided to make a blind attempt to find it, together with Johannes von Buttlar and his wife.

We drove from Albuquerque to Socorro, skirting the Manzano Mountains, in the middle of which is one of the world's largest arsenals for atomic weapons. After lunch we continued towards Magdalena, to find the right dirt road. After two errors, which, however, took us into the picturesque scenery of the Magdalena Mountains and the Cibola National Forest, we knew that we had gone too far. Back toward Socorro, one more dirt road and we found both, the "gateway," actually a small canyon, and, behind it, a dry lake bed (or a wide riverbed, banked up in front of the rocks, before it made its way through it by creating the canyon) of about 150 yards in diameter! Even now one can see the tracks of its former tributaries, one of which probably carved out the mighty opening in the rock. We had found the right spot. The cameraman's description fitted and he must have at least known the place. Later communication with him through Santilli confirmed all other details.

The spot tallied with all the details given by the cameraman. It was near White Sands Proving Grounds (fifteen miles as the crow flies) and the Bosque del Apache National Wildlife Refuge, which Jack (or Santilli) had mistaken for a Reservation. All that underlined the credibility of his story.

Major Jesse Marcel, who made first investigations on the debris-covered field, did mention a second crash site in an interview with the journalist Bob Pratt on 8 December 1979. "It could be clearly seen from which direction it (the object) came and in which it flew. It was flying from northeast towards southwest. . . . I learnt later that further west, Carrizozo way, something similar was found. . . . it was about the same period, sixty to eighty miles west of here."[2] Now Carrizozo lies west of Foster Ranch and the dried-up lake is about eighty miles away in that direction, toward which the object had flown, according to Marcel.

The *Roswell Daily Record* of 10 July 1947 stated that Brazel had discovered the debris already on June 14. But since it was five miles away from his house and he had other things to do, he had not bothered with it just then but had waited till July 4 to go with his children and gather it. Only after he had heard at Corona about "flying saucers" on July 5, and learned that there was a reward of $5,000 for proving their existence, did he report his find to the sheriff.[3] This version had been dismissed as a "cover story" by Roswell researchers—but could be true after all. Perhaps there is no connection between the debris on the Foster Ranch and the delta-shaped object that crashed north of Roswell on probably July 4. In fact Santilli said on the CompuServe Encounters Forum: *"The cameraman confirmed that they had believed that the whole district had been cleared, but then, owing to information that came from Roswell, discovered that they had overlooked a certain area."*[4]

The evidence that something really happened at this lake on 1 June 1947 was strengthened when I was contacted by two local UFO researchers, Llewellyn A. Wykel and Carol M. Kelly of Albuquerque. Wykel and Kelly had heard about our discovering the lake through CompuServe. They asked me for clear directions as to how to get there, in order to investigate the spot personally and more thoroughly. They sounded profession-

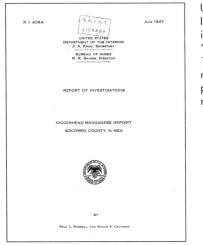

U.S. Department of the Interior document regarding the reopening of the "Niggerhead Mine" on 1 June 1947. We have reason to believe its purpose was to cover up the retrieval operation.

al and reliable, so I told them how to get there, after Santilli's cameraman had confirmed that we had found the right spot. They did not disappoint me.

The first thing they saw at the lake was the entrance to a closed mine in the rocks above. Mines in that area have a history. The excavation of ores, particularly in this region, which was closely connected with the armaments industry, stood under government control and was subsidized during World War II. Besides that, scientists of the Manhattan Project visited the region ostensibly as prospectors and miners, but really to confiscate and isolate land for their experiments.

A visit to the New Mexico Institute of Mining & Technology revealed the history of "our" mine, which yielded manganese ore. The mine was opened in 1937, but closed down soon after that because the ore was very poor in quality and its extraction unprofitable. But during the war that followed, the military armaments industry required manganese for hardening steel so much that every source of this metal, however poor, became valuable. The mine was, therefore, reopened in 1943. The excavation of ore was carried on until 1945,

when the vein finally ran out and the mine was closed again. But later, during peacetime, without any apparent reason, the U.S. Government staked a claim for renewing mining operations and that on 1 June 1947![5]

Was it a coincidence that this was exactly the same day as the UFO wreck was recovered, according to the cameraman? Was the announcement of mining activities only a cover for transporting crew, cranes, trucks and other equipment to the site without exciting suspicion amongst the local population? Was not the mention of blasting operations to widen the mine sufficient excuse to cordon off the area completely and keep off the curious? Robert W. Eveleth, the senior mining engineer in charge of the New Mexico Institute of Mining & Technology in Socorro, produced the relevant document, proof of the claim staked by the U.S. Government. He assured researchers Kelly and Wykel that after that the "reopening" of the mine, no actual mining had been carried out. Two weeks later the whole action was terminated and the mine itself was sold in 1953.

Encouraged by these results, I returned to the site in February 1996. My aim was to find evidence for the recovery operation. All that I had to aid me were two drawings made by an artist based on sketches by the cameraman. With me were the well-known UFO researcher Wendelle C. Stevens with his daughter Cece, Bob Shell, the photographic expert, and a research team from UFO-AZ, a UFO research group of Tucson, Arizona, led by mining engineer Ted Loman and including two professional treasure hunters. It was our intention, using state-of-the-art metal detectors, to find traces of the recovery activities, which could be dated back to 1947.

The expedition began with a mysterious occurrence. Wendelle and Cece Stevens had risen early and were having breakfast at their hotel, when they felt that a

The co-author M.Hessemann in front of the "rock gate", a small canyon through which the retrieval team arrived. The cliff to his left is the impact point of the alien craft.

man sitting three tables away was watching them. Cece, in her very direct manner, went over to him and asked, "And what do you know about these UFOs?" It turned out that he worked for the DNA (Defense Nuclear Agency), the successor of the Atomic Energy Commission, and knew that we would be coming there. The UFO crash in 1947 was known to him and he showed Wendelle and Cece the actual site of the crash on a map. It was the same spot as I had discovered six months earlier. Later, as we met at the car park of the hotel, the man drove past us in his Chevy Blazer more than once, then followed us down to the crash site. He stopped his car a bit higher up and, while we were looking for clues, watched us through a pair of binoculars—which I in turn filmed with my video camera.

But apart from a few old tin cans, which might indeed have dated back to the fourties or fifties, we could find no leftovers from the salvaging team. Instead, Loman made a much more spectacular discovery. He found the possible spot of impact of the disc—and a clear indication that just there someone had tried to eliminate all other traces.

When Santilli sent me the sketches of the crash site by telefax, I was a bit confused. Shortly before that the cameraman had identified the dry lake as being the right crash site, from photographs which I had sent to Santilli. Some of the details of the landscape, such as the mighty rocky "gateway" and the outstanding mountain with the boulder on its top—the "Niggerhead"—were unmistakable. But in the drawings the scene looked quite different. Now the wreck and the camp of the salvage team were in the middle of a canyon, with a rocky wall on both sides. Were the sketches vague or had I been mistaken?

This second visit gave me the answer. For when I looked at the gorge from closer quarters, it turned out in fact to be a small canyon about five hundred yards long and fifty yards wide. It is shown in the topographical map as Box Canyon. I wandered through it from one end to the other, and the closer I came to the lake, the clearer it became to me that this was exactly what the sketches showed. They had been drawn from the perspective of a person approaching the lake through the canyon. Perhaps the camp was laid between the protecting (and hiding) walls of the gorge.

I was trying to figure out the position of the wreck from the sketch, when Ted called out to me: "Mike, have a look at that!" He showed me a part of the steep rock face in the eastern side of the canyon, where heavy boulders had been piled up. "Look at the cliff—the archlike spot there. Obviously someone has chiseled off something. That has nothing to do with mining. That has been knocked off with hammer and chisel. Someone wanted to remove traces from there." Ted knew what he was talking about. He had enough experience in mining, possessed three silver mines in Mexico. I looked at the place and agreed that human hands had been at work there. Then I looked at the sketch and indeed the rock face it showed resembled the rock face in front of me.

"The stones are not lying here by chance," added Ted. "They have been deliberately piled up—as if to prevent anyone from looking for something here. If you ask me, it all looks very suspicious." He could be right. . . .

Back in Socorro I visited the senior mining engineer Robert Eveleth, to check the results of Kelley and Wykel. Eveleth is a friendly and very helpful person who knows the district like the palm of his hand. He recalled the visit of the researchers, and it did not take him long to find the files pertaining to the "Niggerhead" mine. Although we did not talk about UFOs, he seemed to sense what it was all about and remarked that he had noticed that "whatever the reason for it was," it was difficult to get data about the mines in that area, whereas the histories of the mines farther away toward Magdalena were far better documented.

Confirmation of at least some of our findings were made by former radio news reporter and UFO researcher Steven Kaeser. Kaeser informed us:

With directions provided by Bob Shell, (Michael Hesemann) and Ted Loman, I was able to locate the (crash) site with little difficulty. I was able to easily see the section of the cliff face that had been cut out. . . .

I (Kaeser) spoke with Bob Eveleth at the N.M. Bureau of Mines, and he was very helpful. He said that such a cut was very unusual, but not unheard of. Apparently the type of rock there is used for road bedding material, since it doesn't deteriorate when it gets wet. It is possible that someone was involved in a road building project and came to that area to obtain bedding material, but there probably would be no records of that. I found no evidence of that material on the gravel roads that I traveled, but that proves nothing of course.

I took a picture of two large sandstone rocks near the mouth of the hollowed out area, which I found interesting. They were both cracked all the way through in several places, and I would

suspect that was the result of extreme heat. If they had cracked while tumbling to that location they wouldn't have come to rest on one area like that, and they showed no evidence of an impact from above that would crack them. Sandstone tends to retain moisture, and it seems logical that high heat would likely cause it to crack, but I wish I had asked Bob Eveleth to come to the site with me for his opinion. Even if heat is thought to be the cause, that wouldn't prove much, since we do not know if it was five years ago or five hundred years ago. But I found that interesting."[5A]

Were there local witnesses? Five miles west of the crash site there is a ranch, the only one in that area, at which two persons lived during June 1947—Joseph Gianera and his wife Esther. They are no longer alive, but their daughter Betty Pound lives on the ranch today, with her husband "Smoky." Kelly and Wykel paid her a visit. Betty's parents had never spoken about any special incident in summer 1947 to her—perhaps they had really believed that the salvaging activity was the opening of a mine—but Smoky's best friend, Fred Strozzi, claimed to have seen a meteorite falling during the time and over the area in question, which he described as being "bigger than a basketball."[6]

Had others seen this "meteorite crash"? Was there anything in the papers about it? The UFO-AZ team visited the office of the local paper, the *Socorro Sentinel.* There they were told that towards the end of the sixties some of the papers had been destroyed by fire—these were, of all the issues, those between 10 May and 15 June 1947. At the suggestion of a staff member, the team tried the library of the Mining University. Here they found microfilms of all the issues of the paper—with the exception of those between 10 May and 15 June 1947. Bob Shell then tried at the neighboring town Magdalena. The chief editor of the local paper there said that all papers from that period were missing there too. "You won't find them. I have been looking for them for forty years and nobody has them," were her words.

Shell did not give up but asked about papers for the period 31 May to 5 June 1947 at the Zimmermann Library of New Mexico. There too the issues were missing. Equally unsuccessful was the attempt of the UFO-AZ team at the Rio Grande Collection of the New Mexico State University at Las Cruces. There, too, the issues in question were missing.

But we were able to locate additional witnesses for this alleged "meteorite crash" who were able to pinpoint the date more accurately: it happened during the late hours of 31 May 1947.

The witnesses are Laguna Indians, from the Laguna Reservation, who went to school in Gallup and were thirteen or fourteen years old at that time. May 31 had been an extremely hot day and the children had been waiting for the evening to go out and play. When it finally cooled down, it was already quite dark. A dozen or so of the children went out to the water tower of the old railway station belonging to the Santa Fe Railroad. They climbed up the tower, enjoying its coolness, chattering and playing with one another. *"Suddenly the whole sky was lit up as if it was daytime,"* reported a woman witness, *"in less than four seconds a big ball of fire glided silently over our heads, from left to right, i.e., northwest to southeast. My sister had just then stuck a quarter in her mouth and was so frightened that she at once swallowed it. The light was so dazzling that we kids held our hands before our faces to protect our eyes."*[7]

Two days later all the children who had sat on the tower had blisters on their hands and arms. The doctors treated them as burn blisters, but could not determine their cause. The children thought they had scabies—the blisters lasted for a week. One of the girls had kept a diary and had noted down the date of the incident: it was 31 May 1947. The cameraman had repeatedly stressed the point that even at the time of his arrival on the evening of June 1, twenty-four hours after the crash, the wrecked disc was so hot that the retrieval team feared an outbreak of fire. One can, therefore, imagine that it had really "glowed" as it fell and had looked like a meteorite. Besides that, one has never heard of meteorites causing blisters.

A few days later, according to the witnesses, a strange girl had appeared on the scene. Her skin was grayish and she had gray hair, which looked as if she had a wig on. She avoided all contact with grown-ups but sought the proximity of the children who had seen the "ball of fire." Most of them, however, kept away from her for she was so odd, but some played with her. Whoever had contact with her became ill, the closer the contact, the worse was the sickness. After about a week the mysterious girl vanished and was never seen again.[8]

This description of the events was given by an elderly Indian lady, who now lives in Los Angeles. Her daughter had heard the "Art Bell Show" on the radio, in which Bob Shell had been interviewed about the Santilli film, and suddenly her mother's old story made sense. "I've always wondered whether what my mother had experienced had something to do with the Roswell incident," she wrote to Bell, "but neither the date nor the direction in which the object flew tallied. Then I heard in your show about the crash near Socorro on June 1 and now I ask myself whether that was what my mother had seen." Bell sent the letter to Bob Shell, who shortly after called up Los Angeles and spoke to the daughter and then to the mother.

The latter told him her story in detail and also named two more witnesses. Both still live in New Mexico, and after a bit of searching Bob succeeded in getting their telephone numbers. In the course of long telephone conversations both of them confirmed the story of the first witness in all details. Since they both lived in the reservation, they were hesitant to give him a personal interview. But later one of them—let us call her

Theresa—did agree to meet him. When we met in Socorro, Bob invited me to go along. Thus we went together to visit her on February 19, 1996 at her little House in a reservation west of Albuquerque.

Theresa was a cordial little woman with warm brown eyes. I filmed our talk with a video camera, but promised her not to publish it. She was afraid of the reaction of her neighbors and the tribal elders, for she believed that such experiences were still regarded as taboo among her people and one does not speak about them to outsiders.

We lived in those days at Gallup, in a round house, and our father worked for the railroad. I stayed there till my father retired in 1956. I was seven years old at that time and went to school. We were playing out there, near the rail tracks when it appeared. It was white, glowing white, like fire, as if it was burning, and had a sort of smoky film around it—but it had no trail. It was as big as the sun, round, and absolutely silent. It came from the northwest and disappeared towards the southeast direction. I was so frightened that I swallowed a quarter which I had in my mouth. I remember that very well. Some of us had burns after that, but I didn't.

Theresa knew about the strange girl too.

She wore white clothes. She always stayed near the river at night. The men tried once to catch her, but she disappeared. She was small like a little girl and wore wide white clothes and a white veil that hid her face. No one could see her face through the veil and so we did not know whether she was white or Indian. Most of us were afraid of her. Some kids got close to her and they fell sick. Perhaps they saw her face or the color of her skin, but they never spoke about it. She had something eerie about her. But that is all I still recall about her. She always came from the east and went along the river. And one day she was no longer there.[9]

General Twining's report of July 18, 1947 also speaks of an aircraft of the type "flying saucer," which had been found near the White Sands Proving Grounds. He mentions *"a recovered flying disc and the remains of a possible second disc."*[10] No one had ever claimed that Roswell was "near the White Sands Proving Grounds," and therefore he must have been referring to another UFO crash that happened *before* July 18. Interestingly enough, Twining was the commander of the Air Materiel Command at the Wright Field Army Air Force Base, where apparently the "flying saucer type of aircraft" had been examined. The investigation seems to have been finished by about the middle of July. The cameraman said that the wreck had been loaded onto a flatbed truck some time around June 6 and taken to Wright Field, where he had filmed the examination procedures for about three weeks, that is to say, until the end of June.[11]

As early as 1990 I was able to interview Virgil A. Postlethwait, a witness to this occurrence. Major Postlethwait served in 1948 in the G-2 Intelligence Corps of the U.S. Army at the Pope AAF/Fort Bragg Complex in North Carolina. He had a "Top Secret" clearance. He remembers receiving a report in 1948 over the telex, about a UFO crash in the vicinity of the White Sands missile testing range in New Mexico. The telex came from the Headquarters of the Third Air Force in Atlanta, Georgia.

Without specifying the time of the crash, the report described the disc as being about one hundred feet in diameter, thirty feet high, whose *"metallic skin was too tough to be penetrated by conventional tools, although as thin as a newspaper."* Besides that, they had found four *"small humanoid bodies"* about four feet tall, which *"were stuck in close-fitting silvery uniforms. Their heads were big, they had no hair. The ears, nose and mouth were the dwindled remains of what they might have been before. . . . Similarly it was found during the examination of the*

Howard Marston witnessed the arrival of the Socorro wreckage in Wright Field.

inner organs that they were human but in a state of degeneration," reported Postlethwait. *". . . before the bodies could be examined they had to be taken out of their uniforms. Their suits presented a bit of a problem; they had no visible buttons or zips or other means of opening them. An attempt to cut them with a pair of scissors was not successful either. Only metal shears made it possible to remove the clothing. The material behaved in its consistency and properties completely different from anything we know on earth: extremely tough and very light and thin; it withstood all external influence."* Bodies and wreckage, according to Postlethwait, were taken to Wright Field.[12]

In December 1995 I interviewed Howard Marston, now seventy years old, who had been an engineer at Wright Field in 1947. He said: *"I was a civilian, twenty-two years old, just discharged from the army. I was then working for a firm of aircraft builders, testing hydraulic systems for high level flights. I had just come out of the testing laboratory at Wright Field, when they brought in the disc. It was to be examined there at Wright Field; they wanted to see if they could figure out its propulsion system. It was on the trailer of a truck, covered with tarpaulins. They unloaded it in a hangar. I saw it from a distance. One couldn't get nearer on account of security. But I saw it uncovered. It was a metallic disc about thirty or forty feet in diameter. I wasn't near enough to see if it was damaged or not."*[13] Marston heard rumors that the wreck had been found near Roswell, but it can be ruled out that it came from "the" Roswell crash. None of the Roswell witnesses mentions an almost undamaged disc of about thirty-five feet

diameter. On the contrary, the majority of them speak of a "heel-shaped" object. The debris from Roswell was transported by plane to Wright Field, not on a truck. Only our cameraman spoke of a circular disc and a transportation over land; of a crash southwest of Socorro, five weeks before the Roswell occurrence.

This incident may also explain the report given by Barney Barnett, the field engineer of the Soil Conservation Department, which does not really fit into the Roswell scenario. Barnett lived in Socorro and his beat was the plateau of San Augustin, west of Magdalena. Why did he have to go to Roswell, how could he have passed the crash site there? But he drove almost daily on the road to Magdalena, the road from which the track leads off to our dried-up lake! Had he seen the "meteor" and looked for the site of impact? Or had he, early in the morning of June 1, on his way to work, seen a "glow" toward the south and had gone to investigate its cause? We can only speculate, for Barney died before any researcher could ask him.

But there were other civilians who were witnesses to the Socorro crash—Indians in the neighboring Apache Reservation, as Robert Morning Sky, half Apache, half Hopi, told me in December 1995. He claims to have spoken to these witnesses, who however refuse to come out into the open, into the world of the "paleface." They are afraid, afraid of the Government, afraid of the Army, afraid of the soldiers, whose brutality they have seen with their own eyes.

They told me from which direction the disc came and where it crashed and what happened to the Star Beings. There are rumors in the reservations about a number of beings and a number of crashes. Often the beings survived the crash but not the retrieval team. They were beings from the stars, closer to God than anyone else and these soldiers shot them or killed them with blows. What chance have we then as Indians? We are far less important. On a scale of one to ten we can be happy if we had the importance number one. We are afraid of that too: if I gave you names and you went and talked to them—will the soldiers get wind of it and get at them? Perhaps. Do we trust them? No. I am sorry about it all. But when a people have been repeatedly punished, I can understand why they do not want to talk anymore.

Robert Morning Sky says that this was not the only UFO crash the Indians knew about.

What surprises me and other Indians in the reservations is that the majority of UFO crashes—as far as I know there were sixteen crashes between 1945 and 1950 in the U.S.A.—that fourteen out of sixteen crashes occurred on or near reservations and that no UFO researcher noticed this fact and started his researches with us. Indians prefer to sleep under the open sky rather than in a house. It seems to me that those who do UFO research and seek eyewitnesses should at first ask those who live in the open. Especially people whose whole life, whose whole tradition revolves around stellar beings. But strangely enough in the last fifty years, nobody thought of asking us Indians. This is strange for us. And if at all anyone thinks of asking us— during the recent years there have been books about Indians and UFOs—then he already thinks he knows the answer: yes, those are myths and legends.

No, they are not. They deal with real beings. That is why I now turn to the public and say, "Look here, there are many stories and rumors which you have never heard in your 'civilized' world. One of these is that the crash near Roswell on July 4, 1947 was not the only crash that summer. We Indians know of three, and the first happened near Socorro. That was the crash from which the being in the autopsy film came and not

from Roswell. The third crash was in the Four Corners area and there too Indians were the witnesses. But the researchers talk even now only of the Roswell incident. Not even one of them heard about the other crashes, or took the trouble during fifty years, to ask us. . .[14]

But I went, and asked, Robert Morning Sky. And what I learned from him left me no doubts that my efforts to find him had been worth the while.

[1]Personal interview, 14 July 1994.

[2]Pratt, Bob, Interview with Colonel Jesse Marcel, 8 December 1979.

[3]*Roswell Daily Record*, 10 July 1947.

[4]Santilli, Ray on the "Encounters"-Forum on CompuServe 24 June 1995.

[5]Document in New Mexico Institute of Mining & Technology in Socorro, New Mexico.

[5A]Kaeser, Steven, Letter to Philip Mantle, 14 June l996, 20 June l996.

[6]Wykel, Llewellyn and Karol Kelly, "The Six Mile Canyon Crash Site," Report of 24 September 1995.

[7]Letter to Art Bell, 10 September 1995.

[8]Message from Bob Shell, 23 January 1996.

[9]Personal Interview, 19 February 1996.

[10]Twining, General Nathan, "Air Accident Report on 'Flying Disc' Aircraft Crashed near White Sands Proving Grounds, New Mexico," dated 18 July 1943.

[11]"Operation Anvil," transcription of Ray Santilli's interview with cameraman Jack B., published 1995.

[12]Personal Interview, 25 June 1990.

[13]Personal Interview, 2 December 1995.

[14]Personal Interview, 3 December 1995.

15.

The Star Elder

I (Hesemann) had come to know Robert Morning Sky through Lieutenant Colonel Wendelle C. Stevens and met him personally, together with my fiancé Natalia, in December 1995. Robert was born, by a coincidence, in the Roswell year 1947, but as he stood before us in his dancing costume, adorned with innumerable colorful feathers, he looked younger. His skin had been burnt red-brown by the southern sun, his hair was long and black, he had friendly brown eyes and a soft voice. Patiently he explained to us the spiritual meaning of the costume and the dances, which were sacred to him. He was a "spirit dancer," half Hopi, half Apache. After the early death of his parents, he had been taught by his grandfathers from both tribes. When Robert saw the Roswell film, he knew it was real. And he had a number of reasons for his belief.

"I know that many people won't believe me, but that being in the film looked exactly like the Star Elder about whom my grandfather had told me." And then he related a story more incredible than any other we had heard during our by no means tedious search for the truth in New Mexico. But Morning Sky did not in the least look like someone who was trying to tell us a cock and bull story. Moreover, he was willing to take us to witnesses who would confirm his tale, however fantastic it might sound.

"In August 1947, more than a month after the famous UFO crash near Roswell, my grandfather and five of his friends went on a vision quest," began Robert after we had found a shady and quiet spot to sit.

That is an old ceremony, a technique to learn about one's own future, to find out what the stars have in store for you. They saw a light in the sky which descended and crashed. With us the Star People are part of our daily lives. We believe in them, know that they exist, we talk to them, dance with them. So it is no wonder that my grandfather was interested in this light and that he knew there were Star People in it. These young men were very naïve, ignored all rumors that went around the reservations that if a star fell from the sky, one should keep off, for soon soldiers would come there—soldiers and Indians just did not belong together! So my grandfather and his friends went looking for the star and found it too, before the soldiers arrived.

When they examined the wreck they discovered one survivor. But he was injured. They decided to take him with them to their vision-quest camp. There they nursed him. Sometimes he was conscious, sometimes not, and whenever he could, he gave them instructions. After a few months he had recovered his health. During this time they had won his confidence and they called him "Star Elder." One day he produced a small, green crystal. It was round and flat and fitted into his little hand. When he held up the crystal, he was able to project pictures into it. Through these pictures my grandfather and his friends learned who he was, from where he came and what he was doing here. They decided not to talk about him to anybody for they were anxious about his safety. Curious people would come, ask questions and finally the soldiers would come to know of him and come to take him away. When he was in full health again and could have been picked up by his people, he decided nevertheless to stay on for a short while.

The stories he told about his home and mode of life were remarkable, for he spoke of war between the stars. The way of life he and his people lived was very similar to the life we original Americans lead. Our way of a warrior was also theirs, which surprised my grandfather and his friends. But the Star Elder was also astonished that such primitive and wild people like us should know some of his techniques, and that was why he stayed on. After a while he began to tell them the history of the earth and mankind, as he knew it. My grandfather told me some of those stories and that is why I am here. Over many years I tried to tell this story. My grandfather is dead and I had promised to tell his tale. That is why I am here today, to say, "Look, Star People are here, they exist, and we had better listen to what they have to tell us!"

"How did the Star Elder leave your grandfather? Was he collected?" we wanted to know. "He stayed for a while and then felt it would be dangerous if they came to pick him up. So he waited some more time, till he thought it was safe to go." "When was that?" "After the crash he stayed five years with them. Finally one day he just left the camp, but let them know that he had left. But he appeared a few more times after that."

"What did he tell your grandfather?" was our next question. Robert took a deep breath, as if he had a big task ahead of him. Obviously the answer was not easy.

Now, many of those who hear my story are under the impression that Star Beings come to the earth with a wonderful message for humanity, but that is not so. The Star Elder crashed here, but he did not want to be here at all. What he told them was that mankind had been cheated and misled. The Gods and Devils of whom people wrote in the past were stellar beings. We have been misused and manipulated, we were taught to believe in things that are not true, but invented to support the Star beings in their plans. I always wonder why we believe in angels and demons but not in spacemen. We accept the concept of a heaven far above, but not of life on other planets. We even swallow stories of flying carpets and Mickey Mouse, but refuse to believe in flying saucers and Star People. The gist of his words was: We must cease to accept blindly what we are taught, learn to question everything. That which we are told is real, is not real. The reality is bigger and more wonderful than what our books and schools teach us. I don't want to antagonize any of our teachers and professors; many of them are good people, who honestly try, but that which they teach us is not the truth. It is a system, a prison for our thoughts, and their job is to keep this system going. But our job as human beings is to be warriors and renegades in our life, without hurting others but fiery and passionate as individuals.

He also spoke of the history of mankind.

He said that man is not a natural creation, but was developed specially to serve the Star Beings. Man has created the mule as a hybrid race by crossing horses with asses, as well as plants which did not exist in nature. If we can do that, imagine what a scientist with the knowledge of millions of years can do. And that is what happened: man was made to serve as a servant, a slave of the Gods. He was an animal which was genetically manipulated. But that is not bad. Now that we have experience and consciousness, we have broken out of that experiment. Some of us, many of us, have come to the conclusion that life is too important to be spent as slaves. And that was one of the things that the Star Elder was astonished about: that we, born as slaves, have broken our chains and want to live our own lives and also that we are intelligent and earnest enough to do it. In

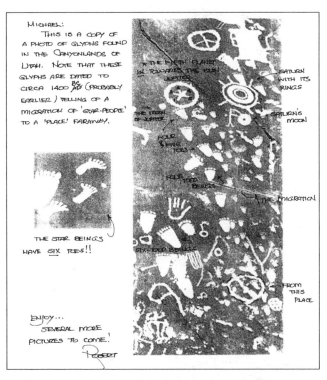

Anasazi petroglyphs in the Canyonland of Utah. Around a wheel animals, people . . . and six-toed footprints are visible.

Another Canyonland petroglyph illustrates the way of the six-toed beings (and other races) to Earth. They passed Saturn (the sixth planet, depicted with its rings and six indents), Jupiter (the five-pointed star in the center = the fifth planet) and Mars (the fourth planet with the four-pointed star in the center).

some cases it happens really. We are in a position to realize our dreams. That is not easy. But if one is a warrior, he has the fire in him and can do it. And he was more than anything else impressed about the fact that we humans carry that fire in us.

"What did he say about his own people, his religion?" we asked. Obviously we had touched a delicate theme with that crunch query.

I hesitate to talk about it, for religion is a delicate subject. It is something that we believe, that we think, that we are taught and

that we have to accept. In his world, there is no religion as a matter of belief, of faith. Their religion is simply the way they live. "We don't have to fight about what we believe, we can discuss what is—and that we shall." Their lifespan is far more than ours; a man of 100,000 years is considered young. What the Star Elder said about that was: the human body is constructed to deteriorate quickly; our food and way of life makes it worse. Actually, our bodies could become two to three thousand years old if we nourished ourselves properly and the environment were right. But we are programmed for self-destruction. Our bodies age quickly, not because they want to but because we push them into doing so. Actually everything that he said about the way of living, the culture and society of galactic beings, with the exception of religion, life expectancy and way of life, is much the same as ours on earth.

However incredible it may seem, Morning Sky maintains that contacts with extraterrestrials or "Star Beings" has a long tradition among his people. Many of the elements of their religion, according to their tradition, have been taught to them by the "heavenly teachers" who visited their forefathers.

What astounded my grandfather was that the Star Elder knew the use of feathers, which is a very important part of our ritual costumes. Legends say that this tradition comes from the stars. It began with the race of the Akhu, the bird people, who carried fire and passion in them. It may irritate other Indians, but in my costume I wear two discs on my back. In one of the dances, the firedance, one dances so quickly that the discs rotate and jump up and down, one goes down to the ground, springs up high. . . . I can only guess—I don't want to get into trouble—that this rotation and bouncing symbolizes something other than fire. To us it is fire, but for me, something else too."[1]

As proof of the antiquity of the legends about the Star Elders who are alleged to have had rounded heads, six fingers and six toes, Robert showed us photographs of petroglyphs from the canyon lands of Utah. They were carved by the Anasazi, one of the oldest peoples of the southwestern states, who lived 1,000 years ago in pueblos (the first stone buildings of North America) until they disappeared completely and mysteriously in the thirteenth century A.D. One of the rock paintings shows six-toed footprints around a big (landed?) wheel, near them other footprints with four or five toes, along with some animals. Another rock painting, at least 1,400 years old, seems to show that the six-toed beings come from outer space. In any case it represent's how they approach the earth from a great distance in a heavenly body and pass by the outer planets, whereby Saturn is depicted with rings and six projections to identify it as the sixth planet, Jupiter with five and Mars with four projections to show them as the fifth and fourth planet, respectively.[2]

Among the Acoma and the Laguna Indians, who are, according to their tradition, related to the Anasazi, there is a tradition regarding beings with six fingers and toes, called "Sky Kachinas" or "celestial spirits." For centuries the Pueblo Indians have carved wooden figures representing these—as also other Kachinas—to make their children familiar with their appearance.

Other Indian tribes also knew about hexadactylic beings. In 1972, a foreign correspondent of the ARD (Germany's radio/television Channel One), Karl Brugger, met a man in Rio de Janeiro who had lived in the jungles of North Brazil since he was five years old. Günther Hauck, who called himself Tatunca Nara, claimed to be the son of a German missionary woman and an Indian Chief. He had lived for a time in Germany, had even married there, but in 1967 he finally went back to the jungle. During many expeditions in the Brazilian/Venezuelan border region he demonstrated to Brugger and other journalists his familiarity with the jungle and the Indians who lived there. In addition he knew the location of two ancient pyramid cities, one at the Venezuelan border, the other in East Peru, which were first discovered through NASA satellite photographs in the early eighties.

Nara proved to have an intimate knowledge of Indian mythology, and his tales were the basis of the book *The Chronicle of Akakor*, which Brugger wrote in 1976. This chronicle is the story of the Ugha Mongulala people, who have lived in the jungles of Brazil since antiquity. It deals not only with the ancient kingdoms of South America, but also mentions the "Earlier Rulers," the "Ancient Fathers" who came from the stars. *"Suddenly there appeared ships in the heavens, shining like gold. Fire lit the plains. The earth quaked and thunder echoed across the hills. The people bowed down in reverence before the mighty strangers, who had come to take possession of the earth,"* begins the chronicle. It gives a fairly good description of the heavenly visitors, who *"settled the nomadic tribes, shared all edible things with them and taught* them their laws, even if they behaved like stubborn children and opposed the teaching." "They differed only a little from human beings. They had slender bodies, the color of their skin was white. . . . like humans they were made of flesh and blood and were vulnerable. But the most significant feature that differentiated the Ancient Fathers from humans was that they had six fingers and six toes, the signs of their divine origin."[3]

The "tabula smaragdina" of Hermes Trismegistos.

Morning Sky concludes: "In ancient Egypt and Sumeria the entire numerical system was based on the number twelve. Our numerical system is based on the number ten. Why? Because we have ten fingers. And I can only ask whether the beings who developed the mathematics of those old civilizations perhaps had twelve fingers. We have evidence from Egypt and Sumeria, we have evidence in ancient America—and suddenly this film appears and shows a creature with six fingers and toes."[4]

Does the creature in Santilli's film point to our own cosmic past? The Sumerians said that the fundamentals of their civilization, their alphabet, laws, mathematics, architecture and agriculture had been brought to them by the "Annunaki," which literally means "Those who came from heaven to the earth." The Bible calls them "nefilim" or "the ones who descended," the ancient Egyptians called them "neteru" or "the watchers."[5] The inventor of the hieroglyphs, the architect of the pyramids and the father of medical science was Imhotep, often referred to as the Leonardo da Vinci of antiquity. But Imhotep, or Asclepios as the Greeks called him, was not himself the universal genius, but only a good student. His teacher was Toth or Tehuti, the Egyptian God of Wisdom, one of the "neteru." The Egyptians believed that the "neteru" ("Watchers," as they called their gods) sailed along the "heavenly Nile"—the Milky Way—in their heavenly barges, just as humans sailed on the Nile. Toth was the one "who knew all secrets" and taught them to mankind. "He divided the day into twelve hours, made the first calendar, taught the people how to write, to count and measure the land. As Lord of the Divine Words, he made the laws and compiled all knowledge in a book of spells, consisting of forty-two volumes. Great indeed was Toth," says an old papyrus. The Greeks revered him as "Hermes Trismegistos," the "thrice-great Hermes," messenger of the gods, whose staff, handed over to Asclepios, is the symbol of the medical profession even today.[6] Later Toth, or Hermes, is supposed to have gone to Phoenicia, where, according to the historian Sanchuniathon, he built a "flying ship" for Cronos. He is also supposed to have put up the legendary emerald tablets there on which the basic theory of a holistic universe was engraved: "What is above is as below. . . ." And naturally the Phoenician script, which is considered to be the oldest alphabetic script by philologists, is also supposed to have originated from him.[7] Indeed for

Rock painting of a deity near Kimberley Ranges, Australia. Note the "protophoenician" writing in his "halo."

historians there is no doubt that the Phoenician alphabet—and all other Semitic alphabets, including the Hebrew and Arabic—was derived from the "hieroglyphic alphabet," consisting of twenty-four vowels and consonants, which is one of the four groups of signs of the hieroglyphic system: the hieroglyphic alphabet, double and triple consonant symbols and ideograms.

As if all this were not interesting enough, the "hieroglyphs" on the "H-beams" shown in Santilli's film seem to be alphabetic script, which resembles the Phoenician. Some of the symbols look like classical Greek letters, which were directly derived from Phoenician—a Delta, a Lambda, a Sigma. It is interesting to note that examples of writing, which appear like the Phoenician, have been found on archaeological artifacts and rock inscriptions in many places around the world. Some of these are much older than the Phoenician script, which was developed about 1100 B.C. from the Canaanite linear alphabet, which is three hundred years older.[8] Amongst these are: the golden plaques of Ecuador, now exhibited in the Gold Museum of Cuenca[9], as well as the writing on the walls of the Pedra Pintada (Painted Rock) Caves in the Amazon region, which French archaeol-ogist Professor Marcel Homet explored during the 1950s and whose petroglyphs he dated as being older than at least 6000 B.C.[10] Inscriptions that the British adventurer Fawcett discovered on a gate, remains of a lost city, in the jungles of Brazil[11], the inscriptions of Ylo in Peru[12], and the script of the Guanches on the Canary Islands[13] are further examples. Also the painted pebbles of Maz d'Azil in France[14], the engraved tablets of Glozel, also in France, which the farmer Emile Fradin discovered on his field in 1924 and was considered by archaeologists to be about 6,000 years old.[15] I call this writing "proto-phoenician," because these inscriptions predate the Phoenician culture.

Was this the "script of the Gods," was it taught by the same stellar visitors to various peoples on earth? Did our alphabet originate in outer space? And have these same "gods" of our forefathers returned today?

Robert Morning Sky, who made a profound study of ancient cultures to check the information the Star Elder had given

Drawing of a stone figure with a "protophoenician" inscription, discovered by the English adventurer Col. Fawcett in the Brazilian jungle.

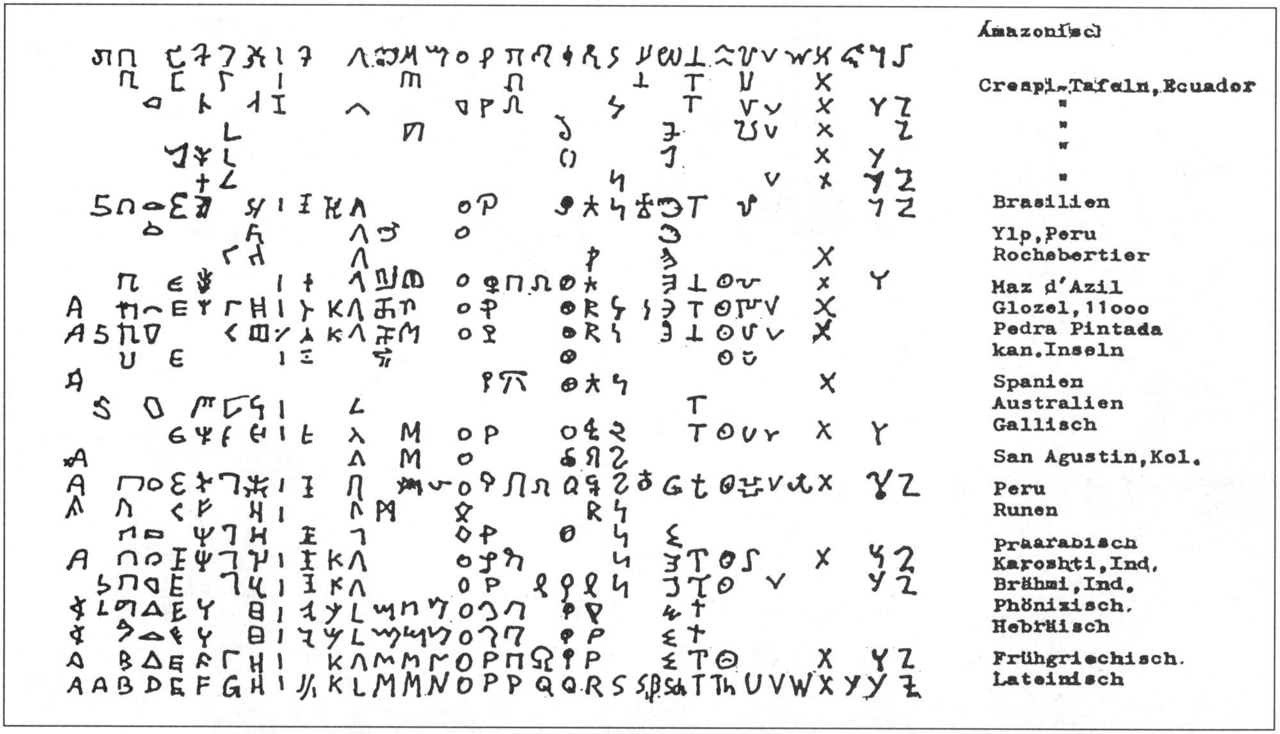
Amazonisch
Crespi-Tafeln, Ecuador
Brasilien
Ylp, Peru
Rochebertier
Maz d'Azil
Glozel, 11ooo
Pedra Pintada
kan. Inseln
Spanien
Australien
Gallisch
San Agustin, Kol.
Peru
Runen
Praarabisch
Karoshti, Ind.
Brähmi, Ind.
Phönizisch.
Hebräisch
Frühgriechisch.
Lateinisch

Proto-Phoenician inscriptions from around the world. Comparison by the author, 1981.

"Proto-Phoenician": the plates from Glozel, France, c. 500 B.C.

"Proto-Phoenician:" letters on the Cuenca plates from Ecuador. (Achive of Erich von Däniken)

Extra-terrestrial script found aboard crashed UFO (copied down from memory). Notice similarity with Santilli hieroglyphs.

Comparison between Semitic and Egyptian (hieroglyphic, hieratic) scripts.

"I had the opportunity to see a form of writing which allegedly came from an extra-terrestrial spaceship," Maggie S stated on April 25, 1995 in a letter to the Roswell Museum. The Government worker remembers fourteen signs, four of which we recognize in the Santilli film.

Das Hieroglyphen-Alphabet
in Vergleich mit dem Hebräischen Alphabet

(E.A. Wallis-Budge: Egyptian Language, London 1910)

The Egyptian hieroglyphic alphabet and its Latin and Hebrew counter parts.

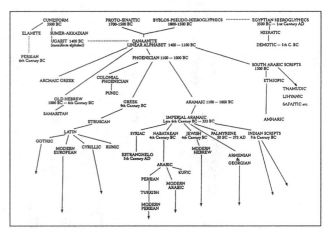

Pedigree of the Semitic and European alphabets.

his grandfather, took over the task of deciphering the nine signs on the T-rods. I too have diligently tried to do the same and have reached a different conclusion. Since both are equally legitimate, I present here our two different interpretations.

To translate the Santilli hieroglyphs, we must try to determine every single sign in the context of early Semitic alphabets and the Egyptian hieroglyphic system. Here we have two premises: First of all, if there are two possible interpretations, we choose the one that makes more sense. And second: A translation has to come from the same cultural context as the writing itself, which means it has to come from ancient Egyptian or a Semitic language.

To decipher an inscription in an unknown script one must first arrange the signs. That is the standard method in archaeology as well as in cryptology. Champollion used this method while deciphering the Egyptian hieroglyphs. One gives each different sign a serial number in its order of appearance. So we have the order:

1 - 2 - 1 - 3 - 4 - 1 - 5 - 6 - 7

There seems to be no doubt about the Santilli hieroglyphs being related to the classical Greek and Phoenician letters. To understand them we have to look at the early Semitic alphabets and the Egyptian hieroglyphic system, which were the forerunners. Owing to this relationship it is legitimate to search amongst all languages and alphabets, which according to legend came from the god Tehuti (Toth).

1: Morning Sky reads this as "Samekh" (Phoenician) or "Xi" (Greek). Both correspond to "S" or "Sh." In the Cretan Linear B script it is read as "Si," in the Coptic

Phoenician	Name	Phonetic value	Early Greek	Classical Greek	Name
ⱡ	aleph		A	A	alpha
◁	beth	b	B	B	beta
∧	gimel	g	𐌂	Γ	gamma
◁	daleth	d	Δ	Δ	delta
∃	he	h	𐤤	E	epsilon
Y	waw	w	𐤟		digamma
I	zayin	z	I	Z	zeta
日	beth	h	日	H	eta
⊗	teth	t	⊗	Θ	theta
ᔦ	yod	y	ᔈ	I	iota
ⱡ	kaph	k	ᔈ	K	kappa
ᒪ	lamed	l	ᒧ	Λ	lambda
ᛘ	mem	m	ᛘ	M	mu
ᒈ	nun	n	ᒧ	N	nu
ᚂ	samekh	s		Ξ	xi
o	ayin	'	O	O	omicron
?	pe	p	ᒈ	Π	pi
ᚕ	sade	s	M		saw
Φ	qoph	q	ᖁ		qoppa
Φ	res	r		P	rho
W	sin	sh/s		Σ	sigma
X	taw	t	X	Y	tau
					upsilon
				X	chi
				Ω	omega

Santilli symbols

Santilli symbol	Reading
△	D — DELTA
(grid)	S — SAMEKH
⊖	T — THETA
◎	Q — QOPH
(grid)	S — SAMEKH
◍	B — BETH or R — RHO
◖◗	K — KAPPA or X — TAU
△	D — DELTA

Comparison between Phoenician, early Greek, and classical ancient Greek alphabet and the Santilli hieroglyphs.

as "Shei" and in Hebrew as "Sin." There is a resemblance also to the Egyptian hieroglyph for "S" or "Sh." On the other hand, the frequency of its appearance rather indicates a vowel. My suggestion is to read it as the Phoenician "He," or the Greek "Epsilon," forerunner of our "E."

2: Although Morning Sky reads this sign, as well as the seventh, as "Delta" (Greek) or "Daleth" (Phoenician), it rather is a "Lambda" or "Lamed," therefore an "L"—or even a "Gamma" or "Gimel," our "C," since in contrast to the symbol no. 7 "Daleth"/"Delta," the lower cross stroke is missing.

3: The first circular glyph looks—to Morning Sky—

like the Greek "Theta" or the Egyptian glyph for "bread," pronounced as a hard "T." The Coptic "Thita" and Phoenician "Teth" are written similarly. I, on the other hand, see it as "Het"/"Heta," the forerunner of our "H."

4: The second circular glyph, with a vertical dividing line, is most certainly a Phoenician "Qoph." In ancient Greek, the forerunner of classical Greek, it was known as "Qoppa."

5: Again there are two possibilities: a Greek "Beta" (Phoenician "Beth"), or a Greek "Rho" (Phoenician "Res"). Comparison with other scripts brings no clarification: it can be an Egyptian "Beh" (a foot) or Cretan Linear B "Po," or a Coptic "Ro" and Hebrew "Resh." One can read it as "B" or "R."

6: Robert Morning Sky reads this symbol either as "Kaph" (Phoenician)/"Kappa" (Greek) or as "Taw" (Phoenician)/"Chi" (Greek). The similarity to the knot-like Egyptian "H" glyph would favor the latter solution. But I see here a "Yod" or "Iota," which corresponds better to the Egyptian "I"—a double reed.

7: The equilateral triangle must be a Greek "Delta"/Phoenician "Daleth." In Egyptian it represents the earth and is also written as a semicircular "hill," which is read as "Ta." It is pronounced as "D" or a soft "T."

Robert Morning Sky reads this inscription as:
(S) D/T-S-T-Q/Kh.-S-B-K/Kh-Dt
I (Hesemann) prefer to read it as:
E-L-E-H-Q-E-R-I-D
or

[DT - S] [T - Q/Kh - S] [B - K/Kh - DT]

Interpretation of Santilli hieroglyphs according to Robert Morning Sky.

E-C-E-H-Q-E-R-I-D
In Phoenician:
Samekh-Daleth-Samekh-Thet-Qoph-Samekh-Beth-Taw-Daleth (Morning Sky)
Or:
He-Lamed (or Gimmel)-He-Het-Qoph-He-Res-Yod-Daleth (Hesemann)

In Classical Greek:
Ξ Δ Ξ Τ Θ Ξ Β Τ Δ
Xi-Delta-Xi-Theta-Qoppa-Xi-Beta-Tau-Delta (Morning Sky)
Or:
Ε Λ (Γ) Ε Η Θ Ε Ρ Ι Δ
Epsilon-Lambda (or Gamma)-Epsilon-Heta-Qoppa-Epsilon-Rho-Iota-Delta (Hesemann)

Robert Morning Sky thinks the following reading is probably correct:
S (DT-S) (T-Q/Kh-S) (B-K/Kh-DT).

DT could mean "Life" in the Sumerian language and in Egyptian "Aware, Prepared, Ready." The Suffix "-S" or "-US" means "those who." Morning Sky reads the first group of letters as meaning "Those who have awareness" or "Those who are prepared."

The second group consists of a combination of "T" = "life" and "K" or "Q" = "cut" or "cleave." The "T-Q"'s are, therefore, the "Cutters of Life," the warrior race of the galaxy, which is responsible for our evolution, according to the Star Elder. The suffix "-S" refers to this race: "those who are cleavers of life."

Thus the first two alphabetic groups refer to two groups of entities: in general, "all who are aware" and in particular the warrior race.

The third group of letters, "R/B-K/Kh-DT," reveals, according to Morning Sky, the identity of the occupants of the spaceship, who had made the inscriptions. Inserting vowels, as is usual in Semitic languages, one can read here "ReKiT" or "BeKuT." Rekit was an Egyptian fire goddess, the Bekut(s) were Falcon-Goddesses. Since the hieroglyph for the root word "beht"—foot, interwoven spirals and semicircle—resembles the inscription on the rods in Santilli's film, the latter reading is more plausible. "We are falcon-goddesses!" Besides that, "behet" can be read as " the ripper" or some kind of bird, which may refer to the "Space-craft of the falcon goddesses."[16]

Since we have an inscription with a relation to the Semetic/Egyptian family of alphabets I read them, as is usual for them, from right to left:

DIREQH-ELE or DIREQH-ECE.

And this makes sense. "Derech" is Hebrew for "way, road, journey" , but as a preposition also "-like" or "in the manner of." "Derech Aretz" means literally "way of the world" and stands for "etiquette," "good manners." The verb "Derach" means "to go, to take a step, to march." "El" is Hebrew for "god" in the singular, the plural being "Elohim." "Derech Elohim" can, therefore, be translated as "the journey of the gods" or "the path/way of god/the gods."—or maybe analogous to the Spanish "Vaya con Dios" as "Go with God." We cannot say which interpretation is the right one, since we don't know the grammar, but it surely is a slogan for this mission, which makes sense. If we read the second word as ECE, then we must go to ancient Egyptian. There "ACA" or "ASA" means "to present, to approach."

Unfortunately Morning Sky has studied only the larger of the struts, not the smaller, which bears four signs. Here we have 6-8-9-10, out of which "6" has been identified as "Yod"/"Iota" on the larger strut. Let us read this the semitic way, from right to left.

10. This is undoubtedly an "Ayin" or "Omicron," which was written in ancient Greek with a dot in the middle.

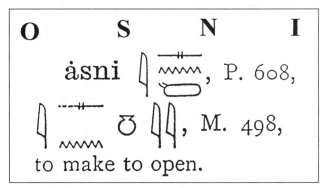

9. The Hebrew and Phoenician "Shin," from which the Greek "Sigma" was derived.

8. A sign that resembles the Egyptian hieroglyph for "N"—"net" = water—is the Phoenician "Nun" or Greek "Ny," despite the strong resemblance with "Sigma."

16. "Yod"/"iota." See above.

That makes the word OSNI (Greek: Omega, Sigma, Ny, Iota: OSNI).

ASNI is an Egyptian word. Sir E. A. Wallis Budge translates the word as "to make to open."[17] That can be interpreted practically as "Open here" or philosophically as "Open the way to other worlds." It makes sense either way.[18]

Is all this a coincidence, or is there here really a connection with the ancient civilizations of Egypt and the Near East, to the cradle of mankind and our own civilization? Do the scenes in Santilli's film take us back to the secret but true history of mankind, our origin in outer space? Or is all this only a clever swindle, aimed at misleading the gullible? Only time can tell.

I am afraid, in any case, that Robert Morning Sky is right in saying, *"Whereas we and other native Americans know about the authenticity of Santilli's film, we believe that in the end it will be proved that the material is a fake. The UFO believers have to be discredited, the contents of the film must be drawn*

Der fernste gemeinsame Vorfahre des arabischen د (dal), des hebräischen ד (dalet) und des lateinischen D ist ein Bild-Buchstabe, der einen Fisch darstellt und zum erstenmal in den protosinaitischen Inschriften auftaucht. Aus dem Fisch wurde in der südarabischen Schrift und in der protokanaanäischen Schrift , die in den ostgriechischen Schriften als delta Δ erhalten blieb und von dort in die klassische griechische Schrift geriet: Δ. In den alten westgriechischen Schriften wurde das Dreieck auf die Seite gekippt ▷. Daraus wurde später D, als das es auch die lateinische Schrift übernahm.

In der phönikischen Schrift wurde der linke Winkel des ursprünglichen Dreiecks rund und die rechte Seite verlängert: . In der althebräischen Schrift wurde der obere Strich ebenfalls verlängert: . Aber die anderen semitischen kursiven Schriften neigen dazu, geschlossene Kreise zu vermeiden. Deshalb ist das phönikische kursive dalet unten geöffnet und das aramäische oben: .

In der neuhebräischen Schrift öffnete sich der Buchstabe ד (ca. 1. Jahrhundert v.Chr. bis 1. Jahrhundert n.Chr.), aus dem dann das moderne hebräische dalet ד wurde. D und R werden auf ähnliche Weise geschrieben und unterscheiden sich in der syrischen Schrift nur durch diakritische Punkte voneinander: ܕ bzw. ܪ.

Das nabatäische kursive dalet wurde zu einem Strich I, das R ebenfalls. Die arabischen D, die daraus entstanden, د dal und ذ dal, nahmen wieder kursive Formen an.

Der älteste gemeinsame Vorfahre des arabischen ي (ya), des hebräischen י (yod) und des lateinischen I war ein Bild-Buchstabe, der eine Hand mit einem Unterarm darstellt: . Im 11. und 10. Jahrhundert v.Chr. das frühphönikische yod und in der späteren phönikischen Schrift , in der althebräischen Schrift , in der samaritanischen Schrift . Die aramäische kursive Schrift reduzierte es auf folgende Weise: . Im 4. und 3. Jahrhundert v.Chr. entstanden zwei verschiedene Formen. Eine glich der Zahl 2 und die andere einem umgedrehten V . In der nabatäischen Schrift entwickelte sich das 2-förmige yod , aus dem dann das arabische ي (ya) wurde. Die neuhebräische Schrift übernahm das aramäische V-förmige yod und machte da-raus , aus dem י wurde.

Aus dem protokanaanäischen yod entstand auch das alte griechische iota , das gleichzeitig den Vokal I und den Konsonanten Y darstellte, wenn es vor oder nach einem anderen Vokal stand. Auf die gleiche Weise wurde das I im lateinischen Alphabet benutzt, bis im Mittelalter die neue Form J das konsonantische I ersetzte, worauf dieses nur noch als Vokal gebraucht wurde.

In den frühen protokanaanäischen und protosinaitischen Inschriften gibt es einen Bild-Buchstaben, der einen menschlichen Kopf darstellt , des hebräischen resh ר und des lateinischen R. Die griechische Bezeichnung rho scheint darauf hinzuweisen, daß der phönikische Name des Buchstabens rosh lautete, was "Kopf" bedeutete. Das aramäische Wort für Kopf, "resh", war wohl auch der aramäische Name des Buchstabens.

In der späten protokanaanäischen Schrift entwickelte sich der Bild-Buchstabe zu einem einfachen , das im griechischen rho (ρ) übernommen wurde. Die altgriechische Variante R war der Vorläufer des lateinischen R.

In der althebräischen Schrift blieb der obere Teil des resh geschlossen: (samaritanische Schrift), in der phönikischen Schrift öffnete er sich im 5. Jahrhundert v.Chr. nach unten: und in der aramäischen gegen Ende des 8. Jahrhunderts mit dem aramäischen bet, dalet und 'ayin). Später neigte die aramäische Schrift dazu, den Buchstaben in einem Zug zu schreiben und dann den Bogen auszuziehen , und daraus entstand das neuhebräische resh ר.

Nachdem resh und dalet sich in manchen semitischen Schriften gleichen, waren diakritische Punkte nötig, um sie voneinander zu unterscheiden (zum Beispiel in der syrischen Schrift: ܕ = dalet; ܪ = resh). In der nabatäischen und dann in der arabischen Schrift wurde das ra (ر) zu einem geschwungenen Strich, von dem das za (ز) sich nur durch einen diakritischen Punkt unterscheidet.

Der fünfte Buchstabe im lateinischen Alphabet, das E, stammt ursprünglich von einem Bild-Buchstaben aus der Zeit um 1500 v.Chr. ab, der eine betende oder rufende Gestalt darstellt . In der südarabischen Schrift wurde daraus , in der protokanaanäischen Schrift ; das griechische und lateinische Alphabet behielten diese letztere Form bei, drehten den Buchstaben aber herum und benutzten ihn als Vokal E, der im Griechischen epsilon heißt. In den semitischen Schriften galt der Buchstabe als Konsonant he. Die protokanaanäische Form wurde auch in der phönikischen Schrift beibehalten , aus der die aramäische Form entstand, die auch im Neuhebräischen so übernommen wurde. Die moderne hebräische Form ist ה.

Aus dem aramäischen he entstand das nabatäische he , und daraus entwickelte sich das arabische ه (ha).

D I R E

Interpretation of the "Santilli hieroglyphs" by Michael Hesemann.

through the mud. The powers that be have to keep their control over the people. I don't know how it will be done, but the film will be, has to be exposed as a fake."[19] But even if this film is proved to be a fake—since what should not be, cannot be— there still remains the question of identities and motives of those who made the film. It seems certain that the film is based on a real occurrence and that factual information and material was used in filming the scenes. Did someone want to test the reaction of the public, before finally revealing the truth? Actually, this "test" has now been made and the results were far from spectacular. Although more than 150 million people all over the earth saw this film—of these twenty-four million in the U.S.A. alone, where "Alien Autopsy—Fact or Fiction?" for the Fox Network reached on that evening the second highest TV ratings ever recorded—the public reaction was a mere "back to normal." On the morning after, everything went on as usual! This would seem to show

Der älteste gemeinsame Vorfahre des arabischen ڧ (*qaf*), des hebräischen ק (*qof*) und des lateinischen Q erscheint in den protosinaitischen Inschriften von etwa 1500 v.Chr. in dieser Form: 𐤒. Später, um 1000 v.Chr., schaut es so aus: 𐤒. In den alten griechischen Schriften wurde das *qoppa* entweder wie in der phönikischen Schrift oder dann Q geschrieben. In der klassischen griechischen Schrift wurde das *qoppa* als Buchstabe gestrichen und nur noch für die Zahl 90 verwandt. Aber das lateinische Alphabet behielt den Buchstaben Q bei, der in etlichen europäischen Sprachen benutzt wird.

In der phönikischen und althebräischen Schrift entwickelte sich das Q im 8. und 7. Jahrhundert v.Chr. auf folgende Weise: Der Kreis wurde geöffnet 𐤒, verwandelte sich in zwei Halbkreise 𐤒, und dann wurde der linke Halbkreis in einem Zug mit dem Unterstrich geschrieben 𐤒. Das Q in der phönikischen (𐤒), in der samaritanischen (𐤒) und in der aramäischen Schrift (𐤒) nahm dann beinahe die Form eines waagrechten S an. In der spätaramäischen und neuhebräischen Schrift wurde der linke Bogen des Buchstabens verkleinert, 𐤒 , und daraus entstand die neuhebräische Form.

Die nabatäische Schrift ging noch weiter und schrieb 𐤒 , aus dem sich 𐤒 → 𐤒 , entwickelte, bis es dem *pe* (𐤐) glich. In der arabischen Schrift mußten zwei diakritische Punkte hinzugefügt werden, um das *qaf* (ڧ) vom *fa* (ڢ) und *waw* (ۅ) zu unterscheiden.

Das arabische ح (*ha*), das neuhebräische ח (*het*) und das lateinische H haben sich aus einem protokanaanäischen Bild-Buchstaben entwickelt, der einen Zaun darstellte 𐤇 , 𐤇 . Daraus wurde später in der phönikischen Schrift ein Rechteck mit einem Strich in der Mitte 𐤇 . Diese Form wurde von den alten griechischen Schriften übernommen und entwickelte sich zum H, das auch in das lateinische Alphabet überging.

Die alten Griechen benutzten diesen Buchstaben nicht wie die Semiten für den Konsonanten H (*het*), sondern für H (*neta*) und verwandelten ihn in den Vokal *eta*, der ein langes E ist, im Gegensatz zum kurzen E *epsilon*. Der Laut H, der vor einem Vokal am Anfang eines Wortes ausgeatmet wird, ist durch ein ʿ gekennzeichnet. Im lateinischen Alphabet ist das H jedoch ein Konsonant.

Die phönikische Schrift behielt die alte Form des Buchstabens bei, aber die Langstriche wurden etwas verlängert: 𐤇 genau wie im Althebräischen (oder auch 𐤇) und in der samaritanischen Schrift 𐤇 . Schon Ende des 8. Jahrhunderts v.Chr. fehlten in der aramäischen Schrift zwei Querstriche, und der Buchstabe schaute so aus: ח . Das ist auch die Grundform des modernen hebräischen ח.

Die arabische *ha* entwickelte sich auf dem Weg über die nabatäische Schrift so: 𐤇 → 𐤇 → 𐤇 . Einzeln geschrieben oder am Ende eines Wortes sieht es so aus: ح . Weil es in der arabischen Sprache noch einen H-Laut gibt, den das aramäische und das nabatäische Alphabet nicht kannten, wird dieses *ha* durch einen diakritischen Punkt auf dem Buchstaben gekennzeichnet: ح . Mit einem diakritischen Punkt im Buchstaben (ج) bedeutet er *jim* (siehe unter C).

Das arabische ل (*lam*), das hebräische ל (*lamed*) und das lateinische L sind aus einem protokanaanäischen Bild-Buchstaben aus der Zeit um 1500 entstanden, der einen Ochsenstecken darstellt, einen Stock mit einem Stachel, um Vieh anzutreiben: 𐤋 , 𐤋 . Vom 11. Jahrhundert v.Chr. an wurde das phönikische *lamed* senkrecht geschrieben und der Bogen nach unten gezogen: 𐤋 , 𐤋 . In der späteren phönikischen Schrift, auch in der althebräischen und in der aramäischen Schrift, bestand die Neigung, den Bogen in einen scharfen Winkel zu verwandeln: 𐤋 . Der diagonale Oberstrich begann an einem höheren Punkt als die anderen Buchstaben, während der untere Querstrich gerade unter der oberen Linie gezeichnet wurde. Im 5. Jahrhundert v.Chr. fügten die Phöniker einen kleinen Schwanz an den Querstrich an: 𐤋 . Eine ähnliche Entwicklung nahm im 4. Jahrhundert v.Chr. das aramäische *lamed* ל , das ein Schwänzchen bekam ל , und sich dann in der kursiven aramäischen Schrift leicht in die Wellenlinie verwandelte ل . Die althebräische Schrift übernahm dieses Schwänzchen am aramäischen *lamed* nicht, wohl aber die neuhebräische Schrift ל.

Die aramäische Wellenlinie blieb auch im nabatäischen *lamed*, aber im arabischen *lām* wurde sie wieder geradegezogen ل .

In den alten griechischen Schriften wurde das *lambda* entweder mit dem Winkel oben Λ oder unten geschrieben. In der klassischen griechischen Schrift überwog die erste Form und wurde Λ . In der lateinischen Schrift wurde der Buchstabe umgedreht und wurde L.

Im lateinischen Alphabet ist der dritte Buchstabe das C, aber im Griechischen ist es das Γ (*gamma*), und im Neuhebräischen das ג (*gimel*), die dem Laut G entsprechen.

Die Grundform des protokanaanäischen *gimel* bestand aus zwei geraden Strichen, die einen Winkel bilden: 𐤂 oder 𐤂 . In den protosinaitischen Inschriften sah es so aus: 𐤂 , in den alten griechischen Schriften wurde es Λ oder Γ oder 𐤂 gezeichnet, und im klas-sischen Griechisch bildete es sich zu Γ . Das lateinische Alphabet übernahm die westliche Form des *gamma* 𐤂 und verwandelte es in C . Die Etrusker hatten keinen G-Laut in ihrer Sprache und verwandten das *gamma* für den K-Laut. Da die Römer das griechische Alphabet von den Etruskern übernahmen, war es naheliegend, daß der Laut des Buchstabens von G zu K wurde (siehe auch G).

Die althebräische Schrift übernahm das protokanaanäische *gimel* 𐤂 . In der phönikischen und der aramäischen Schrift überwog die Form Λ . Daraus entstand das nabatäische 𐤂 und aus diesem das arabische *jim* ج , das am Ende eines Wortes oder wenn es allein steht ج geschrieben wird und sich durch den diakritischen Punkt vom ح (*ha*) und خ (*ha*) unterscheidet.

Das neuhebräische *gimel* entstand auf folgende Weise aus dem aramäischen Λ : λ → λ → λ. Daraus wurde dann das moderne ג.

Q H E L /C? E

Interpretation of the "Santilli hieroglyphs" by Michael Hesemann.

that the fears of those in power are ill-founded. That, perhaps, is the true message of the film: we are ready for the truth.

The big question in government circles—and the main reason for the secrecy—was always: how will people take the news that extraterrestrial forms of life had been discovered? Will there be a panic, will the stock exchange collapse, will the faith in religion and the authority of the state be shattered? This question was the main theme of three international conferences held in connection with the NASA project SETI (Search for Extra Terrestrial Intelligence) during the eighties in Brighton, Innsbruck and Bangalore.[20] More recently in May 1995, international experts, including psychologists, anthropologists, sociologists, political scientists—and my humble self (Hesemann)—met in Washington, D.C. at the invitation of the Human Potential Foundation, which is financed by Laurance Rockefeller, to discuss the ques-

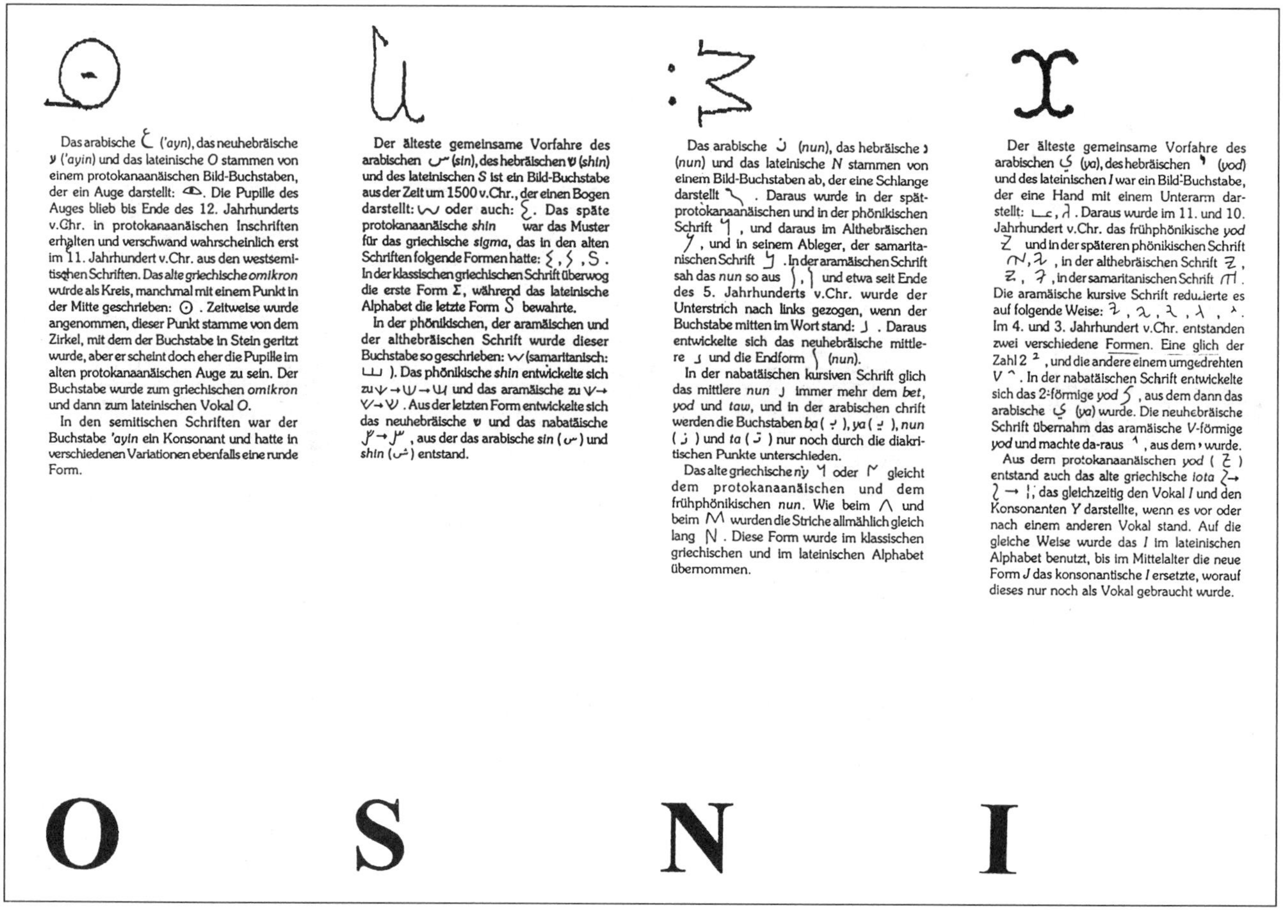

Das arabische ع ('ayn), das neuhebräische ע ('ayin) und das lateinische *O* stammen von einem protokanaanäischen Bild-Buchstaben, der ein Auge darstellt: . Die Pupille des Auges blieb bis Ende des 12. Jahrhunderts v.Chr. in protokanaanäischen Inschriften erhalten und verschwand wahrscheinlich erst im 11. Jahrhundert v.Chr. aus den westsemitischen Schriften. Das alte griechische *omikron* wurde als Kreis, manchmal mit einem Punkt in der Mitte geschrieben: ⊙ . Zeitweise wurde angenommen, dieser Punkt stamme von dem Zirkel, mit dem der Buchstabe in Stein geritzt wurde, aber er scheint doch eher die Pupille im alten protokanaanäischen Auge zu sein. Der Buchstabe wurde zum griechischen *omikron* und dann zum lateinischen Vokal *O*.

In den semitischen Schriften war der Buchstabe *'ayin* ein Konsonant und hatte in verschiedenen Variationen ebenfalls eine runde Form.

Der älteste gemeinsame Vorfahre des arabischen س (*sin*), des hebräischen ש (*shin*) und des lateinischen *S* ist ein Bild-Buchstabe aus der Zeit um 1500 v.Chr., der einen Bogen darstellt: oder auch: . Das späte protokanaanäische *shin* war das Muster für das griechische *sigma*, das in den alten Schriften folgende Formen hatte: , , S . In der klassischen griechischen Schrift überwog die erste Form Σ, während das lateinische Alphabet die letzte Form S bewahrte.

In der phönikischen, der aramäischen und der althebräischen Schrift wurde dieser Buchstabe so geschrieben: (samaritanisch:). Das phönikische *shin* entwickelte sich zu → → und das aramäische zu → → . Aus der letzten Form entwickelte sich das neuhebräische ש und das nabatäische → , aus der das arabische *sin* (س) und *shin* (ش) entstand.

Das arabische ن (*nun*), das hebräische נ (*nun*) und das lateinische *N* stammen von einem Bild-Buchstaben ab, der eine Schlange darstellt . Daraus wurde in der spät-protokanaanäischen und in der phönikischen Schrift , und daraus im Althebräischen , und in seinem Ableger, der samaritanischen Schrift . In der aramäischen Schrift sah das *nun* so aus , und etwa seit Ende des 5. Jahrhunderts v.Chr. wurde der Unterstrich nach links gezogen, wenn der Buchstabe mitten im Wort stand: . Daraus entwickelte sich das neuhebräische mittlere נ und die Endform ן (*nun*).

In der nabatäischen kursiven Schrift glich das mittlere *nun* immer mehr dem *bet*, *yod* und *taw*, und in der arabischen chrift werden die Buchstaben *ba* (ب), *ya* (ي), *nun* (ن) und *ta* (ت) nur noch durch die diakritischen Punkte unterschieden.

Das alte griechische *ny* oder gleicht dem protokanaanäischen und dem frühphönikischen *nun*. Wie beim Λ und beim M wurden die Striche allmählich gleich lang N . Diese Form wurde im klassischen griechischen und im lateinischen Alphabet übernommen.

Der älteste gemeinsame Vorfahre des arabischen ي (*ya*), des hebräischen י (*yod*) und des lateinischen *I* war ein Bild-Buchstabe, der eine Hand mit einem Unterarm darstellt: , . Daraus wurde im 11. und 10. Jahrhundert v.Chr. das frühphönikische *yod* und in der späteren phönikischen Schrift , , in der althebräischen Schrift , , , in der samaritanischen Schrift . Die aramäische kursive Schrift reduzierte es auf folgende Weise: , , , , . Im 4. und 3. Jahrhundert v.Chr. entstanden zwei verschiedene Formen. Eine glich der Zahl 2 , und die andere einem umgedrehten *V* ^ . In der nabatäischen Schrift entwickelte sich das 2-förmige *yod* , aus dem dann das arabische ي (*ya*) wurde. Die neuhebräische Schrift übernahm das aramäische *V*-förmige *yod* und machte da-raus , aus dem י wurde.

Aus dem protokanaanäischen *yod* ( ) entstand auch das alte griechische *iota* → → ¦, das gleichzeitig den Vokal *I* und den Konsonanten *Y* darstellte, wenn es vor oder nach einem anderen Vokal stand. Auf die gleiche Weise wurde das *I* im lateinischen Alphabet benutzt, bis im Mittelalter die neue Form *J* das konsonantische *I* ersetzte, worauf dieses nur noch als Vokal gebraucht wurde.

O S N I

Interpretation of the "Santilli hieroglyphs" by Michael Hesemann.

tion of how humanity will react to—or how it can be prepared for—a "contact with cosmic cultures."[21] We were all conscious of the risk of panic and even worse, the danger that we would be so overwhelmed by the technical superiority of the aliens that it would lead to a cultural shock, a cultural paralysis or identity crisis.

But no one will panic at the sight of this pitiable, wounded creature on the autopsy table in Santilli's film. That is the good part of it: that the truth comes to light in this manner, in a context where the "human" vulnerability of this being is exhibited. They are human beings likes us, only born on another planet. They are not gods and will certainly not deprive us of the golden privilege of learning and helping ourselves.

But the knowledge that we are not alone, that we are only one group of human beings among—possibly—millions of human groups in the universe, opens up new perspectives as to who we ourselves are: not German,

The "Very Large Array" (VLA) Radiotelescope used in NASA's SETI (Search for Extra Terrestrial Intelligence.)

Baptist church in Roswell warns of the invasion.

not English, not American, Czech or Chinese, but—as they must see us—Earthlings. One humanity, Children of the Earth. That is what we must most urgently grasp, at the threshold of the third millennium, if we really want to survive. For all our global problems—overpopulation, greenhouse effect, environmental pollution, ozone layer depletion, etc.—cannot be solved by one country alone and must be tackled by all nations, by mankind in its entirety. If only we can discover our innate oneness, our true nature... then the "dialogue with the universe" can be the biggest chance and challenge of our generation. And that is what the Roswell film can teach us: that we are, in fact, not alone.

On the other hand, I was shocked and thoroughly disgusted by the brutal treatment given to the obviously peaceful visitors from another world as recorded by the cameraman. Does this explain why there has been no open contact until now, why they have never landed in front of the White House ? This all-too-close first meeting must certainly have taught them that man has not yet learned to live in peace with other races. They

landed in the darkest decade of this century, just after a devastating war, the worst in our history. The inhuman behavior of the invaders in Europe and in Asia forced the democracies of the world to develop weapons more brutal and inhuman, capable of destroying thousands of human lives in a moment. The sick and diabolic ideology of the Nazis had, in its racist madness, developed "death factories" to destroy those who belonged to other races and religions. Auschwitz and Hiroshima represent two phases of that black era, the latter becoming possible through a weapon developed to end the first. Dark indeed was that decade. Shortly after winning the war, still proud of her victory and emergence as the most powerful nation of the earth, the U.S.A. committed this act of inhumanity against the peaceful, innocent visitors who were stranded in New Mexico, on our inhospitable planet . They treated these strangers from space, who sought help and protection, as potential enemies, without even attempting to learn their intentions. This was the third sorry phase of that dark decade. Through this crime, committed by citizens of the most powerful nation of this world, mankind has, at least for the time being, lost its claims to possessing humaneness as its characteristic quality.

Ready we may be for the truth—for knowledge of their existence and presence—but we are, in reality, unfit for contact with populations from other worlds, and will remain so until we learn to live in peace with one another and develop tolerance, respect and kindness for other forms of life and customs.

[1] Personal Interview, 3 December 1995.

[2] Written message, 12 January 1996.

[3] Brugger, Karl, *Die Chronik von Akakor*, Düsseldorf, 1976.

[4] Sitchin, Zecharia, *The Twelfth Planet*, New York, 1976.

[5] Hesemann, Michael, *A Cosmic Connection*, Bath, 1995.

[6] Hessman, "Das Land der Götter," in *Magazin 2000*, no. 90, Düsseldorf, November 1992.

[7] Tomas, Andrew, "Die Smaragdene Tafel des Hermes Trismegistos," in *Magazin 2000*, no. 93, Düsseldorf, May 1993.

[8] Robinson, Andrews, *Story of Writing*, London, 1960. Naveh, Joseph: *The Origin of the Alphabet*, Jerusalem, 1994. Zauzich, Karl Theodor, *Hieroglyphs without Mystery*, Austin, 1992.

Watterson, Barbara, *Introducing Egyptian Hieroglyphs*, Edinburgh, 1993.

Wallis-Budge, E. A., *An Egyptian Hieroglyphic Dictionary*, vols. 1–2, London, 1920.

—*Egyptian Language* (reprint), London, 1966.

[9] Däniken, Erich von, *Meine Welt in Bildern*, Düsseldorf, 1973.

[10] Homet, Marcel, *Die Söhne der Sonne*, Olten, 1958.

[11] Berlitz, Charles, *Mysteries of Forgotten Worlds*, New York, 1972.

[12] Charroux, Robert, *Vergessene Welten*, Düsseldorf, 1974.

[13] Herrera, Salvador Lopez, *The Canary Islands through History*, Santa Cruz (n. d.).

[14] Berlitz, Charles, *Der 8. Kontinent*, Hamburg, 1984.

[15] Charroux, Robert, *Das Rätsel der Anden*, Düsseldorf, 1978, and "Glozel Tafeln doch echt!" in *Magazin 2000*, no. 97, Düsseldorf, January 1994.

[16] Morning Sky, Robert, *The Santilli Hieroglyphs*, 1996.

[17] Wallis-Budge, E. A., 1920.

[18] Zauzich, Karl-Th., 1992.

Naveh, Joseph, 1994.

[19] Morning Sky, Robert, 1996.

[20] Tarter, J. C./Michaud, M.A., *SETI Post Detection Protocol*, Washington, D.C., 1990.

[21] Jones, C. B., *When Cosmic Cultures Meet* (conference program), Washington, D.C., 1995.

16.

Chronology of Events

Saturday, 31 May 1947

At approximately 9 P.M. 12 Indian children playing in Gallup, New Mexico, on the water tower of the Santa Fe Railroad, see a "big ball of fire" shooting across the sky over their heads. Some of them, who hold their hands before their faces, get blisters on their hands on the following day. The fiery ball disappears in the direction of Socorro. Southwest of Socorro Rancher Fred Strozzi observes the falling of a "meteorite," bigger than a "basketball."

Sunday, 1 June 1947

At about 8 A.M. cameraman Jack B. is ordered by Gen. McMullen, deputy-commander of the SAC, to go on a special mission to Socorro. There he must film the recovery of "a crashed Soviet spy plane." At 10 A.M. a C-54 starts with 16 officers and medical personnel and during an intermediate stop-over at Wright Field at 12 noon technical personnel and equipment are taken aboard. At about 3 P.M. the plane lands at Roswell, New Mexico. The retrieval team drives in a convoy to the crash site. The "spy plane" turns out to be a big disc, which apparently collided against a cliff, turned over and now lies on its back, surrounded by debris—and four humanoid beings, small, but with big heads and large black eyes. They lie face down, screaming loudly and holding on tightly to metallic boxes, which have indentations to fit their hands.

Monday, 2 June 1947

6 A.M.: The recovery begins, after the disc has cooled down sufficiently. At first the beings are relieved of their boxes by strikes with the butt of a rifle, whereby one of them dies. The other three are dragged away and secured with rope and tape. Then the debris is collected, logged and loaded onto trucks.

Thursday, 5 June 1947

A complete retrieval team comes from Washington. The disc is lifted with a crane and loaded onto the back of a truck and taken to Wright Field, the seat of the Air Materiel Command (Air Technical Intelligence Center) of the Army Air Force, for closer inspection. The site of the crash is cleared of all traces of the wreck and the recovery.

Sunday, 8 June 1947

The disc arrives at Wright Field and is taken to a large hangar. A thorough investigation begins, with the assistance of scientists of the Manhattan Project and Operation Paperclip.

Saturday, 14 June 1947

According to the *Roswell Daily Record* rancher William "Mac" Brazel finds mysterious wreckage on his land (see 5 July).

Tuesday, 24 June 1947

Private pilot Kenneth Arnold sees a formation of 9 objects over Mt. Rainier, Washington, which a reporter later describes as "flying saucers." During the following weeks mysterious flying objects are sighted all over the country, which carry out unbelievable maneuvers.

Monday, 30 June 1947

Cameraman Jack B. gets orders to go to Ft. Worth AFB near Dallas to film an autopsy.

Tuesday, 1 July 1947

10 A.M.: The first autopsy on one of the crew of the crashed disc is performed by Prof. Detlev Bronk and Dr. Robert P. Williams. It lasts two hours and serves mainly to determine the cause of death of the humanoid due to the risk that the rest of the crew dies before one can find out with what intention they came to earth.

Wednesday, 2 July 1947

9:50 P.M.: The Wilmots sit on a veranda in Roswell, New Mexico, and see a big, glowing, oval object which flies at a very high speed northeast.

Thursday, 3 July 1947

10 A.M.: The second autopsy is carried out at Ft. Worth AFB.

Friday, 4 July 1947

11:15 P.M.: The Franciscan nuns of St. Mary's Hospital at Roswell see a "flaming object that comes down in a curve north of Roswell." It is also seen by William Woody and his father from their ranch south of the town. At the same time a thunderstorm is raging in the Corona district, 75 miles northwest of Roswell. Rancher William "Mac" Brazel, foreman of the Foster Ranch, and his neighbors hear an explosion. Jim Ragsdale and his girlfriend, who are camping in the desert, caught in the storm, observe the crash of a bright object.

Saturday, 5 July 1947

Early in the morning Brazel rides with William "Dee" Proctor, the seven-year-old son of a neighbor, to check for thunderstorm damage. He finds an area of his ranchland, about 200 yards wide and three quarters of a mile long, covered with wreckage: metallic, foil-like material "which, if crumpled and let loose, regained its original shape again," rods like balsa wood which one could neither cut nor burn, and "which had violet hieroglyphlike signs on them." When he brings Dee home to his parents, Floyd and Loretta Proctor, he shows them a few of the fragments. They advise him to report this to the authorities. In the afternoon Brazel transports some of the wrecked pieces to his shed, among them a piece about 4 feet long. His sheep refuse to cross the field of wreckage. But since their water is on the other side he has to load them on a truck and bring them over there. In the evening he drives over to Corona to do shopping. There he tells his friends and neighbors about this and they too tell him to inform the authorities—there is also a reward of $5,000 for anyone helping to solve the mystery of the "flying saucers" offered by the Army Air Force.

Sunday, 6 July 1947

7:30 A.M.: Brazel drives to the office of Sheriff George Wilcox at Roswell and arrives there at 11 A.M. He has taken a few of the fragments with him and shows them to Wilcox, his wife and his daughter, who think they are pieces from a flying saucer. Wilcox sends his deputies to the ranch. They do not find the field of debris but instead of that "a big, circular, black" spot, in which the sand has melted and turned to black glass. While Wilcox is talking to Brazel, he gets a call from Frank Joyce, reporter of the radio station KGFL, and puts him on to Brazel. Joyce is the first one to announce this news. At his suggestion Wilcox calls the Roswell AFB and speaks to Intelligence Officer Major Jesse A. Marcel. Around 1 P.M. Marcel drives to the Sheriff's office, sees the fragments and takes them to the base. Col. Blanchard orders him to go with a captain of the CIC to the Foster Ranch. Blanchard then calls Brig. Gen. Roger Ramey, Commander of the 8th Air Force at Ft. Worth and tells him about the find. Ramey informs the Pentagon. At about 3 P.M. chief of staff Col. Thomas Jefferson DuBose receives a call from Gen. Clements McMullen, deputy commander of the Strategic Air Command, from the Pentagon, ordering that the material found by Brazel should be flown without delay to Andrews Air Field near Washington (via Ft. Worth), where he, McMullen, would personally collect it. According to DuBose, McMullen sent it to the deputy commander of the Air Technical Intelligence Corps, Brig. Gen. Benjamin Chidlaw at Wright Field.

A transport plane is made ready to start at 4:00 P.M.

Marcel and the captain go in different vehicles to the Foster Ranch with Brazel and arrive there at about 8 P.M. Brazel shows them the pieces in the shed, Marcel checks them for radioactivity and finds none. The men sleep at the ranch.

What they do not know: on direct orders from the Pentagon, at 5 P.M. an aerial search for wreckage has begun. They find a wreck and its crew 40 miles northwest of Roswell. At once a salvage team is brought there to secure the wreck and make preparations for the retrieval next day. They meet a group of civilians at the site, archaeologists led by W. Curry Holden, who have come upon the wreck accidentally while searching for pre-Columbian Indian pottery.

Sheriff Wilcox also makes a discovery: near the burnt spot he finds wreckage and four "beings from space. One of them was still alive. Their heads are big and they wore silvery suits," his wife years later tells her granddaughter

Monday, 7 July 1947

7 A.M.: The three men at the ranch ride over to the debris-covered field and load as much as they can onto their vehicles. They find something like tough parchment, more rods with "hieroglyphs," and the foil-like material. Meanwhile Col. Blanchard starts a big action. Early in the morning he orders road blocks to be put up at all approach roads, starting from 20 miles north of Roswell on State Road 285 up to 10 miles north of the 247 crossing. The sheriff's deputies, rancher Bud Payne and William Woody and his father, are all stopped at the road blocks and told to turn back.

At 1:30 P.M. Glenn Dennis of the Ballard Funeral Home, the undertakers who have a contract with the Roswell AFB to provide mortuary services, gets a call from an officer at the base: "How big is the smallest hermetically sealed coffin you have?" Dennis: "Has there been an accident?" Officer: "No, we only want to know for an eventuality."

At about 1:55 P.M. Gen. Curtis LeMay, deputy chief of staff for research and development of the AAF has a meeting with air chief of staff Gen. Hoyt Vandenberg at the Pentagon, the subject: "flying saucers." At the same time Gen. Nathan F. Twining, commander of the

ATIC, changes his plans and prepares for a flight to New Mexico.

At around 2:30 P.M. the officer at Roswell AFB calls Dennis again and asks how bodies can be preserved that have been lying in the desert for long and whether the chemicals used would change the chemical composition of the body. Dennis recommends freezing and offers his assistance, but this is waved off because "the information is required only for eventualities." An hour later Dennis is called to the base to deal with an injured soldier. He renders first aid and takes the GI to the base infirmary at 5:00 P.M. There he passes by an ambulance, the door of which is open. Inside it he sees various metal pieces. One of them looks like the stern of a canoe, 3 feet long, like stainless steel but reddish, as if it had been exposed to high heat, covered with "hieroglyphs." He goes into the staff room to meet a 23-year-old-nurse. She comes out of an examination room, with a mask on, sees him and cries out, "My God, get out of here or you'll get into serious trouble!" She goes into a room, out of which a captain barks at him to get out and not to talk to anybody about what he has seen at the base. By late evening the Army Air Force officers at the ranch have collected a large part of the debris, drive back to Roswell at 10 P.M. Before Marcel gets to the base, he stops at his house after midnight and shows his wife and son some of the wreckage, saying, "This is something very special, it does not come from this earth. I want you to remember this all your life."

Tuesday, 8 July 1947

6:00 A.M.: Confidential meeting between Blanchard and Marcel, who shows him the fragments. The CIC captain goes with a colleague to the ranch to cordon off the area, collect the rest of the wreckage and keep a watch on Brazel.

7.30 A.M.: Staff meeting in the office of Col. Blanchard.

9 A.M.: Sheriff Wilcox looks for Dennis's father and tells him that his son seems to be in trouble. "Tell him that he has seen nothing at the base and knows nothing. They also asked about your name, your wife's and those of your other children."

9 A.M.: As a maneuver to divert the attention of the public away from the dead bodies, and as a reaction to the rumors already afloat in Roswell about Brazel's find—about which Joyce had already reported on Sunday—Blanchard decides to make a press announcement, which he dictates to press officer Lt. Walter Haut:

"The many rumors regarding the flying discs became a reality yesterday when the intelligence office of the 509th Bomb Group of the Eighth Air Force, RAAF, was fortunate enough to gain possession of a disc through the cooperation of one of the local ranchers and the sheriff's office of Chaves County.

"The flying object landed on a ranch near Roswell sometime last week. Not having phone facilities, the rancher stored the disc until such time as he was able to contact the sheriff's office, who in turn notified Major Jesse A. Marcel of the 509th Bomb Group Intelligence office.

Action was immediately taken and the disc was picked up at the rancher's home. It was inspected at the RAAF and subsequently loaned by Major Marcel to higher headquarters."

11 A.M.: Lt. Haut goes to the radio stations KGFL and KSWS and the local papers *Roswell Daily Record* and *Morning Dispatch* to hand in the announcement. The former, an evening paper, publishes it the same day.

The stations cable the news to Associated Press; from there it goes around the world. During the following hours the radio stations, the sheriff's office and Roswell AFB are bombarded with calls from London to Tokyo.

But soon after Frank Joyce from KGFL has telexed the news to United Press, he receives a call from Washington. A "Col. Johnson" wants to know from where he got the news. Joyce names Lt. Haut. The colonel puts the phone down without saying another word. An official caller tells the *Dispatch* that Lt. Haut's statement is an error. Johnny McBoyle, reporter and part owner of the KSWS drives out to the cordoned-off area, looks around, calls the telex secretary of the station KOAT, Albuquerque, Lydia Sleppy, to tell her what he could find out. While she sends the report on the telex the machine stops suddenly and types out "Attention Albuquerque, this is the FBI. Stop transmitting repeat stop transmitting. Matter of national security." McBoyle tells Sleppy on the phone, "Forget it! You have never heard of it, speak to no one about it."

Also at 11 A.M., Glenn Dennis gets a call from the nurse. They decide to meet for lunch. There she tells him that she had assisted at an autopsy on the previous day. Two doctors from Washington had dissected three little beings, which had very big heads, sunken eyes, and only four fingers. The creatures had stunk so badly that soon the autopsy was carried out in a hangar. After an hour Dennis and the nurse part. The same evening he reads in the paper the report about the retrieval of a "flying disc." The next day he calls the nurse, but she is "not available." Shortly afterwards he hears that she has been transferred overseas. Two weeks later he gets a letter from her from England. He writes to her but the letter is returned with a stamp on it saying "Deceased."

Around 12 noon: A plane from Washington lands at Roswell AFB, bringing a special expert and a team of photographers.

The UFO wreck is loaded into a plane, piloted by Capt. Oliver "Pappy" Henderson, taken to Wright Field. During the loading Henderson is able to see three extraterrestrial bodies still in the hangar, kept in ice.

Gen. Twining lands at the Kirtland Air Base at Albuquerque. From there he goes to Alamogordo AFB, the closest base to Roswell AFB.

Around 12 noon: The chief editor of the Dispatch sends reporter Jason Kellahin together with photographer Robin Adair to the Foster Ranch. They get through because they come from the north, where there are no blockades, and reach the ranch at 4 P.M. They find Mac Brazel, his wife and young son. Brazel declares that it was a mistake to have informed the authorities, and the next time he won't say anything unless it was a bomb. They see three or four officers who are searching on the field, as well as a lot of debris. Nobody stops them in their work. They try to interview Sheriff Wilcox, but he refuses to talk since "he has been forbidden by the Army to talk about the matter." The soldiers leave the ranch, taking Brazel with them to Roswell. An interview with Brazel is recorded in the house of Walt Whitmore, the owner of KGFL, but the next morning a call from the office of the congressman for New Mexico, Clinton Anderson, stops the broadcasting of the interview. "We assure you that if you send it, your broadcasting license will be withdrawn." Two calls follow from Washington, one of them from Senator Dennis Chavez personally, bearing similar threats.

At about 3 P.M.: A plane arrives from Washington, is loaded with more debris, and leaves again.

Also at 3 P.M. Major Marcel flies with some fragments to Ft. Worth. He shows them to Gen. Ramey and then leaves his office. He is recalled to the office to attend a press conference that Ramey has arranged. Instead of the wreck fragment, there lies a crashed weather balloon with a radar reflector on the floor. Major Marcel has to suffer with patience the humiliation of his find being presented to reporters as "a big error," the "disc" is only a weather balloon. The news is spread all over the country right in time for the morning newspapers to print it.

6:17 P.M. An internal telex from the FBI states that the weather balloon explanation is not true.

Brazel is intimidated and compelled to give Frank Joyce an interview, which is then broadcast, in which he has to tell a very different tale from that he told Joyce from the sheriff's office on the previous Sunday. He is not allowed to go home, is kept in custody at the guest house at the base under continuous watch. "It was like being in prison," he says later.

During this period he is interrogated by experts from the Kirtland Base and Prof. Lincoln LaPaz of the University of New Mexico. Gen. Ramey and Charles Lindbergh also visit the base, probably on July 9.

In Roswell the wildest rumors are going around: there is talk about recovered Martians, even that one of them had still lived and shrieked like an animal the whole night. Others say a "green man" escaped and ran through the town in the night, before being captured again.

Wednesday, 9 July 1947

8 A.M.: Col. Blanchard leaves Roswell and visits the crash site to supervise the final clearing of the place and after that goes on "leave."

8 A.M.: Three C-54 transport planes are loaded with wreckage. Armed MPs and "inspectors" from Washington supervise the loading, which is unusual. At about 3 P.M. the planes leave in the direction of Kirtland Air Base, where Gen. Twining is staying.

Gen. Leslie Groves, commander of the Armament Development Project at Los Alamos, flies in the company of Gen. Montague, commander of the Army Guided Missiles School at Ft. Bliss, Texas, to Washington.

9 A.M.: Walt Whitmore and his reporter Jud Roberts want to drive to the Foster Ranch, but are stopped by the road block put up by the Army.

10 A.M.: A plane from Washington lands, bringing a secret service man who officially represents President Truman.

10:30 A.M.–11:00 A.M.: President Truman receives Senator Carl Hatch of New Mexico.

Lt. Gen. James Doolittle and Deputy Army Air Force Chief of Staff Gen. Hoyt S. Vandenberg meet Army Air Force Secretary Stuart Symington.

10:50 A.M.: Doolittle, Symington and Vandenberg confer with Gen. Loris Norstad and the Chief of Staff of the Army, Gen. Dwight D. Eisenhower, in his office.

11:48 A.M.: Vandenberg calls the president.

12 noon: The bodies of the UFO crew are made ready for transport.

12:50 P.M.: Gen. Vandenberg and Secretary Symington meet again and go to attend a meeting of the chiefs of staff of all the forces at 12:57 P.M.

1 P.M.: Officers of the Roswell AFB go to the papers and radio stations to confiscate Lt. Haut's announcement.

2:30 P.M.: Third meeting between Vandenberg and Symington.

Gen. Schulgen, chief of the Air Force Intelligence Requirements Division, requests the FBI to aid in the matter of "flying discs." He assures FBI director J. Edgar Hoover that the discs do not originate from the Army or the Navy.

4 P.M.: The corpses are flown out in two planes, one going to Washington and the other to Ft. Worth.

6 P.M.: Three MPs, two secret servicemen and the mortuary officer at Ft. Worth AAF receive the ET bodies. One of the crew members says, "We have just made history." The machine flies back to Roswell with Major Marcel and lands there at 8 P.M.

Thursday 10 July 1947

10:30 A.M.: Generals Groves and Montague meet Generals Vandenberg and LeMay at the Pentagon.

12:15 P.M.: Generals Doolittle and Vandenberg meet President Truman at the White House.

Gen. Twining returns from New Mexico to Wright Field.

2:40 P.M.: Defense Secretary Robert P. Patterson meets Generals Grove and Montague.

Friday, 11 July 1947

The "debriefing " of all the soldiers who took part in the salvaging operations is conducted. They are taken into a room in small groups, and an officer declares, "That was a matter of national security and stands under absolute secrecy. Talk to no one about it. Forget everything that happened and all that you saw."

Tuesday, 15 July 1947

Mac Brazel is warned again, but is allowed to go home. Although he was so poor before this that "he never had two nickels to rub together," he now returns with a brand-new truck and has enough money to buy a new house at Tularosa and a cold store at Las Cruces.

Wednesday, 16 July 1947

Gen. Twining visits Roswell AFB. Within one month, all MPs involved in the retrievals are transferred to other bases.

Wednesday, 13 August 1947

The third UFO crashes on the lands of the Hopi reservation near Flagstaff, Arizona. One of the crew survives, is saved by six young Indians, and lives with them for five years.

September 1947

Prof. Lincoln LaPaz tries to determine the course of the Roswell object and discovers in the presence of CIC Sgt. Rickett the circular spot of an impact, where the sand has melted and turned into blackened glass. He tells Rickett that he still believes that the object was an unmanned reconnoitering device from another planet.

Wednesday, 24 September 1947

President Truman creates the super-secret Operation Majestic 12 to coordinate the evaluation of the Roswell find.

Thursday, 30 October 1947

Brig. Gen. Schulgen writes a memorandum, classified as SECRET, in which he instructs the Air Force Intelligence Service to gather all available information about "aircraft of the type 'flying saucer.'" In this memo he lists construction details: sandwich construction utilizing various combinations of metals, metallic foils, plastics and perhaps balsa wood or similar material. . . unusual fabrication methods to achieve extreme light weight and structural stability." Since this agrees fairly accurately with the descriptions given by the Roswell witnesses, in the opinion of the Pentagon it is still a "flying disc" and not a balloon. Schulgen emphasizes that "it is the considered opinion of some elements that the object may in fact represent an interplanetary craft of some kind."

March 1948

A "war scare" is initiated, so that Congress grants the finances required for the investigation of the wrecks as well as for armament.

5 September 1948

Project Sign comes to the conclusion that the UFOs are interplanetary spaceships. Gen. Vandenberg refutes this report and has all copies of the report destroyed.

September 1949

Bill Brazel, Mac Brazel's son, tells in a bar at Corona that he still finds now and then fragments of the wreck. On the next day he gets a visit from "Capt. Armstrong" and three MPs, who take away the pieces.

22 March 1950

FBI Director Hoover learns from the Air Force that three so-called flying discs have been retrieved in New Mexico.

15 September 1950

Wilbert Smith of the Canadian Ministry of Transportation learns in Washington from U.S. Government scientists that they had salvaged UFO wrecks and were keeping them under lock and key. "The matter has the highest classification, even higher than the H-bomb."

1978–1994:

UFO researcher and nuclear physicist Stanton Friedman locates Major Marcel and interviews him about the Roswell incident. The silence is broken. In the next 16 years 5 books appear, based on the statements of over 300 witnesses (Schmitt/Randle alone name 273 in *UFO Crash at Roswell*, 1991), TV clips, and in 1994 a TV series on the subject. Roswell gets two UFO museums.

11 December 1984

U.S. film producer Jaime Shandera gets the controversial Majestic 12 documents. U.S. secret service contacts promise further exposures.

Senator Steven Schiff of New Mexico initiates an inquiry into the incident through the General Accounting Office of Congress. Thereupon the U.S. Air Force declares that a balloon of the Project Mogul had crashed at Roswell.

July 1994

The mayor of Roswell declares July 2 as official anniversary day of the event.

December 1994

After two years of wrangling, British film producer Ray Santilli buys from a former U.S. Army cameraman a film that is supposed to show the recovery of the Roswell UFO wreckage and the autopsy carried out on two of its four occupants.

5 May 1995

The alleged Roswell autopsy film is shown for the first time to experts and journalists from all over the world. Later it becomes clear that the film has nothing to do with the Roswell crash, but deals with the first crash on May 31, 1947, near Socorro.

28 July 1995

The GAO report is handed over to Republican congressman Steven Schmitt. All documents of the relevant period, including those which could have thrown light on the matter, have apparently been destroyed.

28 August 1995

The Roswell autopsy film is shown in 18 countries of the world and sets off a lively debate.

October 1995

Alleged piece of Roswell UFO crash debris given to U.S. UFO researcher Derrel Sims.

24 March 1996

Alleged Roswell UFO crash debris handed in at the Roswell UFO Museum and Research Center, Roswell, New Mexico.

10 April 1996

Alleged Roswell UFO crash debris mailed to U.S. radio host Art Bell.

APPENDIX A

The Roswell Fragments

In 1996 for the first time alleged samples of the Roswell crash debris were given to journalists, researchers and members of the UFO community. Some of them are rather dubious, others have a potential of being "the real thing." Since only material evidence could prove beyond all doubts that indeed two alien spacecraft crashed near Roswell and Socorro in the summer of 1947, let's have a look at them:

Roswell UFO Museum:

According to an Associated Press wire report, on Sunday, March 24, 1996, a man who wishes to remain anonymous walked into Roswell's UFO Museum with a piece of metallic debris allegedly recovered from the 1947 crash of a UFO. The anonymous donor of this material was described as a local citizen.

One of the museum's administrators, Secretary and Treasurer Max Littel, was quoted in the AP report: *"From the information we have,"* he said, *"this is from a man who was stationed here and was part of the crew that helped pick it up. We are not saying one way or another that this is what it is, but we are going to do everything we can to find out."*

Photographs of the framed specimen were soon circulating on the WWW (Internet). The specimen is made of copper and silver. The specimen has been ana-lyzed by X-ray fluorescence at the New Mexico Bureau of Mines and Mineral Resources in Socorro, and appears to be composed of a thin sliver of silver coated with copper on one side.[1]

An official release from the Roswell UFO Museum and Research Center attempted to clarify matters and provide an update on the analysis of the specimen.

In answer to many, many calls concerning the piece of metal brought into our museum concerning the 1947 incident, this information is to give an answer to the inquires that have been made. On Sunday, March 24, 1996, this gentleman brought in the item, in a frame with a glass face so it was protected. His story was that he received it from a person we will refer to as No. 2. No. 1 was the person in the military stationed at Roswell Army Air Field in 1947 and was one of the GIs who helped clean up the debris. It is obvious to accomplish getting the piece of wreckage he did, it had to be small enough to be placed in a pocket to avoid detection. So, No. 1 gave the material to No. 2, who placed it in a frame. No. 2 then gave the item to No. 3, who brought the material to this museum on March 24, 1996. No. 3 has presented the museum with the item and it will remain in our possession permanently.

On Friday, March 29, the Roswell chief of police and one of the volunteers of the museum took the item to New Mexico

Tech in Socorro, New Mexico, for an analysis that had been scheduled at our request. The formal results will be available in a few days, but it was determined the metal was copper with silver on each surface. All metals were very thin and when all three were as indicated, the thickness was still less than a dime would be in thickness. When the formal results are obtained (and we also ask for a layman's interpretation) the experiments and research can and will continue in any direction that might lend information. Further, we will not release the names as indicated above as No. 1, 2 & 3 to ANYBODY, as we all know the press would crucify anyone to get one of their 'scoops.'... [1A]

Further details came from the *Roswell Daily Record*, the local newspaper, on April 5, 1995:

Analysis of metal fails to refute claims of crash. Wherever it came from, somewhere along the line it fell down and went boom. Analysis of the piece of metal reportedly linked to the alleged 1947 Roswell UFO crash reveals that the sample was part of a larger object that did indeed suffer some kind of disaster. "It obviously came from a larger piece and the way it came from there was from a catastrophic event," analyst Chris McKee said. "What that really means, I have no idea. It could be from an explosion, it could be from a crash." The piece, which was turned in to the International UFO Museum and Research Center on March 24, by an anonymous source, was tested last week by McKee at the New Mexico Institute of Mining and Technology in Socorro. Initial results revealed that the sample was composed of silver and copper, but a written report lists traces of sodium, aluminum, silicon, iron, chromium, sulphur and chlorine as also present on the piece.

*According to McKee, the origin of those elements is unknown. "It could just come from handling or soil, we didn't clean the sample or anything so we have no idea what was on the surface," McKee said. Since the components of the piece are all natural elements, and could be found throughout the uni-*verse, the composition of the metal does not provide proof one way or another about what crashed in 1947. "It doesn't really help decide whether it is extraterrestrial or not," McKee said. One thing is for sure though, it did not come directly from the weather balloon experiments known as Project MOGUL that the United States Air Force claim is responsible for the crash. According to Max Littel of the UFO Museum, Charles Moore, a member of the team that designed and worked on Project MOGUL, was at the test in Socorro. "He said it was not a part of the balloon, and he worked on the project before it was even known as MOGUL," Littel said. "It could have been part of extra instrumentation attached to it, but it wasn't part of the balloon, nor was it part of its inner workings." Although the findings are promising, Littel noted that there is still no conclusive evidence that what crashed in the desert all those years ago was a UFO. "There are still a lot of 'could-be's' and 'maybe's' but no absolutes yet," Littel said. The next step in verifying the origin of the piece is tracking it back to its original owner. Littel said the museum is currently working toward that end.*[1B]

On April 24, 1996 Michael Hesemann visited the Roswell UFO Museum and went with Max Littel to the local police station, which had the framed fragment in its safe. Hesemann was rather unimpressed by the piece, since it did not have any of the characteristics reported by the Roswell eyewitnesses and rather looked like an ordinary terrestrial piece of metal. The main body was of silver, covered with a fine level of copper on top and was 79 x 43 mm in size. As Hesemann learned, the results of the fluorescence analysis in Socorro were that the "front side" consisted of 50% copper (Cu) and 50% silver (Ag), the back side of 87% silver, 12% copper and 1% traces. Its weight is 16.16g. According to these results the specimen is not unusual at all, and there is no indication that it has any connection with the Roswell incident other than the alleged anonymous witness's claim.

In the meantime the case could be solved. On September 6, 1996 the "Albuquerque Journal" revealed that the piece was created by artist Randy Fullbright, who manufactures jewelry of silver and copper according to an old japanese method, and gave the piece to Blake Larsen just before the latter moved to Roswell. Larsen was the person who handed it over to Max Littell. According to Fullbright, he already informed the museum about the origin of the metal when he saw its picture in a newspaper, but nobody was willing to set the records straight. According to Littell the museum made more than $1500—by selling pictures of the "Roswell fragment".

Art Bell Radio Show:

Further alleged debris from the 1947 Roswell UFO crash was sent to American radio show host Art Bell. The following letter was received by Art Bell on April 10, 1996, along with an amount of specimens.

Dear Mr. Bell,

I've followed your broadcasts over the last year or so, and have been considering whether or not to share with you and your listeners some information related to the Roswell UFO crash.

My grandfather was a member of the retrieval team sent to the crash site just after the incident was reported. He died in 1974, but not before he had sat down with some of us and talked about the incident.

I am currently serving in the military and hold a security clearance, and do not wish to "go public" and risk losing my career and commission.

Nonetheless, I would like to tell you briefly what my own grandfather told me about Roswell. In fact, I enclose for your safekeeping "samples" that were in the possession of my grandfather until he died, and which I have had since his own estate was settled. As I understand it, they came from the UFO debris and were among a large batch subsequently sent to Wright-

Patterson AFB in Ohio from New Mexico.

My grandfather was able to "appropriate" them, and stated that the metallic samples are "pure extract aluminum." You will note that they appear old and tampered, and they have been placed in tissue-paper and in Baggies for posterity.

I have had them since 1974, and after considerable thought and reflection give them to you. Feel free to share them with any of your friends in the UFO research community.

I have listened to many people over the years discuss Roswell and the crash events as reported by many who were either there or who heard about it from eyewitnesses.

The recent Roswell movie was similar to my grandfather's own account, but a critical element was left out, and it is that element which I would like to share.

As my grandfather stated, the team arrived at the crash site just after the AAF/USAF reported the ground-zero location. They found two dead occupants, hurled free of the disc.

A lone surviving occupant was found within the disc, and it was apparent its left leg was broken. There was a minimal radiation contamination, and it was quickly dispersed with a water/solvent wash, and soon the occupant was dispatched for medical assistance and isolation. The bodies were sent to Wright-Patterson AFB for dispersal. The debris was also loaded onto three trucks which finished the onload just before sunset.

Grandfather was part of the team that went with the surviving occupant. The occupant communicated via telepathic means. It spoke perfect English, and communicated the following:

The disc was a "probe ship" dispatched from a "launch ship" that was stationed at the dimensional gateway to the Terran solar system, 32 light years from Terra. They had been conducting operations on Terra for over 100 years. Another group was exploring Mars and Io. Each probe ship carried a crew of three. A launch ship had a crew of 100.

The disc that crashed had collided with a meteor in orbit of Terra and was attempting to compensate its flight vector, but because of the collision the inter-atmospheric propulsion system malfunctioned and the occupants sent out a distress signal to their companions on Mars. The launch ship commander made the decision to authorize an attempted soft-landing on the New Mexican desert. At the same time, the inter-atmospheric propulsion system had a massive burn-out, and the disc was soon virtually helpless.

There was another option available to the occupants, but it involved activating the dimensional power-plant for deep space travel. However, it opens an energy vortex around the disc for 1,500 miles in all directions. Activating the dimensional power-plant would have resulted in the annihilation of the states of New Mexico, Arizona, California and portions of Mexico. Possibly even further states would have been affected.

Thus, the occupants chose to ride the ship down and hope for the best. They literally sacrificed their lives rather than destroy the populations within their proximity.

The dimensional power-plant was self-destructed, and the inter-atmospheric propulsion system was also deactivated to prevent the technology from falling into the hands of the Terrans. This was done in accordance with their standing orders in regard to any compromise with contact experiences.

Grandfather spent a total of 26 weeks in the team that examined and debriefed the lone survivor of the Roswell crash. Grandfather's affiliation with the "project" ended when the occupant was to be transported to a long-term facility. He was placed on-board a USAF transport aircraft that was to be sent to Washington, D.C.

The aircraft and all aboard disappeared under mysterious and disturbing circumstances en-route to Washington, DC.

It may interest you that three fighter aircraft, dispatched to investigate a distress call from the transport, experienced many electrical-malfunctioning systems failures as they entered the airspace of the transport's last reported position. No crash or debris of the transport was ever found. The team was disbanded.

Well, I realize I have likely shocked you with this bizarre and incredible account, and seeking a remaining "unknown"

likely doesn't do anything for my credibility, eh? And the metal "samples" only will likely add to the controversy.

But, I know you will take this with a "grain of salt," and I don't blame you, Mr Bell. I just hope that you can understand my reasons and my own desire to maintain my career and commission.

I am passing through South Carolina with an Operational Readiness Mobility Exercise and will mail this just prior to this exercise, possibly from the Charleston area. I will listen to your broadcast to receive any acknowledging or confirmation that you have received this package.

This letter and the contents of the package are given to you with the hope that it helps contribute to the discussion on the subject of UFO phenomena.

I agree with Neil Armstrong, a good friend of mine, who dared to say, at the White House no less, that there are things "out there" which boggle the mind and are far beyond our ability to comprehend.

Sign me, A Friend.[2]

A second letter followed on April 22. This time the sender claimed that the investigative team consisted of scientists, military and intelligence personnel of the University of Colorado, the Atomic Energy Commission, NASA, the University of California, Los Angeles (UCLA), the ONR (Office of Naval Research), OSRD (Office of Scientific Research and Development) and, of course, the Army Air Force. They came to the conclusion that the fragments were "pure extract aluminum" and served "as a conductor for electromagnetic fields their propulsion system created." The surviving alien was not willing to deliver any technological data, in spite of "many attempts to interrogate him . . . the survivor had the ability to receive thoughts and questions before they were asked. Sometimes this became quite frustrating." They also found fiber-optical material aboard the craft plus "control panels in shape of the hand of the Extraterrestrial," definitely a hint to the Santilli debris footage. The space program, he claimed, was only started to track down aliens.

Although this story sounded rather incredible and is most probably full of disinformation, when the samples were analyzed by a Midwestern University, they turned out to be interesting, as reported by journalist Linda Moulton Howe. Bell published the results of the analysis on his homepage on the Internet:

Three types of specimens were received for analysis. We refer to them here as:

1: the chips.

2: the metal strips.

3: the vent.

The chips corresponded to 5 squares, 1 circle and 2 ellipsoid items. All 5 square chips appeared essentially identical with respect to size and physical appearance. All 5 weighed 160 mg. The diameter of the circular chip and the smaller diameter of the ellipsoid chip were similar in size to the lengths of the sides of the square chips. The circular chip weighed 119 mg, and the 2 ellipsoid chips weighed 168 mg (these measurements are all within plus or minus one milligram for each type).

At this point, analyses have been conducted only on the square chips, using a micrometer, a representative square chip had the dimensions: 6.368 mm x 6.361 mm x 1.596 mm. This gives a volume of 64.65 mm³. Using a weight of 160 mg, this would correspond to a density of 2.47mg/mm³. The squares had two distinguishable sides: a "top" side with rounded edges, and a "bottom" side that was squared off—as if they had possibly been "punched out" from the top. Using a scanning electron microscope (SEM), photographs of the top side and the bottom side were generated.

The SEM was configured for energy dispersive spectroscopy (EDS) which allows determination of the elemental content of the area being scanned by the electron beam. The bombardment of electron results in the release of X-rays whose wavelengths are characteristic of the elements being targeted. A detector is able to translate this information into specific "peaks" which are then recorded. The analyses showed that over a broad (averaged) area on the surface of the top and bottom of the square chips, only aluminum could be detected. It was also noted that despite the differences in apparent texture on the sides of the chips, the EDS spectra were essentially identical—i.e., only aluminum was detected in both the rougher and smoother portions. The density of aluminum is 2.7 and thus close to the value of 2.47 determined from our calculation. The curved top edges might contribute to the small difference.

High magnification showed granular particles embedded in the surface of the squares. These had sizes of just a few microns (um). EDS showed that these contained silicon (Si).

A square chip was embedded in epoxy, cut through the middle and polished in order to obtain a good cross section for SEM and EDS analyses. The SEM was done using a "backscattering" configuration which allows heavier elements to look brighter than less-heavy elements. A photo of this shows that there are white (ie, brighter) particulate flake-like materials scattered through the aluminum. These particles had an iron (Fe) content where the area measured was within a single particle. Small amounts of silicon (Si) and manganese (Mn) were also evident. The elements in these particles wee not detectable when EDS was measured over a broad area of the chip cross-section, presumably because of their small respective areas.

The strip measured 25.3 cm (10 inches) by 3.8 cm (1.5 inches), the thickness was 0.165 mm (average of 5 measurements). The weight was 4.04 gm. A computation of density using these values and assuming a uniform thickness comes to 2.54 gm/cc. A corner of the strip was removed manually by bending several times until it broke off. EDS was done on the removed piece, with a broad area showing primarily aluminum. Small granules could be detected on the surface; EDS showed these to contain small amounts of iron (Fe), manganese (Mn), calcium (Ca), and silicon (Si).

The vent, so called because of its vent-like appearance, had dimensions of 4.9 cm by 6.2 cm; the thickness was 0.157 mm (average 3 measurements) on the edge (ie, not over slits). The thickness over the slits was 0.304 mm (average 6 measurements). The weight was 1.24 gm. Using the edge-thickness we calculate a density of 2.60 gm/cc. (If assumed that the slits are just cuts in the metal they should not effect the overall density).

The slits are in 24 groups with 10 parallel slits one mm apart in each group. The lengths of the slits are 8 mm. When held up to the light at an angle, light can be seen through the parallel slits. The slits in each group appear orientated opposite to those in the adjacent group. That is, if considered to act in a vent-like manner, air going through the slits would be directed "up" in one group and "down" in the adjacent group.

A small piece of the vent on one corner was removed for analysis. One edge of this piece corresponds to a slit edge. EDS showed it to consist primarily of aluminum. This was similar for the three different sections that seemed to have a different external appearance. In this case the granules showed a content similar to the metal strip granules—ie, aluminum with small amounts of iron, manganese, calcium and silicon.

Samples of material newly acquired by Art (Bell) were obtained (from Art) on May 31, 1996. These were very different from the aluminum specimens received earlier. The material was in two main pieces, one, designated sample 1, was approximately 6 cm by 3 cm and about 3–4 mm in thickness; the other sample, sample 2, was about 5 cm by 2.5 cm and again 3–4 mm in thickness. Sample 1 weighed 6.23 gm; and sample 2 weighed 6.9 gm. The shape of each sample was quite irregular, and the thickness in each case varied in different areas. It is emphasized that these measurements are meant to provide only some notion of the general size of the specimens.

Each sample had a "silvery" shiny side with a rough (granular) appearance. The other side was blackish-gray. Looking at the samples edge-on, numerous layers can be seen. The samples were hard but brittle, and a few small pieces could be broken off using a small hand vice and manual pressure. Two such samples broken off were analyzed (side by side) by scanning electron microscopy (SEM); one was shiny side up—the other was dark side down. Energy dispersive spectroscopy (EDS) revealed the shiny side contained more than 95% magnesium and a small amount (2-3%) of zinc. The dark side contained a significant amount of bismuth.

A small piece was embedded in epoxy, cut through, and polished in such a way that a cross section of the layering could be visualized. In these cases we utilized a backscattering mode which shows heavier elements to be brighter than less-heavy elements. As seen in the photo's there are layers of lighter (less bright) material separated by much thinner layers of heavier (brighter) material. When EDS scans were done on the light material, a high level of magnesium was observed, again with a small amount of zinc; whereas scans of the bright material showed a significant content of bismuth. The thickness of the "bismuth layers" appears to be only a few microns. There are apparent "bismuth layers" that appear less bright than others. Possibly this relates to a lower concentration of bismuth, or the bands occur slightly below the surface being examined. Additional studies will be necessary to determine which, if either, of these interpretations is correct.

Thus the material appears to represent layers of a substance consisting mainly of magnesium and a small amount of zinc separated by thin layers containing a high bismuth content.[2A]

Journalist Linda Moulton Howe added, at an online conference in the CompuServe UFO Forum:

The aluminium pieces which the biologist and metallurgist at Midwestern University have had to examine all appear to be above 99% aluminium with a hardness value based on the Vickers Diamond Hardness test to be an average of 48 in 5 averages. The normal hardness for 99% above Aluminium is 19. The 48 might be explained by iron flakes that show up on the EDS analyses at more the center of the little squares. The iron could be contaminants—a common contaminant in aluminium—or could be a manufactured alloy. . . . Then on May 28, Art Bell received a third letter and another shipment from the anonymous source whose envelopes have a South Carolina post mark. The letter said: "I now include the enclosed, and can only say that these scrapings came from the exterior underside of the Disc itself. It literally was a 'shell-like' shielding of the Disc. Brittle and layered, almost with a prefabricated design and placing. Keep in mind, Mr. Bell, that these are the last of Granddads samples. They have sat for years inside a closet, with his personal effects."

Since receiving that letter and getting two of those pieces to the same university lab for scanning electron microscope and EDS analyses, I can say that I have not been able to find anyone in university research, Sandia Labs, Los Alamos Lab, exotic metal manufacturers, and many other people with metal knowledge who can tell me who is laying down thin layers of pure bismuth with layers of magnesium-zinc. . . . The frosting between layers is 1 to 4 microns of pure bismuth. We have not found anything else yet in the bismuth layers and a wave Dispersive Spectroscopic analysis was performed to look with more refinement. Then above the 1–4 micron bismuth layer is a 100 to 200 micron layer of magnesium and zinc, which are mixed this way: 95 to 96 % magnesium and about 3–4% zinc. We have looked for other trace elements including oxygen and zirconium, but nothing showed up in the WDS. . . . Nobody could give me a current day manufacture working with these elements in this kind of layering and might be able to say what the use is. Hypotheses that have been presented across the range of metallurgists and scientists including Dr. Paul Chu who discovered the 1,2,3 superconductor at the Univ. of Houston thought it might be an electrical-thermo material:

1) Electro-thermo-material-heat induced electricity.
2) Magnetic shielding.
3) A power source such as a battery. . . .
4) A possible self-cooling super-conductor.

It's interesting to note that when Dr. Paul Chu and Robert Hazen at Carnegie Institute in Washington discovered the 1,2,3

superconductor in the 1988–89 time frame and it was considered a major breakthrough because the combination of yttrium, barium and copper brought the temperature for the superconductor efficiency up to a warmer working point than ever before—that within a short period of time after their discovery was announced, European superconductor researchers announced that they had made more breakthroughs on the temperature functioning by adding BISMUTH to their element mix. . . . (so they seem to be) very provocative pieces of material.

UFO Researcher Derrel Sims:

Yet another alleged piece of Roswell UFO crash debris was given to U.S. UFO researcher Derrel Sims. In an interview with Philip Mantle Sims highlighted how he had come into possession of the specimen.

Sims: The object came into my possession in October 1995. A gentleman came to me and he mentioned that he had such an object (debris specimen) and wanted to know if I would be interested in reviewing it, and said he wanted to give it to me for that purpose, and I said why would I want to do that, and he said it was part of the—he felt the Roswell crash. He agreed to give me the object and allow me to have it analyzed. . . . I then asked the individual about the person's background and he said, "Well, here are the rules concerning the object," he said, "the object is yours," he said, "I know that you have an investigative background and know that you are a private investigator and a trainer for people in need of protection, I know you are a military police officer and I know you were also in the Central Intelligence Agency," he said, "now that qualifies you to do all the background work you need on me." He said, "you are going to find what you want." He said, "I do not want it public." He said, "I do not want to be involved in this in any way, shape or form."

Mantle: But you know who this individual is?

Sims: Oh yes, yes I do. I said I have to follow that back as far as I can and all the way through the person who gave it to *you. He said, "That's fine, I just don't want my name involved in any of this." He went onto say, "I am perfectly willing to give whatever you need to explore me and the situation." He said, "What you have in your hands . . . is all the proof you are going to need."*

Mantle: Just to interrupt, you know when you said he came to you, was this at your home, your office?

Sims: I met him in California, I was touring from a university in Oregon down, doing five conferences, and I met him as part of a meeting during this five-conference tour from Oregon to California. At that point this was the second time that we'd had our meeting and that's when he finally gave me the object (specimen), at that point we made a call and verified the stuff, the content and so on.

Mantle: You were saying that you were attempting to have this material analyzed at an institution.

Sims: At this point, and I'll make it available to you as soon as it gets to me, I have two labs and a university who have samples (of the specimen). . . . they will give us independent reports. . . . [3]

Indeed the "Sims fragment" has all the characteristics of the reported Roswell and Socorro Crash debris, as described by the witnesses and visible on the Santilli debris footage: it is extremely light, reflective, and tough. When Sims presented it at the European UFO Conference, organized by the Ministry of Transportation of the Republic of San Marino, on May 10–12, 1996, the specimen, about 38 x 32 x 12 mm large, had a shiny, reflective surface and a dim underside with sharp edges. The stainless-steel-colored surface had traces of a bluish-violet discoloration, probably caused by heat. It is extremely light and weight's less than 20 g, and is extremely hard; it cut glass easier than a diamond and caused a deep scrape on researcher Johannes von Buttlars Titanium watch. Indeed it resembled the descriptions given by the Roswell witnesses:

"It looked like quicksilver . . . it had jagged edges and was a dull grayish-silver color." (Frankie Rowe)

"It was a gray lustrous metal resembling aluminum, but lighter in weight and much stiffer." (Dr. John Kromschroeder)

"Very light in weight, metallic . . . it looked like a little piece of rock . . . even the heaviest hammer or the best knife couldn't scratch it." (Sgt. Thomas Gonzales)

From all the alleged "Roswell fragments," Sims's is closest to be genuine. Only time will tell us more about its origin.

On 24 September 1996 Derrel Sims informed the authors that an Isotope analysis in a laboratory in New Mexico reveled indeed a non-terrestrial isotope configuration, similar to that found in meteorites, in his fragment. He decided to wait until further tests from different laboratories check these results before he will make them known to the public.

[1]Mutual UFO Network: *Ufo Journal*, no. 337, May 1996.

[1A]Roswell UFO Museum and Research Center Press Release, not dated.

[1B]*Roswell Daily Record*, 5 April 1996.

[2]NEXUS New Times, vol. 3, no. 4: June/July 1996. (Source downloaded from the Art Bell web site.)

[2A]Art Bell web site, 6 April 1996.

[3]Mantle, Philip: Personal Interview with Derrel Sims, 10 May 1996.

APPENDIX B

The Search for the Cameraman

Since Ray Santilli published his spectacular footage of the alleged alien autopsy, researchers tried to identify his source Jack, the cameraman. This indeed proved to be difficult, since it was one of the conditions for Santilli's deal that he keep his identity strictly confidential, a condition the Brit carefully fulfilled. Those who insisted in asking received misleading answers, and to give him a name he started to call him "Jack Barnett." This was not coincidental, since there was a Universal News cameraman by this name, who indeed filmed Elvis Presley at a high-school concert in the summer of 1955. But when the "King of Rock 'n' Roll" gave a second concert open air, the organized cameramen were on a strike and our cameraman took over the job for Barnett. Barnett, indeed, as the researchers quickly found out, had died in 1969 and was therefore out of question to be Santilli's source.

When the truth about "Jack Barnett" came out, some researchers started to claim there was no cameraman at all, alleging the autopsy footage being either an orchestrated hoax or Santilli being a frontman for the intelligence community which tried to test the public reaction on the release of new UFO evidence by the release of the "Roswell" footage.

But there is a cameraman, and he is by now eighty-six years old. There have been a number of people who, besides Ray Santilli, have spoken to him or other members of his family, on the phone. Gary Shoefield, formerly of Polygram, confirmed he had a date with the cameraman, when he suddenly got sick and had to go to a hospital. He spoke with his worried wife, and got quite convinced that nobody was playing a comedy on his expense. John Purdie producer for Union Pictures and maker of "Incident at Roswell" for Channel Four in the UK, spoke to him, and also the secretary of David Roehring (Kiviat Green Productions, makers of "Alien Autopsy—Fact or Fiction?" for the Fox Network in the USA). Because Santilli asked him to do so, he had called Roehring, who tried to trap him and trace back the call by electronic means, but when Jack heard the suspicious sounds in the line, he hung up.

More fortunate was one of the authors of this book, Philip Mantle, who had asked Ray Santilli to ask the cameraman to give him a call. On June 22, 1995, Santilli phoned Mantle at around 7:30 P.M., informing him that the cameraman would call later that evening. At around 8:50 P.M. a man did call Mantle and introduce himself as the cameraman, still using the pseudonym Jack Barnett. The telephone conversation between Mantle and the cameraman lasted for about fifteen minutes, during which time the cameraman reaffirmed some of his earlier statements, but did add that he would no rule out a face-to-face meeting with Mantle in the USA at some date in the future.

When we requested details of the crash site in New Mexico, we were convinced that the cameraman has an excellent knowledge of the area in question. With Santilli as the go-between (Santilli knows nothing about the area in question) the cameraman even described a ruined bridge that we could only locate on the third attempt. The cameraman knew exactly what he was talking about.

A different approach was tried by Bob Shell. In his report, published by Santilli in August 1995, the cameraman said he had polio as a child and only got into the military because his father was a cameraman and he knew how to handle a camera. Polio victims at that time usually had an affected limb as a result of the illness. In this instance it could not have affected the cameraman's hands/arms, otherwise he would not have been able to work as a cameraman in the first place. Could he possibly have had an affected leg? The movement of the cameraman in the autopsy film could indicate this since he doesn't appear to move too easily around the room. Bob Shell made enquiries among a number of U.S. military cameramen and asked if they remembered a colleague from the 1940s who had a bad leg. They knew one, he lives in Florida today and has the exact age claimed by Santilli for the cameraman. Did Shell find the right man? Obviously he did.

On Monday, April 15, 1996 Shell received a phone call from Capt. John McAndrews of the U.S. Air Force, who claimed he was investigating the Santilli footage for the Clinton Administration. According to Capt. McAndrews, President Clinton asked his Science Advisor John Gibbons to find out if the film is authentic or not and if there is further footage in the military archives. Gibbons requested a comment from the secretary of the Air Force, who was commissioned for this job.

The result according to what he told Shell: At least parts of the footage are authentic, further reels of the autopsy were allegedly located in the U.S. Air Force Archives. The being in the film, so he said, is no dummy and no human being, but also not an extraterrestrial, whatever that means. Did it come from another dimension, the future, is it a biorobot—or did McAndrews try to spread new disinformation? We don't know, but perhaps are inclined to believe the latter. To make it even more mysterious, McAndrews claimed the debris footage is "ridiculous" and fake, although there is no doubt that it comes from the same stock.

Shell added that if McAndrews was contacted about this subject he would deny making any such statement to Bob Shell. McAndrews went on to say that he was looking for the cameraman, and believed he knew his name. McAndrews had been unable to locate this man's military records, as part of these records had been destroyed by fire some years ago at the Military Records Center in St. Louis, Missouri. McAndrews had been unable to locate the cameraman despite knowing that he now lived in Florida.

Indeed one of the authors (Hesemann) had written to President Clinton on December 12, 1995 and sent him a full copy of the Santilli footage:

Dear Mr. President,

On your recent visit to Ireland on a public speech in Belfast, you replied on the request of Ryan, a 12-years-old-boy, regarding the alleged crash of an alien spacecraft near Roswell, New Mexico, in July 1947. You said, quote, "if the United States Air Force did recover alien bodies, they didn't tell me about it, and I want to know."

After talking to about 30 eyewitnesses I am convinced that indeed TWO alien spacecraft crashed in the summer of 1947, one at May 31st southwest of Socorro, NM, and one at July 4th north of Roswell, NM. The Generals of the Army Air Force and Strategic Air Command involved in the retrieval operation were Gen. Clements McMullen, Gen. George C. Kenney, General Carl A. Spaatz and General Nathan F. Twining. Unfortunately, as reported by the General Accounting Office (GAO) this summer, in 1953 all records in the archives of the USAF were destroyed. It is unclear who gave the order, because the order was destroyed, too. But we have reasons to believe there still is a higher authority in existence, code-named MJ12 or PI-40, who knows and has the documents.

Enclosed I send you a tape of the autopsy of one of the creatures retrieved from the wreckage of the first craft. The autopsy was supervised by the Physiologist Dr. Detlev Bronk, chairman of the Natl. Research Council, and took place at Fort Worth AFB on July 3rd, 1947.

The tape was made from the original 16mm film taken by a Army Air Force cameraman under order of General McMullen. He kept some of the reels and sold them last year to an English producer, because he felt the time for the truth has come. The original material was verified by Mr. Bob Shell, phototechnical consultant of the FBI (he is 95 % sure it was produced, exposed and developed in 1947). Leading pathologists (Prof. Cyril Wecht, USA; Prof. Christopher Milroy, GB; Prof. B. Ballone, Italy) confirmed it is a biological entity but "not a member of the human race as we know it."

Eyewitnesses told us they saw the rest of the footage in the CIA Headquarter or during their service at the US Airforce. This makes me sure that you, if you inquire, will have the possibility to see the complete footage. Last May the respected "Human Potential Foundation" organized a conference "When Cosmic Cultures Meet" and I was one of the speakers—discussed ways to prepare mankind for the most important event in the last thousand years, the recognition that indeed we are not alone. We know of the concern of many official studies that indeed a culture shock could result from this announcement, but we think it's time to prepare the public for the truth. The time for the truth has come . . . and it takes a courageous democratic President like you to get your place in history as the man who finally revealed it to mankind.

Yours sincerely
Michael Hesemann
Cultural Anthropologist, Historian

Obviously the letter was forwarded to the U.S. Air Force, maybe together with Clinton's/Gibbon's requests. The answer at last came from Major Robert T. Wimple, "Chief, White House Inquiries, Office of Legislative Liaison," dated February 29, 1996: "On behalf of President Clinton, thank you for your letter regarding the Roswell Incident. Your letter was provided to the Department of the Air Force for response" and included the obligatory "Project Blue Book Fact Sheet," claiming that the U.S. Air Force "no longer investigates unidentified flying objects" and did not find any indication of a threat for national security.

Whatever role my letter and videotape played, the reply went the same way as the alleged White House request regarding the footage.

On May 29, 1996 I (Mantle) telephoned Captain James McAndrews at his office to see if he would indeed deny having made such statements to Bob Shell. Some of McAndrews comments are listed here below:

Mantle: I dare say you know what I am calling about.

McAndrews: Flying Saucers and aliens and extraterrestrial biological entities.

Mantle: Well, you said that, not me.

McAndrews: All right.

Mantle: No I was just curious at some of the things that Bob (Shell) was saying about the so-called Santilli autopsy film. Bob has told me that perhaps you have an interest in it. Is that correct ?

McAndrews: Sure, you know any fraudulent thing like that is always interesting.

Mantle: You think the film is a fraud.

McAndrews: Without a doubt, yes it is.

Mantle: Is there any way we can prove that, though.

McAndrews: Well, it didn't happen, so that's a good place to start.

Mantle: So you are convinced it is a hoax then.

McAndrews: Oh, without a doubt, yes.

Mantle: Have you yourself contacted Santilli to try and find this man (cameraman).

McAndrews: No, I've told anybody who talks to him, I've said have him (Santilli) call me. He hasn't called.

Mantle: Well alright, I will do, I'll try and speak to him (Santilli) tomorrow.

McAndrews: Have Ray call me and we'll discuss it, but I don't believe that it's authentic, it doesn't even look authentic, but I've studies when I did that other report (Official U.S. Air Force Report on the Roswell incident), I've studied thoroughly what the U.S. military was doing in that part of the world in that time frame and quite a bit of time surrounding that too and I came up with nothing like that. There were a lot of interesting things but nothing like that and like I told Bob (Shell) I don't believe that this is an authentic film, I believe that you know there is a possibility other things could have inspired someone to hoax this film, that's what I would, but you know that's not based on anything, that's based on my thorough knowledge of what's going on there at that time and I'll tell you that didn't go on and you know I was cleared to look in anything I needed to look at with full authority and we did. People weren't always happy, people like keeping secrets so we got in where we needed to go and we looked at where we needed to look at and you know, was called names and things, but you know we did it.

Mantle: OK.

McAndrews: So that's that, but it doesn't even look real to me.

As Bob Shell had previously informed us, McAndrews would indeed deny everything and indeed he did.

In the meantime Jack agreed to be interviewed on camera for a future TV program. On August 7, 1996 one of the authors (Hesemann) was able to watch the full interview in Ray Santilli's office in London. The cameraman, indeed a small, stocky old gentleman in his mid-eighties with a friendly, round face, wearing a baseball cap, was clearly visible, neither his face nor his voice were disguised. Hesemann: "I could look straight into his eyes. The way he spoke, the way he answered the questions, at least for me there is no doubt this guy is the real cameraman and not an actor, and is telling the truth."

On December 19, 1996 the interview with the camerman was broadcast in Japan by Fuji TV. He begins by saying he is reading from notes and that his son helped him. He admits: "I am the person who shot the film. I will not tell you my name, but I want you to know that I am not happy that I have betrayed my country. Our United States of America is the greatest country in the world and I am proud to be an American. I do not want that to change." The interview does not deliver any new information. The cameraman confirms that the crash site was "just ouside Socorro, New Mexico". He answered 14 questions before he ended with the words: "Frankly, I wish I has never sold the film. He (Santilli) came back to me until I sold him the film. I sold the film because I needed money. I'm not proud of it. Santilli took about 25 rolls. That's it. I'm going to bed. No more questions. Turn it off. No more questions."

A picture from the film appeared on the Internet, and American ufologists started a "manhunt" for the cameramen. It seems to be just a question of time until his identity is revealed.

APPENDIX C

Santilli Autopsy Film Ananlysis

by Professor Corrado Malanga (University of Pisa, Italy)

Background: Testing of the film provided by Philip Mantle was done the first week of July at the laboratories of the Chemical and Industrial Chemistry Department at the University of Pisa, Italy, by Professor Corrado Malanga.

What follows is a translation of Professor Malanga's report. Translation by Maurizio Baiata.

"The film frame has been analyzed through infrared spectroscopy by Fourier Transforms on the film base. The film base has been obtained by cutting away a portion of the film not covered by emulsion under the optical microscope and microbistoury (unknown term?).

"The segment (some tenths of a millimeter in size) has been compressed in a diamond cell in order to minimize its thickness to the necessary limit. The infrared spectrum obtained has been recognized by the data bank of the analytic computer as generic polyacetate. Analysis of the literature enables us to define the unknown sample as Cellulose Polyacetate produced by Eastman Kodak, of the series "n," where "n" stands for the sequential number.

"At present we can surely exclude Kodapak 1 and 2, and we believe with a 5% margin of error that the examined product can be Kodapak 3, 4 or 5. The uncertainty is only due to the fact that, while for Kodapak 4 the infrared spectrum is known in the literature, we will have to make a direct comparison with samples of Kodapak 3 and 5, which have been requested from Kodak, to be certain of the correct polyester type match. In any case, for Kodapak 4 we have a total superimposition of the infrared spectrograph bands with our sample.

"As to synthesis, the analyzed material, being known in the literature since the first half of the fifties, seems to possess the following composition: cellulose acetate (2.5 acetile group per glucose (starch, sugar)) unit, with added esthers of phosphoric acid as platecisers."

NB: Professor Corrado Malanga is a chemical researcher of the Chemistry & Industrial Chemical Department at the University of Pisa, Italy. He is a professor (that is to say, a degree superior to a Ph.D. which was introduced in the Italian universities only six years ago). As a teacher Malanga is a prominent figure and for the last fifteen years has taught an average of 200 students per academic year. Malanga has published dozens of works in the international chemical literature, including the UK, with thirty-six publications within the Royal Chemical Society's *Tetrahdron*. As part of his work he has conducted over 800 analyses in the infrared spectrum, so he possesses a more than extensive background in this field. However, in order to correctly analyze the film strip in question, he was assisted by Professor Enzo Benedetti, head of the Chemical Spectroscopic Analysis Department of Pisa University.[1]

Comments by Bob Shell, August 1, 1996.

"What this means in plain English is that this sample matches the specific acetate batches made by Eastman Kodak and used as film base (Kodapak 1, 2, 3 etc). This sample most closely matches Kodapak 4 from the published literature, but examples of Kodapak 3 and 5 are not in the literature. This information has been requested from Kodak (USA and UK) so that a comparison can be made. Also, dates of manufacture of these various types of Polyester must be obtained from Kodak. Bob Shell."[2]

At least the analysis proves the footage was shot on material sold by Kodak before 1956. Since it and a limited "life-time," it was exposed and developed before 1958.

[1]Malanga, Professor Corrado: "Results of Film Testing," University of Pisa, Italy, July 1996.

[2]Shell, Bob: Comments on film test results in a letter to Philip Mantle dated 1 August 1996.

APPENDIX D

Further Medical Opinions

On the Santilli Autopsy Film

Russia:

Professor Anatoli Smolyannikov, surgeon general of the Soviet Army (Russian) from 1989 to 1994:

"The body on the slab doesn't differ considerably from a human creature in appearance, in height and size. However, it has such deviations as a relatively big head and six digits on each of its hands and feet. The only other unusual detail of the autopsy which attracts my attention is the investigation of the (creature's) eyes."

Dr. Sergei Morots, surgeon-pathologist, Russian Academy of Sciences 1976–1993 (various positions), Murmansk Psychiatric Clinic 1993–1996:

"All aspects and details of the (Santilli) film point out that the autopsy was real and it has been conducted by professionals. . . . In my opinion (of course it is not the last point) the lady in the film has human origin in reality."

Norway:

On September 19, 1995, the Santilli autopsy film was shown to two Norwegian pathologists in Oslo. Section leader of the Autopsy Department of one of the main hospitals in Oslo is Dr. Tor Carsten Nygren, who has conducted over 3,500 autopsies, and Dr. Jan Marius Junge (physician and psychiatrist) with many years experience in the same pathological department as Dr. Nygren.

Both physicians commented on various parts of the Santilli autopsy film, and when seeing the brain removed in the film, Dr. Nygren stated, "This is not a human brain. It is completely polished (slippy clean) and much too dark." Both physicians agreed that they did not believe the film was a hoax but would of course not draw any conclusions about the being on the table.

Japan:

On February 2, 1996 the FUJI TV network in Japan aired its own program on the Santilli autopsy film. In its program it showed, for the first time on TV, the so-called "tent footage." Commenting on the tent footage was a former forensic pathologist with the Tokyo Forensic Institute, Dr. Masahiro Ueno.

Dr. Ueno states, *"We see two persons wearing a white over-all. Something is lying on a bed, covered with a sheet. I think the intestines are being extracted. I think it is the intestines. Small intestines. In this case, unlike the dissecting (autopsy) scene, they are not wearing the protective suits. As we see it (the film), they are standing on the left side of the corpse, although usually the doctor stands on the right-hand side. I think they are assistants, and the doctor is standing on the opposite side."*

USA:

Dr. Roger K. Leir, doctor of pediatric medicine,

Thousand Oaks, California:

"... The handling of the alleged body by the individual in my opinion is not an autopsy surgeon but most likely perhaps a general surgeon or someone in a medical speciality. ... I would like to mention the handling of the tissue seems to be real and what I mean by that is that the tissue pressures both from the instrumentation, cutting through the tissue looks like what you see in cutting through normal tissue, not through pieces of rubber, silicone or other artificial materials. ... the other things in the film, for example, if you run it in slow motion at a frame at a time in the beginning when he is looking at the body in general and flexing the knee you can see that the thigh externally rotates and he would have to be a pretty smart director to have the services of a physiologist and God knows what other expertise to build a dummy so that there is external rotation of the thigh during flexing of the knee. ..."

At the request of Bob Shell, a number of physicians have been asked to comment on the Santilli autopsy film. At their request their identities are being kept confidential. The comments they have had to make are as follows:

" ... In the dissection of the thorax, the surgeon exposes a mediastinal structure located in the left midline of the anterior mediastinum. He then opens it in the left anterolateral aspect of the structure and removes a structure through which he inserts a finger. This looks remarkably similar to exposing the left side of the heart. The position of his cardiac incision would place it in the vicinity of the mitral valve. The structure that is removed is most likely the valve. It appears of unknown material as nothing else in the mediastinum is of the same reflectivity. The surgeon also makes special note of it in his handling. Its shape and the fact that it separates from the other tissues so easily is suggestive that it is a prosthetic valve. The aorta is then severed in clear focus.

"In the opening of the cranial vault, the duramater is shown being opened with Metzenbaum scissors and the cerebrum then removed. This is seen collapsing in the pan under its own weight as you would expect in a human specimen. In the pan the surrounding dura and arachnoid membranes are seen. The question of what is the upper abdominal mass still remains. It may represent an enlarged lobe of the liver. After the mediastinal structures are removed, the surgeon removed a structure in the left upper abdominal quadrant by severing two small vascular pedicles. This is very suggestive of the spleen. So far, based on these assumptions I feel that the film is highly suggestive of human anatomy with many anatomical relationships maintained. Obviously more footage would be a great benefit. As to the origin or nature of the specimen I don't know."

"Basically, it doesn't surprise me that a surgeon describes the contents of the thorax/abdomen as at least humanoid and possibly even ... highly suggestive of human anatomy with many anatomical relationships maintained ... After all, as many of the critics have already pointed out ad nauseum, the body, whatever it is, is very humanoid in appearance. The question is what do we do with the fragments of information we have? Or, in modus Sherlocki, what is impossible and what is possible?

"I think we can begin by saying that there must be a physical relationship, however distant, between the entity on the table and the entities watching the film. At least in terms of appearance it is certainly at the very least as similar to us as we are to chimps, for example, and we and chimps share around 98% genetic code. If the organs have the same shape, consistency, position and size this would seem to give another strong indicator in this direction. I'd be quite willing to be proved wrong on this one, but if it doesn't originate on earth I think the odds against independent parallel development producing results that similar are pretty massive. The next question is, what is the physical relationship, given that it exists? The possible hypotheses range from mundane to outrageous."

"The brain does look a bit odd as it is removed from the calvarium. The film shows the cerebrum removed and handed off with what looks like the arachnoid layer still adherent. What appears to be numerous vessels on the meninges can also be seen. Sulci and gyri are not seen. Later, the dissector reaches into and removes another structure that would correspond to the cerebellum and brain stem that do show some gyri. I don't know what to make of this. If this were a child I would speculate that hydro-

cephalus may have caused the lack of these surface details but I don't think that we are looking at a child. Another possibility would be hypertrophy of the cerebrum. (As to could this be a visitor from an evolved human or hybrid with these neurologic changes, got me!) One thing in the dissection of the head that I did not see is that there is a significant dural sinus in the midline of humans and almost every animal that I have seen. This was absent on the specimen that was dissected. Oh, in regards to the lack of scars. The thing that is removed from the mediastinum looks very much like a prosthetic valve to me. I showed the tape to a friend who is a cardiothorasic surgeon, and he felt that if you had a normal valve and removed it with some tissue surrounding the annulus that it might have the appearance of the one in the film. Thank you for the information on the suits! It makes sense that they are fueling suits or fire fighting gear."

"Responding to a question about the tube that is seen being cut, and could it be the esophagus or trachea instead of the aorta, since no blood flows out when it is cut: I really don't think that it is the esophagus, for the following reasons. First there is a shot that shows the tubular structure arising from what appears to be an anterior mediastinal mass which I believe to be the heart. Also, the aorta is relatively thick and maintains its shape secondary to its strong muscular media. An argument could be made that as this structure is anterior in the mediastinum that it may be the trachea, however no ring structures are seen. Furthermore the tracheal rings are incomplete. They are open posteriorly where there is a common party wall with the esophagus. This structure is clearly round. Lastly, the esophagus in both the in-vivo and post-mortem state is flat. It lacks a serosal layer to maintain its shape. It only assumes a round tubular shape when it becomes distended with air or a food bolus. Lastly, the esophagus is extremely thin also because of a lack of this serosal layer and is relatively difficult to dissect free from the deep cervical fascia.

"As to the lack of blood, there is oozing from the cadaver as the skin incisions are made. This is not uncommon in the early to middle post-mortem state. Blood becomes pooled in the venous sinusoids in the skin and cutaneous tissue where at first clotting

occurs. As the body cools, calcium sequestion occurs resulting in clot lysis and oozing. In addition, at this time some liquification necrosis may occur, also accounting for this. The lack of blood in the "aorta" may be due to removal of clot prior to our visualization as no clot is seen to be removed from what appears to be the heart.

"Looking at the tape it is hard to analyze as it seems we only see what we want to see. I asked one of our visiting research fellows to view the tape and he concluded many of the same points. He has also suggested that when the structure which we are calling spleen is removed, there may be a structure similar to a pancreas visible although I have a hard time discerning this. Our general opinion is that this specimen is anatomically very similar to a human with gross morphometric anomalies. This is a broad statement that can go many ways but either this is indeed real, an extremely competent attempt to replicate human anatomy in an altered fashion, or an undescribed syndrome. I continue to be happily encouraged by the number of people who I show this to who are initially extremely skeptical but who then offer similar conclusions on anatomic details."

"Recently, a question arose as to the identity of the anterior mediastinal structure that is shown to be cut early in the dissection process. At present I feel that this most likely represents the aorta if some of the other human anatomic relations hold. I base this on the following points. The structure is relatively thick-walled, suggestive of a strong media and that it appears to enter a structure in which I believe a valve is removed as demonstrated by the dissector inserting his finger into it. The tubular structure does not show any ring structure or any posterior wall flattening that would be consistent with trachea. Furthermore, the esophagus lacking a serosa is flat in the in-vivo and postmortem state and I would not expect it that anterior."

"Just a quick question on the Santilli film. In Europe the film has been 'written off' by the mainstream media on the basis of some doctor who claims to have 'proven' that the body is simply a young, female progeria sufferer.

"Frankly, even to the casual observer and on the basis of the

photos they actually published with the articles on this new angle, I think the whole theory is a load of hooey. Progeria patients look about as much like the entity in the film as my Aunty Ros looks like Jimmy Durante. What I don't understand, again, is that people seem to be buying it. They look at the photos and say, yes, of course. This is totally, totally weird. Are they literally not seeing what is before their eyes? Puts a whole new angle on 'The Emperor's New Clothes.'"

Responding to my comments on progeria:

" . . . I agree with you that the progeria argument is without basis. As a disease of early degeneration, patients with progeria have at first a normal appearance following which their normal anatomy just assumes a more aged appearance. This would not account for polydactily and the significant enlargement of the calvarium seen in the tape.

"It has always amazed me that the anatomy of mammals is so similar with the same set of organs attached the same way doing the similar functions. With slight modifications these organ systems can be applied to reptiles, etc. The specimen that is dissected to me at least clearly shows mammalian if not human anatomy. When I reviewed congenital syndromes I did not find any that would give the phenotype of the specimen being dissected. I would like to think that it would be unnecessary to have to prove the authenticity of the film. However, there seems to be so much unwillingness of government agencies and press to disclose or openly discuss possibilities of UFOs that it may take undeniable evidence to prompt their action. This film I hope may be the start of a movement towards disclosure at least to bring the issues out further in the press. "Oh, before I forget, both congenital and sporadic cases of progeria maintain normal skeletal development. . . ."

" . . . I think that if we first assume that we are viewing the dissection of an individual afflicted by a genetic syndrome, a logical question would be why it is necessary to perform the postmortem using protective suits. Secondly, when looking at the specimen many developmental anomalies are clearly seen before the dissection begins. These include: hypotelorism, bilateral microtia, maxillary hypoplasia, mandibular hypoplasia, calvarial bossing, polydactily, etc. The subject must then have lived to at least prepuberty and obtained age-appropriate stature. These specific anomalies do not correspond to any known syndromes, either genetic or developmental. Spontaneous mutations can occur however again though I know of no report cases.

"In regards to the question if this is a 'dummy' or some device constructed to fool us: The oozing seen upon incision is very consistent with a fresh, hours to few days postmortem examination. In particular, footage showing the peeling back of the pericranium to expose the periosteum is very similar to that of standard surgical procedure, as is the remainder of the craniotomy. From my experience, these particular areas which are seen relatively clearly are consistent with a real specimen as opposed to a constructed device. The picture quality of the remainder of the film is without adequate quality to determine further. On of many things about the dissection that bothers me is that when the corneal shields are removed, the eyes are in upward gaze. In an acute fatal injury, the eyes remain fixed in near normal gaze. As we fall asleep or loose consciousness gradually, the eyes roll upward to protect the cornea (modified Bell's phenomenon). This is in no way absolute, but it suggest that the specimen expired either while asleep or unconscious after its injury. . . ."

" . . . I ran a copy of the tape by one of my associates who is a general surgeon also presently on a research rotation. He agreed that the specimen appeared as a fresh dissection specimen would appear. In regards to the abdominal anatomy, it was his opinion that what I thought to be the spleen may be in fact a stomach with significant gastric contents. He based this on its position and the presence of the vascular pedicles. He also pointed out that in one view there appears to be almost two stomachs with very little intestines and mesentary visible. Given that this was seen for only a few views he could not say for sure. Again, I don't know what all this means. I am more and more convinced that we are seeing something real dissected, the implications of which I find amazing. . . ."

APPENDIX E

Discussion of Debris Details: "Santilli Alien Dissection Film," by Dennis W. Murphy

I would like to present some observations on the "Santilli Alien Dissection Film," specifically the "Debris" footage portion of the film that shows the two tables with the "Panels" on the table on the right and the H-beams on the table on the left. These observations are based on the Fox video "Alien Autopsy—Fact or Fiction?" and several framed grabbed images from the "Roswell Footage LTD" video. These comments were initially offered up for discussion in the CompuServe Encounters Forum, section 15—MUFON.

The "Santilli Film" is either a scripted fictional film or film documentation of a real event. In my mind the film exists as both a very elaborate hoax and a real event. Some of my observations are based on the assumption that the "debris" are real and some are based on the assumption that the film was hoaxed. As of the writing of this presentation the "Santilli Film" has not been conclusively proved a fake or a real event.

I have an A.S. degree in Marine Diving Technology from Santa Barbara City College. My commercial diving experience was geared toward the offshore oil industry. One of my skills as a diver was welding. My welding experience involved stick arc, brazing, MIG (Metal Inert Gas), resistance, friction and TIG (Tungsten Inert Gas) processes. I have welded materials as thin as $1/16$-inch aluminum and laid down welds to fillet a three-inch steel beam. I have taken a course on magnetic particle and ultrasonic weld inspection at the Welding Institute in Cambridge, England. I have had a machine shop course where I learned to use metal lathes, precision grinders, milling machines and drill presses. Currently, my company "Murphy Studio Furniture" designs and markets studio furniture layouts to radio stations nationwide using Autocad. The ergonomic layout of the "Panels" and the possible proof that life exists on other planets or dimensions were the original sparks that ignited my interest in the Santilli Film. I am not a Ufologist, but I have always been intrigued with the UFO sightings reports and the movies they have spawned.

H-BEAMS DETAILS

An H-beam has two flanges that are connected by the web. The first anomalous detail is found at the root portions of the H-beams. The root is where the web meets the flanges at a right angle. What I do not see at these locations on the H-beams is a radius. You would have a radius at that point (the root) to prevent cracks from forming. Any material that I know of, that has a crystalline structure, will develop cracks if two planes meet at right angles. I am assuming from the appearance of the break in the H-beams that the material has a crystalline structure.

The second detail is the thickness of the web, in relation to the thickness of the flanges. I have not seen an H-beam that has a web that is as thick as the ones in the Santilli film as compared to the thickness of the flange faces. I have never seen anything that resembles the manufacturing technique used in the construction of the H-Beams in the Santilli film wreck debris footage. I know of no manufacturing process that could produce the multitude of details found on the H-beams.

DEBRIS MANUFACTURING OPTIONS

Milling. Could the beams have been milled? When milling something you start with a block of solid chunk of material and remove everything except that which you need. Milling would be a good option if it were not for the thinness of some of the beams and the raised letters on both sides of the beams. When milling, the cutting tool is forced against the material. If the material is thin, especially at a root meeting at acute right angles, the force of the tool against the material will cause it to break. The raised lettering would have to be done with a very precise CNC (computer numeric control) machine. When I look at the lettering I see precise rounds as parts of the symbols. I do not think that you can do this with current milling machines. Extrusion. Extrusion is out again because of the acute right angles of the roots and the raised lettering. There are some H-beams in the film that have more than two right-angled roots. The raised lettering would be impossible.

Rolling. Rolling is out because of the acute right-angle roots and raised symbols. Rolling implies that the final material shape is formed by passing hot material back and forth through rollers. Again if there are acute right angles the material will break at the root during manufacturing. To form the raised symbols the hot material would have to be passed through rollers with the symbols engraved into them. This would mean you would only be allowed one pass through the rollers and you would have to keep the rollers clean through-out the run. The detailed definition of the symbols would argue against this as a possibility.

Molding and Casting. At first glance molding or casting would seem the only way to make the H-beams and the panels. Molding and casting fall apart for a number of reasons. The things that argue against the molding are the apparent lack of weight for all the pieces that get moved around, the acute right angles at the roots, the thinness of the flanges of the H-beams and the finely detailed definition of the raised symbols. The detail of the symbols on two sides of the H-beams would mean that if the H-beams were molded or cast you would have to use a very high density material to get the detail exhibited in the raised symbols. High density means that the pieces would be much heavier than the indicated weight (the way in which the panels are handled). The H-beams are handled many times and there are several times when a piece is held in one hand by pinching it between the thumb and fingers. The material that the H-beams are made of appears to be very rigid and does not show any indication of bending while being handled in this manner.

Laser Milling. Now this might be a valid process to form these H-beams if it was not for the super-smooth appearance on the flat surfaces. The raised symbols have many multifaceted details that exhibit a smooth fine finish to tiny areas of their facets as well. I think all these surfaces including the ones in the symbols are too smooth for laser milling.

Foam Core. I could see the stuff being made of foam core paperboard to solve the weight issue, but the following reasons argue against foam core:

The symbols are present on both sides of the webbing on the H-beams. The crystalline nature of the break in the broken beams. The reflectivity of the material in the break. The rigidity of the H-beams.

When considering any of the above-mentioned processes one must think of cost. I do not see how any of the above-mentioned processes would work, and if they could be made to work, who would spend enough money to make them work. If you could produce this type of detail with some process, you would be making money on producing things that would reap far greater profits than an Alien Dissection hoax film.

FILM DETAILS

There is a small H-beam that has been broken. The broken end is on the right. The break goes right through one of the symbols. The break is not straight. The break would have been straight if it had not broken in the middle of one of the symbols. You can clearly see that the fracture line starts straight down (perpendicular to the flange faces) the face of the web of the beam until it gets to the raised symbol. The fracture line then shifts just to the right of a raised portion of a symbol. The fracture line skirts the raised portion of the symbol and then it jumps back to the left and continues down to the next flange face. The reason that the fracture line would take this course is because it is the path of least resistance for the fracture. When the fracture line encountered the raised symbol, which can be thought of as increased thickness of the H-beam at that point, the fracture line shifts away from the thicker material. You would have to be looking at the debris footage to understand this fine a point. It is a very small detail, minute, but this is the type of detail that says this

is a for real fracture in a for real manufactured H-beam. I cannot imagine someone planning to put such a small detail in a hoax film. One of the H-beams I reviewed was about 5 cm from flange to flange. This is one of the smaller H-beams. I noticed that it had a melted circular-shaped puddle on the left end (it was orientated with the symbols going from left to right). I have seen this puddle shape before in melted aluminum. The thing that caught my eye was that the puddle had collapsed and the puddled area appeared thinner than the unmelted part of the H-beam in the same area. An analogy would be if you took a thin piece of Styrofoam sheet and heated the sheet with a flame just enough in one area so that the foam lost its trapped air form. When the area cooled off it would be thinner than the rest of the Styrofoam sheet (meaning lost volume in that area) but it would still weigh the same.

There are a lot of melted looking pieces of debris on the table. The large blobs of debris material seen on the table look like puddles that formed when the debris material melted. The curious thing about some of the smaller melted pieces is the shape they took after they cooled. What catches my eye is the thickness of the puddles. The surface tension was strong enough to counter gravity, making some of the smaller pieces thick. Think of small drops of water in a clean pan. If the drops are small you get a fairly round droplet. But as you increase the size of the droplet by adding more fluid, the droplet starts to flatten out and turn into a puddle because gravity pulls on the center of the droplet and forces it down. A water droplet turns into a thin puddle. In order to keep the appearance of the debris droplets round and thick, the material would have to have a very high surface tension or be really light or be really viscous. The debris objects maintain consistent appearance characteristics in the "look" of the way they melted and cooled.

There are large puddles of melted looking debris on the right and left side of the table on the left. The puddle on the right appears to be a melted H-beam because it has a hemispherical ridge running through the center of it. This detail matches hemispherical ridges found on one flange face of all the other H-beams. The puddle on the left end of the table does not have a ridge detail like the one on the right. I am not sure if it is a piece of material that was sheetlike or if it is just another puddle. It looks as if there is the reflection of a face in the left puddle in about the nine-o'clock position.

The raised symbols communicate some type of writing. Each symbol has a myriad of details and appears to be machine perfect. The symbols are located on the web of the H-beams and are the same symbols on both sides, except they are in reverse order. I cannot think of a harder detail to want to undertake from a time and money standpoint if this is a hoax. The symbols do not look phoney to me.

The detail that puzzles me most is the lack of mass that the panels and H-beams exhibit when they are moved. I cannot think of a material I have handled or seen handled that would be this light, exhibit properties of rigidity, reflectivity and the ability to show fine detail. I get the impression from watching the film that these things are so light that the only thing that impedes their movement is air resistance. Anything structural that exhibits a lack of starting and stopping momentum that these objects exhibit must be very light.

The soldier handles the large H-beam by squeezing the flanges between his thumb and fingers. Most of the time he holds the H-beam with two hands. There are several instances, including one where the large H-beam is held vertically and he is only holding on to the H-beam with one hand. The way in which the solider handles the large H-beam with a couple of fingers says that this H-beam is very light. Here is a problem for the hoaxer. The bigger H-beam would have to be made out of some type of foam to make it as light as it appears. Foam that is as thin as that on the large H-beam flanges would flex if it was twisted, squeezed or handled like the soldier does in the film. This stuff is so reflective, you would see it bend, especially if you pinched it between two fingers at the very edge of the flange faces. This stuff appears to be real stiff.

The soldier handles the large H-beam with two hands most of the time so he is sure he will not drop it. When the soldier holds the H-beam with two hands it has nothing to do with the weight of the H-beam. When he transfers the large H-beam from hand to hand, the receiving hands never drop or twist like they would if these H-beams weighed anything. The best example of this is when the large H-beam is held vertically.

The panels exhibit the same weight qualities as the big H-beam. I have made a list of the details of these "panels" with the six-fingered hand impressions. I am attaching an addendum to this presentation that describes those details. One of the interesting things about the "panels" is that they were all different. It was a nice "touch" to make all the panels different from one another if this is a hoax. If they are props then the prop maker had to make three different molds. Two for the undamaged panels and one for the damaged panel.

The item that gave me some indication that the panels could be props was that they never showed the backside of the undamaged panels. If the panels were hollow it would make the prop maker's job much simpler.

I tried to think of a test that would prove that the panels were hollow and had no back. I looked for something like seeing the soldier's fingers curl up inside a panel as he was handling them. I went through the footage frame by frame over and over. It always looked to me like his fingers never go up inside the backs of the panels, in fact I think I see just the opposite.

I did see something that I think proves that the panels have a backside that is as reflective as the front side. It is a detail that is hard to catch because of where it happens in the video.

As you are watching the video, the entity dissection ends and the wreck debris footage starts. The soldier is handling the forward most undamaged panel. The lighting is coming in from the right side of the table. The shadows from the panels on the table indicate to me that there are two light sources separated by a foot or so. Just as the guy sets that forward most complete panel down on the table you can see the light reflecting off the table, onto the back of the panel and then back onto the table. If you look closely you can see that there must be a shiny surface that reflects the light from the surface of the table back down to the surface of the table and that this reflecting surface must be located on the underside of the panel.

Tying The Debris Footage to the Dissection Footage and the Cameraman's Statement

The "panels" that have indentations for the six-fingered hands in the debris footage are the most obvious link to the dissection footage that features an entity with the six fingered hands. The dissection shows how the SUE's (Santilli Unidentified Entity) bodies are put together, the debris show the workings of the entity's mind. What I would like to do now is to tie the debris footage to the entity in the dissection footage. To do this I would like to present a chain of logic that fits a consistent theme I see reoccurring throughout both the debris and dissection footages.

I used the Fox video "Alien Autopsy—Fact or Fiction," several framed images from the Roswell Footage LTD video and the "Cameraman's Statement." The "Cameraman's Statement" is the story that explains when, where and why the Santilli film was shot. This was the story given to Ray Santilli by the cameraman, the person who shot all the footage in the Santilli film.

I am impressed by the reflectivity of all the debris and the panels. Why would you make something so reflective? I see two initial options to explain this reflectivity. The first is that the debris material naturally happened to have a high reflectivity. The second option would be that you wanted the debris to be very reflective, so you would pick a highly reflective material to make the debris.

Let's think about the second option. You have a creature with very large eyes and pink skin. The entity has contact lenses that are very dark. I am assuming that these contacts are sunglasses for a world that is brighter than its home environment. These details indicate that this creature came from somewhere with less light than our planet.

Let's think for a moment what requirements a low light environment might place on a technologically advanced species. By looking closely at the panels we find that there are twenty raised buttons per hand or forty raised buttons per panel. When the hands are placed in the hand positions of the panels, there are fourteen raised buttons in constant contact with each hand. The raised buttons are situated so that there are eight buttons that touch the base of the fingers and the palm of the hand only. It's like these eight raised buttons are not there to be pushed because they are situated in the palms and at the base of the fingers. So if these eight buttons are not there to be pushed by the hand then they must be there to push against the hand.

When we look at the H-beams we see raised symbols and keyed type detail such as the raised hemispherical ridge that runs along the middle of one of the flange faces. All this tells me that these SUEs used a form of

Braille. They appear to be very tactile creatures. The panels were not only keyboards, they appear to be a tactile interface.

A human hand is fairly sensitive and can feel something as small as .001 of an inch (.0025 cm). I would guess that the SUE's hands were less sensitive than human hands. I base this opinion on the size of the panel buttons and on the size of the raised symbols on the I-beams. Compared to Braille these features appear very course.

Other Details

The debris footage looks as if shot in a tent. The tent is seen to billow in and out. The tent pole that has the gas mask hanging from it moves when the walls of the tent move. This detail would indicate that this tent was set up outside and not on some sound stage. The soldier holding the debris for the cameraman has large sweat stains around his armpits. This would tie in with the cameraman's story that states that the film was shot in the desert in the month of June.

The debris materials look manufactured because they have a radius at the ends of the flanges, machine produced raised symbols, fracture lines and highly uniform reflectivity.

What these small details argue for is a unique material with special properties. Let me list a few of what I would call unique properties.

The material appears to melt, but it does not appear to be burnt. I do not see any oxidation on the melted stuff. When the stuff breaks it does not bend or shatter. I do not see anything that is bent. I see only fractures along a jagged line.

The puddle of stuff on the left side of the left table has the same reflectivity as the unmelted stuff. What tells me this? You can see the reflection of a man's face in about the nine-o'clock position of this puddle.

Conclusion

The Santilli footage consists of four different films that include the debris footage, the tent footage, and the dissections of two different entities. Every detail that is put in a hoax film costs money and increases the risk of exposure as a fraud. It would seem that if this film was a hoax that there would be as little detail as possible. There is enough detail in the debris footage to convince me that it would be expensive to produce. If this film is a hoax it was well researched, elaborately scripted and was therefore an expensive undertaking.

"Santilli Film" Panels Debris Observations

The panels are about $1\frac{1}{2}$ inches thick, are 25 inches wide at the top of the panel and 20 inches wide at the bottom of the panel.

The panels appear to be really light. My guess is that they weigh less than two pounds. The panels have six sides. I would label the six sides as follows. Imagine putting a panel on a table with the hand indentations on top. The hands in the panels are orientated as you would lay your hands in them with the left hand on the left and the right hand on the right.

The face that the hands are in I would call the Hands Face.

The face that was against the table I would call the Bottom Face.

Going clockwise around the perimeter starting at the top at twelve o'clock, I would call that the Top Side. At three o'clock would come the Right Side. At six o'clock would come the Bottom Side, and at nine o'clock would come the Left Side.

The sides are perpendicular to the top and bottom faces. The edges where the sides meet the top and bottom faces of the panels have a $\frac{3}{16}$ inches quarter round radius on the edges. The panels are curved slightly in an ergonomic manner, "curved" meaning arced slightly.

The panels have a skin or what might be called a shell that appears to be about $\frac{3}{16}$ inch thick. You can see this in the edge view of the broken panel. The skin of the panels appears to have a shiny metallic crystalline composition. It appears crystalline from the jagged way the panel broke.

The panels are not identical.

There are six-fingered hand indentations in the panel's Hands Face.

The panel indentations appear to be cast. They are not stamped because the wrist area indentation protrudes down into the bottom side. They are not milled because from the side view of the broken panel the skin appears to be of a uniform thickness. I would guess that the panels are custom-fitted to the individual who was to use that particular panel.

There are raised buttons in the hand indentations and in a row above the tips of the finger indentations. Let's call this the first row.

The left and right hands are not the same size in a given panel. It appears that the left hand has longer fingers and a longer palm indentation than the right hand in the same panel. It appears that the left hand in the other panel also has the left hand longer than the right hand. You can also look at how close the top indentation comes to the top side of the panels. In at least two of the panels this top row left indentation is closer to the top side of the panel than the top row of the right-side indentation.

The left and right hands are not symmetrical in layout of the buttons in the hands.

There are four raised buttons on the panels in the palms of the hands. One button is located where the heel of human hand would be. One button is located in the center of the palm in line with the outside base of the thumb. Two buttons are in a row straddling the center of the palm and in line with the inside base of the thumb. This layout appears to be the same from hand to hand and from panel to panel.

There are four raised buttons just below the point where the base of the fingers meets with the palm of the hand.

There are five raised buttons, one at the tip of each of the five fingers.

There appear to be different numbers of buttons in the first row arc indentation just above the finger tip indentations. I count five buttons on one in the right hand and six buttons on the left hand in one of the panels. In another panel I count six buttons in the top row on the right hand and three buttons in the top row of the left hand.

The panels are hollow or what I would call chambered at the top. The chambers are separated by a $\frac{3}{16}$-inch wall and run from left to right of the panels. There are three chambers. The first chambered area is formed and starts at the inside of the panel's skin at the top side of the panel and goes to a chamber wall that follows the indentation arc that follows the bottom edge of the top row. The second chamber starts after the $\frac{3}{16}$-inch wall that follows the arc of the bottom of the top row and stops at a wall that follows the arc of the very tips of the fingers. The third chamber starts on the other side of the second wall and ends at a wall the follows the arc of what would be on a human hand the row of first fingertip joints. The buttons appear to be centered in the chambers. These observations are based on the side view of the broken panel.

Below the chambered area the panels are filled with a dark substance that has some light colored stringy stuff mixed in with the dark stuff. From the way the dark stuff broke I would say it was hard, not soft or mushy.

INSIDE THE ALIEN SPACECRAFT: PERFECTLY FUNCTIONAL APPARATUS WITH INTERACTIVE LINK TO A CENTRAL COMPUTER.

By Adriano Forgione and Cristoforo Barbato, Centro Ufological Nazionale (C.U.N.), Naples, Italy

The Santilli autopsy footage is the target for researchers to define its originality and authenticity. Our investigation is dedicated to the control panels shown in the debris section of the footage. We have separated this investigation into two parts: the first one of an anatomical type, the second of a technological type.

Anatomical Characteristics of the Control Panels

The panels depicted in the Santilli debris footage are three in number and appear to be very light in weight and can be easily lifted using just one hand, this in spite of the apparent remarkable size and dimension of the panels and its apparent metallic composition. The panels are a solid structure having four sides, whose upper surfaces have two marked "hand prints" in relief. Right and left hands each with six fingers.

There are also three "bows" above the hand prints, one above the other, forming a double bow shape above the hand prints, while the third is near the thumb area. Every one of these bow-shaped marks is complemented with a number of raised areas rather like "buttons." These "buttons" could well be "digital sensors." Four of these sensors are positioned on the palm of each hand print, one on the thumb, five on the bow above the fingers, and a variable number from four to seven in the longer bow.

Two of the control panels are apparently undamaged in the film. They appear almost as if they were constructed for ease of removal. Only one of the three panels is damaged. This enables us to look at the cross section of the panel's construction. Looking closely at this damaged panel, we can see what appears to be "white cables" or something similar, which emanate from inside of the panel exactly in line with the digital sensors. This takes us to believe that the control panels function as a kind of control mechanism linked to a central apparatus or computer.

At this point we must try and understand how such "orders" from the control panels could be linked to a computer and how they in fact worked. It is quite possible that we can compare these panels with a kind of "anatomical keyboard" linked to a central computer which in turn controls the total working of the vehicle (UFO).

The keyboards could be used in the following way:

The hands are placed into the hand-print areas on the panels, and increasing the pressure on various parts of the hand or fingers activates certain commands. To activate the censors contained within the bow shapes above the hands, one would have to remove the hand from the hand print area. It is possible that the bow closer to the fingers is used for making frequent commands. This sounds like a complex technological piece of hardware but we will see that it might not be so. . . . By measuring the angles of the hand prints and fingers we can see that they are positioned in the correct anatomical position, which would ensure easy access to the panels and surrounding censors.

Technological Characteristics of the Control Panels

A possible confirmation of the function of these panels and their advanced technology comes from the USA, where an important hardware and software company, Data Hand System of Scottsdale, Arizona have projected and produced a new and revolutionary computer keyboard that does not require movement of the hands, but only the fingers. The hands are placed in two anatomical hand-shaped guides very similar in appearance to the panels depicted in the Santilli film.

In this way every finger controls a certain amount of keys, moving in a variety of directions with varying degrees of pressure applied. Data Hand System states that this keyboard will guarantee a stress reduction of 96% compared to traditional computer keyboards.

Modern technology currently at use in various air forces exhibit some apparatus that could reflect the working of the control panels in the Santilli film. In fact, we have determined that such technology is already at work. For example; this same system is used in aircraft such as the "AWACS" (Airborne Warning And Control System). Part of the AWACS system consists of nine consoles called "SDC" (Situation Display Console). Every console imparts a variety of data and instructions for the crew, permitting every operator to work with different data. The SDC consoles are linked in a series, by an interface connection with a unique central computer forming an interactive homogeneous system. The central computer gives an overall figure of the large mass of data elaborated by every single SDC console. This function could be the same as used by the "alien space craft" whose control panels are depicted in the Santilli film.

Adriano Forgione and Cristoforo Barbato,
February 1996

APPENDIX F

Roadmap of "Alien Autopsy" Film

by Bob Shell

The purpose of this preliminary study of the film is to provide some useful information which I hope will be helpful to others in making their own evaluations. Consider it a "roadmap" with travel notes as you look at the film. I have remarked on points of particular interest to me and have indicated their location on the tape of the second autopsy. My time index begins with the first actual film frame on the video, and others should be able to use my index numbers to locate the points I am calling attention to. When referring to directions, all references to left and right are the creature's left and right; except when otherwise noted. I have tried to avoid technical terms as much as possible, but a few were inevitable, and I hope are not confusing. I have used terms which would apply to a human or mammal body, but it must be remembered that this is not a human or mammal body, so these terms will be approximations rather than accurate descriptions. For the purpose of this report, I have assumed that this is a real non-human body, but I ask that you look at the film and my comments and make your own decisions, as this point is by no means fully established.

I have referred to the man who appears to be in charge as the "surgeon" and his assistant as the "doctor", although it is unclear if the assistant is the same person throughout, since there is a third person in the room at times who also seems to be assisting.

When I use the term "break in film" this does not refer to a physical break but to a noticeable change of camera position in an otherwise continuous roll of film. It is my speculation that some of these breaks were made by the cameraman so that he could change his position for a better view. Others, made for no apparent reason, may have been pauses to allow still photography to be done. I would appreciate any feedback, comments, criticisms of this report, which I stress is a preliminary document.

00:00-First images. Camera pointed at floor, moves up to creature's head, on creature's left side. In this brief opening sequence the steel frame support for the autopsy table is clearly visible, as well as the drain pan on the floor underneath. The pan appears to be pretty empty at this time. As camera moves up from the floor a wall-mounted electrical outlet can be seen on right. It is a horizontal type mounted on the wall, not recessed into it.

00:02-Creature's head just comes into frame. Camera moves to show head and torso of creature. In the background, against the far wall is a small table covered with a white cloth. On this table is a Bunsen burner (not lighted) with a flask stand next to it, two metal bowls, a test tube rack with what appears to be five test tubes in it, two of them with stoppers, a large beaker half filled with a dark fluid, a large flask, and some other glassware.

00:06-Camera pans down body. Dark area, perhaps a bruise is seen on the side where lower edge if rib cage would be on a human. Another "bruise" can be seen just above the iliac area. The cameraman walks around the body in a clockwise direction, showing the left thigh which appears to be badly bruised and swollen. In this and subsequent scenes, the creature's distended belly is quite striking, and there is no evidence that I can see of a navel.

00:09-As cameraman comes around the body, it can be clearly seen that the right hand is almost completely severed at the wrist, and appears to be held on only by a strip of skin. The wound in the right thigh is also clearly seen in this sequence.

00:11-Wound under right armpit is clearly seen.

00:12-A "bruise" is visible on the right side in exactly the same place as on the left side. May not be bruises, but some natural pigmentation or organ of the creature.

00:13-Cameraman begins to circle back around in the opposite direction, at which time you can see that the thigh wound is a penetrating wound with a smaller "entry wound" on the outer side of the thigh.

00:17-Drain holes in table clearly visible as cameraman shows close views of legs and feet.

00:23-Chest or cooler visible under the table holding the tray of surgical instruments.

00:25-Electrical outlet behind table seen, same as one mentioned earlier. Clock is plugged into this one.

00:29-As camera is pointed more upwards, clock and microphone are seen for the first time. Clock shows 10:06.

00:35-Starting with close-up of head from right side the cameraman circles around the body again.

01:01-Surgeon appears for first time. Comes in from the right. Begins examining creature's head and neck.

01:16-Break in film—surgeon now on opposite side of creature, feeling neck with left hand while holding head with right hand. Man behind window appears to be watching intently.

01:25-Surgeon looks into mouth for six seconds, points to mouth and speaks into microphone emphatically. Looks again, points again, and appears to be talking to someone on opposite side of table. It is important to note that this man I am calling the surgeon, who appears to be in charge, has some very characteristic hand gestures, including an emphatic, stabbing motion when pointing things out. This may help establish his identity.

01:43-Break in film-surgeon lifts and flexes injured leg which seems to be slightly stiff. Looks hard at wound.

01:53-Roll of film ends in whiteout. This is characteristic of the Bell & Howell Filmo 70 cameras which often come to a stop with the shutter open.

01:55-Next roll starts. Now two people visible in room. Camera on left side of table looking across creature. One, apparently the original surgeon (based on his gestures), studies leg wound intently, then indicates by gesture and comments directed to the microphone where the dissection will be made. Clock on wall reads 10:20.

02:25-Surgeon feels over abdomen, perhaps trying to determine cause of distension, while making comments into microphone.

02:41-Surgeon points to something on right side of creature's head out of camera range and speaks about it. Clock reads 10:23.

02:44-Break in film—view from foot of table. Surgeon pulls pubic slit open, looks intently inside, speaks toward man behind glass who responds to the comments. Man behind glass glances down periodically during this sequence as though making notes. Pubic slit examination can not be seen clearly because the surgeon's hands and arm are in the way, but careful examination of single frames seems to indicate that the area inside the upper part of the slit is featureless and smooth. This requires additional study.

03:20-Surgeon returns to leg wound and moves his hand around top of it while making comments toward the microphone. Appears to be describing wound. Second doctor appears at foot of table.

03:30-Surgeon again feels abdomen while talking to second doctor. Appears to be describing the planned dissection procedure.

03:36-Second doctor points to pubic slit with odd hand motion. Holds hand palm up, folds all fingers

except pinkie, and points with that. (Who points like this?? Gesture looks very odd to me.)

03:37-Break in film.

03:38-Close-up from bottom of table looking at wound. Surgeon has scissors and forceps (Someone has said that he holds the scissors wrong, but I have no idea what they are talking about. He holds them the same way I always did when making dissections, just the ordinary way you pick up scissors when cutting paper or cloth. I can't see how else you could hold them.) Surgeon lifts what appears to be burned skin tissue at top of wound with forceps and begins to snip off a sample with scissors.

03:59-Break in film—slightly closer view from left side of table as tissue is cut.

04:01-Break in film—still closer view from across table. Tissue sample is lifted and deposited in glass container resembling a very deep Petri dish which appears to have some liquid in it.

04:05-Break in film—view from over surgeon's left shoulder as he inspects the burned tissue around the top of the "entry wound" on the outer side of the right thigh, moving the tissue with his forceps. Looks as though he is about to cut a sample with the scissors but changes his mind. Interior of wound shows odd looking, spongy, shiny tissue under muscles. This is not seen very clearly, but can possibly be enhanced for detail.

04:11-Roll of film ends in whiteout.

04:17-Next roll begins. View from left of table looking toward head of table. Semi close-up as surgeon lifts hand of creature and describes. Then moves down body to left foot and points out six toes while speaking. (An odd point: There is no view from the head of the table of the surgeon holding the hand. Yet one of the stills from Merlin's web page clearly shows this. Why is it not here? Perhaps this is accounted for by the fact that this video is one minute and fifteen seconds shorter than the stated 18 minutes length.)

04:26-Break in film—view from left of table looking toward feet. Surgeon points to features of foot while speaking and gesturing to second doctor. Foot clearly has six toes, and human-like toenails.

04:34-Break in film—close-up side view of creature's head and neck from left, low angle. Surgeon begins first cut behind left ear, down neck and across upper chest. Then cuts down center of abdomen. This is a superficial cut only, just through the skin, and establishes the position of the cuts. When the skin is cut it bleeds.

04:38-The "nipple" is clearly seen. However this feature appears only on the left side of the chest, and there is no matching feature on the right. In a bilaterally symmetrical creature like this, a nipple on only one side is highly unlikely. I consider this some sort of skin injury, but it will require more study and enhancement to make a positive determination. During this sequence at about 04:50, a "wound" in the form of a small round depression about the size of the end of the surgeon's thumb is clearly visible on the creature's left temple area. This does not appear to be a natural feature, since there is no matching one on the right side of the head. It has been speculated that this is the rifle butt would, but it is too small and the wrong shape. Could possibly be a wound caused by striking with a barrel of a rifle.

At about 04:54 the doctor's features can be seen through the face mark briefly.

05:09-Break in film—second cut down midline of chest and belly shown in close-up. This is a deeper cut, made with a sawing motion of the scalpel, to penetrate the subcutaneous muscle layer and tissue. Sequence ends with camera panning up to surgeon's face. His eyes and part of his face are briefly visible during this.

05:25-Break in film with whiteout. Final abdominal cut made. Surgeon hands scalpel to other doctor, who appears to be female. Film is denser during this sequence reflecting uneven development characteristic of hand processing. Abdomen does not deflate when final cut is made. Clock shows 10:40. During this sequence some things can be seen better due to the denser film. First of all, the top of the head part of the suits can be seen to puff in and out with the breathing of the doctors. The sign on the wall can be seen to read DANGER. Under this are two lines of large type, which I cannot make out, and a shorter line of smaller type under these. It should be possible to read this sign with some computer enhancement.

05:32-Surgeon begins reflection of skin and muscle layer from upper chest by lifting and pulling while cutting it free underneath with a scalpel. Revealed underside of this layer as well as internal chest structure is smooth and glistening, wet. View is from upper left.

05:56-Break in film—skin and muscle layer on chest and belly fully open. "Ribcage" fully visible but shows no definition of individual ribs. Looks like a fused structure. View is from lower left. Cameraman moves to right during sequence. Surgeon is busy pointing to things, manipulating some, and speaking toward microphone.

06:12-Break in film–view from lower left. Organs clearly visible, with large oblong dark organ protruding from under ribcage, apparently swollen, may be cause of swollen belly. Camera moves in close and then moves toward head. Sternocleidomastoid muscles very prominent, tubular not flattened as in human, very long. Appear to arch over clavicle ends and attach directly to "sternum." Clavicles show deep V-shape, attaching to "sternum" much lower than in a human and appearing to actually have their points of attachment inside the ribcage. Top of ribcage seems to have solid, transverse structure, and ribs seem to begin lower than in humans. Could not see any "Adam's apple" or indication of voice box, but difficult to see between the sternocleidomastoid muscles. This whole neck and upper chest muscle and skeletal structure is very odd in appearance and very non-human.

06:32-Break in film—close-up of neck from upper left, pan down over body and organs.

06:38-Break in film—close-up of chest, pan up to head.

06:47-Break in film—looking down from upper left on neck. Muscles clearly visible. Pan down body.

06:53-Break in film—looking up from lower left. Doctors reappear, one working on tray of instruments.

07:05-End of roll. Whiteout.

07:10-Next roll begins in whiteout.

07:13-View of table from lower left, low angle. Surgeon asks other doctor for scissors, again using his forceful shaking finger as he points. Removes small organ which is not seen clearly and drops into glass dish held by other doctor. Camera moves to higher angle and begins pan to cameraman's left. You then see that the front of the "ribcage" has been cut away and removed. Surgeon points to "heart" and speaks while pointing.

07:46-Break in film—view from upper left as surgeon begins to cut connective tissue above "heart."

08:03-Break in film-Surgeon works with fingers and scalpel to remove "crystal" from heart. At the early part of this sequence, the cut ends of the ribs on the left side of the body can be seen, but not clearly. The "crystal" object is triangular in shape, transparent and hollow (surgeon pokes his finger inside to demonstrate this). Looks to be about two inches across. Very strange object, whatever it is. Throughout this sequence you can see clearly inside of the body cavity.

08:16-Break in film—camera back on left side. Moves to foot of table. Man behind window can be seen intently observing the doctors at work, and then glancing down. Motion of his arms suggest that he is either typing or using a steno machine.

08:37-Break in film—view from right side, close-up of chest cavity. There is no sign of any lungs, trachea, bronchial tubes or associated structures. I could not see any sign of a diaphragm. There is also no sign of an esophagus. The large organ which is sticking out from under the ribcage earlier has also been removed. This all could have been removed during the missing roll in the earlier gap, when the ribcage was also cut and removed. Surgeon lifts a pale-colored tube which looks like aorta above heart and cuts it with scissors. There appears to be no blood inside. Camera pans down as surgeon cuts connective tissue under a large firm organ with scissors. This organ might possibly be the liver, but its placement is lower than expected and it is not shaped exactly as expected.

08:54-Break in film—surgeon lifts this organ from body cavity and places into steel pan held by other doctor.

09:05-End of roll. Whiteout.

09:08-Next roll starts. Close-up from right side of lower abdomen. Surgeon lifts spongy mass from belly area and puts in bowl held by other doctor. Other doctor turned and places it on table and then makes note on pad of paper (on clipboard ? Not clear). Other writing is clearly visible on this paper and could probably be read with enhancement. Camera pans back to surgeon who is feeling around inside abdomen. He grasps another organ and cuts under it. Camera pans away and down leg. It is important to note that these large, spongy organs fill up the lower abdomen, and that there is no sign that I can detect of small or large intestines, which would fill up the lower abdominal cavity in a human. I cannot relate these abdominal organs to anything familiar in human anatomy.

09:33-Break in film—view from upper left over surgeon's shoulder as this organ is lifted out and put in bowl held by doctor.

09:48-Break in film—view from left foot of table. Man behind window seems to be typing. Surgeon on the left of table, doctor on the right. Two small organs (kidney's?) removed from upper abdomen, put in pan, and taken to table by doctor.

10:05-Break in film—close-up of head from lower left. Surgeon looks hard at eyes, says something to man behind glass, asks nurse for forceps. Takes forceps and looks hard at left eye from several angles.

10:22-Break in film—closer view from same angle. Surgeon deftly lifts black cover from left eye and drops it into a glass dish half filled with clear liquid. Dish is held out for him by doctor.

10:27-Break in film—view from other side of table as procedure is repeated on right eye.

NOTE: These segments are NOT out of sequence as some have claimed. The neck skin has simply been rolled back down into place.

10:38-Break in film—close-up of head from left. Slow pan across face shows rolled up eyes and part of iris. Camera pans around head to show surgeon starting transverse cut across scalp, from ear to ear across top of head.

10:47-Break in film—close-up of cut being made from over surgeon's right shoulder.

10:55-Break in film—same view as cut is made deeper. Some bleeding from cut.

10:57-End of roll. Whiteout.

11:03-New roll begins. View from foot of table as surgeon cuts scalp. Doctor on right side of table holds head at chin. Camera pans to cameraman's right. Man behind window moves around to get a better view. Cameraman walks to left of table and then back showing someone making notes on the table, and for the first time showing that there are three "doctors" participating in this dissection. Surgeon still working on scalp.

11:35-Break in film—close-up from left as surgeon peels scalp forward.

11:41-Break in film—view over surgeon's right shoulder as scalp is peeled forward while scalpel is used to free it from the rough textured skull.

11:56-Break in film—view from foot of table. Cameraman moves around left side of table for close-up while surgeon works and doctor steadies head. Cameraman seems to be jockeying for a good view while staying out of surgeon's way.

12:07-During a pan to the cameraman's left, a chest or cooler is seen under the table holding the instruments and against the wall. It is fitted with metal carrying handles.

12:09-View from left close-up, surgeon still peeling scalp.

12:12-Break in film—view from foot of table, right. Doctor still holding head as surgeon works on scalp. Man behind glass has eyes down. Blood clearly visible between creature's legs draining into holes in table.

12:24-Break in film—view over surgeon's right shoulder. Still peeling scalp. Cameraman walks to his left behind surgeon's back to show view from surgeon's left side. Still appears to be looking for a good angle to film from.

12:40-Cameraman apparently bumps surgeon, who turns and appears to be angry, waving his hand in the cameraman's face and pushing him back. Cameraman moves back to his left, camera tilts up and off subject. This looks to me like a flare-up of temper from the sur-

geon, either from the discomfort of the suit or the tension of the procedure.

12:46-Break in film—doctor is now where surgeon was. Camera view from lower side of table at left. Surgeon walks around table in front of camera, camera follows him to table where he makes notes on pad.

13:06-Person I have been calling the doctor leans forward over the table clearly showing breasts pressing against cloth of suit. Obviously a woman.

13:10-Roll ends. Whiteout.

13:12-Roll begins on creature's leg then camera pans to head. Close-up view from left as back flap of scalp is peeled down. Doctor still steadying head. Cameraman walks to foot of table and then across to right.

13:51-Break in film—close-up of cutting and peeling scalp from right side.

14:00-Break in film—view from foot of table. Surgeon still cutting scalp.

14:03-Break in film—close-up of head from left side. Scalp fully peeled. Doctor hands bone saw to surgeon. Cameraman moves behind surgeon to get vantage point over surgeon's right shoulder. Surgeon begins to saw at front of skull.

14:37-Surgeon's back and arm block shot. Cameraman moves to his left around back of surgeon for shot over surgeon's left shoulder. Can't get good shot from here, so goes back around surgeon's back to shoot over surgeon's right shoulder. Cameraman moves back to left again apparently trying to find good shot then back right again. Surgeon is still sawing hard at 15:14, so this skull must either be very thick or very hard. A human skull is very thin in front and would not be this difficult to cut through.

15:17-Break in film—very brief view which seems to be of the top of the head as the surgeon works to free the skullcap.

15:22-Break in film—side view from left. Skullcap has been removed and brain is exposed, covered by membrane. Surgeon uses fine scissors to cut through brain membrane.

15:30-Membrane pushed aside by surgeon's fingers, brain fully exposed. Surgeon reaches inside membrane and works his fingers around and under the brain, working to free it.

15:39-Surgeon takes instrument from doctor and cuts brain free underneath. Hands back instrument.

15:45-Break in film—view from right side of head over doctor's left shoulder as surgeon uses a spatula tool to further free brain.

15:49-Break in film—view from left toward head, high angle. Surgeon eases brain out and slides into enamel tray held by doctor.

16:05-Break in film—brain shown in tray on table as doctor makes notes.

16:14-View from right side close-up as lower brain is lifted from skull by surgeon and placed in tray with rest of brain. By comparison with a human brain, this brain shows a proportionally smaller upper brain and larger lower brain. The upper brain appears not to be split into separate hemispheres, nor does it show the characteristic furrows seen on the brains of humans and all advanced mammals. This is definitely not a human brain.

16:25-Break in film—view from lower left shows surgeon pointing out something inside the empty brain cavity to the man behind the window, who then looks down and appears to be typing. Clock, reflecting in glass, appears to show 11:45.

16:45-End of film. Whiteout.

Biography of Bob Shell

Background: If you have *Who's Who in the World* you will find my bio in a recent copy. I am also in *Who's Who of Emerging Leaders in America, Who's Who in the South and Southwest, 3,000 Personalities of the World,* and *American Artists.* To summarize, I am schooled in zoology and fine art, and after college I worked for the Smithsonian Institution in Washington, which also published several of my scientific papers (on insect coloration, Indo-Australian butterflies, etc.). I've always had a strong interest in photography, and after a lengthy struggle, photography won out over zoology, and I left the Smithsonian (and Walter Reed Army Medical Center, where I also worked briefly for the CIA) and moved back to Virginia to work in photography.

I operated a photo studio and camera store for some time, opened a photographic import and distribution business, and began writing for photo magazines. Ten years ago I sold the photo import business and have been a full-time magazine writer/editor ever since. For the last five years I have been editor of *Shutterbug,* the world's third-largest monthly photo magazine. I am also technical editor of *Outdoor & Nature Photography* magazine. I was publisher of *PIC* magazine in the UK for all of 1994, as well as 50% owner of that magazine, and have sold the magazine recently. I am on the technical staff of *Color Foto* in Munich, Germany's largest photo magazine.

I am highly regarded as a technical expert on photography and have authored more than a dozen books on photographic subjects, including *Canon Compendium* (a complete history of the Canon Camera Company) with English and German editions, *Pro Guide: Mamiya Camera Systems* (English and German editions), *Pro Guide: Canon EOS Systems* (English and German editions). At present I am under contract to write four more photographic books.

I have also kept my fine arts interest alive, with painting, drawing and sculpting. In 1995 I won an international graphic design award from *Graphics* in Switzerland for a magazine cover I designed.

Through my company, Bob Shell Ltd., I do consulting on product design and technical photographic problems for major camera companies, other firms, government agencies, etc. I am also sometimes called to testify as an expert witness in federal court cases involving photography, and have also testified in patent courts on technical photographic patent interpretation.

APPENDIX G

Autopsy Creature Reconstruction

In order to try and visualize the creature in the autopsy film, which, incidentally, has been called S.U.E. (Santilli. Unidentified. Entity), the authors have commissioned two British artists to reconstruct S.U.E. in an upright condition, and obviously alive.

Both professional artists were given the same brief: from the stills and the video film, reconstruct S.U.E. to see what she might possibly look like while alive and walking around. The results are interesting if nothing else.

Both artists have estimated that S.U.E. would still have a slight double-chin, small low-set ears, six digits on hands and feet, legs being narrow at the front but wide at the sides, large cranium, and a reduction in the size of the pot-belly.

Both artists have made three drawings, S.U.E. from the front and

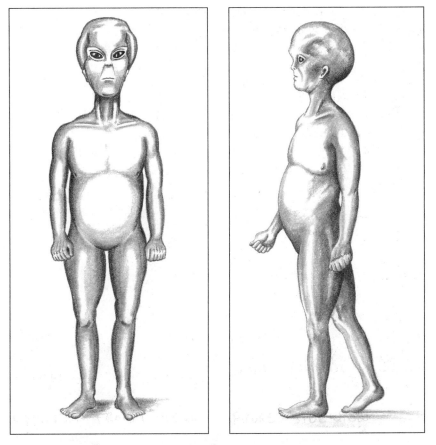

Origional artwork by Mark Spain

side (full-length) and a portrait.

Rick Jones: Dover, Kent, England.

Rick Jones is a professional illustrator and cartoonist. Aside from general commercial illustration work he also works for a number of UK-based UFO magazines, including *UFO Reality* and *UFO Times*.

Mark Spain: Gateshead, Newcastle-Upon-Tyne, England.

Mark Spain has a B.A. (Hon.) degree in art and design. As a freelance professional illustrator he has worked on a large variety of commercial projects. He is a regular illustrator for *Ufo Times* magazine and has formed his own company, Flights of Fancy, to produce UFO merchandise such as posters and postcards.

Both artists can be contacted via Philip Mantle.

Origianal artwork by Rick Jones

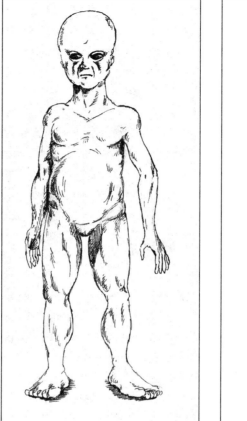
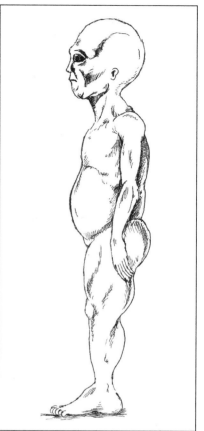

CALL FOR WITNESSES

The authors of this book and all others involved around the world in the research and investigation of the events contained within these pages, would like to appeal to anyone who has any information on the content of this book.

Were you one of the military personnel involved at the time? Was it perhaps your parents or grandparents who were serving in the military in 1947, and may have witnessed the events in question?

Were you one of the staff that later worked on the recovered wreckage, or perhaps you were one of the physicians who worked on the bodies? Perhaps you even know the identity of the autopsy cameraman?

We would like to appeal to anyone who has any information to come forward now. The events in New Mexico in 1947 have been kept secret for fifty years now, surely it is time for the truth to be told!

Anyone with any information can contact any of the three addresses to the right. We guaranty complete confidentiality in all cases. If you have any information that you think might be of help, please contact us now, and help us solve this fifty-year-old mystery.

USA:
Bob Shell,
P.O. Box 808
Radford, Virginia 24141

EUROPE:
Michael Hesemann
Worringer Strasse 1
D-40211 Düsseldorf
Germany

GREAT BRITAIN:
Philip Mantle
1 Woodhall Drive
Batley
West Yorkshire
WF17 7SW
England

Michael Hesemann:

Futurologist, cultural anthropologist, expert for frontier sciences and extraterrestrial phenomena, bestselling author and award-winning film producer, Hesemann studied cultural anthropology and history at Göttingen University. He lives in Düsseldorf, Germany. Since 1984 he has published *Magazine 2000* which comes out in German, English and Czech. His international bestsellers *UFOs: The Evidence, A Cosmic Connection* and *UFOs: A Secret Matter* were published in fourteen countries with a circulation of more than 500,000 copies. Hesemann produced several award-winning documentaries and worked for TV programs in Germany, Japan and the U.S. He spoke at international conferences in twenty-two countries on all five continents, at thirty universities, and at the United Nations.

Philip Mantle:

Philip Mantle from Batley, West Yorkshire, England. Married with a family, he has worked for the last 17 years as a lithographic plate preparer for a larger company in Leeds, West Yorkshire. Philip Mantle currently holds the postion as Director of Investigations for the British UFO Research Association, is the Mutual UFO Networks representative for England, and is a honorary member of the Research Institute on Anomalous Phenomena in the Ukraine.

Philip Mantle has published one book entitled *Without Consent* a study of UFO abductions in UK which he co-authored with Carl Nagaitis. An international lecturer on the subject of UFOs, Mantle has also worked for a variety of TV and radio companies around the world.

INDEX